1984

(cont.
ON back)

Management
in Marketing
Channels

McGraw-Hill Series in Marketing

Consulting Editor

Charles Schewe, *University of Massachusetts*

Bowersox, Cooper, Lambert, and Taylor: Management in Marketing Channels
Britt and Boyd: Marketing Management and Administrative Action
Buskirk and Buskirk: Retailing
Buzzell, Nourse, Matthews, and Levitt: Marketing: A Contemporary Analysis
DeLozier: The Marketing Communications Process
Howard: Consumer Behavior: Application of Theory
Kinnear and Taylor: Marketing Research: An Applied Approach
Lee and Dobler: Purchasing and Materials Management: Text and Cases
Loudon and Della Bitta: Consumer Behavior: Concepts and Applications
Monroe: Pricing: Making Profitable Decisions
Redinbaugh: Retailing Management: A Planning Approach
Reynolds and Wells: Consumer Behavior
Russell, Beach, and Buskirk: Textbook of Salesmanship
Schewe and Smith: Marketing: Concepts and Applications
Shapiro: Sales Program Management: Formulation and Implementation
Stanton: Fundamentals of Marketing
Star, Davis, Lovelock, and Shapiro: Problems in Marketing
Stroh: Managing the Sales Function
Wright, Warner, Winter, and Zeigler: Advertising

Management in Marketing Channels

Donald J. Bowersox

M. Bixby Cooper

Douglas M. Lambert

Donald A. Taylor

*Professors of Marketing and
Transportation Administration
Michigan State University*

McGraw-Hill Book Company

New York   St. Louis   San Francisco   Auckland   Bogotá   Düsseldorf
Johannesburg   London   Madrid   Mexico   Montreal   New Delhi
Panama   Paris   São Paulo   Singapore   Sydney   Tokyo   Toronto

MANAGEMENT IN MARKETING CHANNELS

1 2 3 4 5 6 7 8 9 0   DODO   7 8 3 2 1 0 9

This book was set in Times Roman by Progressive Typographers.
The editors were John F. Carleo and Elisa Adams;
the production supervisor was Donna Piligra.
The drawings were done by ANCO/Boston.
R. R. Donnelley & Sons Company was printer and binder.

Library of Congress Cataloging in Publication Data

Michigan. State University, East Lansing. Dept. of
    Marketing and Transportation Administration.
    Management in marketing channels.

    (McGraw-Hill series in marketing)
    Bibliography: p.
    Includes index.
    1. Marketing channels—Management.   2.   Marketing
management.   3.   Marketing management—Case studies.
I.   Bowersox, Donald J.   II.   Title.
HF5415.125.M5   1980   658.8′4   79-13610
ISBN 0-07-006740-6

Contents

v

Preface

We believe that the management of interfirm relationships is an important day-to-day activity for a successful business, since smooth functioning of the distribution channel is a vital link in a firm's total marketing effort. This belief applies not only to manufacturing organizations but to all institutions that deal with others in their quest for success.

Our conviction has influenced the development of this book in three ways. First, we have tried to maintain a distinctly managerial orientation. No attempt has been made to organize or compare materials along a purely institutional, functional, economic, behavioral, or social approach. In practice, a marketing channel is a vital part of all these and more. Although the distinctive features and contributions of each alternative study approach are of interest, comprehensive coverage and comparison would have limited benefits for the person dedicated to a management career. Thus, where appropriate, we have attempted to utilize all study approaches to aid in understanding particular aspects of channel management.

This managerial orientation has, in turn, influenced the second unique aspect of the book. Incorporated within this text are a number of situational illustrations that focus upon the role responsibilities, problems, and opportunities involved in channel management. Our objective in including such illustrations is to demonstrate the application of concepts in an interorganizational setting and to develop an appreciation for the specific decision-making activities in channels. The chapters are supplemented by case studies so that the reader can apply the concepts in the text to new and different situations in an effort to sharpen problem-solving capabilities.

The third unique aspect of the book is that its coverage is limited to channel management concerns. Each reader comes to this book as a student or manager already having some knowledge of basic marketing elements. Thus, no attempt is made by the authors to provide comprehensive treatment of managerial marketing. Rather, we have given relatively short and crisp coverage of basic marketing concepts that respects the reader's previous training and experience.

The development of a text is certainly an evolutionary process. In this respect, all authors owe a debt of gratitude to many other individuals. We must thank all those upon whose previous work we have drawn to crystallize our thinking and give substance to our efforts. Special thanks are due to Felicia Kramer, whose assistance in preparing this manuscript went far beyond normal expectations.

Considering the number of individuals who have provided input, it is difficult to offer an excuse for any shortcomings that might follow. That responsibility, however, lies solely with the authors.

Donald J. Bowersox
M. Bixby Cooper
Douglas M. Lambert
Donald A. Taylor

Management
in Marketing
Channels

Chapter 1

Contemporary Marketing Channels

In writing this book, we have assumed that you, the reader, have previously studied or worked in the marketing field. Thus, you bring to this discussion a realistic understanding of what a marketing channel is and how it operates. We anticipate you are well aware that the practice of marketing is less formally structured and sloppier in operation than the mythical manufacturer to wholesaler to retailer to consumer distribution channel described in basic marketing textbooks.[1] Our objective in this book is to integrate channel-related issues and research to better explain how channels function and how managerial strategies can be formulated and executed in a dynamic channel environment. This initial chapter provides definition and gives an overview of the materials that follow.

Marketing in an advanced industrial society combines the efforts of many different business and public institutions. For purposes of discussion, a marketing channel is defined as *a system of relationships that exists among institutions involved in the process of buying and selling.*

The marketing channel system focuses on the process of ownership and physical transfer of commodities, products, and services. In marketing any

---

[1] This point of view is clearly made by a number of authors. See: Philip McVey, "Are Channels of Distribution What the Textbooks Say?" *Journal of Marketing* (January 1961), p. 61–65.

group of items or services, it is typical for a number of different enterprises to be involved. Many marketing channel members are not aware of how many other organizations or individuals constitute the total channel, beyond the direct face-to-face buyer-seller relationship. From the vantage point of many participants, the so-called channel may not exist. In other words, many institutions involved in marketing goods or services may not acknowledge or identify themselves as channel members. When viewed as channel participants, these firms or individuals come and go according to their perceived needs and relative stake, or degree of risk, in channel success. Thus, channels are dynamic. Many channels are relatively loose and ever-changing arrangements. Concern over the channel's direction of change and overall well-being is only important to management when it is actively involved as a participant.

In extreme contrast to the loose channel arrangement discussed above are the highly visible and organized arrangements dominated by large retailers, wholesalers, or manufacturers. Organizations such as K-Mart, Sears, General Motors, Ace Hardware, and McDonald's offer all channel partners a sense of stability in that they retain their identity over time. Such channels are identified by the dominant organization that provides leadership and direction for the activities and practices of all channel participants. However, the actual degree of stability over time between loose and dominated channels is relative. While the dominant organization may enjoy stability, a closer look at other channel associates often reveals considerable instability and desire for change over the same time period.

To further complicate an understanding of marketing channels, many institutions are simultaneously members of a number of different channel arrangements. For some, the involvement in two or more channels reflects a specific managerial policy to engage in segmented marketing or dual distribution.[2] For others, involvement in multiple channels is more accidental than strategic. The practice of scrambled merchandising has created some strange relationships wherein the point of final product sale to consumers is duplicated widely in a single market.[3] Although it is common to find the same brand of a manufacturer's product selling in directly competitive retail outlets, a less obvious fact is that many manufacturers market competitive products within the same retail store. For example, national brand and private label food products processed by the same packer are frequently offered for sale side by side on the retailer's shelf. Similar contradictions can be observed in industrial and service marketing arrangements. For example, American Hospital Supply Distribution Corporation markets to hospitals products made in their own manufacturing divi-

[2] The terms "segmented" and "dual" marketing are used to describe the process of selling the same product to one or more different industries or markets. For a related discussion of market/product adjustment considerations, see: Wendell R. Smith, "Product Differentiation and Market Segmentation as Alternative Marketing Strategies," *Journal of Marketing* (July 1956), pp. 3–8.

[3] Thomas A. Staudt, Donald A. Taylor, and Donald J. Bowersox, *A Managerial Introduction to Marketing,* 3d ed. (Englewood Cliffs, N.J.: Prentice-Hall, Inc., 1976), pp. 320–321.

sions as well as items manufactured by Johnson & Johnson's Surgikos Company.

Finally, in most situations, channel codes of conduct or rules of the game appear to exist which extend far beyond legal regulations and requirements. In part, organization of channel affairs results from the cultural and social setting of the specific nation in which the channel functions. However, in multinational situations, channels cross international borders and appear to retain their structural and functional ordering. Thus, the prevailing relationships between the institutions that constitute a channel are both formal and informal with respect to rules and expectations of conduct. Conflict does arise, but it is most often resolved on the basis of mutual satisfaction before it becomes dysfunctional or destructive. *Although far less dramatic to describe than conflict, the prevailing state of affairs within a channel is cooperative.*

In an effort to characterize the anatomy of contemporary channels more clearly, numerous authors have developed ways to view such arrangements. Among the most popular is to describe the channel as a system with particular emphasis on the behavioral, social, economic, ecological, or strategic managerial forces that result in channel design and mode of operation.[4] In contrast, we place emphasis on concepts that can be observed to be integral parts of numerous channel arrangements. Attention is directed to description and illustration of these concepts in a variety of channel situations. Two major advantages are gained by this treatment.

First is the recognition that specific managers need to formulate channel strategies for their enterprises. Such channel strategies ideally will be innovative and insightful if the manager involved has a comprehensive understanding of the fundamental forces at work in channel design. Such channel strategies represent only one aspect of the enterprise's total marketing effort and must be fully integrated with all other elements of the marketing mix.[5]

Second is the recognition that the aggregation of individual channel decision making should be viewed by managers from an overall societal perspective. To retain a strong free market system, a relatively high degree of economic and social efficiency must exist between the independent firms participating in channel arrangements. The alternative distribution arrangements available are based on clear-cut ideological choices.[6] It should be fully understood by the individual manager that the ultimate maintenance of a selected distribution arrangement is the by-product of prevailing as well as future business practices. Extensive review of this accumulation of insightful and innovative history constitutes the foundation for formulating distribution channel arrangements.

---

[4] For a comprehensive review of alternative approaches to channel study, see: Ronald Mitchman, *Marketing Channels* (Columbus, Ohio: Grid Publishing, Inc., 1974), pp. 3–6.

[5] For elaboration of the marketing mix concept, see: Staudt, Taylor, and Bowersox, op. cit., pp. 72–74.

[6] This point is further developed in Chapter 2, pp. 29–32.

NATURE OF CONTEMPORARY CHANNELS

To set the stage, we will examine in this section six fundamental environmental and behavioral relationships reflective of contemporary marketing channels. These six relationships—legal-social setting, complexity, specialization, routinization, dependence, and disproportionate risk—are, to a greater or lesser degree, common to all channel arrangements.

Legal-Social Setting

Although marketing channels reflect a wide variety of differences, a vast number of common features prevail. The most apparent common features are those stemming directly from the legal-social setting within which channels are designed. All enterprises, regardless of size, are subject to the judicial, legislative, and administrative laws of the legal authorities under which they operate, whether they be state, federal, or international. Although enforcement does indeed vary, the legality of a specific act does not. With increasing frequency, executives are being held responsible for their managerial actions and their subsequent impact upon society. The past few years have seen direct prosecution of corporate executives for enterprise activity judged to be in violation of antitrust laws. The recent prosecution of General Electric executives for alleged price fixing is typical.[7] An example of the extent to which the doctrine of public trust has expanded is typified by the 1975 Supreme Court ruling that a firm's chief executive officer was responsible for the failure of subordinates to comply with federal food laws.[8] This doctrine of executive responsibility in public corporations was further institutionalized by passage of the Foreign Corrupt Practices Act on December 19, 1977 (Public Law 95-213). This act holds executives responsible for up to 5-year jail terms, with personal fines of up to $1 million for violations of bribery or accounting provisions of the law.

The force of cultural impact upon channels is less apparent than the direct impact of the law. Many traditions of a society are reflected in the ways and means of commerce. These traditions extend from such simple practices as selling in specific units of measurement, such as dozens and quarts, to very complex but, in many cases, unwritten rules regarding the responsibility of merchants to customers. For example, beer is typically sold in units of six (sixpacks) in the United States, while in most Latin American countries it is common practice to buy by the individual bottle. Likewise, the responsibility of the retailer to stand behind the product varies considerably from one nation to another. A limit exists regarding which marketing practices will be tolerated by channel participants or consumers. The very manner by which a transaction is completed is based upon the fundamental economies of exchange. Shopping is

[7] "Justice Department Charges General Electric with Sherman Antitrust Violation," and "U.S. Charges Reciprocity on Purchasing," *Wall Street Journal* (May 19, 1972), p. 2; and "Turbine Makers Get Sued Again: Antitrust Suit against General Electric and Westinghouse," *Business Week* (January 8, 1972), p. 24.

[8] "The Growth Years 1952–77," *Supermarket News,* Section 2 (October 24, 1977), p. 58.

one of the most visible forms of human interaction and, to a significant degree, is a form of learned behavior.[9] This behavior pattern serves as an operational constraint on the degree of change that a society is willing to accept in its marketing methods.

The important point regarding legal and social settings of channel management is that they are universal to all distribution relationships. Channels that operate in a multinational climate must be sensitive to individual countries' legal and social constraints since planned strategies often must accommodate contradictory behavior patterns.

Complexity

A second common denominator among contemporary marketing channels is their complex nature. A prime example is the food distribution business. On one hand, large retailers have expanded to stock over 12,000 items in the typical line of merchandise. As would be expected, these super-supermarkets dominate volume and market share in this industry. The contradiction in complexity is that miniature convenience stores and out-of-home eating represent two of the fastest growing forms of food marketing. Thus, with each passing day channels of food distribution in the United States become more complex.

In 1972 within the United States one retail establishment existed for every 109 persons.[10] To provide the necessary logistical support, the ratio of trucks to consumers was 1 to 8.[11] As expected, wholesale level sales far exceed retail sales as ownership of products is transferred several times throughout the marketing channel. To say the least, the marketing situation in terms of numbers of participants within the United States is complex. The prevailing manufacturer practice of new product introduction as a prime growth strategy, coupled with expansion of retail merchandise lines, has resulted in a wide variety of nearly duplicate items being sold at many locations throughout a market area.

All managers concerned with developing a marketing channel strategy confront the same degree of structural complexity. To a large extent, the above characterization of contemporary marketing channels is a reflection of the basic nature of modern marketing complexity.

Specialization

Specialization is a basic characteristic of an advanced industrial society. That one specialist can perform a specific activity for many organizations at a lower per-unit cost by virtue of economy of scale is a notion of long standing in economic and business literature.[12] The fact that, in 1975, 62.3 percent of all inter-

[9] James F. Engel, David T. Kollat, and Roger D. Blackwell, *Consumer Behavior* (New York: Holt, Rinehart and Winston, Inc., 1968), p. 117.

[10] Based on U.S. Bureau of Census, *Census of Retail Trade 1972*, which reported 1,912,871 retail establishments and a 1972 population of 208.8 million persons.

[11] *Transportation Facts and Trends*, 12th ed. (Washington, D.C.: Transportation Association of America, 1976).

[12] George E. Stigler, "The Division of Labor is Limited by the Extent of the Market," *Journal of Political Economy* (June 1951), pp. 185–193.

city freight ton-miles was hauled by federally regulated motor common carriers is a prime example of such specialization.[13] While not traditionally viewed as channel members, transportation carriers and public warehouse facilities are important elements of marketing channels. In terms of ownership transactions, the fastest growing marketing channel participants are merchandise agents and brokers.[14]

Specialization as the dominant form of economic activity extends far beyond institutions that perform services within the marketing channel. In fact, manufacturing firms which represent locations of product origin within the channel are, for the most part, specialists. The vast arena of industrial marketing wherein the product of one enterprise represents an input to another firm reflects this extensive specialization. In the assembly of a television set, several hundred component parts manufactured by different firms may be required to produce a set suitable for retail sale. Beyond assembly, the services of specialists are required for packaging and all aspects of physical distribution. The specialist finds economic justification until such time that individual users require sufficient volume to perform the activity for themselves with maximum benefits of scale. At this point of feasible vertical integration, the specialist stands in jeopardy of either being absorbed into the buyer organization or being eliminated.

In terms of marketing channel structure, the specialist serves to combine the output of varied manufacturers into an assortment for sale at the retail or industrial market level. In fact, as we will elaborate in Chapter 2, the economic justification of wholesale trade is based upon the capability of efficiently offering an assortment for sale at a price which reflects the economies of scale inherent in a large-volume operation.[15]

A significant social concern is the survival of specialists in an industrial society characterized by gargantuan organizations.[16] This question of survival is the bedrock of antitrust policy. The small-scale specialists are protected and can remain competitive with large organizations provided that they add an element of efficiency to the marketing process. Preservation of such specialists provides a benefit to society, but it also intensifies complexity.

Specialization serves to create economic opportunity. The result is a sufficiently large and varied assortment of institutions performing as channel members. Specialization is a common factor throughout marketing channel management.

Routinization

The benefit of routinization of activities is one of the primary reasons why enterprises form the coalitions we have described as marketing channels. A seri-

---

[13] *Transportation Facts and Trends.*
[14] Reavis Cox, *Distribution in a High-Level Economy* (Englewood Cliffs, N.J.: Prentice-Hall, Inc., 1965), p. 56. These specific terms are defined in Chapter 2, pp. 43–48.
[15] See Chapter 2, pp. 36–37.
[16] John W. Gardner, *Self-Renewal* (New York: Harper & Row, Publishers, Inc., 1964), p. 85.

ous question can be raised regarding why such coalitions evolve in the first place. Evidence suggests that the traditional motive behind routinization is much more production-oriented than it is market-oriented.[17]

Routinization in marketing eliminates the requirement to search out a new specialist and negotiate a transfer price each time a need is experienced. To the extent that a relationship is routinized, the opportunity exists to increase the efficiency of joint operations. For example, if sufficient business volume exists between two parties, specialized equipment can be introduced to reduce the cost of materials handling and information flows. Indeed, the advent of routinization between buyer and seller forms a cohesive bond between the two organizations because it reduces uncertainty by creating dependence.

Dependence

A logical extension of specialization and routinization among business firms is dependence. The state of dependence is created when the management of two or more enterprises formally acknowledges that it is in their best joint interest to perpetuate a business relationship. Such dependence can result from common practice or may be formalized in legal agreements. Dependence is viewed as the first indication that a marketing channel has emerged. At the most basic level, the involved managements develop a set of expectations regarding the role each will perform in future marketing efforts. Such roles may specify activities or they may relate to specific products or territories. In all cases, they will identify dependence. Establishment of a commonly acknowledged role not only provides the incentive for cooperation but also provides seeds for conflict between channel participants. The development and resolution of conflict is treated in Chapters 3 and 4.

Disproportionate Risk

Coexistent with the development of dependence is the acknowledgment that very seldom, if ever, will two organizations have equal risk in a channel arrangement. The fact is that one enterprise involved in a two-party arrangement normally will have more at stake than the other. Among multiple participants in the same channel, a wide variance may exist in perceived and actual risk in channel success. Four points are of concern in the relative balance of risk.

First, if the channel relationship has not evolved from the state of routinization to acknowledged dependence, then one of the channel participants can be assumed not to feel extensive commitment. For example, a trucker may provide specialized services on a routinized basis but not perceive a dependence on the channel or any degree of risk beyond performance of single shipment requirements. Such a carrier would be a weak channel member in terms of unwillingness to compromise individual goals for any specific channel because of continued involvement with many different shippers in many different

---

[17] Wroe Alderson, *Marketing Behavior and Executive Action* (Homewood, Ill.: Richard D. Irwin, Inc., 1957), p. 296–304.

channels. However, if the carrier was under contract to haul freight exclusively for one firm, the risk would become clear as a result of formalized dependence. The advent of dependence can be formal or informal. The acknowledgment of disproportionate risk either provides the force for greater cohesiveness or may dissolve the channel arrangement if not acceptable to all parties concerned.

Second, open acknowledgment of disproportionate risk creates the opportunity for leadership and the formulation of the channel as a behavioral system. Acknowledgment of disproportionate risk and the development of operational plans on a joint enterprise basis results in open identification of a channel relationship. Most manufacturing firms that produce private label merchandise under contract for large retailers participate in joint planning of product design, packaging, and quantities to be produced for a specific selling season. Agreements related to these and other issues can and are discussed on an open basis. Little, if any, question exists concerning who is the formal leader and where the risk exists in such formalized channels. Unless a level of disproportionate risk exists and each member's position is clearly articulated, the channel cannot be identified as a vertical marketing system.

Third, the joint concepts of dependence and disproportionate risk form the basis for identifying primary and facilitating channel participants. At the most basic level, those enterprises acknowledging dependence and assuming risk are *primary participants*. All other channel members are classified as *facilitating participants*. As a general rule, facilitating participants are more inclined to engage in multiple channel relationships because they do not accept the risk involvement necessary to qualify as a primary participant.

A fourth and final point is the role of consumers as channel members. A number of authors have discussed the merit of including consumers as members of the channel structure based upon their participation as terminal points for the flow of products and services.[18] Although the concept has social appeal, once again, the degree of relative risk must be the guiding criterion. In selected situations when commitments are made in advance, consumers assume considerable risk in the overall marketing process. In this case, they should be viewed as active channel participants. When involvement is limited to low-risk shopping, however, no justification exists to include the consumer as a channel member. Indeed, becoming a channel participant would negate the lofty position of prime benefactor and final judge of the desirability of a given marketing process. To date, little evidence exists to suggest that consumers themselves have any desire to advance their channel participation beyond the role of ultimate critics.

In summary, the six aspects briefly introduced—legal-social setting, complexity, specialization, routinization, dependence, and disproportionate risk—

---

[18] For varied discussions see: Louis W. Stern and Adel I. El-Ansary, *Marketing Channels* (Englewood Cliffs, N.J.: Prentice-Hall, Inc., 1977), pp. 345–346; J. Taylor Sims, J. Robert Foster, and Arch G. Woodside, *Marketing Channels* (New York: Harper & Row, Publishers, 1977), pp. 17–18; and G. Glenn Walters, *Marketing Channels* (New York: The Ronald Press Company, 1974), p. 13.

are readily observed in contemporary marketing channels. These concepts form the nucleus around which channels emerge or are strategically planned. The result may be an informal or a highly formal channel arrangement subject to substantially different survival time spans. The degree of visible and formal interorganizational behavior serves as a foundation for channel classification.

CHANNEL CLASSIFICATION

Following the discussion of contemporary marketing channels, we can now offer a formal classification of channels based on participant acknowledgment of dependence. Three channel classifications are specified for managerial purposes: (1) vertical marketing systems, (2) free-flow channels, and (3) single transaction channels. Each is discussed in this section.

Vertical Marketing Systems

The essential feature of a vertical marketing system is that the primary participants both acknowledge and desire interdependence.[19] As such, they view their best long-term benefits resulting from participation in what is commonly described as a behavioral channel system.

In order to participate in a behavioral channel system, each channel member must accept a role. The assumption is that the mutual relationship is greater than a non-zero-sum game.[20] In other words, the participants feel that as active channel participants their organizations will be better off than they would be standing alone or participating in a competitive channel. In this sense, the relevant competitive unit becomes the channel system.

For the channel to function as a vertical marketing system, one of the member firms must be acknowledged as the leader. The leader is typically the dominant firm and can be expected to take a significant risk position. Likewise, the leader typically has the greatest relative power within the channel.[21]

While dependence is the cohesive force in a channel organization, it also serves as the source of potential conflict. The fundamental perception is that all who enter into a formal channel organization desire to benefit from cooperative behavior. However, conflicts evolve occasionally and must be resolved if the channel is to survive over time. One of the primary roles of channel leadership is to resolve conflict and thereby maintain stability for the channel.

Another important role of the leader is to plan change for the channel. The importance of achieving direction and planned change by the leader is second only to providing stability.

[19] Louis P. Bucklin and Stanley F. Stasch, "Preliminary Considerations," in Louis P. Bucklin, ed., *Vertical Marketing Systems* (Glenview, Ill.: Scott, Foresman and Company, 1970), p. 2.

[20] The concept of zero-sum games is treated in many texts. For the original treatment, see: J. von Neumann and O. Morgenstern, *Theory of Games and Economic Behavior* (Princeton: Princeton University Press, 1947).

[21] The concept of channel leadership is further developed in Chapter 4, pp. 105—107.

Many behavioral channel systems are classified as vertical marketing systems because they enjoy the common feature of functioning as integrated combines of two or more independent enterprises. The concept of vertical marketing systems is further classified as corporate, contractual, or administered on the basis of formal cohesive devices over and above acknowledged dependence.

Corporate   The corporate vertical marketing system is one which is operated as a single business by virtue of ownership. Such corporate systems are rare because few, if any, firms can command the resources to perform at all levels of market channel operations where a primary participant must function. Perhaps the closest example to a fully integrated channel of distribution was achieved by Ford Motor Company during the early 1930s. Firms that approach this type of channel in today's competitive environment are Singer, Otis Elevator, A&P, and Thom McAn Shoes. For practical purposes, the corporate vertical marketing system is defined as one that owns and operates two or more traditional levels of the marketing channel.

Contractual   A contractual vertical marketing system is one in which the acknowledgment of dependence exists in a formal contract. The most common forms of contractual arrangements are franchises, exclusive dealerships, and cooperative and voluntary groups. The essential difference between a corporate and contractual arrangement is the absence of ownership. In many cases, the operating arrangement under a contractual vertical marketing system is more clearly stated than within a corporate channel system. The prime examples of contractual channels are found in the automotive industry. However, all voluntary chains such as Tru-Value, Spartan Stores, and IGA fall in this channel category. Likewise, the franchise arrangements in the fast-food industry represent contractual channel arrangements.

Administered   The administered vertical marketing system typically does not have the formalized arrangements of the contractual system or the clarity of power characteristic of the corporate system. The member firms acknowledge the existence of dependence and adhere to the leadership of the dominant firm. This type of system is capable of retaining operational stability over an extended period of time based upon attainment of joint rewards. The dominant firm may operate at any level of the channel. However, large retail organizations such as Wards, Sears, K-Mart, and J. C. Penney offer the best examples of administered vertical marketing systems. A situation which illustrates the power of mutual recognition without formal contractual arrangement is the Sears-Whirlpool channel. Although the two firms have never had a formal contract, their active business relationship spans more than 20 years during which Whirlpool has been the prime supplier of Sears brand appliances.

Free-Flow Marketing Channels

The channel classified as free flow is typically called the conventional channel. The free-flow concept is adopted because it captures clearly the nature of the channel arrangement. Firms engaged in free-flow arrangements do not reach the level of dependence characteristic of vertical marketing systems. They do, however, acknowledge the benefits of specialization and focus their activities to a specific area of total channel performance. The enterprises that participate in a free-flow marketing channel attempt to enjoy the benefits of specialization whenever and however possible. Thus, when participants in a free-flow channel seek to improve marketing efficiency, they do so without becoming fully committed as members of a behavioral marketing system.

It follows that, over time, a free-flow marketing channel would demonstrate less stability than one would expect to observe in a vertical marketing system. The primary force for solidarity in the free-flow system is the perception of two or more firms that they are enjoying a satisfactory arrangement. The arrangement can be terminated rapidly by either party if and when the business relationship loses its appeal.

Three points should be noted. First, shortages in the economy during the mid-1970s encouraged a widespread practice of "contract selling." Under a contract sell or purchase, the buyer and seller agree to a specified price and quantity to be exchanged over a given time period. In effect, such contracts are buy and sell agreements, similar to the contractual source of vertical marketing systems. No expectation exists regarding mutual business arrangements following the contract expiration. The typical duration of such arrangements is one year or less with specified terms of cancellation.[22]

Second, a great many enterprises that function on a free-flow basis do conduct regular business with vertical marketing systems. However, because of their failure to acknowledge dependence or to formalize arrangements, the free-flow firms do not become full participating members of the behaviorial channel system.

Third, the term "free-flow channel" is not meant to include all channel participants who perform a service. For example, a common carrier transportation company would not necessarily qualify as a channel member by providing a transportation service to a single manufacturing firm. However, the combination of a buyer, a seller, and a carrier would constitute a free-flow three-party channel. Thus, the free-flow classification is related to primary channel participants.[23]

Single Transaction Channel

A great deal of marketing performance is negotiated wherein a transaction is formulated and executed with no plan or expectation to extend or perpetuate

---

[22] If the performance contracts were of longer duration then the channel arrangement would be classified as a contractual vertical marketing system.

[23] See Chapter 2, p. 44 for a clarification of primary participants.

the business relationship. This form of negotiated business usually involves a full or partial search for a buyer or seller for each transaction. Prime examples of the single transaction channel are real estate sales, stock and bond purchases, and selected forms of industrial equipment procurement. For example, the sale of asphalt mixing plants is a single transaction negotiation.

In a technical sense, no channel arrangements of lasting duration are required by the parties in a single transaction channel. However, at the time of transaction negotiation, a full channel capability may be required to meet and fully execute the terms as specified in the transaction negotiation.

In summary, existence of dependence and willingness to participate on a more or less formal basis as a member of a behavioral system are the main features that result in vertical marketing systems. The size and relative volume of vertical marketing systems make their performance a major concern to the formulation of a channel strategy and evaluation of the social and economic efficiency of channels in general. However, it would be incorrect to assume that all marketing transactions are dominated by the various forms of vertical marketing systems. The channels classified as free flow and single transaction constitute major segments of marketing activity which cannot be ignored in formulation of a channel strategy. Likewise, the relative efficiency of these traditional channels must be evaluated in comparison to the various vertical marketing arrangements when formulating a channel strategy.

CHANNEL STRATEGY FORMULATION

As indicated earlier in the chapter, formulation of a channel strategy represents only one part of the overall marketing posture of an enterprise. However, the channel strategy is fundamental because it provides the structure of institutions through which the marketing plan must be orchestrated. From a managerial viewpoint, the formulation of a channel strategy involves four considerations which are briefly discussed in this section:

1 It is necessary for the management of an institution to evaluate the enterprise's relative power position from the perspective of channel alternatives. All channels result from negotiated effort. In single transaction channels, the negotiation may be limited to the price and terms of physical transfer. In a more formalized channel arrangement, negotiations extend beyond transactional terms to encompass performance expectations and determination of who will perform specific functions. The bedrock of formulating a channel strategy is the assessment of an enterprise's relative negotiating position.

2 A second aspect of channel strategy formulation is the arrangement of channel commitments and the design process by which alternatives are evaluated. In this sense, any given channel strategy consists of two parts which are logically separated. One part of the channel is viewed as concerned primarily with selling transactions, whereas the other part constitutes the physical distri-

bution structure.[24] The design of transaction and physical distribution channels represents a number of unique features that should be reviewed in formulating a channel strategy.

3 The third aspect of channel strategy formulation is accurate measurement of channel performance. Performance measurement requires both financial and physical assessment of past activities for the individual participant as well as the overall channel. The performance base provides motivation to either maintain or modify existing channel arrangements.

4 The final step in channel strategy formulation is evaluation of change potential and the related dynamics of change management. Few, if any, channels are designed from ground zero level; most evolve from a number of years of participation in marketing relationships. The degree to which such evolution gives way to planned change can be directly related to innovative behavior on the part of one or more channel members. Thus, the change of institutional arrangements is viewed as the culmination of effective channel strategy planning.

ORDER OF PRESENTATION

The following chapters are divided into two groups. Chapters 2 through 5 provide the interdisciplinary foundation necessary to understand the operation of channel systems. Chapters 6 through 11 are directed to managerial considerations in channel strategy formulation and evaluation. The content of each group of chapters is briefly reviewed below.

Understanding the integral nature of channel relationships requires a combination of insights. In Chapter 2, we initiate the interdisciplinary treatment by examining the economic foundations of exchange systems. The emergence of channels originates from the benefits to be gained from specialization. Chapter 3 introduces the relationship of dependence, which is spawned by specialization, and the inevitable emergence of conflict. The causes and impact of conflict represent important aspects of understanding channel solidarity. Chapter 4 treats interorganizational behavior from the viewpoint of leadership and power. Of primary concern is an examination of how conflict is resolved in mature channel situations. The process of interorganizational management rests upon acknowledgment and direction of dependence. Chapter 5 concludes the foundations portion of the text with a review of the legal environment of the channel. Regardless of the particular nature of the channel system which evolves or is planned, in the final analysis it must function within a triad of judicial, legislative, and administrative law.

The second major grouping of chapters explores the managerial process of developing channel strategy. Chapter 6 is concerned with development of a negotiation posture. Regardless of the degree of permanence involved in a partic-

---

[24] This concept will be identified as channel separation in Chapter 7. For a history of the concept, see: Donald J. Bowersox, *Logistical Management,* rev. ed. (New York: The Macmillan Company, Inc., 1978), p. 37.

ular channel relationship, the rules for conducting business result from negotiation. In Chapter 7, a normative model is presented to guide the process of
organization and design of a channel strategy. Chapters 8 and 9 provide parallel
treatment of strategic elements that may or may not be included in a specific
channel plan. Chapter 8 develops the channel perspective from the viewpoint
of the manufacturer. Chapter 9 examines similar material from the vantage
point of retailers, wholesalers, and third-party institutions. In addition, the special case of franchise arrangements is treated in Chapter 9. In Chapter 10, we
examine the important subject of channel performance measurement. Performance measurement provides the basis for evaluation of potential innovation.
Inadequate performance is the prime force leading to a search for channel alternatives. The subject of planned change of channel arrangements is treated in
Chapter 11. The object of channel strategy formulation and execution is to arrive at a new arrangement of affairs that results in greater overall distribution
productivity.

Our coverage of channel management concludes with a brief chapter dealing with future distributive arrangements. Over the past decade a great many
forces have been at work in our economy which are now beginning to alter the
traditional way that products and services are marketed. Chapter 12 reviews
selected forces of change and concludes with examples of potential future distribution arrangements.

At the conclusion of each chapter, one or more cases are presented to illustrate the concepts developed in the chapter. These cases are based on business
situations and illustrate the concepts in a practical setting. The case we have
selected for Chapter 1 describes the failure of W. T. Grant. Although the
focus of the case is retailing, the channel issues are equally applicable to
wholesalers and manufacturing organizations. Despite one-time size and
strength, all business organizations can fall victim to a variety of fatal forces,
some of which stem directly from channel decisions. During the past few years,
W. T. Grant has been joined in bankruptcy by such other "household word"
firms as Federal Department Stores, Robert Hall, Interstate Stores, and Aber-
crombie & Fitch.

QUESTIONS

1   What are the primary factors which have complicated the study of marketing chan-
    nels?
2   Describe the impact of the cultural environment upon marketing channels.
3   Why is it expected that wholesale level sales would far exceed retail sales?
4   Should consumers be included in discussions of the roles of channel participants?
    Why or why not?
5   What is a vertical marketing system? Compare and contrast the three types of verti-
    cal marketing systems.
6   What are the four basic considerations involved with formulation of a channel
    strategy?
7   What is meant by *complexity* as a common feature of marketing channels?

8   How do the concepts of specialization and routinization lead to dependence in marketing channels?

9   Why is an understanding of disproportionate risk important in understanding channels of distribution?

10 What are the primary differences between free-flow marketing channels and vertical marketing systems?

CASE 1-1: W. T. Grant Company

On February 6, 1976, the committee of secured creditors, composed of six bankers and five merchandise suppliers, voted 7–4 for liquidation of W. T. Grant. Thus, the doors were closed on the nation's seventeenth largest retailer. The collapse of W. T. Grant Company represents the biggest retailing failure in the history of the United States, and the closing of Grant's 1,073 retail stores meant that 80,000 employees lost their jobs. The demise of the giant retailer, whose 1973 sales were $1.8 billion, is a classic example of mismanagement. Facing changing channels of distribution at the retail level, Grant countered with vigorous expansion in the absence of management information systems, controls, well-conceived performance measures, or a management team trained in basic merchandising principles.

BACKGROUND

The first W. T. Grant store was opened in Lynn, Massachusetts, in 1906 by William T. Grant, who invested his entire savings of $1,000. Grant, aged 30, had more than a decade of retailing experience and believed that there was a market for a retailer offering prices in the range above those of the five-and-ten-cent stores such as Woolworth's and Kresge's, but below those of the expensive department stores. The concept was a success and first-year sales of $99,000 were achieved.

Between 1907 and 1917, twenty-nine stores were added and sales reached $4,511,000. The chain grew to 157 stores by 1927 with sales of $43,744,000. However, in 1924, the founder gave up active management for the position of chairman of the board, which he held until 1966. Grant built a successful retail giant on the sales of basic, staple merchandise such as infants' wear, children's wear, white goods, and curtains and draperies, which had provided the basis for growth.

The year 1966 represented W. T. Grant Company's sixtieth year and the chain boasted 1,104 "Friendly Family Stores in 46 States" and sales of $920 million. In 1968, sales passed the $1 billion mark and the company made the following statements in the annual report:[1]

> Credit service is available at all stores, with approximately 25% of all sales being sold on credit.
>
> Over half of the present company stores have been opened during the last 10 years. There has been a rapid increase in the size of the average store opened. These newer stores, free-standing and in shopping centers, are complete promotional department stores offering broad merchandising assortments and services.
>
> Over half the stores have restaurants.
>
> More than one-third offer major appliances and have outside garden shops.

[1] W. T. Grant Company 1968 Annual Report.

There are over 60 auto service centers.

17 appliance service centers inspect, deliver, install, and service our "Bradford" brand of appliances.

Five major distribution centers warehouse and deliver merchandise to the stores.

Net earnings for the year were almost $38 million and management made the following projection:[2]

Having reached this significant milestone of one billion dollars in sales, the company will continue to build a bigger and stronger company for the benefit of Grant customers, stockholders, vendors, and employees.

A CRITICAL CHANGE IN TOP MANAGEMENT

On June 27, 1966, on the occasion of his ninetieth birthday, William T. Grant resigned as a director and chairman of the board. He was replaced by his brother-in-law, Edward Staley, formerly vice chairman of the board. Staley, a long-time Grant employee, was president of the company from 1952 to 1959. Louis C. Lustenberger remained as president, a position he had held since 1959. However, a number of organizational changes took place that would shape the future destiny of the firm. For example, in October 1966, Harry E. Pierson, former president of Pacific Coast Properties, Incorporated, and prior to 1960, a Grant real estate attorney and negotiator, was elected vice president, store expansion. Also, effective February 1, 1967, James G. Kendrick, formerly sales and store expansion vice president, again became president of Zeller's Limited, Grant's Canadian subsidiary. Kendrick was previously president of Zeller's Limited from 1958 until 1964. Richard W. Mayer, financial vice president and treasurer, who had set up the company's credit operation and had held the positions of national credit manager and treasurer, became sales vice president. John G. Curtin, formerly president of Zeller's Limited from 1965 to 1967, was elected financial vice president and treasurer.

Effective February 1, 1968, Louis C. Lustenberger, president of the company since August 25, 1959, retired under the terms of the employees retirement plan. Under his direction, W. T. Grant's sales had more than doubled and earnings had increased from $9,850,000 to over $32,000,000. In addition, new Grant stores had tripled in size, and total selling area had more than doubled. In the 1967 fiscal year, W. T. Grant Company set all-time records in both sales and earnings.

Lustenberger's choice for his successor was James G. Kendrick, then president of Zeller's Limited. Kendrick had joined Grant's store management program in 1935 after completing his education at the University of Minnesota. However, Lustenberger and Staley, the chairman of the board, had long been rivals on whether Grant was competing for the same market as K-Mart or if its target market was the same as Ward's and Penney's. Kendrick had openly dis-

___
[2] Ibid.

agreed with Staley over the direction of the company's expansion program. He believed that store interiors should be upgraded to match the change in merchandise mix. By changing store interiors, Kendrick felt they would create a consumer image that would be consistent with the objective of selling better merchandise. Staley, on the other hand, wanted to keep opening costs per store to the barest minimum and was against upgrading the interiors.[3] Also, Staley was not about to let Lustenberger's retirement slip by without strengthening his own position. Consequently, "a Staley man," Richard W. Mayer, was elected as Grant's ninth president on August 27, 1968.

THE STALEY–MAYER EXPANSION YEARS

Under the direction of the Staley–Mayer management team, Grant began an ambitious expansion program that "placed a great strain on the physical and human capability of the company to cope with the program. These were all large stores we were opening—6 million to 7 million square feet per year—and the expansion of our management organization just did not match the expansion of our stores."[4]

During the six years from 1968 to 1973 inclusive, Grant opened 410 new stores, enlarged an additional 36, and in the process spent $117,284,000 (Table 1 contains a summary of Grant's store growth from 1964 through 1973). The new stores ranged in size from 60,000 square feet to Grant City "superstores" of 180,000 square feet. The smaller stores were built in neighborhood and convenience shopping centers and the big stores were either free-standing or in medium-sized malls, with Sears, Ward's, or a discounter as coanchor.

The merchandise mix in the larger stores emphasized major appliances,

Table 1   Store Growth Program, 1964–1973

Year	Number of new stores opened	Number of stores enlarged	Capital expenditures	Store closings	Net number of stores at year end
1973	77	4	$23,537,000	96	1,189
1972	92	5	26,983,000	52	1,208
1971	83	5	26,476,000	31	1,168
1970	65	8	15,995,000	44	1,116
1969	52	3	13,668,000	49	1,095
1968	41	11	10,625,000	35	1,092
1967	24	13	7,792,000	42	1,086
1966	51	11	14,856,000	35	1,104
1965	27	13	7,846,000	31	1,088
1964	31	12	5,262,000	20	1,092

Source: W. T. Grant Company Annual Reports.

[3] Based on information obtained from James G. Kendrick during a telephone conversation on December 19, 1977.
[4] James G. Kendrick in "How W. T. Grant Lost $175 Million Last Year," *Business Week* (February 24, 1975), p. 75.

televisions, stereo equipment, automobile accessories, furniture, sporting goods, and camera equipment. Major appliances and televisions were sold under Grant's private label, called Bradford. While this was similar to the Sears position with its Kenmore line, it was in contrast to K-Mart's strategy of marketing a line of major appliances under the Whirlpool brand name.

By the early 1970s the average store stocked over 21,000 items, 71 percent of which were private label goods. Family fashions, which had once contributed about one-half of Grant's annual sales volume, represented less than 25 percent of sales in the early 1970s. In an effort to stimulate sales of big-ticket items, credit sales were emphasized. One former finance executive said: "We gave credit to every deadbeat who breathed."[5] Credit sales continued to account for as much as 25 percent of Grant's sales volume.

THE BEGINNING OF THE END

The year 1969 represented a significant turning point for Grant. It marked both the eighth consecutive year of improved sales and profit and the last year that such a claim could be made. A summary of selected financial data covering the years 1969 through 1973 is contained in Table 2. Although sales increased by almost 53 percent from 1969 to 1973, credit accounts receivable rose 62 percent, merchandise inventories more than doubled, short-term and long-term debt combined more than tripled, and earnings per share fell from $2.99 to $0.59. Perhaps even more significant, income before taxes from retail operations fell from $.0649 per dollar to $.008 per dollar of sales.

As early as 1971, significant dangers were evident. Sales per square foot reached an abysmal $30.74, less than one-half the rate achieved by Grant's major competitors. Return on net worth was 10.8 percent, down from 14.4 percent, and inventory and credit accounts receivable were increasing as a percent of sales. Also, short-term and long-term debt increased 68 percent on sales increases of 13.5 percent over 1969 levels. Alarmed by the direction in which the company was moving, former president Lustenberger and Raymond H. Fogler, also a past president and a Grant director, tried unsuccessfully to mobilize the outside directors. A former board member said: "The outside directors had to become more active if they were going to fulfill their responsibilities as company directors."[6]

THE 1973 ANNUAL REPORT

On October 1, 1973, Edward Staley retired as chairman of the board of directors and became chairman of the executive committee. Mayer became chairman of the board and chief executive officer, and Harry Pierson was elected

---

[5] "Investigating the Collapse of W. T. Grant," *Business Week* (July 19, 1976), p. 61.
[6] "How W. T. Grant Lost $175 Million Last Year," *Business Week* (February 24, 1975), p. 74.

Table 2 W. T. Grant Company: Selected Financial Data, 1969–1973

	1973	1972	1971	1970	1969
Sales	$1,849,802,346	$1,644,747,319	$1,374,812,791	$1,254,131,857	$1,210,918,068
Cost of merchandise sold, buying and occupancy costs	1,282,944,615	1,125,261,115	931,237,312	843,191,987	817,671,347
Interest expense	51,047,481	21,127,084	16,452,635	18,874,134	14,919,228
Net earnings	8,429,473	37,787,066	35,212,082	39,577,087	41,809,300
per common share	.59	2.70	2.51	2.87	2.99
Dividends paid per preferred share	3.75	3.75	3.75	3.75	3.75
Dividends paid per common share	1.50	1.50	1.50	1.50	1.40
Employee compensation and benefits	434,368,156	397,133,721	336,311,735	295,882,263	271,650,884
Cents per sales dollar	23.5	24.1	24.5	23.6	22.4
Accounts receivable, net	598,798,552	542,751,365	477,324,069	419,731,126	368,267,131
Merchandise inventories	450,636,556	399,532,793	298,676,170	260,492,329	222,127,620
Store properties, fixtures and improvements	100,983,800	91,419,748	77,173,498	61,832,352	55,310,732
Short-term commercial notes and bank loans	453,096,715	390,033,500	237,740,700	246,420,216	182,132,200
Accounts payable for merchandise	58,191,731	60,973,283	Unavailable	80,681,456	70,853,108
Long-term debt	220,336,000	126,672,000	128,432,000	32,301,000	35,402,000
Net worth	323,738,431	334,338,566	325,745,094	302,036,424	290,688,499
Income from retail operations before taxes*	1,502,000	59,901,000	59,059,000	69,806,000	78,598,000
Cents per sales dollar	.08	3.64	4.30	5.57	6.49
Percent earned on net worth	2.6%	11.3%	10.8%	13.1%	14.4%
Inventory as a percent of sales	24.4%	24.3%	21.7%	20.8%	18.3%
Cost of goods sold as a percent of sales	69.36%	68.42%	67.74%	67.23%	67.52%
Accounts receivable as a percent of sales	32.37%	33.00%	34.72%	33.47%	30.41%
Square feet of store space at year end	56,224,000	50,618,000	44,718,000	38,157,000	33,855,000
Sales per square foot	32.90	32.49	30.74	32.87	35.77
Dividends pair—common	20,828,989	20,806,653	20,793,621	20,426,251	19,279,815
—preferred	293,054	344,709	345,813	395,031	456,858

* 1973 Annual Report, Comparative Statement of Operations, p. 27.

president and chief operating officer, effective February 1, 1974. These changes were no doubt related to the 1973 performance of the firm.

Sales for 1973 increased to $1,849,802,346, but profits fell 78 percent to $8,-429,473, the lowest profit since 1961 when sales were $574,502,000. Short-term commercial notes and bank loans and long-term debt reached $673,432,715, more than twice the net worth. It is interesting that on profits of less than $8.5 million, the company continued to pay dividends in excess of $21 million.

In the 1973 annual report, Mayer and Pierson addressed the issue of the company's lack of image at the consumer level:[7]

> During the last six years your Company opened 410 large stores of over 50,000 square feet, enlarged 36 successful stores, and closed 307 smaller units. In view of the decline in earnings in 1973, you might well ask . . . WHY?
>
> Retailing is synonymous with change. Selling methods, size and types of stores, and lines or departments of merchandise change as the demands of the American Consumer dictate. The Management of your Company recognized this inevitable shift from smaller, limited stores to larger "full line" stores and committed itself to the complete restructuring of the Company.
>
> As this proceeded, a frequent question asked was "We do not understand or recognize your image." Ten years ago, the Company had been "understood and recognized" as a large chain of Variety Stores. Our image was clear. We sold limited price items in smallwares, wearing apparel and soft goods for the home. Times changed and retailing changed . . . to the one stop, complete store of over 50,000 square feet which we call Grant City and that is the direction your Company followed.
>
> To convert a chain of approximately 1,000 successful limited variety stores to a Company with approximately half of its units composed of Grant City or "full line" stores, while at the same time adding all of the necessary back up services, merchandise distribution centers, data processing, and major appliance warehousing, home delivery and service in a relatively short span of time was not easily accomplished. Our image may have become blurred. We do have both small and large stores. This has to be. Ten years ago, from Maine to California, Grant operated small stores with limited merchandise assortments. Today in hundreds of communities the Grant City store is recognized as a store with complete assortments of merchandise for the home and family. Our Grant City stores may not yet have the general acceptance of some of our major competitors, but we firmly believe our quality is good, our pricing and values excellent and that our reputation and acceptance as a Grant City full line store improves each year. We are still relatively new to the full line store field, but we intend to stay—and to improve each year.
>
> In this letter to Stockholders we will cover more fully the factors influencing operations in 1973 and our prospects for the future.

In addition, Mayer used the opportunity to attempt to justify the ill-fated credit system which he had expanded, promoted, and directed for a number of years:[8]

[7] W. T. Grant Company 1973 Annual Report, p. 2.
[8] Ibid., pp. 2–3.

In 1946, the Company first introduced a credit service to aid its customers to purchase wanted merchandise and pay on an installment plan. The stores were small and stocked with merchandise limited in lines and price. The credit coupon book was selected as the most practical method as these coupons could be used as cash and the customer did not have to wait for individual sales slips on each item purchased. It gave us a method of granting credit without incurring the expense of a sophisticated credit system to keep customer credit limits under control. For smaller stores, this type was not only popular with customers—but it was tailor-made for the simplified operation of this small unit. However, as the Company developed new full-line Grant City stores, customers indicated a preference for the revolving credit charge plan. In addition, governmental regulations have made it increasingly difficult and expensive to administer the coupon-type credit plan. Primarily, in recognition of the customer preference for revolving credit charge accounts, this plan was promoted in 1973, and this emphasis will continue in the future. This change from the credit coupon book plan produces less service charge revenue and is more expensive to operate. During 1973, although credit sales were $45,000,000 higher, service charge revenues were down by over $7,000,000. On the other hand, our experience in the past year indicates that Grant City customers prefer the revolving credit charge and will purchase more merchandise with this plan.

In spite of the looming financial disaster, Grant continued with its expansion plans for 1974 and its diversification into catalog showroom stores:[9]

In 1973 the Company opened 77 new stores and enlarged 4 existing units, for an additional 5,606,000 square feet of new store space. In addition, construction of the new 475,000 square foot Distribution Center in Windsor Locks, Connecticut, was completed in late Fall 1973.

In 1974, we will open approximately 45 new stores and enlarge 1 unit for approximately 3,000,000 square feet. The reduction, both in number of stores and square footage from 1973 levels, is due to developers encountering difficulty in securing necessary materials to complete centers on schedule, inability to start some projects because of the high cost of interim financing, and the increased time required to be spent before beginning a project in satisfying environmental control requirements. It is our estimate at this time that the 1975 program will be of the same magnitude as 1974, or smaller, and management feels that this is a more workable program in view of present conditions. This will, of course, reduce pre-opening costs and the additional funds required for investment in capital expenditures, inventories and to carry customer receivables, from the peaks of the last few years.

The program of closing older Grant stores, typically of a smaller size, was accelerated in 1973 with 96 closings. All expenses pertaining to this program were charged to the year of closing. Since the closing of unprofitable stores not only reduces investment in inventory but eliminates the burden of operating costs, this program will be continued in 1974.

In 1973, GranJewel, the company's joint venture participation in catalog showroom retailing with Jewelcor, opened 11 stores and purchased Edison Jewelers and Distributors Co. of Fort Worth, Texas, which operates 4 units. In 1974, an additional 7 catalog showroom stores are planned.

[9] Ibid., p. 4.

Table 3 Grant Directors as of 1973 Year-End with Company Affiliations

Richard W. Mayer	Chairman of the Board and Chief Executive Officer
Harry E. Pierson	President and Chief Operating Officer
Edward Staley	Chairman of the Executive Committee
A. Richard Butler	Executive Vice President—Merchandising
Joseph W. Chinn, Jr.	Director and Chairman, Consulting Committee, Wilmington Trust Company
Raymond H. Fogler	Retired, former President of W. T. Grant Company
John D. Gray	Chairman of the Board and Chief Executive Officer, Hart, Schaffner & Marx
Joseph Hinsey	Partner, White & Case
James G. Kendrick	President and Chief Executive Officer of Zeller's Limited
E. Robert Kinney	President and Chief Operating Officer of General Mills, Inc.
John J. LaPlante	Personnel Vice President
Robert A. Luckett	Corporate Services Vice President and Comptroller
Louis C. Lustenberger	Retired, former President of W. T. Grant Company
DeWitt Peterkin, Jr.	Vice Chairman of the Board, Morgan Guaranty Trust Company of New York
Charles F. Phillips	President Emeritus, Bates College
Clarence W. Spangle	Executive Vice President of Honeywell, Inc.
Asa T. Spaulding	Consultant to Boyden International Group, Inc., of Los Angeles

Mayer and Pierson concluded their message to the stockholders as follows:[10]

> We will continue opening full-line Grant City stores and will continue to expand our revolving credit charge account plan. This year, the economy will be uncertain, but Management will continue to take aggressive steps to strengthen its entire operation, whether in limited or full-line Grant City stores. We will continue to change the Company to meet the demands of customers. In the final analysis, our customers will determine the success of the Company. We feel that Customers are aware of the positive changes that are occurring and that, as a result, the acceptance of the Grant City stores—as full line stores—will continue to increase.

Table 3 contains a list of Grant directors as of the 1973 year-end.

CRISIS MANAGEMENT AT GRANT

The dismal 1973 financial performance was followed by a $10 million loss for the first 6 months of 1974. Effective June 30, 1974, Richard Mayer resigned as chairman and chief executive officer of Grant's and Edward Staley resigned as a director. Fogler and Lustenberger also resigned from the board. One former director made the following observation about the reorganization:[11]

[10] Ibid., p. 5.
[11] "How W. T. Grant Lost $175 Million Last Year," *Business Week* (February 24, 1975), p. 76.

. . . it is a pretty safe bet that Staley's resignation would not have been forthcoming if his old foes didn't leave, too.

On September 3, 1974, James G. Kendrick became chairman and president
of W. T. Grant after leading Zeller's Limited for a total of approximately 13
years of impressive sales and profit growth. He believed that the most critical
problems facing him were: (1) to increase the company's sales per square foot,
(2) to revise significantly the merchandise program back to the basic lines that
the company had built its reputation on, (3) to reduce the substantial losses associated with the company's credit operation, and (4) to revise and strengthen
its financial policies and controls.[12]

One of Kendrick's first accomplishments was refinancing the short-term
notes with a $600 million line of credit with 143 banks headed by Morgan Guar-
anty Trust Company. Three banks put up $300 million, eleven banks doled out
about $200 million, and the remaining $100 million came from 129 banks. Grant
used its 50.2 percent interest in Zeller's Limited and $600 million in credit ac-
counts receivable as collateral.

Kendrick planned to reduce the company's reliance on private label merchandise and to replace an inventory of slow-selling items with fresh, new,
wanted merchandise. With rising credit delinquencies, Grant began accepting
BankAmericard and Master Charge sales. In addition, nervous suppliers had to
be assured that Grant would continue to pay its bills since the American Credit
Indemnity Company had canceled its credit insurance policy.[13] In an effort to
gain immediate consumer support, $6 million was budgeted for television
advertisements in thirty-five major markets in fall 1974.

In spite of these changes, Grant suffered losses in 1974 of $175 million on
sales of $1.7 billion. Contributing to the massive loss were credit losses of over
$90 million, $24 million in store closing expenses, heavy interest charges, and a
substantial markdown budget. Also, Grant filed suit against three former real
estate employees, including John A. Christensen, former real estate vice president, for taking what Kendrick described as "hundreds of thousands of dollars
in bribes in connection with store leases."[14]

THE COLLAPSE

In 1975, Kendrick began a program to close another 126 stores and the maturity
date on Grant's agreement with the banks was extended from June 1975 to
March 31, 1976. To satisfy the banks, Robert Anderson, former vice president
of Sears, was hired as president and chief executive officer in April 1975 for a
guaranteed salary and pension totaling $2.5 million. At this point, any anxious

[12] Based on a telephone interview with James G. Kendrick on December 19, 1977.
[13] "It's Get-Tough Time at W. T. Grant," *Business Week* (October 19, 1974), p. 46.
[14] "How W. T. Grant Lost $175 Million Last Year," *Business Week* (February 24, 1975),
p. 74.

supplier could have brought down the company by filing a Chapter X proceeding.

By October 1975 losses were mounting and Grant was having great difficulty obtaining merchandise from suppliers. As a result, the company filed under Chapter XI. Under Chapter XI, stores west of the Mississippi River were closed and plans were initiated to reduce further the number of stores to 359 in the Northeast. However, questionable financial data and an uncertain future resulted in liquidation:[15]

> The final blow came when the consultants cautioned the creditors that it would take six to eight years to determine whether Grant would survive. The bankers favored liquidation and were hungrily eyeing the $320 million in cash accumulated from store closings and liquidations. Trade creditors, by contrast, were uncertain. They were fully secured and doing business with Grant. But on Feb. 6, the committee voted 7–4 for liquidation.

EPILOGUE

In December 1977, former president Kendrick was asked whether he believed in September 1974 when he returned to Grant's from Zeller's that he could save the company. He replied: "I would not have accepted the job if I had not. However, at that point in time I was not aware of just how bad the credit situation was." In addition, Kendrick was asked whether he could have accomplished his objectives if he had been named president 7 months earlier (on February 1, 1974, Pierson became president). Keeping in mind the impending legal cases, he observed that, with the benefit of 20/20 hindsight, it might be possible for some people to reach that conclusion.

CASE 1-1: QUESTIONS

1 What channel decisions do you see in the W. T. Grant Company case?
2 When did it become evident that Grant was headed for financial trouble? What were the danger signs? What measures of financial performance would have provided management with additional useful information?
3 What were the primary causes of the bankruptcy of the W. T. Grant Company?
4 What role did the American Credit Indemnity Company play in the collapse of the W. T. Grant Company? The decision to private label big-ticket items? Grant's credit department?

---

[15] "Investigating the Collapse of W. T. Grant," *Business Week* (July 19, 1976), p. 62.

Channel Structure
and Participants

Why is it that some countries have highly developed, efficient distribution systems, while others, particularly the developing countries, lose up to 50 percent of their food supply due to spoilage before it can be consumed? Why is it that some countries have modern supermarkets while others still rely upon the native trader to satisfy distribution requirements? Is it simply a matter of institutional capability, or something as basic as marketing attitude? In areas such as Colombia, Bolivia, and northeastern Brazil, there is virtually no distribution infrastructure.[1] What exists are central food supply warehouses run by the government and built at the insistence of United States or French foreign aid agencies. In addition, market preferences are not an integral part of the distribution process, since legislation governs the size of inventories wholesalers are al-

---

[1] Studies in food distribution were conducted by the Latin American Market Planning Center of Michigan State University in northeastern Brazil, Bolivia, and Colombia. The findings of these studies are reported in *Market Processes in the Recife Area of Northeast Brazil,* Marketing in Developing Communities Series, Research Report No. 2, Latin American Studies Center, Michigan State University, East Lansing, Michigan; *Market Processes in La Paz, Bolivia,* Marketing in Developing Communities Series, Research Report No. 3, Latin American Studies Center, Michigan State University, East Lansing, Michigan; *Market Coordination in the Development of the Cauca Valley Region, Colombia,* Marketing in Developing Communities Series, Research Report No. 5, Latin American Studies Center, Michigan State University, East Lansing, Michigan.

lowed to carry. In some countries the wholesale supply is as small as 2 days of retail demand.[2] In such situations, wholesalers and retailers are viewed as parasites, and the result is a large number of small, inefficient organizations, or what might be termed a minidistribution system.[3] In some developing countries, it is common practice for such items as cigarettes to be distributed one at a time by an individual trader whose total supply is limited to one or two packages. In contrast, the United States distribution system is massive and highly efficient and performs a well-defined set of marketing functions. In completing its distribution job, the United States distribution system accounts for 50 percent of the selling price of goods.[4]

In these contrasting situations, each country began with similar economic foundations, but diverged somewhere along the way. In this chapter we shall examine the ideological origins of the free market distribution system, the emergence of channels and their basic activities, and the dynamics of the activities and structures that evolve.

ECONOMIC FOUNDATIONS OF THE FREE MARKET SYSTEM

To fully appreciate the origins of a free market system, it is necessary to review economic history. As we observe the evolution of our distribution channels from the era of feudal rulers to our contemporary market system, we can gain an understanding of why the structure exists as it does today. In this section, we examine the competitive foundations of our distribution system by exploring the basic forces of scarce resources, freedom of choice, division of labor, exchange, and conflict.

Scarce Resources

Contrary to the utterings of the avant-garde denouncing the competitive system, most Western economies still function on the basis of historical ideological foundations that resulted in the development of the free market system. The free market system is grounded in the belief that society must always cope with a condition of scarce resources. Contemporary shortages of energy and raw materials reflect that condition.

Although many social, political, and economic differences exist among societies, there is one common element: the basic economic requirement to cope with scarce resources. The problem was articulated by Adam Smith in his *Wealth of Nations* and well stated by Professor Lionel Robbins in his classical

---

    [2] *Market Coordination in the Development of the Cauca Valley Region, Colombia,* Marketing in Developing Communities, Research Report No. 5, Latin American Studies Center, Michigan State University, East Lansing, Michigan, p. 326.

    [3] *Market Processes in the Recife Area of Northeast Brazil,* Marketing in Developing Communities, Research Report No. 3, Latin American Studies Center, Michigan State University, East Lansing, Michigan, pp. 6–24, 25.

    [4] Reavis Cox, *Distribution in a High-Level Economy* (Englewood Cliffs, N.J.: Prentice-Hall, Inc., 1965), chap. 1.

definition of economics: *"Economics is the science which studies human be-havior as a relationship between ends and scarce means which have alternative uses."* [5] If resources are scarce, then wants will be insatiable. Unraveling and solving this demand-supply dichotomy is a major objective of an economic system.

To understand the full impact of scarce resources, we should contrast the era of mercantilism, in which societies equated the accumulation of treasure with wealth, with the modern era of capitalism, in which societies equate the accumulation of material goods with happiness. [6] At the turn of the eighteenth century a great deal of philosophical debate centered on the justification of the new social contract theories which had as their objective the attainment of individual economic freedom. The nonrescindable contractual arrangement in which individual rights were relinquished to a feudal ruler in return for protection was under attack by a new doctrine based on the individual wills of the members of the population. A variant of the individual theme was a doctrine by which the sum total of individual wills was combined into a "state" will for the good of all concerned. In classical terms, these two ideologies were identified as capitalism and socialism. Remarkably similar are the Ideology I and Ideology II themes elaborated by Lodge in 1975 in *The New American Ideology*. [7]

In England, the new social contract theory of individual will led to the overthrow of the Stewarts and the establishment of a government representative of the people during the latter half of the eighteenth century. It also glorified the individual. Production and commerce flourished and all activity was directed toward wealth accumulation. The new social organization and resultant behavior of the citizens created another philosophical issue: Just how free should individuals be to accumulate wealth?

Freedom of Choice

With the removal of political oppression and the general acceptance of individual rights, people began to exercise their new-found freedoms. The most notable displays of this new freedom were in the economic areas of consumption and production. That is, producers became free to produce what they wanted to and consumers were free to select from a variety of production alternatives those goods they wished to consume. The forces of the free market system were put into action and the result was heterogeneity of demand.

As might be expected given human nature, the accumulation of the greatest wealth possible became one of the primary goals of powerful individuals. Once again, the issue of wealth accumulation became a matter of social con-

[5] Lionel C. Robbins, *An Essay on the Nature and Significance of Economic Science*, 2d ed. (London: Macmillan & Company, Ltd., 1952), p. 16.

[6] Mercantilism was used to characterize the period from the downfall of the feudal system in Western Europe to about the beginning of the 16th century. It was followed by commercial capitalism until about the end of the 19th century.

[7] George Cabot Lodge, *The New American Ideology* (New York: Alfred A. Knopf, Inc., 1975).

cern among the philosophers of that day. Economists began to realize that greater and greater individual wealth accumulations made possible by a free market system did little, if anything, to increase the happiness of the very rich. At the same time, the poorer element of society became worse off due to the scarcity of resources. The presumption that the increased output of society would spill over to the poor who needed additional increments of wealth did not materialize. Society now faced a new dichotomy. Income redistribution did not happen automatically, nor was the underlying basic economic doctrine well understood. The paradox was ethically resolved by many but was publicized in 1759 by Adam Smith in his *Moral Sentiments*. Around 1790, the logic was resolved by Jeremy Bentham with his law of diminishing utility. This development of economic understanding helped explain and justify the rationale of the free market system and pointed out the importance of the insatiability and heterogeneity of human wants to economic growth. Attention was turned to the best economic system to overcome the problem of scarce resources.

Division of Labor

The frenzy for wealth accumulation soon established the practice of division of labor, or specialization. Specialization remains an important part of all contemporary political and economic systems. At the same time, however, it creates some basic distribution problems. First, specialization in production results in specific manufacturers limiting output to selected products. From the viewpoint of the total society, this results in heterogeneity of supply. Products in the United States are produced and distributed by approximately 11.8 million establishments. These establishments represent a source of supply and demand to each other as well as to the 66.6 million households.[8] Specialization creates a basic problem since each unit of supply and demand is in a different geographic location. However, location factors tend to concentrate industries in specific geographic areas. For example, the shoe industry is concentrated in the Northeast and Central Midwest, the furniture industry in the South, and the rubber industry in Ohio.[9] Regardless of selected economic concentration, however, the fact still remains that some mechanism must be found to match *heterogeneous supply* with *heterogeneous demand*.

Second, if individuals or firms are willing to specialize, and if they have the freedom to produce and consume what they wish, the result could be utter chaos unless some ordering mechanism exists to allocate resources. The *exchange mechanism* provides the matching force. *Exchange* is the means by which heterogeneous supply and heterogeneous demand are matched. The specific quantities of commodities and finished goods exchanged are determined by the calculation of value for each transaction. The determination of value through a system of free markets and free prices is the enabling mechanism. It

[8] Figures are compiled from data in the *Statistical Abstract of the United States,* 1974.

[9] For a comprehensive review of location theories, see: M. J. Webber, *Impact of Uncertainty on Location* (Cambridge, Mass.: The MIT Press, 1972), chaps. 2–3; and Melvin L. Greenhut and H. Ohta, *Theory of Spatial Pricing and Market Areas* (Durham: Duke University Press, 1975).

is this simple fact that led Professor Boulding to write: "Indeed it is hardly too much to say that the study of exchange comprises nine-tenths of the economists' dominion."[10]

Exchange

One objective of economic activity is to maximize satisfaction from scarce resources. In an economic organization characterized by a division of labor, this satisfaction is achieved by an exchange mechanism. The exchange mechanism, through the determination of value, is used "to guide the choices economic specialists make among alternative uses of their resources and to exchange among them the goods and services they produce."[11]

Exchanges do not just happen. Specialization through the division of labor and demand creates barriers to exchange. Specifically, four problems exist. The first problem results from the location of sources of supply and centers of demand. Because the sources of supply are dispersed geographically throughout the world, there is a need for physical movement. The transport problem is further aggravated by the fact that buyers distant from producers often require only small quantities of a product, which results in high costs of transportation.[12] This problem is often referred to as a spatial discrepancy between the points of production and consumption of a product.

The second problem results from the fact that goods are produced at different times from the time of demand. Agricultural output is seasonal, but consumption is constant. Mass-produced manufactured goods must be fabricated and assembled far in advance of consumption. Inventory stocking and related risk become a major requirement in such marketing systems. This problem is often referred to as a temporal discrepancy between the time of production and consumption of a product.

The third problem results from the quantities and assortments demanded. Manufacturers typically specialize in production of a large quantity of an item while consumers purchase only one or a few at a time. For instance, Genesco produces several million pairs of shoes in a year, but consumers buy only one pair at a time. In addition, manufacturers usually specialize in production of a few product items while consumers need thousands of different products. From the range of products produced, specific quantities and unique assortments must be assembled to meet demand requirements. This problem is often referred to as a discrepancy of quantity and assortments.

The fourth problem is to stimulate the exchange process. Resolution of the first three problems provides no guarantee that exchange will take place. In a free market society where the output sector makes available to buyers an almost

---

[10] Kenneth E. Boulding, *Economic Analysis,* 4th ed. (New York: Harper & Row, Publishers, Inc., 1966), p. 4.

[11] Cox, op. cit., p. 14.

[12] For an elaboration of the impact of size of shipment on transportation cost, see: Donald J. Bowersox, *Logistical Management,* rev. ed. (New York: The Macmillan Company, Inc., 1978), chaps. 5 and 8.

endless number of products, it is paramount that suppliers seek to identify needs and then influence the exchange process toward their individual market offerings. Thus, the solutions to the four problems of exchange create a basic element of conflict within a free market system.

Conflict

An outstanding feature of a free market system is conflict between firms as they bid for buyers' patronage, and among buyers as they bid for scarce resources. An exchange system based upon negotiated price provides a basis for resolving such conflicts. This form of conflict, identified as competition, is essential to the operation of the free market system.

Another form of conflict is also present. To the extent that specialization exists, it creates dependence among participants. This dependence carries with it the potential for conflict. Conflict may be within a channel of distribution or external to channel participants. An example of external conflict is a strike by dock workers, which can cripple retail trade. When governmental policies are enforced to prevent such occurrences, a degree of freedom is lost. To the extent that freedom is maintained, exposure to external conflicts remains a vital management concern. It is important to realize that government regulations reduce the freedom of some participants to function. While some restriction is in the public interest, the greatest part of our economic life has remained relatively free. The impact of the legal setting on market channels is developed in Chapter 5.

Conflict that results from dependence within a particular channel is of critical importance to managers. This form of conflict is discussed in depth in Chapters 3 and 4. Resolution of conflict either by power or by cooperation is necessary for a distribution channel to function effectively.

In summary, the objective of economic activity is to maximize satisfaction from scarce resources. In an economic arrangement characterized by specialization, the objective is achieved by an exchange mechanism. Exchange systems must overcome some basic problems which are created by heterogeneity of supply and demand. The solution to these problems creates friction in the form of conflict and, to a degree, places restrictions on the individual freedoms of production and consumption choice. The manner in which channel structures emerge to satisfy the objectives of a free market system is discussed in the next section.

EMERGENCE OF CHANNELS OF DISTRIBUTION

In this section we examine the development of modern distribution channels which satisfy the basic needs of a free market system. The emergence of channels is viewed from the perspective of structure and the activities performed by an exchange system.

Structure for Exchange

In primitive societies a high degree of specialization through division of labor in production can exist without the presence of an efficient means for matching supply and demand. In the "cottage" economies, families may have specialized output, but distribution is costly and time-consuming unless specialists are used. In this part, decentralized versus a central marketplace is discussed and the evolution to multistage distribution systems is examined.

Decentralized versus Central Marketplace   Figure 2-1 illustrates three possible forms of exchange for an economy with five households. Assume each household produces a product desired by all other households. In the decentralized structure, each producer must visit or be visited by the other producers to exchange products. Thus, this decentralized structure requires ten trips and ten transactions in order to satisfy everyone's demand. The number of transactions can be found by the formula

$$\frac{n(n - 1)}{2}$$

where n represents the number of producers. Of course, such a structure would be impractical today, but years ago such systems existed and represented the

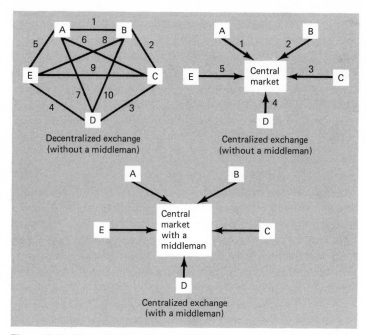

Decentralized exchange
(without a middleman)

Centralized exchange
(without a middleman)

Centralized exchange
(with a middleman)

Figure 2-1   Alternative exchange patterns.

primary means of exchange. The initial institutional arrangement which evolved to promote efficiency was the central marketplace.

A central marketplace evolves when the five producers in our hypothetical example decide to meet in one spot at a given time. At the market, they set up their own stalls since no middlemen* exist. This central market offers a distinct advantage in comparison to a decentralized system. The number of trips required to complete exchange is reduced from ten to five, with resulting savings in transportation. However, the number of transactions, as illustrated in Figure 2-1, remains at ten since each producer must still trade with the others.

Further refinement of the institutional structure occurs when a middleman emerges in the central marketplace. In this situation, each producer comes to the market and, instead of setting up an individual stall, goes to the middleman to exchange surplus products for needed products. Since each producer turns in surpluses, the middleman maintains an inventory so that the number of transactions required to satisfy demand is reduced from ten to five.

In many developing countries (and in the United States not too many years ago), a large portion of the food supply moved through a central market reminiscent of the system described above. The primary difference is that the market is usually owned and operated by the local government. Foodstuffs, household utensils, textiles, and clothing are brought to the central marketplace by producers for sale to buyers. The producer either sells through a private stall or sells outright to a stall operator. These systems, compared to modern distribution, are grossly inefficient. The stall operators are small, partially subsidized by local governments, and have high variable costs which make price reductions an impossibility. They have poor price communication and usually inadequate sanitary conditions.[13] Still, these central markets offer some distinct advantages in comparison to a decentralized system:

1 Products move in large quantities to market with potential savings in transportation.
2 The number of transactions is reduced.
3 A convenience is introduced for producers and consumers.

The cost of such a market is establishment of the physical facility and payment to the distribution specialist who, in the above example, is the stall operator.

A vestige of the central market system of exchange exists in the farmer's markets operating in several towns and cities in the United States today. Only a very minute portion of our food supply moves through such systems. A more elaborate variation is the Furniture Mart in Chicago. Another highly sophisticated permanent central market is the Chicago Board of Trade, one of the

---

* The term "middleman" is used by convention in marketing literature and practice. It refers to individuals, firms, or corporations that stand between prime producers and ultimate consumers. It is not intended to be gender-specific.

[13] High variable costs result in such a steep total cost line that any attempt to reduce prices pushes the break-even point beyond the capacity of the stall operation.

larger grain exchanges in the world. Sophistication is introduced in a central market like the Chicago Board of Trade in that there is no need to move the actual product to the marketplace. Buying and selling is conducted on the basis of well-established grain grades.

Other variations of the central market system are the periodic trade fairs such as the Machine Tool Trade Fair held annually in Chicago, or the trade fairs sponsored by foreign governments in different countries, such as the Brazilian Trade Fair in Brussels in 1974. In these cases, producers exhibit merchandise for buyer examination and potential purchase. These modern variations on the central marketplace are efficient for selected forms of exchange. However, the dominant means of modern distribution is the multistage exchange structure.

Multistage Structure The burden on producers to transport products to the central market was soon assumed by specialists, or intermediaries, who contacted each producer and purchased goods for future resale. Such specialists would then sell an assortment of goods to stall operators who operated in the central marketplace. In many developing countries, independent truck operators perform this collection when production is distant from the central marketplace. Unlike transportation companies in the United States, these independent truck operators actually purchase the goods and therefore assume a significant element of risk.

Just as producers welcomed a specialist to ease their burden, some stall operators saw greater opportunities in moving away from the central marketplace and providing buyers with a purchasing "location convenience." As more and more entrepreneurs began to seek this opportunity, the multistage distribution structure evolved.

Today vast numbers of intermediaries or specialists exist within distribution channels. Most producers rely on some type of specialist for sale of their products to consumers or other industrial firms. The central marketplace has been replaced by wholesalers and retailers, who have emerged to bring assortments closer to buyers. Over the years, many variations have been introduced which add additional layers of specialization, but the characteristic exchange system of today remains a multistage structure.

Exchange System Activities

Four problems of exchange were identified earlier in this chapter:

1 The need to match heterogeneous supply, caused by specialized production, with a heterogeneous demand caused by freedom in consumption: a discrepancy of quantity, assortments, and search problem.

2 A need for economic physical movement of goods because of the separation of production and consumption: a spatial problem.

3 The need to match supply with demand when supply is produced at one point in time and demand is manifest at another point in time: a temporal problem.

4 The need to stimulate exchanges because of the multiplicity of suppliers offering alternative goods to potential buyers: a demand-stimulating problem.

As noted earlier, these problems are resolved by the distribution capabilities of the free market system. In this part, we review the activities which the aggregate distribution system must accomplish to realize effective exchange.

Discrepancy of Quantity and Assortment-Search Activities   We have already seen that output is heterogeneous because of specialization. Producers supply large quantities of a specialized product that is demanded by a wide variety of other producers, intermediary specialists, and consumers. Each buying unit desires a unique assortment of goods. Within the assortment the quantity of each individual product demanded is much smaller than the quantity typically manufactured. Furthermore, as noted earlier, specialized production tends to be geographically concentrated. In contrast, demand units are widely scattered.

Figure 2-2 illustrates numerically the demand and supply situation of the United States economy. A major activity of the exchange system which is required to overcome the inherent discrepancy of assortments and searching is *sorting*. The sorting activity was first described by Hovde and later developed by Alderson.[14] It is divided into four basic processes: sorting out, accumulation, allocation, and assorting. Each is described below.

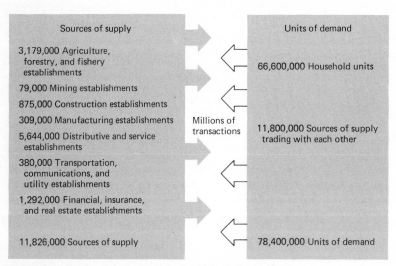

Figure 2-2   Demand and supply in the United States today.

[14] The concept of sorting was first developed by Hovde in: Howard T. Hovde, special ed., "Wholesaling in our American Economy," *Journal of Marketing*, supplementary issue (September 1949), pp. 84–107. It was later articulated by Alderson in: Wroe Alderson, *Marketing Behavior and Executive Action* (Homewood, Ill.: Richard D. Irwin, Inc., 1957), chap. 7.

Sorting out   This is the task of selecting from a heterogeneous supply of a given product class an assortment of homogeneous goods within that class. The idea first developed in agricultural goods whereby different quality levels or grades were assembled to represent a homogeneous supply of grain or fruit. In an industrial context, this can be expanded to illustrate selection of a homogeneous supply from the total supply of textiles: for example, a supply of synthetics versus wool or cotton textiles. The concept can also be illustrated in industrial goods, such as the sorting of malleable, gray, and ductile iron. Any business performing sorting out may elect to work in more than one quality grade or class of product but probably will not elect to do business in all available products.

Accumulation   Because of the vast size of an economy such as the United States and the fact that buying units are scattered throughout the nation, it makes sense that no single business will corner the entire supply of any specific class of product. Accumulation is left to businesses which assemble homogeneous supplies into larger quantities than are typical of sorting out. Accumulation of homogeneous stocks typically is performed closer to the demand centers than sorting out. It is a process designed to reduce transportation costs, since goods of a certain class can move closer to the demand centers in larger quantities. If output moved directly from the relatively small stocks gathered in the sorting-out process to the demand units, a large number of small shipments would be required. Accumulation allows unique assortments to be achieved while retaining the inherent economies of transportation.

Allocation   Allocation is the act of selecting an assortment of goods related to a specific demand from a number of homogeneous supplies gathered at the accumulation stage. The allocation process results in a broad assortment of goods that a retailer or an industrial purchaser may wish to acquire. For example, tools, housewares, and building materials may be brought together to assemble a line of hardware. Similarly, carpets, drapes, and furniture may form a stock of goods that has some association in purchase. This is characteristically the wholesaler's task in a given line of trade.

Assorting   The last process in the sorting activity brings together a final assortment of goods for exchange. The retailer, a department store for example, has to select an assortment that consumers will purchase. Department store buyers must select a merchandise assortment from the available range of men's and women's clothing, appliances, hardware, furniture, and the like. With the final task of assorting, the retailer obtains a final selection of goods that matches consumer demand as closely as possible.

The overall activity of sorting is a process of conversion and dispersion. It converts heterogeneous supply into customized quantities and assortments in an efficient manner. The sorting activity not only matches heterogeneous supply and demand, but also bridges the distance gap between production and consumption.

Figure 2-3 illustrates the sorting activity. A furniture assortment has been selected for this example. We start with a number of specialized industries such

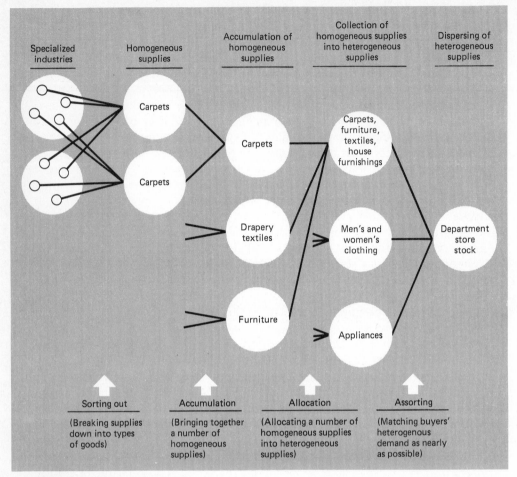

Figure 2-3 The sorting solution.

as carpets, textiles for drapes, and furniture. At the sorting-out stage, two homogeneous supplies of carpets are assembled from the twelve suppliers of carpets. At the accumulation stage, another homogeneous supply of carpets is assembled from each of the two homogeneous supplies. At the same time, a similar process of sorting out and accumulation is occurring for drapery textiles and furniture. At the allocation stage the carpets, drapery textiles, and furniture are combined into a heterogeneous supply identified as household furnishings. At the assorting stage, the unique assortments buyers want are matched, and the house furnishings assortment will be combined with clothing, hard goods, white goods, and so on. Our example describes a consumer good, but the same process applies to industrial goods.

The sorting activity is the solution to the discrepancy of assortments problem created by modern exchange. It must be performed in a specialized society. Who performs this activity is not important at this time, but we cannot do without it.

Related to discrepancy of quantity and assortment is the search aspect of exchange. In an economy with freedom of both consumption and production, uncertainty arises. Producers are not certain exactly which products buyers want, and buyers are not certain that they can find what they want. Those engaged in the sorting activity try to anticipate the assortment of goods wanted. Likewise, the producer tries to anticipate before production the goods that will sell. Much of the skill in sorting lies in correctly assembling a heterogeneous supply that matches reasonably well the unique assortments that will be demanded. This process is called *search* and both suppliers and buyers engage in it.

Spatial Activity   An analysis of the sorting activity highlights the need to overcome the problem of space. In this section the decentralized, central, and multistage market systems are examined from the viewpoint of space closure.

In Figure 2-1 five producers in a decentralized system require ten transactions to complete supply and demand matching. Because of the small size of the quantities to be moved to each household, the total cost per movement would be high. In the decentralized system, assume that each movement will cost $5.00 and each transaction will cost $1.00. The total movement cost will be $50.00 (ten movements at $5.00) and transaction cost will be $10.00 (ten transactions at $1.00) for a total cost of $60.00. With a central marketplace, assume movement from the points of production to the central marketplace will be in large quantities at $8.00 per movement. The per-movement cost is higher, but the unit cost of movement in the system will be less.[15] The cost of movement from the central marketplace to the buyer is a nondollar cost borne by the buyer. The transaction cost is still $1.00 per transaction. Movement cost will be $40.00 (five movements at $8.00). Transaction cost will be $10.00 (ten transactions at $1.00) or a total of $50.00. The central marketplace system achieves a reduction of $10.00 in comparison to the decentralized system when overcoming the problems of space. With the emergence of a middleman, cost is reduced to $45.00 because the number of transactions required decreases.

As the multistage exchange system develops, additional complications are introduced. Such a system is illustrated in Figure 2-4. In this system, the economy has grown and further specialization has developed. For illustration, we have assumed six producers—two in food, two in textiles, and two in household utensils. Each specialist in searching out goods has concentrated on one of the three product lines. To complete the distribution process, the exchange structure consists of one central market and nine retailers. Figure 2-4 assumes thirty consumers. The three specialists must make two transactions with each producer-specialist for a total of six, and each will make a transaction with the central market, or three more, for a combined total of nine transactions. The nine retailers need to make nine transactions to purchase goods from the cen-

---

[15] Bowersox, op. cit., chaps. 2 and 5.

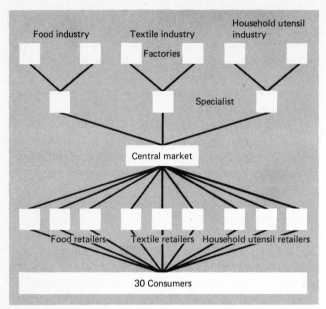

Figure 2-4 A multistage system.

tral market. Thus, the total system will require twenty-four transactions to complete spatial closure to the retail level. To complete retailer-to-consumer linkage, a total of 270 additional transactions (9 × 30) may be necessary if each consumer finds it necessary to visit each retail outlet.

To evaluate the cost of this more complex exchange system, assume transaction cost is $1.00, except for those transactions between consumers and retailers, which are assumed to cost $0.50 each. Assume movement from the producer through the specialist to the central market costs $4.00 because of large quantities and long distances, and that all other movements cost $2.00 per movement. How efficiently has the system worked?

Transactions
Producer-specialist, central market
  Nine transactions at $1.00   = $ 9.00
Central market retailer
  Nine transactions at $1.00   =   9.00
Retailers-buyers
  270 transactions at $0.50   =   135.00
                                    $153.00

Movements
Producer-specialist, central market
  Six movements at $4.00   = $ 24.00
Central market retailer
  Nine movements at $2.00   =   18.00
                                    42.00
  Total cost $195.00

In contrast, a system using only a central marketplace would require six movements at $4.00 each and six transactions at $1.00 each by the producers to the market. If each consumer wished to benefit from the production specialization available at the central market, 180 transactions would be necessary (six producers' output and thirty consumers) at a cost of $1.00 each. The total cost would be $210.

The concept involved is the *principle of minimum total transactions,* which has been articulated by a number of authors.[16] It is an extension of the central marketplace into a multistage exchange system for the purpose of overcoming spatial problems. The introduction of specialists reduces the number of transactions while allowing goods to move in large quantities over long distances, thereby reducing the total cost of transportation. There remains, however, a nagging question. Is it possible to have so many intermediaries in the system that the cost of a multistage system is greater than a decentralized or central marketplace system? It is possible. In the illustration, a further increase in intermediaries could require more transactions and a greater number of movements. Both would tend to increase total cost. Thus, a complexity of structure exists beyond which the introduction of more intermediaries will increase the cost of exchange.

There is yet another consideration. Each distribution system has certain outputs, termed *service outputs* by Bucklin.[17] These include *lot size,* or the ability to buy in small quantities; *waiting time,* or the length of time it takes to gain physical possession of goods after purchase; *market decentralization,* or the proximity of goods to the buyer and convenience in buying; and *product variety,* or combinations of products that most closely match the unique assortments desired. As service outputs increase, more middlemen are likely to be involved and distribution costs can be expected to increase independently of the economics of minimum total transactions.

Temporal Activity   The temporal aspects of distribution result in additional requirements to be satisfied by the exchange system. Since production in a mass-producing system does not take place at the same time as consumption, the first temporal problem is storing produced goods until they are needed for consumption. The second temporal problem is in organizing flows of goods throughout the system so that a satisfactory level of convenience can be provided to buyers and consumers. Since both temporal problems require storage, the cost of carrying inventories must be borne by society.

On the surface, it may appear that increasing the number of distribution specialists will increase the amount and cost of goods in storage. On the contrary, storage cost is lower in a multistage distribution system. If the only stocks available are at the producer's location, each purchaser will be required

[16] Margaret Hall, *Distributive Trading* (London: Hutchinson's University Library, 1951), p. 80.

[17] Louis P. Bucklin, *A Theory of Distribution Structure* (Berkeley: IBER Special Publications, 1966).

to carry a much larger inventory in an effort to reduce the inconvenience and cost of excessive market trips. In societies with poorly developed exchange systems, consumers carry large stocks, as evidenced by the presence of large pantries in homes. Since there is a much larger number of consumer buyers than distribution specialists and producers, the total stock of goods for the economy will be greater. The cost of household storage is hidden since it is not reported as warehousing. If a multistage system is working efficiently, the flow of goods—particularly manufactured goods—can be calibrated to meet demand with a minimum of total inventory stock. This is known as the *principle of massed* reserves.[18] In addition to keeping storage costs down, the multistage system increases buyer convenience.

Demand-Stimulating Activity Thus far, we have been discussing the physical task of bringing products closer to buyers. However, transactions do not just happen. A number of other activities must be consummated before ownership transfer takes place. These activities are identified as *marketing flows*. For purposes of discussion, the marketing flows related to demand stimulation are negotiation, ordering, financing, service, information, and, in some cases, security. Each is examined.

Negotiation Flows Sorting and search activities make available attractive assortments of merchandise, whereas spatial and temporal activities increase the service outputs of the exchange system. All activities assist in stimulating demand, but before any negotiation begins, potential buyers must become aware of available goods. In consumer marketing, stimulation is usually accomplished through advertising and promotion. As awareness develops among consumers, personal selling is used to intensify the desire and to set the stage for transaction negotiation. The negotiation may not result in a transaction. To a large degree, completion of a transaction will depend upon how satisfactory the other flows are to the potential buyer.

Ordering Flows The potential buyer is interested in waiting time. How quickly can the system process the order and have goods available for physical possession? Increased use of computer systems to process orders has substantially reduced traditional ordering times in many distribution channels. Even with consumer goods, certain aspects of the ordering flow present problems. Consider the time required to get through a supermarket checkout line after all buying decisions have been made.

Financing Flows Financing requirements are important to exchange in two ways. Storage of inventories in the distribution system, which includes costs of pilferage, spoilage, breakage, insurance, and storage, requires an extensive tie-up of working capital. To the extent inventories are stocked in anticipation of sales, the inherent risks create substantial cost. Unless adequate finances are available, sorting activity will not be performed efficiently.

Financing flows are important to both buyers and sellers. From the buyer's

---

[18] Hall, op. cit., p. 81.

point of view, negotiation usually is desired regarding time and terms of payment as well as credit availability. As will be discussed in Chapter 6, agreement to financial arrangements is one of the major sources of negotiation within mature distribution systems.

Service Flows To ensure consumer satisfaction with many manufactured products, it is necessary to provide a service organization which offers repair, spare or replacement parts, and, in many cases, ability to train personnel in the use of equipment. In the case of highly technical industrial machinery, availability of a service flow may be the determining factor in a purchase. The dollar cost of downtime on industrial equipment can be very great.

Another aspect of the service flow is ability to handle warranties and guarantees quickly and to the buyer's satisfaction. This aspect of service is so critical that many manufacturers, such as General Electric, maintain authorized service facilities throughout the nation to handle warranty repair work.

Information Flows Information of many kinds must flow up and down the exchange channel. An example of a downward flow in an exchange channel is the communication of price change information. Many participants, such as retailers, are closer to consumers, and information regarding which products are most popular must then be communicated upward to other channel members.

Security Flows With all goods, a need exists to maintain security for products flowing through the system, but special types of security are required under some circumstances. Products with a high potential for improper use, such as automatic check writers and postage and excise stamp machines, or products upon which a government tax must be paid, such as alcoholic beverages and cigarettes, must be surrounded by security as they flow through the system. In those instances where the system is set by design to a limited number of participants, it is important to ensure that the system is not broadened through certain participants acquiring products as back-door merchandise.

In summary, all the above flows must be completed many times at each stage in the exchange system. They are essential if the system is to perform efficiently. They may be performed by anyone, including producers, but they must be done.

All these suggested activities have been incorporated into the traditional functions of marketing, such as buying, selling, transportation, storage, finance, risk taking, standardization and grading, and marketing information. We will begin to use this traditional functional breakdown in Chapter 3.

CHANNEL PARTICIPANTS

Many times in this chapter we have referred to participants in the system. You will recall that a distinction was made in Chapter 1 between primary and facilitating participants.[19] Participants engage in sorting and search, spatial and temporal closure, and demand-stimulating activities. In this part, the primary

[19] See Chapter 1, p. 8.

Table 2-1   Methods of Retailing, 1972

Methods of retailing	Number of establishments	Retail sales (in $ millions)
Mail-order houses	7,982	4,574
Automatic merchandising machine operators	12,845	3,010
Direct selling establishments	141,294	3,984
Retail establishments	1,750,750	447,472
Total	1,912,871	459,040

Source: U.S. Bureau of the Census, Census of Retail Trade, 1972, United States Summary.

participants are classified as retailers, wholesalers, and agents. To standardize terminology, the definitions used by the Bureau of the Census are used whenever possible.[20]

Retailers

Retail trade is defined by the Bureau of the Census as "all establishments engaged in selling merchandise for personal or household consumption and rendering services incident to the sale of such goods." In 1972, the last complete Census of Business reported retail trade amounting to $459 billion conducted by 1.9 million establishments and employing approximately 11.2 million people.[21] Four types of retailers are distinguished, with the number of establishments and sales of each shown in Table 2-1. Methods of retailing other than through retail establishments are described in the Standard Industrial Classification Manual as follows:[22]

Mail-order houses. Establishments primarily engaged in retail sale of products by catalog and mail order.

Automatic merchandising machine operators. Establishments primarily engaged in retail sale of products by means of automatic merchandising units, also referred to as vending machines.

Direct selling establishments. Establishments primarily engaged in retail sale of merchandise by house-to-house canvas. Included in this industry are individuals selling products by this method who are not employees of the organization which they represent, and establishments which are retail sales offices from which employees operate to sell merchandise door-to-door.

Wholesalers

Wholesale trade is defined by the Bureau of the Census as "all establishments or places of business primarily engaged in selling merchandise to retailers; to

[20] This section was developed from the most recent U.S. Bureau of the Census, *Census of Retail Trade, 1972,* Summary Statistics, the *Census of Wholesale Trade, 1972,* Summary Statistics, and the *Standard Industrial Classification Manual,* 1967, Executive Office of the President, Bureau of the Budget (Washington, D.C.: Government Printing Office, 1967).
[21] *Census of Retail Trade, 1972.*
[22] *Standard Industrial Classification Manual,* pp. 240–241.

Table 2-2   Wholesale Trade by Type of Operation, 1972

	Establishments		Wholesale sales	
Type of operation	Number	Percentage of total	$ Millions	Percentage of total
Merchant wholesalers	289,980	78.4	353,316	50.8
Wholesale merchant and distributors	274,733	74.3	305,182	43.9
Grain elevators (terminal and country)	5,811	1.6	11,441	1.6
Importers	6,786	1.8	23,092	3.3
Exporters	2,650	.7	13,601	2.0
Manufacturers' sales branches and offices	47,191	12.8	255,562	36.7
Manufacturers' sales branches with stocks	32,611	8.9	124,458	17.9
Manufacturers' sales offices without stocks	14,580	3.9	131,104	18.8
Merchandise agents and brokers	32,621	8.8	86,952	12.5
Merchandise brokers for buyers or sellers	4,770	1.3	20,398	2.9
Commission merchants	6,940	1.9	18,971	2.7
Manufacturers' agents	16,529	4.4	23,345	3.4
Selling agents	1,723	.4	6,990	1.0
Auction companies	1,769	.5	8,170	1.2
Import agents	265	.1	3,619	.5
Export agents	440	.1	4,694	.7
Purchasing agents and resident buyers	185	.1	765	.1
Total	369,792	100.0	695,830	100.0

Source: U.S. Bureau of the Census, Census of Wholesale Trade, 1972, Summary Statistics.

industrial, commercial, institutional, or professional users; or to other wholesalers; or acting as agents in buying merchandise for or selling merchandise to such persons or companies.''

In 1972, the census reported wholesale trade amounting to $695.8 billion conducted by 369,792 establishments and employing approximately 4 million people.[23] Three types of wholesale establishments with numerous subdivisions exist. The number of establishments and sales of each are shown in Table 2-2. The various types within each wholesale category as described by the Bureau of the Census are discussed in the following sections.

Merchant Wholesalers This group consists of wholesale establishments engaged primarily in buying and selling merchandise on their own account, including farm products merchants who do not buy primarily from farmers. Included in this group are the following types of operations:

[23] *Census of Wholesale Trade, 1972.*

Wholesale merchants and distributors. Establishments primarily engaged in buying and selling merchandise in the domestic market and performing the principal wholesale functions—buying, stocking, selling, etc. Several wholesale merchants perform their functions in a specialized way. The following are some of the more significant categories:

Rack merchandisers. Establishments primarily engaged in placing their goods on display racks or shelves in retail stores for sale.

Cash-carry wholesalers. Establishments primarily engaged in selling on a cash-carry basis.

Wagon, truck distributors. Establishments primarily engaged in selling their merchandise from trucks or other vehicles, combining functions of sales representatives with those of delivery personnel, and carrying a limited assortment of well-known, fast-moving items.

Other limited-function wholesalers. Included here are other types of wholesale establishments buying and selling, at wholesale, merchandise on their own account and performing limited services—includes establishments known as drop shippers, desk jobbers, retailer cooperatives, consumer cooperative wholesalers, etc.

Terminal grain elevators. Establishments with sizable storage space buying and selling grain received primarily by rail or barge, rather than direct from farmers via truck or wagon.

Importers. Establishments buying and selling goods at wholesale on own account, whose principal source of purchases is foreign.

Exporters. Establishments primarily engaged in purchasing goods in the United States and selling to foreign customers.

Manufacturers' Sales Branches and Sales Offices   These wholesale establishments are distinguished by the fact that they are owned by manufacturers or mining companies and maintained apart from producing plants primarily for selling or marketing their products at wholesale. Branch stores selling to household consumers and individual users are classified within retail trade. Sales branches or sales offices located at plants or administrative offices are included where separate records were available and reported. In Table 2-2, data are shown separately for manufacturers' sales branches and for sales offices. They differ in that sales offices normally do not carry stocks of merchandise for delivery to consumers.

Sales as recorded for sales branches include direct deliveries from plants on orders from branches as well as deliveries from branch stocks. Sales as shown for sales offices generally represent the value of orders written or booked by employees at the offices, including sales representatives, working out of the offices.

Merchandise Agents and Brokers   This group of channel participants includes establishments whose operators are in business for themselves and are primarily engaged in selling or buying goods for others. "Sales" as shown in census publications for agents and brokers represent sales or purchase value of goods in the transactions negotiated. These sales data include some approximation as many agents and brokers do not maintain accurate records of dollar sales.

Merchandise brokers. Wholesale establishments primarily engaged in buying or selling merchandise in the domestic market on a brokerage basis, but not receiving goods on consignment.

Commission merchants. Wholesale establishments operating in the domestic market, receiving goods for sale on consignment.

Manufacturers' agents. Wholesale establishments in the domestic market, selling for a limited number of manufacturers on a continuing agency basis.

Selling agents. Wholesale establishments primarily engaged in selling, on an agency basis in the domestic market, all or the major portion of clients' output.

Auction companies. Wholesale establishments primarily engaged in selling merchandise on an agency basis by the auction method.

Import agents. Merchandise agents and brokers in the domestic market, buying merchandise from or selling merchandise for foreign firms.

Export agents. Merchandise agents and brokers in the domestic market, selling to or buying for foreign customers.

Purchasing agents, resident buyers. Wholesale establishments primarily engaged in buying merchandise on an agency basis, in the domestic market, for a limited number of customers on a continuing basis.

Facilitating Participants

A large number of establishments other than retailers and wholesalers are equally important to the smooth functioning of our exchange system. These institutions are identified as facilitating participants. The most common facilitating participants are financial institutions, public warehouses, transportation companies, and advertising agencies. Many services provided by facilitating participants can be provided as part of the activities performed by primary channel members. For example, a merchant wholesaler can operate private warehouses and trucks. Nevertheless, facilitating participants do provide "for-hire" services. In terms of channel organization, the essential feature of facilitating participants is that they assume limited or no risk in the functioning of the channel.

Financial Institutions   These institutions are essential to finance primary participants within the channel system. A significant function of financial institutions is providing capital for inventories which must be financed at many levels within the channel as they move from production to consumption. You will recall from the W. T. Grant case that financial factors played an important role in the ultimate decision to file bankruptcy.[24]

Public Warehouses   The public warehouse rents space to owners of inventory, thus avoiding the need to invest in storage facilities. In selected situations, public warehouses are involved in financing in that some warehouse re-

[24] See Case 1-1, p. 16.

ceipts are negotiable instruments that may be discounted at a bank. The use of negotiable receipts can free working capital while inventory is awaiting sale.

Transportation Companies The efficiency of transportation has a direct influence on the cost of the entire channel. The most current estimate of annual transportation expenditure for intercity freight and local delivery is approaching $200 billion.[25] In a direct way, the efficiency of the transportation system influences the size of inventories which must be maintained in a channel system. If transportation is immediately available, products can flow through the channel at a constant rate, thus minimizing the need for maintaining large inventories.

Advertising Agencies These facilitating participants are instrumental in the initial step in negotiation. They are specialists in creating awareness of products and stimulating demand. They function at each level of the system for producers, wholesalers, and retailers. Without some kind of organized information dissemination, seeking and selecting product sources would be a very time-consuming undertaking for buyers.

In summary, primary and facilitating channel participants join with manufacturers to comprise all channel systems. They are the business units that provide search and sorting, spatial, temporal, and demand-stimulation activities. Without such channel participants, it would be impossible to enjoy the many advantages of specialized production. There is a well-established marketing truism: You can eliminate marketing middlemen (channel participants), but you can't eliminate the functions they perform.

CHANNEL ORGANIZATION

In Chapter 1, a channel of distribution was defined as "the system of relationships that exists between institutions involved in the process of buying and selling."[26] The institutions engaged in a specific set of marketing relationships on a collective basis represent the channel structure. In many situations, a single participant takes the leadership in arranging the relationships among channel participants. Craig and Gabler, as far back as 1940, argued that the United States is a manufacturer-controlled economy.[27] From this viewpoint, one would expect that basic producers would be the driving force in organizing channels of distribution. In many cases, such as in the automotive industry, the manufacturer is the dominant force in establishing channel structure. On the other hand, this is not likely to be the case with agricultural products. Some middlemen, usually assemblers of agricultural output, organize the channel. As

[25] *Transportation Facts and Trends,* 14th ed. (Washington, D.C.: Transportation Association of America, July 1978).

[26] Chapter 1, p. 1.

[27] David R. Craig and Werner Gabler, "The Competitive Struggle for Market Control," in *Marketing in the American Economy,* vol. 209, *The Annals of the American Academy of Political and Social Science* (Philadelphia: American Academy of Political and Social Science, May 1940).

pointed out in Chapter 1, in vertical marketing systems of the administered variety, a large retailer such as Sears or J. C. Penney may determine the channel composition. The Thom McAn shoe stores are an example of a retailer that has integrated backward to manufacturing to form a corporate vertical marketing system. The free-flow and the single transaction channel may not require a single or dominant participant to provide leadership in organizing the channel. Rather, specialists exist to do a number of jobs. They negotiate to buy goods and, in turn, negotiate to sell goods.

Today, any participant within the distribution network can attempt to take the lead in arranging a set of institutions for performance of necessary exchange activities.[28] Given the number of specialists in the system, the alternative arrangements are endless. Figure 2-5 illustrates some ways in which participants are arranged into channels of distribution. The combinations can consist of relatively few participants (short), such as from producer to end user; or many participants (long), with merchandise agents, brokers, wholesalers, and retailers between producer and consumer. The longer the channel in terms of levels of participants, the more *indirect* it is, and the fewer participants, the more *direct* it is.

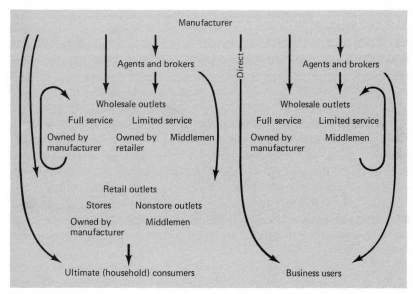

Figure 2-5 Schematic diagram of alternative marketing channels for manufactured goods. [*John B. Mathews, Howard D. Buzzell, Theodore Levitt, and Ronald C. Frank, Marketing: An Introduction Analysis (New York: McGraw-Hill Book Co., 1964), p. 263.*]

[28] Considerable debate has arisen in recent years concerning the topic of channel organization. The controversy involves both who does organize the channel system and who should take responsibility for channel organization. For varying viewpoints, see: Craig and Gabler; Robert W. Little, "The Marketing Channel: Who Should Lead This Extra-Corporate Enterprise," *Journal of Marketing* (January 1970), pp. 31–38: Bruce Mallen, "A Theory of Retailer-Supplier Conflict, Control, and Cooperation," *Journal of Retailing* (Summer 1963), pp. 24–33ff.

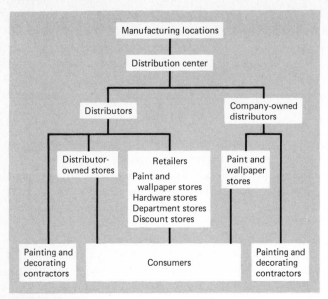

Figure 2-6   Channels of distribution for residential and commercial wallcovering. [*Douglas M. Lambert, The Distribution Channels Decision* (*New York: The National Association of Accountants, 1978.*)]

Figure 2-5 provides insight into how channels organize into combinations of institutions. However, in practice, channels are much more complicated than the diagram indicates. First, more than one channel is typically used for a given class of goods. Producers of competing goods will use different channels. Second, even one producer may use many channels in a form of dual distribution to move products from production to consumption. Channels of distribution will more likely reflect the combination arrangements for wallcovering illustrated in Figure 2-6. In this example, the product line is sold through distributors, some of whom are company-owned, to retailers and painting and decorating contractors. Products move from the plants to one centrally located distribution center from which weekly shipments are made to distributors. All plant-to-distribution center shipments and 95 percent of shipments to distributors are made via private truck fleets.

Another complicated channel is that typically found in international trade. Figure 2-7 shows the channel for the import of shoes into the United States. This type of channel is usually a free-flow channel and is frequently organized around a single negotiated transaction. Curiously, the participants are so specialized they rarely know what specific functions were performed by the other channel members.

We have purposely treated the topic of channel organization in a structural context. However, once a channel is described as a set of participants interacting with each other, behavioral relationships develop which introduce a variable aspect to the management of marketing channels. The structural ar-

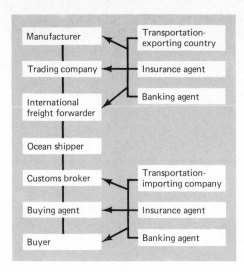

Figure 2-7 Typical channel participants in international trade.

rangements of channels evolve or are planned to accomplish exchange activities. Once these arrangements are established, behavioral relationships become an important consideration for efficient channel operation. We will explore the nature of these relationships in Chapters 3 and 4. The organization of channel activities is also important because of the influence it has on the dynamics of channel structure. This is the topic of the final section of this chapter.

DYNAMICS OF CHANNEL ACTIVITIES AND STRUCTURE

Channels of distribution change over time. In the household appliance industry, we can identify nine different channels which have functioned since the turn of the century.[29] It is difficult today to find a free-standing hardware store, once a major participant in the channel for hardware. As a matter of fact, the number of lumber, building materials, hardware, garden supply, and mobile home dealer retail establishments dropped from 108,300 in 1958 to 92,700 in 1963, to 86,400 in 1967, and to 76,800 in 1972.[30] However, sales between 1958 and 1972 increased from $14.6 billion to $25.5 billion.[31] A similar reduction took place among wholesalers in this line of business.

    Why do these changes take place? There are many explanations of channel change, but one overriding consideration is the relationship between activity and structure. As institutions are arranged in a channel of distribution, relationships emerge between the buying and selling sets involved. These relationships

---

[29] David Adams, *A Study of Institutional Change Processes Within the Appliance Industry* (unpublished doctoral dissertation, Department of Marketing and Transportation Administration, Michigan State University, East Lansing, Michigan, 1977).
[30] *Statistical Abstract of the United States,* 1976.
[31] Ibid.

result from expectations concerning performance of distribution activities. The jobs which must be performed to achieve distribution objectives determine the actual channel structure. The channel of distribution will change if a potential participant is successful in convincing a seller that a job or activity can be performed better. Sometimes the need to perform traditional activities in a channel is reduced, resulting in new forms of channel structure.

In the first case, a retailer may decide that wholesalers are not performing their jobs satisfactorily. The result may be that the retailer selects to absorb those activities previously performed by the wholesaler, and establishes direct negotiation with manufacturers. The wholesaler is thus replaced. For example, in processed foods, wholesalers were used extensively until the emergence of the supermarket food chain. Large chains, in an effort to reduce costs, established distribution centers and began to buy direct. To retain a position in the channel, wholesalers were forced to concentrate marketing efforts with independents and cooperative groups of retailers who faced direct chain competition. The result was the development of multiple channels.

In the second case, channels for radios have changed significantly in the past 40 years. The radio as a consumer product was initially introduced in the 1930s. It was a technically complex product of high unit value and required installation, service, and a large investment in channel inventory. As a new product, it needed demonstration and aggressive selling. The channel which initially organized included a producer and a limited number of retailers, who then used house-to-house selling to explain, demonstrate, and install the product. As the radio began to gain market acceptance, the product was technically simplified, cost was reduced, and channels began to adjust. The need for aggressive selling disappeared. The market broadened and wholesalers were introduced to complete distribution to a large number of retailers. Today, radios are sold in every imaginable type of retail outlet. In this case, the activities required for effective distribution changed. Consequently, there was a structural adaptation in the channel.

SUMMARY

The economic foundations of the free market system are essential to understanding channel structure. The transition from the wealth-treasure goal to the wealth-happiness objective resulted from a change in social perspective. The political and economic organizations which evolved to satisfy new social perspectives emphasized freedom of choice in production and consumption and recognized the dual constraints of scarce resources and insatiable wants. After philosophically and ethically justifying the appropriateness of wealth accumulation, division of labor, or specialization, was introduced as a means to achieve economic growth. Specialization in output required development of an exchange system whereby people could satisfy their needs in varying degrees. The exchange system not only allocated output through the mechanism of value determination, but it also emerged as the means by which goods produced in a specialized way could be matched with the unique assortments demanded. Conflict developed as a pervasive characteristic of the exchange system.

Four problems inherent in operation of the exchange system of a specialized economy are: (1) matching heterogeneous supply with heterogeneous demand, (2) overcoming the distances over which output must move from production to consumption, (3) matching time of production with time of consumption, and (4) stimulating exchange. To solve these problems, three typical channel structures have evolved: (1) decentralized systems, (2) central marketplaces, and (3) multistage distribution channels. In a decentralized structure there are no middlemen. Each producer must visit or be visited by other producers to exchange each other's specialized output. The number of transactions is high. In a central market structure without middlemen, each producer assembles output in a central location and sets up a stall from which to conduct business. The number of trips required to complete an exchange is reduced and transportation costs are reduced. The number of transactions is the same as in the decentralized structure. In a central market structure with middlemen, producers bring their output to the central market but, instead of setting up a stall, surplus output is sold to middlemen in the central market. The producer purchases needed goods from the middlemen. The middlemen carry an inventory, and the number of transactions is reduced over a decentralized structure. The central market structure, with or without middlemen, does offer a savings in transportation cost since products move in large quantities to the central market. Also, there is a convenience to buyers and producers. In the decentralized and central market structure, the producers must transport products to other producers or the central market. In a multistage structure, specialists are introduced who purchase goods from producers for resale. These specialists then sell the goods to stall operators who act as middlemen in the central marketplace. Just as producers welcomed the specialists who purchased their output, some stall operators in the central marketplace moved away and offered a location convenient to potential buyers.

All exchange channels must perform basic activities. These are described as sorting and search, spatial, temporal, and demand-stimulation activities. Sorting involves sorting out, accumulation, allocation, and assorting. The overall sorting activity requires considerable search on the part of channel participants. The spatial activity involves the use of structure to achieve movement at minimal transaction cost. The temporal activity involves flow of goods through time and minimization of inventory and associated cost. Demand-stimulation activity deals with negotiation, ordering, financing, service, information, and security flows to encourage exchange.

As the need to perform these activities was recognized and acknowledged, specialists developed. Retailers, wholesalers, and facilitators such as financial institutions, public warehouses, transportation companies, and advertising agencies emerged as marketing channel participants.

The organization of participants into either direct or indirect channels of distribution, either at the initiative of the producer or other participants, is the basis of channel structure. The basic theory that the activities which must be accomplished determine the most appropriate channel structure helps to explain dynamics of channel change.

QUESTIONS

1 Explain the role of scarce resources and freedom of choice in the emergence of channels of distribution.
2 Discuss the four barriers to exchange and how the structure for exchange attempts to overcome them.
3 What is the difference between a decentralized and a central marketplace system?
4 How does sorting overcome the problems inherent in heterogeneous supply and demand?
5 Is sorting a function designed to cope with the discrepancy of quantity, assortment, and search activities? Explain.
6 It has been said that "the exchange system is designed to achieve spatial and temporal closure in the economic sector." Explain what is meant by this statement.
7 Given the principle of minimum total transactions, is it possible to have too many intermediaries? Explain.
8 In many countries intermediaries are considered parasites without whom the cost of goods would be reduced. Is this statement valid?
9 Explain the marketing flows involved in the demand-stimulating activities of the distribution system.
10 Why would a manufacturer elect to use multiple channels of distribution for the same product?

CASE 2-1: Distribution System Modification

Early in 1974, officers of the Inter-American Development Bank were considering a joint loan request for $18 million from the Government of Colombia, the municipality of Cali, Colombia, and the state government of Valle. The basis for the request was the construction of a new central marketplace in the city of Cali. The background leading to the request follows.[1]

GEOGRAPHIC AREA

Cali is a city with about 1 million inhabitants located in the southwest area of Colombia. It is the principal commercial center in the Cauca Valley, which extends about 125 miles north and south. The valley is about 9 miles wide and bounded on both sides by mountains which reach approximately 3,000 feet. The climate is tropical, with a mean temperature of about 77°F. Most of the agricultural land is concentrated in large acreage, with the exception of fruits and vegetables, which are grown on very small landholdings. The valley is the principal food source for the city of Cali.

ECONOMIC CHARACTERISTICS OF CALI

A wide distribution of income exists in Cali. Table 1 describes the dispersion of monthly income per household and per capita. Given the fact that the exchange rate, at the time the data in this table were collected, equaled 16.90 pesos to the U.S. dollar, the income level was low. The distribution of the labor force in Cali

Table 1   Per Capita and per Household Income (in Pesos) and the Population Distribution Classified by Level of Disposable Cash Income, Cali*

Range of per capita income	Percent of households	Percent of people	Income per capita		Income per household	
			Mean	Median	Mean	Median
1 Less than 125	20.3	25.5	86	92	686	600
2 126–240	27.8	29.1	176	167	1,167	1,000
3 241–500	28.7	25.3	352	333	1,962	2,000
4 More than 500	23.2	20.1	1,157	893	6,340	5,000
All Families	100.0	100.0	395	214	2,500	1,500

* Based upon reports of the 520 out of 625 households who provided income information on the Proyecto Integrado de Mercadeo Urbano y Rural General Consumer Survey in Cali.

[1] This case is based on facts presented in *Market Coordination in the Development of the Cauca Valley Region, Colombia,* Marketing in Developing Communities Series, Research Report No. 5, Latin American Studies Center, Michigan State University, East Lansing, Michigan, 1970. However, the situation illustrated concerning the construction of a new central market and the loan request is fictitious. All data contained in the tables build upon this earlier study but do not reflect current demographics.

Table 2   Distribution of Labor Force by Type of Economic Activity, Cali

Economic activities	Percent
Agriculture, forestry, and fishing	1.8
Extractive industries	0.7
Processing	34.1
Construction	6.9
Electricity, water, gas, and sanitary services	0.2
Commerce	18.1
Transportation, storage, and communication	5.4
Services	22.2
Public services	5.4
Armed forces (excluding police)	0.8
Other activities	4.3
Total	100.0

Source: Centro de Estudios sobre Desarrollo Económico (CEDE). *Encuestas Urbanas sobre Empleo y Desempleo, Apéndice Estadístico,* Bogotá.

Table 3   Sectoral Origin of Gross Internal Product at Current Market Prices for the Department of Valle del Cauca

Sector	Value added (million pesos)	Percent
Agriculture	1,525.8	20.70
Mining	41.7	0.57
Industrial manufacturing	2,270.9	30.80
Construction	325.5	4.42
Electricity and water	64.8	0.88
Transportation, storage, and communication	653.8	8.86
Commerce	1,164.3	15.80
Banking, insurance, and finance	133.4	1.80
Housing	348.0	4.72
Public administration	364.6	4.94
Services	479.6	6.51
Total	7,372.7	100.00

Source: El Centro de Investigaciones Sobre Desarrollo Económico (CIDE) de la Universidad del Valle, *El Por Que de Un Plan de Desarrollo Económico y Social Para el Departamento del Valle del Cauca,* Cali.

is illustrated in Table 2. Although agriculture is not important in the labor force of Cali, it is important in the Cauca Valley. Table 3 illustrates the origin of gross internal product for the entire region.

CALI URBAN FOOD DISTRIBUTION SYSTEM

For many of the inhabitants of Cali, a significant proportion of family income (42 percent) is spent on food. However, the lowest quarter of the population spends 80 percent and the second lowest quarter spends about 66 percent of its income on food.

The distribution system which evolved to supply food to the city consisted of a central marketplace with five satellite public markets, a combination of retail outlets, and wholesalers. The characteristics of each set of institutions are described below.

The Central and Satellite Markets

The central market, the *Galeria Central,* was located in the center of the business district and was operated by the municipality. The facility itself housed 2,410 retail operators selling all types of food products. In addition, five satellite public markets ringing the city included an additional 1,345 retail operators. In combination, these institutions represented the legal retailers operating in the public market system. However, a large number of mobile vendors, particularly in fruits and vegetables, operated on the sidewalks near the public markets. The public market retailers constituted 42 percent of all food retailers in the city and handled 20 percent of all food sales through retail outlets. The average public market retailer occupied an area of about three square meters. These retailers had an average monthly sales volume of about 7,300 pesos at a gross margin of from 8.78 to 14.5 percent.

System of Retail Outlets

In addition to retail operators located in the public market areas, there were a number of retail food stores in Cali. These stores differed substantially in their methods of operation and could be classified as personal service stores, self-service stores, or specialty stores.

Personal Service Stores   There were 4,241 personal service stores scattered throughout the city, with the larger stores concentrated around the *Galeria Central.* These stores, as the largest single retail element, sold about 50 percent of all food in the system. They carried a complete range of food products but were relatively unimportant in sales of fruits and vegetables. They could be subclassified by types of products handled into *tiendas,* carrying a narrow line of processed foods and grains as well as some household cleaning and personal care items; small and large *graneros,* which handled a broader product line than the *tiendas;* and meat outlets specializing only in meats. The average monthly sales for the personal service stores was 17,850 pesos and they occupied about 26 square meters with 6.7 to 12.9 percent gross margins.

Self-Service Stores   Self-service had not come of age as yet. Only fifty-four such stores existed in Cali, doing about 13 percent of the food business, primarily to high-income families. Nineteen supermarkets operated with a full line under a self-service policy. There were also seventeen cooperatives with retail food stores run by paid managers. In addition, four full-service supermarkets were operated by the government and fourteen general merchandise stores were owned by five chains. The high-volume stores did sell at lower margins, using some items as price leaders. On the average, they operated on about 258 square meters, with an average monthly sales volume of 318,000 pesos with 7.5 to 13.3 percent gross margins.

Specialty Stores   As in most developing countries, a high degree of retail specialization existed. There were 864 stores specializing in poultry, eggs, dairy products, and meats which, along with twenty-four retailer-wholesalers, represented 17 percent of total food sales through retail outlets.

In total, there were 8,914 retailers in the city, the majority of which were small, low-volume, high-cost operations. About 42 percent, the public market operators, were subsidized by the municipal government. It was believed that the retail sector was in a state of equilibrium with a low level of throughput. As in any system, a major barrier to large-scale retailing was the problem of supplying large-scale outlets through a wholesale system.

The Wholesale Structure

The area around the *Galeria Central* was the focal point for the wholesaling of most food products. Seventy percent of the total city food supply passed through this area. Only liquid milk, poultry, eggs, soft drinks, and processed foods, distributed directly by manufacturers, moved through other channels.

All this wholesale activity occurred around the *Galeria Central,* either in *depositos* or on the street. Ninety percent of the fruits and vegetables, 80 percent of the total volume of meat, and 90 percent of all grains and basic staple processed goods were handled by specialized wholesalers and wholesaler-retailers in the area. The *Galeria Central* had been erected in 1897 and had become the trading hub of the city. Most of the buildings were old houses inadequate for wholesale operations. A wide variety of related businesses such as hardware stores, drugstores, packaging materials outlets, restaurants, bars, and transportation companies were also attracted to the area.

Of 868 wholesalers in the area, 103 specialized in grains and processed foods, 231 in meats, 450 in fruits and vegetables, and 84 in poultry and eggs. Similar to the retailers, each wholesaler was small and highly specialized. With the exception of grains and processed foods, wholesalers operated in outlets of only 5 to 30 square meters. Grains and processed food wholesalers operated establishments of about 300 square meters. The size of the operations provided little opportunity for storage and only about a 2-day supply was carried. Average monthly volume was 914,400 pesos for a grain and processed foods wholesaler, 106,600 pesos for a meat distributor, and 30,000 pesos for a fruit and vegetable wholesaler. Margins varied depending upon products handled, but were higher than in retail trade.

Retailer-Wholesaler Relationships

The scale of wholesaling made it very difficult for the wholesaler to supply expected services such as consistent availability and quality, credit, and delivery

Table 4   Average Number of Purchases per Month per Item within Product Group by Type of Retailer, Cali

	Self-service	Personal service	Public market
Grains	3.0	3.2	4.0
Processed staples	2.5	3.2	3.0
Fruits and vegetables	15.0	25.0	20.0
Meat	20.0	25.0	30.0
Poultry and eggs	7.0	6.0	9.0
Milk	30.0	30.0	—

Source: Proyecto Integrado de Mercadeo Urbano y Rural, retailer survey.

and price stability. The high degree of specialization made it imperative that the number of purchases by the retailer be very high to round out the line. Table 4 shows the average number of purchases per month per item for different types of retailers. It is estimated that a *tienda* operator handling five fruits and vegetables would have to conduct 125 transactions per month in order to acquire the needed products. Only four wholesalers had sales personnel to call on retailers, requiring retailers to come to the wholesaler's establishment. A related problem was transport of so many small purchases from the wholesaler's place of business to the retail store. This was not as much of a problem for those retail-

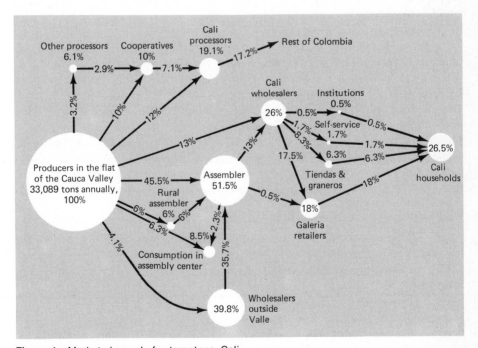

Figure 1   Market channels for tomatoes, Cali.

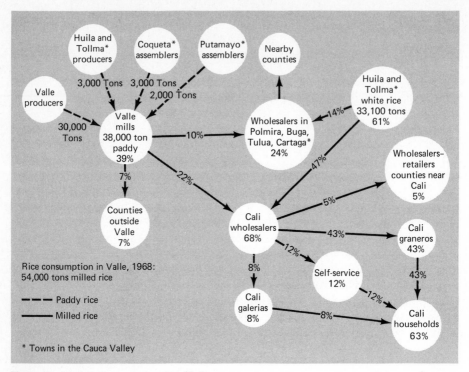

Figure 2   Market channels for rice, Valle.

ers located close to the *Galeria,* where most purchases were transported by pushcart. Those retailers farther away were forced to rely on taxis or bicycles. The retailer owner-operator, a class which included most retailers, spent about 75 percent of the time supplying the store.

Continuous availability was another problem. The small size of both retail and wholesale establishments made storage almost impossible. With 2 days' rain, roads from the agricultural areas were impassable and the city would be without a food supply. The flow of products from the agricultural regions to the city and the flow of agricultural inputs, such as agricultural equipment, feed, seed, and fertilizers, were equally important parts of the system.

Wholesaler-Supplier Relationships

Figures 1, 2, and 3 depict channels of distribution for tomatoes, rice, and fertilizers and are representative of all the fruits and vegetables, processed grains, and agricultural inputs. In many respects, the primary supply channels match the miniretailing and wholesaling structure of the urban distribution system. Table 5 shows supply relationships of fruit and vegetable wholesalers in Cali. The number of purchases was great but transport was a problem. Sixty-two percent of the specialized wholesalers made their purchases FOB the supplier's warehouse, forcing the risk and cost of transportation onto the wholesaler.

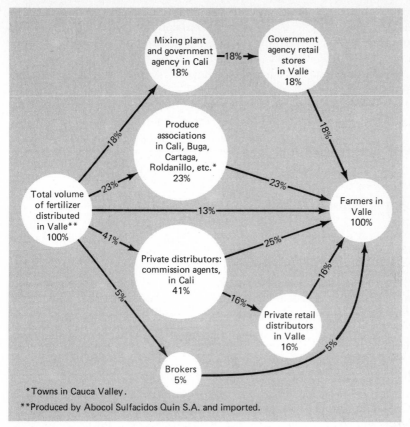

Figure 3 Market channels for fertilizers, Valle.

Table 5   Supplier Relationships of Fruit and Vegetable Wholesalers, Cali

	Potatoes	Tomatoes	*Plátanos*	Other
Major supply sources:				
Direct from farmers	10%	30%	38%	32%
Negociantes outside Cali	83	31	37	43
Negociantes in Cali	7	—	—	7
Truckers in Cali	—	21	15	9
Other	—	18	10	9
Percentage buying from one supplier	8	28	39	22
Average number of suppliers talked to before buying	3.2	3.0	3.0	3.6
Percentage of purchases on which credit is obtained	76	83	82	89
Average number of days credit received	9.6	3.5	4.6	5.2

Source: Proyecto Integrado de Mercadeo Urbano y Rural, wholesaler study.

Products moved into the city by truck. Most truck operators were independents who sometimes purchased products outright for sale in Cali. Products moved from growing regions to the vicinity of the *Galeria,* frequently passing many of the retail outlets (such as the retailers in the five satellite public markets) which eventually had to be supplied from *Galeria* wholesalers. Likewise, wholesalers in Cali supplied retailers in small towns in the valley. Consequently, food may have been grown very close to a small town, transported into Cali, and then moved back to the small town. There was much cross-hauling. Even though most product movements into the city occurred at night, about 330 trucks still entered the area of the *Galeria Central* every day. Congestion from trucks, pushcarts, and taxis was unbelievable.

ORIGIN OF THE LOAN REQUEST

The *Galeria,* with its narrow sidewalks and streets, its refuse from fruit and vegetable wholesalers operating in the streets, and its inadequate structures, was clearly undesirable for handling food products.

In anticipation of the Pan-American games in 1971, the city fathers closed the *Galeria Central* and reassigned the retail stall operators to other public markets. Unfortunately, these public markets were not as well served by bus lines and were somewhat inconvenient for a large number of purchasers. By 1973, consumer shopping patterns were shifting to the satellite markets and the higher-cost neighborhood stores. Yet, the supply system was inadequate. It was felt that a need existed for an institution similar to the old *Galeria Central* but located in a different part of the city. A proposal was thus developed to construct a new central market structure on the outskirts of the city. An architectural plan was drawn up incorporating the latest innovations at a cost estimate of $36 million. On a matching funds basis, the request was made to the Inter-American Development Bank.

CASE 2-1: QUESTIONS

Of course, the major question is whether the loan should be made, but several questions must be answered before arriving at a final decision.

1 What were the major distribution problems associated with the old system when the *Galeria Central* was in operation?
2 What solutions to these problems do you suggest? Would you have recommended closing the *Galeria* as a solution? How would you recommend that the problems be solved?
3 Will construction of a new central market on the outskirts of the city solve some of the distribution problems?
4 If the loan is made and the new central market is constructed, what activities would you recommend be conducted in it?

Chapter 3

Foundations of Interorganizational Behavior: Dependence, Cooperation, and Conflict

Although the basis for channel organization lies in the economic benefits to be gained from specialization, the resulting combination of institutions possesses a number of characteristics whose behavioral nature must be understood by managers involved in formulation of channel strategy and policy. As an operating system, a channel can be viewed as consisting of interrelated components (institutions) striving to achieve mutually acceptable goals, with delegated activities to be accomplished. It also should be noted that participation in a channel is usually voluntary, that one firm often takes on an administrative role, and that an overall code of conduct or set of group norms may arise.[1] These operational characteristics bring into focus the importance of behavior and behavioral relationships among channel members. These behavioral relationships have received increasing attention in recent years as marketers have recognized their importance to effective channel management.

This chapter will examine the underlying foundations for behavior among organizations in a marketing channel. In order to do so, we will build upon the basic ideas developed in previous chapters. Our objective is to construct a

---

[1] Bert C. McCammon and Robert W. Little, "Marketing Channels: Analytical Systems and Approaches," in *Science in Marketing,* ed. George Schwartz (New York: John Wiley & Sons, Inc., 1965), pp. 329–333.

framework for understanding types of behavior most frequently experienced in channel relationships. Fundamental to this framework is the concept of mutual dependence among institutions in channels. Dependence creates the need for cooperation and the potential for conflict, and serves as the ultimate source of power or authority in channel systems. Conflict is treated in this chapter as a behavior pattern arising from the dependence existing in the channel relationship. Power, leadership, and authority, as well as cooperation as the prevailing situation in channels, are discussed in Chapter 4.

AN INTERORGANIZATIONAL BEHAVIOR FRAMEWORK

Figure 3-1 presents an overview of interorganizational behavior. Before examining cooperation, conflict, and power utilization in a channel setting, this section outlines the concepts which provide the basis for this behavior. Each important concept of interorganizational behavior is introduced briefly. The interrelationships are illustrated in Figure 3-1.

Marketing Functions

Chapter 2 presented the basic economic foundations and exchange concepts which give rise to the need for a channel of distribution. In order for the chan-

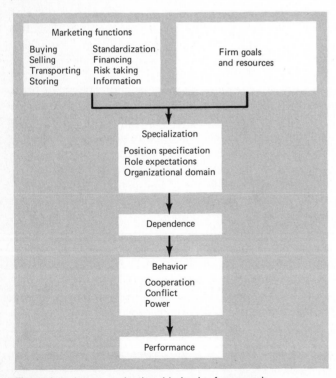

Figure 3-1 Interorganizational behavior framework.

nel system to fulfill its role and provide the exchange mechanism, a number of specific operations or functions must be performed by firms in the network. Although many different classification schemes for marketing functions exist, the most commonly accepted list includes selling, buying, transportation, storage, financing, standardization, risk taking, and market information.[2]

Selling and buying can be considered complementary functions and have been called the functions of exchange. The *selling* operation seeks to cultivate demand for a product through the process of product development in order to match needs of the market, and through various techniques of demand stimulation, such as advertising and personal selling. The *buying* function, on the other hand, consists of operations designed to assemble proper varieties and assortments of goods so that they are available to the buyer at the time and place needed. Buying involves, then, planning assortments so that proper quantities and qualities of desired goods are available. These two functions are related to solving the discrepancy problems discussed in Chapter 2.

Transportation and *storage* are known as functions of physical supply. In many contemporary treatments, the term *physical distribution* is used to describe these functions. Because the production location of a product is rarely the same as the location of consumption, goods must be physically transported to complete the exchange process. Storage is also essential in marketing because of differences in times of production and consumption. Goods produced seasonally, such as fruits and vegetables, must be held in inventory until they are demanded. Goods produced continuously but demanded seasonally, such as toys or lawn furniture, must also be stored until demand occurs. These functions relate directly to the solution of spatial and temporal problems discussed in the previous chapter.

The other four functions—financing, standardization, risk taking, and market information—are often referred to as facilitating functions because their performance is necessary to complete exchange and physical supply activities. Since marketing involves vast resources of machines, materials, land, and labor, capital must be supplied to finance the smooth functioning of the system. *Financing* is also required because of the existence of inventories in storage and due to the widespread extension of credit in our economic system. *Standardization* refers to development of product standards and the process of sorting products into useful or usable quantities for consumption. *Risk taking* is an inherent factor in the marketing process. The nature of risk ranges from possible physical losses, such as from fire or theft, to misjudging consumer needs. One or more firms within the channel system must assume the burden of these risks. Collection, interpretation, and communication of *market information* are critical to effective operation of a channel system. Because business decisions are based on information concerning market size, needs, and supplies available, accurate data must be available to the decision maker.

[2] The following discussion of marketing functions is based on: Rayburn D. Tousley, Eugene Clark, and Fred E. Clark, *Principles of Marketing* (New York: The Macmillan Company, 1962), pp. 14–20.

Performance of all these marketing functions is critical to the completion of an economic transaction. Of primary importance is the understanding that each function must be performed by some individual(s) or institution(s) in the channel system. For the moment, we are not concerned with which firm performs the functions but with the fact that all functions must be performed.

Firm Goals and Resources

Although all functions must be performed in a channel of distribution, each firm may have different goals and varied capabilities to perform these functions. The management of a specific firm may simply not desire to perform certain functions or may feel that attempting to do so will jeopardize the firm's overall profitability. For example, some retailers have determined that it is in their best interest to lease rather than own locations. Their feeling is that they should limit themselves to performing retail functions and avoid risks associated with real estate ownership. The recent move by Dayton-Hudson to sell its vast real estate holdings is a good example of a decision to limit functional involvement. Even if a firm desires to perform certain activities, it may lack the capability or resources to do so effectively. In such cases a firm is forced to limit the scope of its participation in a channel.

Specialization

As discussed in previous chapters, specialization of functions is a natural characteristic of an advanced economic system. It is not important for the moment whether a firm specializes in particular functions because of its own goals or because it possesses specific skills and resources. It is important to note, however, that the specialization process leads to some important behavioral concepts: position, role, and domain.

Position and Role Each channel member chooses a position or location in the channel system. Attendant with each position is a role or a set of roles. In a channels context, "role" refers to the functions and degree of functional performance expected of the firm filling a position.[3] For example, a firm may choose to occupy a channel position as a manufacturer's agent. The role of this position is well defined by convention in industry. It is generally known that a manufacturer's agent will have a limited sales territory and little control over prices, and will be responsible for only part of the manufacturer's output. In contrast, a firm fulfilling the position of selling agent has a different channel role. A selling agent, although having little control over output, may have an unlimited territory and normally is expected to have considerable control over prices. In a similar manner, all channel positions have specified roles defining the type of behavior expected of occupants of those positions.

[3] Louis W. Stern and J. L. Heskett, "Conflict Management in Interorganizational Relations: A Conceptual Framework," in *Distribution Channels: Behavioral Dimensions,* ed. Louis W. Stern (Boston: Houghton Mifflin Company, 1969), p. 157.

Domain Domain refers to the claims a channel member stakes out in terms of: (1) range of products, (2) population (customers) to be served, and (3) services or functions to be accomplished.[4] Each organization in the channel, by nature of the process of specialization, defines its domain in relationship to the domains of other channel members. The concepts of position, role, and domain will be developed fully in a later section of this chapter because of their importance in understanding the total interorganizational behavior model.

Dependence

As a consequence of specialization and the development of organizational positions, roles, and domains, a channel system must be formulated that performs all the necessary marketing functions and satisfies individual firm goals at the same time. The fact that usually no one firm can perform all functions places all channel members into a state of dependence, and mutual dependence has far-reaching ramifications for all behavior observed in a channel system.

Behavior

The most important aspect of interorganizational relationships is the behavior of channel members. Three types of behavior within a channel are typically observed:

1   First, because each firm depends on the others to perform their duties and fulfill their roles adequately, *cooperation* among channel participants is necessary and vital behavior. Cooperation is the prevailing situation in any given channel, and it is necessary so that all channel members can achieve their goals.

2   A second type of behavior observed in channel systems is *conflict*. Seeds of conflict develop from the dependence relationship of firms in the channel. If no dependence existed, no firm would have to cooperate or rely on the performance of others. Involvement creates conflict.

3   The third behavioral pattern observed in channels is the utilization of *power* and emergence of *leadership*. Power, similar to conflict, exists in channels as a result of dependence. The concept of power-dependence behavior is explored fully in Chapter 4.

Performance

The ultimate objective of the channel is to perform adequately to achieve goals. The interaction of cooperation, conflict, and power results in a level of channel performance. If that performance is viewed by all members as satisfactory, the channel relationship will most likely continue. Whenever performance is viewed by one or more members of the channel as unsatisfactory, attempts may be made to realign functions and/or change goals, positions, and roles. Monitoring of performance is necessary to identify the need to adapt to outside conditions which may call for new institutional arrangements.

[4] Ibid.

In summary, this section has introduced a basic framework for understanding behavior in channel relationships. Central to understanding channel behavior is the concept of mutual dependence. Dependence exists as a result of specialization in functions, positions, and roles of channel members. Specialization, in turn, occurs because of the number and complexity of necessary marketing functions to be performed and the goals and capabilities of individual firms. Each firm also monitors performance of the overall channel based on individual goals. If performance is satisfactory for all members, realignment of the relationship is unlikely. Unsatisfactory performance, however, may result in new forms of behavior (i.e., conflict or utilization of power to induce better performance) or may ultimately lead to a reexamination of existing relationships with the intent to form an alternative channel arrangement.

Interorganizational Behavior—an Example

An example which clarifies the nature of interorganizational relationships is the distribution channel for frozen orange juice concentrate.[5] The channel itself is simple. A number of growers in Florida raise oranges, several processors extract the juice and freeze it, and retailers such as A&P, Safeway, and Kroger purchase the concentrate for resale to consumers. Depending upon specific circumstances, the channel may also include various brokers and/or agents as intermediaries between processors and retailers. The apparent simplicity of this channel belies the complex nature of relationships among participating firms.

Approximately 80 percent of the orange crop is sold to processors under contracts which do not specify prices. A grower will sign a contract in June or July to deliver oranges the following year. The processor will then make partial payment to help finance the grower's harvesting operations. However, after this initial payment, the grower will receive no further financing from the processor until the crop is available and wholesale price levels are established. The elapsed time from original commitment to final conclusion of the processor-grower negotiation is over 1 year. The revenue which the grower ultimately receives is calculated by the processor, who deducts cost and traditional profit from the wholesale price. Because of this arrangement, the grower has a guaranteed market before the size of the crop is known. In negotiating wholesale prices with retail chains, processors must attempt to obtain prices which will return adequate revenues to growers in order to be able to attract new contracts. On the other hand, pressure exists from grocery chain buyers to keep prices low to stimulate consumer demand. The grocery chains will also seek alternative sources of supply in order to be in a better position to negotiate with existing processors.

Although the orange juice concentrate channel is unique to that industry, it serves as an illustration of the concepts of interorganizational behavior. Readily apparent are the marketing functions, goals, and capabilities of various

---

[5] The facts in this example were developed from Billy Schwartz, "Florida Growers Say Citrus Processors are Keeping Demand High, Prices Low," *Wall Street Journal* (August 18, 1975).

firms, and resulting specialization. Of particular interest in this example are the functions of financing and risk taking and the manner in which firms specialize in these activities.

It is also obvious that a great deal of mutual dependence exists among firms. Growers are highly dependent upon the ability of processors to effectively negotiate for higher prices. In turn, processors are dependent upon retail chains to sell their product, as well as dependent upon growers to maintain an adequate supply. Because of the structure of this industry, the need for cooperation and the potential for conflict are obvious. In addition, the potential for utilization of power clearly exists because of the high degree of dependency. Nevertheless, as long as all channel members are satisfied with overall performance, there will be little impetus for conflict and cooperation will prevail. Imagine, however, a situation in which wholesale (and retail) prices for orange juice concentrate remained relatively stable over a period of 3 years while growers' costs rose by 60 percent. Because of the manner in which growers' revenues are calculated by processors, it would not be surprising if growers became dissatisfied and came into conflict with processors and retailers. The result could be an attempt to find some means to reduce or alter dependence on the traditional channel.

The above illustration is simplified. It does not include the importance of buying and selling futures in the concentrate commodities market, nor does it elaborate the many institutional arrangements that exist in addition to growers, processors, and retailers. Many grower cooperatives exist to perform the function of the processor. In other situations, processors sell to wholesale mixers who, in turn, sell bottled juice to retailers. Nevertheless, the example does serve to illustrate the risk and potential conflict that can evolve in a channel.

CONFLICT

Based upon the preceding discussion of interorganizational behavior, it is now possible to examine in depth the behavior most often experienced in channels. While a fundamental thesis of this book is that cooperative behavior is most prevalent, attention is focused first on conflict because of its potential ramifications for marketing management.

Types of Channel Conflict

Conflict in distribution channels can occur in many different forms. In his pioneering work on conflict, Joseph C. Palamountain identified three types of distributive conflicts: (1) horizontal, (2) intertype, and (3) vertical.[6] Before we expand on the nature of vertical conflict, which is of primary importance to channel management, an examination of the two other forms of conflict will provide useful background for understanding.

[6] Joseph C. Palamountain, Jr., *The Politics of Distribution* (Cambridge, Mass.: Harvard University Press, 1955).

Horizontal Conflict   Horizontal conflict is normally treated in microeconomics because it relates to competition. The term *horizontal conflict* is used because it occurs among similar firms on the same level in distribution channels. Retailers such as two drugstores in competition with each other for the consumer's dollar are involved in horizontal conflict. Similarly, wholesaler competing against wholesaler or manufacturer versus manufacturer are manifestations of horizontal conflict.

Intertype Conflict   Intertype conflict refers to competition occurring among different types of middlemen at the same level in a channel. As such, some people view it as a type of horizontal conflict occurring between dissimilar institutions which compete for the same customer. The emergence of warehouse furniture outlets has spurred development of new channels which compete with traditional forms of distribution. Intertype competition has intensified since the advent of scrambled merchandising by retailers. Scrambled merchandising refers to the practice among retailers of adding new product lines which are unrelated to their normal lines of business. Some supermarkets, for example, have added housewares and clothing to their product lines in an effort to achieve higher margins. In doing so, they compete with traditional channels for those products. Manufacturers may also spur intertype competition when they attempt to develop new means of distribution. An excellent example is the Hanes Hosiery Company and their development of L'eggs pantyhose. Until Hanes introduced L'eggs, most hosiery was sold in department and specialty stores. Total sales of hosiery in supermarkets were very small and no effort had been made to develop this form of distribution. Hanes developed a new product and a new method of distribution to cultivate retail exposure. Today, about 50 percent of all hosiery sales take place in grocery and drugstore outlets.

Intertype competition is a significant form of conflict because it reflects one manner in which industries remain efficient and respond to changing market conditions.[7] It is also significant for the ramifications it has on a firm's existing channel relationships and its potential for breeding the third type of competition, vertical conflict.

Vertical Conflict   Vertical conflict refers to competition among different levels within a given channel of distribution. When Hanes decided to develop new retail outlets for hosiery, management expected and received considerable negative reaction from department and specialty store buyers who had traditionally handled their products. Such problems among channel members are potentially devastating to the cooperative relationships existing within a channel. Because of the disruptive nature of aggression among channel members, the remainder of this chapter is devoted to a detailed investigation of the vertical conflict process.

[7] Fred C. Allvine and James M. Patterson, *Competition, Ltd.: The Marketing of Gasoline* (Bloomington, Ind.: Indiana University Press, 1972), p. 107.

Conflict Defined

Thus far, we have avoided a formal definition of conflict, relying instead on the reader's intuition and experience to define the term. In fact, there appears to be a lack of agreement among social scientists as to the type of behavior which can be classified as conflict. One common conception of conflict is that it consists of hostile behavior by one party in a relationship which is designed to injure, thwart, or otherwise harm another party.[8] However, this definition is deficient in that it connotes that conflict only exists when incidents of hostile behavior can be observed. It overlooks not only the existence of a covert state of disagreement but also the extreme importance of the subjective perceptions of involved parties.[9] For our purposes, therefore, conflict is defined as *a situation in which one member of a distribution channel perceives another member as an adversary engaging in behavior designed to injure, thwart, or gain scarce resources at its expense.*[10] To gain a deeper understanding, it is useful to review the complex process by which conflict develops, flourishes, and is ultimately resolved. The marketing student will observe that, just as products and institutions follow a distinct life cycle, so does the conflict process.[11]

Many fundamental situations aid in the birth and development of hostility among channel members. It is important to note, however, that rarely is there a single reason for conflict. Rather, the process is typically characterized by multiple causation.[12] Arising from these fundamental situations is a feeling of stress among managements of channel institutions. This stress may exist and conflict be present in a covert state for an indefinite period of time. Although conflict exists, in many cases the frustrated members will take no specific action to change their behavior or the behavior of other channel members.[13] But stress must exist as a prelude to overt behavior on the part of any channel members.[14]

The stress which exists among channel members may ultimately build to a peak, particularly during times of change.[15] By change, we mean that some incident or issue arises, usually a change in the behavior of the frustrated channel member, which brings stress into the open and causes overt hostility among channel members. Conflict then erupts over these issues. Although the distinc-

---

[8] See, for example, Raymond Mack and Richard Snyder, "The Analysis of Social Conflict: Toward an Overview and Synthesis," *Journal of Conflict Resolution* (June 1957), p. 219.

[9] Kenneth E. Boulding, "Organization and Conflict," *Journal of Conflict Resolution* (June 1957), pp. 131–132.

[10] This definition, which relies on the perceptions of involved channel members, is developed from a generalized definition of social conflict posed in Ralph Goldman, "A Theory of Conflict Processes and Organizational Offices," *Journal of Conflict Resolution* (September 1966), p. 335.

[11] Kenneth E. Boulding, *Conflict and Defense* (New York: Harper & Row, Publishers, Inc., 1963), p. 307.

[12] Ronald J. Fischer, "Third Party Consultation: A Method for the Study and Resolution of Conflict," *Journal of Conflict Resolution* (March 1972), p. 67.

[13] Stern and Heskett, op. cit., p. 292.

[14] Robert A. Robicheaux and Adel I. El-Ansary, "A General Model for Understanding Channel Member Behavior," *Journal of Retailing* (Winter 1975–1976), p. 22.

[15] Wroe Alderson, *Dynamic Marketing Behavior* (Homewood, Ill.: Richard D. Irwin, Inc., 1965), p. 253.

tion between causes and issues of conflict may not be obvious, the difference is important because issues are the *stated* claims or grievances of the channel members and may be quite precise. The causes, however, are generally vague. Channel participants are usually unable or unwilling to express to each other the real causes of conflict. The issues may be considered symptoms of the conflict causes, and treating the conflict issues may have little, if any, effect on removal of the underlying causes.[16] To distinguish between causes and issues, a medical analogy may be useful. Treating a patient's fever does little to remove the serious infection which might be causing the fever. Similarly, in distribution channels, dealing with a retailer's specific claim that a manufacturer's required order sizes are too large would do little to remove the conflict caused by the retailer's goal of minimizing investment. Although the one issue may be treated, it is likely that others will arise unless the two parties reach an understanding concerning the basic cause.

When hostile behavior erupts among channel members, some mechanism is required to end conflict. Different methods of conflict resolution exist, including techniques of problem solving, persuasion, negotiation, and political action.[17] The conflict process, once ended, may be evaluated in two ways. First, and of importance to channel members, is the effect of conflict on their individual roles and ability to achieve goals. Second, from the viewpoint of the total channel, hostility is important in terms of its effects on total performance and customer satisfaction.

The conflict process described above is extremely complex. The remainder of this chapter is thus devoted to an in-depth examination of the stages of this process.

Causes of Conflict

A basic tenet of conflict theory is that if no interdependence exists in a social system, there is no basis for conflict. Thus, it could be argued that mutual dependence is the cause for conflict. Such a conclusion overlooks the fact that conflict does not always result from a state of dependence and that cooperative behavior is more likely to prevail. Therefore, some reason or combination of reasons must also exist which cause disagreement.

Social scientists have studied the primary causes of conflict. From the viewpoint of distribution channels, conflict causes can be grouped as:

1 Goal incompatibility.
2 Domain-position-role incongruence.
3 Communication breakdowns.
4 Differing perceptions of reality.
5 Ideological differences.

---

[16] Larry J. Rosenberg, "An Empirical Examination of the Causes, Level, and Consequences of Conflict in a High Stake Distribution Channel" (unpublished Ph.D. Dissertation, The Ohio State University, 1969), p. 24.

[17] James G. March and Herbert A. Simon, *Organizations* (New York: John Wiley & Sons, Inc., 1958), p. 129.

Goal Incompatibility   All members of a distribution channel presumably share a common goal: maximizing the effectiveness of the total system. It may be assumed that each firm's management anticipates that channel membership will also aid its organization in achieving objectives and obtaining satisfactory profits. However, each firm also exists as a separate legal entity. Each has its own employees, stockholders or owners, and other interested groups who help shape goals and strategies of the institution. Thus, each firm has a set of goals, some of which may overlap or be incompatible with the goal-sets of other channel members. This incompatibility may be a primary cause of stress which will ultimately cause conflict within the system.

Examples of goal incompatibility leading to conflict may be seen in disagreements over distribution of channel profits. Each institution may desire the highest possible profit for the channel as a whole and the natural tendency will be to cooperate in achieving maximum channel profits. However, each individual firm can be expected to also desire the largest obtainable share of total channel profits. The predictable result is conflict over the allocation process. Disagreement over the size of margins allowed each channel member is one form of such conflict.

Another form of conflict may result from the amount of aid or support to be granted for performance of marketing functions. Some retailers feel that traditional cooperative advertising agreements calling for 50 percent support from manufacturers are inadequate due to the higher costs of color newspaper advertisements. The retailer may feel that the manufacturer should pay for part of the cost incurred in color production in addition to the traditional support. The retailer may reason that all parties benefit from color ads, therefore all should share in increased expenses. Such disagreements are, of course, rooted in the objective of each firm to obtain high profits.

Even when goals of firms in a distribution channel are compatible, disagreement may exist as to methods.[18] All channel members may agree that volume increases are desirable but will disagree on the means to accomplish them. Manufacturers might desire more shelf space for better positioning of their products in retail stores to achieve the desired sales increase. Retailers, on the other hand, might feel that more advertising effort by the manufacturer would accomplish the objective. The result may be conflict over which method to utilize. One author has suggested that since goals are rarely clear-cut or simple, conflict over means can move into the more fundamental arena of conflict over goals.[19] Thus, in the above example, conflict over which method to utilize in order to secure increased sales may eventually lead to conflict concerning the division of the increase once it has been obtained. For instance, if better shelf position is given to products, the retailer may raise prices to compensate for the improved space and precipitate conflict concerning the objectives of the two firms.

---

[18] Bertram Raven and Arie Kruglanski, "Conflict and Power," in *The Structure of Conflict,* ed. Paul Swingle (New York: Academic Press, Inc., 1970), p. 70.
   [19] Alderson, op. cit., p. 255.

Position, Role, and Domain Incongruency   The concepts of position, role, and domain must be recognized and agreed to by channel members.[20] Suppose that in a channel consisting of a manufacturer using wholesale distributors to sell to retail dealers, consensus exists among all institutions concerning the roles and domains of each party. If, however, the manufacturer decides (as often happens) to serve larger dealers directly, positions, in effect, are respecified. Changes in position specification or poorly defined positions may precipitate conflict among channel members. In the above example, it would be expected that wholesaler distributors would react with hostility to the manufacturer's redefinition of positions. Yet, the fact remains that a firm can perform or fill a position only if all other channel members agree.

Often, the position may be clearly specified but the expected behavior of the firm filling that position may not be. In fact, there may be considerable ambiguity among channel members concerning appropriate behavior of firms filling each position. It was suggested earlier that the role of a manufacturer's agent is clearly specified by custom and convention in industry. However, it may be expected that this traditional role will be modified in each situation. Rarely are the roles of channel members static. They can vary over time and under different circumstances. In cases where roles vary, all channel members must understand and agree upon the expected behavior of the respective firms. When consensus does not exist, conflict can be expected.

Because each role represents a code of conduct defining the channel member's expected contribution, adequate performance is critical to maintain harmony in the system.[21] The roles specified for a position in the channel allow other members to predict behavior and measure performance of their counterparts. A wholesaler, for example, expects certain types of behavior and levels of performance from both the manufacturer and the retailers in the system. Manufacturers might be expected to ship products within 48 hours after receipt of an order. The wholesaler formulates ordering patterns around such expectations. If the manufacturer consistently fails to meet the expected performance level, the wholesaler will seek alternative suppliers. At the very least, conflict will exist between the two channel members. Inadequate role performance or failure to behave in the prescribed manner frustrates attempts by one firm to predict what the other will do. This frustration is a major cause of channel conflict. Of course, actual role behavior or performance will frequently deviate from the expected since a firm's ability to perform is the result of many situational factors.[22]

Conflict may also arise in distribution channels which lack agreement concerning organizational domain. Domain dissension is a likely precipitator of

[20] F. Kelly Shuptrine and J. Robert Forster, "Monitoring Channel Conflict and Evaluations from the Retail Level," *Journal of Retailing* (Spring 1976), p. 57.

[21] Louis W. Stern and Ronald Gorman, "Conflict in Distribution Channels: An Exploration," in *Distribution Channels: Behavioral Dimensions,* ed. Louis W. Stern (Boston: Houghton Mifflin Company, 1969), p. 157.

[22] Robicheaux and El-Ansary, op. cit., p. 18.

hostility in two situations. First, when channel members do not know or do not agree on the domains of other firms in the system, lack of the support necessary for the organization's claimed domain will cause frustration and an inability to achieve goals. Second, if domains overlap and two or more firms lay claim to the same functions, products, or customers, stress or tension will be created. Of course, some dissension concerning domain is likely to exist in all channels, but extreme disagreement will most likely result in open hostility among channel members.

An excellent example concerning role and domain dissension arose with Quaker State Oil and a group of its distributors and jobbers. Quaker State adopted a policy discouraging its distributors from selling its oil to discount stores. This policy was especially important to retail service station operators who felt they were losing sales to discount houses. Nevertheless, some distributors were willing to sell to discounters in violation of the restrictions imposed by Quaker State. Apparently these distributors believed that the manufacturer (Quaker State) had no right to limit the domain of customers who could be served in their daily business. As a result, the distributors failed to conform in their role and behaved in a manner which caused dissension with Quaker State. In order to determine which distributors were violating the prescribed behavior, Quaker coded its packages with ink visible only under special lighting. Once the violators were traced, Quaker responded with threats to reduce or terminate deliveries. The legal implications of this conflict episode are discussed in Chapter 5, but it should be noted that the basic cause of hostility was dissension concerning organizational domains and role performance.

Communication Breakdowns The importance of communications to the smooth functioning of a channel system is well documented.[23] Communications breakdowns may cause conflict in two distinct ways. The first is simply failure of one firm to pass on vital information to other channel members.[24] A manufacturer wishing to maintain competitive advantage may decide not to announce a new product until a national distribution program is developed. Retailers, on the other hand, want information about new products as soon as possible to prepare their own strategy for the introductory period. Another example of potential conflict arising from failure to pass along vital information may occur when the manufacturer announces product recalls. These recall notices often appear in newspapers and may be given prominence in other media. Some cases have occurred in which consumers were instructed to return the product to the retail outlet for refund or replacement. The retailers' first notification of the situation came when consumers entered the store demanding compliance with the manufacturer's instructions. In such instances, retailers can be

[23] John R. Grabner, Jr., and L. J. Rosenberg, "Communication in Distribution Channel Systems," in *Distribution Channels: Behavioral Dimensions,* ed. Louis W. Stern (Boston: Houghton Mifflin Company, 1969), pp. 227–252; Robert W. Little, "The Marketing Channel: Who Should Lead the Extra-Corporate Organization," *Journal of Marketing* (January 1970), p. 32.
[24] Grabner and Rosenberg, op. cit., p. 240.

expected to complain to manufacturers concerning the breakdown in the communication system.

The second way in which communication creates conflict is through the various types of noise and distortion within the message process.[25] In a distribution channel, "noise" commonly arises from confused language connotations in communications.[26] When various members of a distribution channel attach different meanings to language and terminology, the potential for stress increases. Warren Wittreich offers the example of brewery executives trying to communicate with tavern owners:[27]

> To him [the tavern owner] "profit's a highfalutin' word used by wise guys who think they are better than he is." Being in business to "make money," he is more likely to respond to arguments or appeals which are supposed to lead to "better profits." By the same token, talk about "merchandising" or "promotion" is likely to sail over his head. In order to get him to act you have to speak to him in terms which are familiar and meaningful to him and which promise concrete rewards that he can grasp and understand.

Such communications breakdowns are rather common in business. Often this type of noise arises because certain functional specialists develop a terminology of their own which may mean little to anyone except another specialist. (Academicians are noteworthy for their development of specialized languages.) Confused meanings which occur when communicating with a nonspecialist may play a major part in developing conflict. Recognizing this potential for conflict, the specialist should seek a means of ensuring that communications are understood. A major advertising agency realized recently that many nonadvertising executives did not understand such terms as "weighted target audience" and "pulsing." Consequently, the agency published a twelve-page brochure which defined key advertising terminology and explained methods of computation for such figures as "readers per copy." In this manner the agency is attempting to avoid conflict resulting from misunderstood communications with its clients.

Of course, noise can occur in many other ways in the communications process. The fact remains that any time a message is not received with the meaning the sender intended, conflict is a potential result.

Differing Perceptions of Reality   Just as conflict may occur when channel members differ in their methods of achieving mutual goals, different solutions to mutual problems can also lead to conflicting behavior.[28] Even when channel members have a strong desire to cooperate and goal agreement exists, conflict

---

[25] Grabner and Rosenberg, op. cit., p. 239.

[26] Warren J. Wittreich, "Misunderstanding the Retailer," *Harvard Business Review* (May–June 1962), p. 147. Copyright © 1962 by the President and Fellows of Harvard College; all rights reserved.

[27] Wittreich, op. cit., p. 150.

[28] Stern and Heskett, op. cit., p. 294; March and Simon, op. cit., p. 121.

can occur when perceptions of the "real" facts differ.[29] The problem of varied perceptions occurs because each channel member brings to the relationship a different background and prejudices. In any given situation, facts are likely to be interpreted in light of that prior experience. All members may agree that the channel is not functioning as effectively as desired. The situation itself is not in question. However, each channel member may perceive a different reason for this lack of effectiveness. The manufacturer may feel that the retailer's stockouts are caused by a failure to maintain adequate safety stock levels and realistic reorder points. The retailer may feel that inventory policies are realistic and that the problem is caused by the manufacturer's inability to meet scheduled delivery times. Each party is interpreting the situation based on experience as well as the natural prejudices associated with the position and role each fills.

An interesting example of conflict because of differing perceptions by channel members occurred when Cotton Incorporated, the marketing arm of the cotton industry, became angry with one of the primary users of cotton, Levi Strauss & Company. When Levi began making and promoting a line of denim jeans which contained 35 percent polyester, Cotton Incorporated began an advertising campaign using network television, trade journals, and such consumer magazines as *Sports Illustrated* and *Playboy*. Although Levi was not specifically named in the advertisements, the basic theme of the ads was that unless denim jeans are 100 percent cotton, they are not denim jeans. Believing that the cotton-polyester blend is easier to care for than pure cotton, Levi countered with: "It's the performance of the fabric and the weave that makes it denim."[30] Thus, conflict was spurred by a very basic difference in perception as to which characteristics constitute denim fabric. The cotton industry feels that denim must be pure cotton; Levi considers performance and weave the determinants of the fabric. Perhaps the most interesting sidelight in this conflict is that, although Levi began using a blend, its consumption of cotton increased because of sales growth. Nevertheless, cotton industry representatives had most likely feared that Levi would switch to polyester blends for other product lines and that cotton consumption would decrease over time.

Ideological Differences Ideological or value conflicts are, to some extent, similar to conflicts concerning roles and expected behavior of channel members in their selected positions. Assael has identified a fundamental ideological conflict in channels which stems from big-business and small-business perceptions of management.[31] Specifically, this difference is observed in views concerning the appropriate level of sales effort.[32] For example, a manufacturer may be so satisfied with the performance of a wholesale distributor in a given territory that pressure is then exerted on the wholesaler to expand the line of business,

---

[29] Robicheaux and El-Ansary, op. cit., p. 23.

[30] *Business Week* (April 11, 1977), p. 78.

[31] Henry Assael, ed., *The Politics of Distributive Trade Associations: A Study in Conflict Resolution* (Hempstead, N.Y.: Hofstra University Press, 1967), p. 413.

[32] Assael, op. cit., p. 416.

hire new employees, and move into new territories. The wholesaler, on the
other hand, may be satisfied with allowing business to continue in its present
form. For the small business, expansion may mean a loss of personal control
resulting from the need for additional managerial talent. Or the expansion may
be resisted because it would require longer working hours and cause more personal frustration with the business. The small business owner may indeed value
leisure time and fewer headaches and thus will resist pressures exerted by big
business. In such a situation, management of the larger organization may fail to
understand the value system of the small business and conflict can be expected.

In summary, conflict has many origins. Although specific issues which
may precipitate conflict among channel members are limitless, mutual dependence in the channel system carries with it the potential for stress and conflict
concerning incompatible goals, position-role-domain incongruence, communications breakdowns, differing perceptions of reality, and different ideological
values of the involved institutions.

Results of Conflict

Precipitation of a conflict episode with overt hostile behavior among channel
members requires some mechanism to bring hostility to an end. A number of
methods for conflict resolution are available. However, most of the means by
which conflict is resolved rely to a greater or lesser extent upon some form of
power or leadership. Because of the close relationship between power and the
resolution of conflict, the discussion of resolution methodology is delayed until
Chapter 4.

Regardless of the method by which conflict is resolved, the resulting behavioral adjustment determines whether the conflict episode was functional or
dysfunctional.[33] Early literature viewed conflict as dysfunctional or disruptive
because it forced channel members away from their preference for a stable relationship.[34] More recently, however, conflict has been considered to have certain beneficial qualities which can enhance the solidarity of a channel.[35] In fact,
absence of conflict may breed passivity and complacency in the channel with a
resultant lack of innovation.[36]

Kenneth Boulding suggests that both situations may be valid. He argues
that a certain level of conflict is necessary and healthy for channel survival, but
he stresses the need to identify the level above which conflict will have dysfunctional consequences. The normal assumption in marketing literature is that

[33] Stern and Heskett, op. cit., p. 292.
[34] Lewis Coser, *The Functions of Social Conflict* (Glencoe, Ill.: Free Press, 1956),
pp. 16–26; Bengt Hoglund and Jorgen Ulrich, "Peace Research and the Concepts of Conflict," in
Conflict Control and Conflict Resolution, eds. Bengt Hoglund and Jorgen Ulrich, (Copenhagen:
C. Olsen and Co., 1972), pp. 21–22.
[35] Robert A. Levine, "Anthropology and the Study of Conflict: An Introduction," *Journal of
Conflict Resolution* (March 1962), p. 7.
[36] Stern and Heskett, op. cit., p. 292.

conflict will influence the operating performance of channel members.[37] Although conceptually appealing, attempts to identify a level of conflict which promotes greater goal attainment for individual channel members generally have been unsuccessful.[38]

There is no doubt, however, that in some situations dysfunctional conflict may be so pronounced that an effective channel can scarcely be said to exist.[39] The results of functional and dysfunctional conflict are discussed below.

Functional System Results Functional consequences of channel conflict are observed in two distinct situations. The first situation involves unification of the channel system.[40] Channel members may eventually conclude that no alternative relationship exists which could satisfy goals as adequately as the current alignment. A retailer may determine that, although the supplier delivers a high percentage of damaged or defective merchandise, no other manufacturer exists who could promise better performance. In such a situation, the basic issue still exists but stress between the parties is reduced. Cooperation may be fostered in such a situation if the retailer's satisfaction with the manufacturer is increased as a result of the search for alternative supply sources. Increased cooperation may produce more unified efforts to solve other problems in the channel system.

The second situation in which channel conflict produces functional consequences occurs if system adaptation is the result. If the conflict episode precipitates changes in the system which improve performance in distribution, then the conflict can be judged functional. For example, a conflict episode may lead a retailer to integrate operations and reduce dependence on suppliers. If the integrated retailer is able to operate more efficiently, the outcome of the conflict is positive. *In essence, contrary to popular belief, conflict which results in the disintegration of old alliances and relationships is not necessarily dysfunctional.* Rather, such consequences may be positive if the new alliances enable the channel members to better satisfy their own goals or better meet the needs of customers.

Dysfunctional System Results Under what circumstances, then, might channel conflict be considered dysfunctional or harmful? To answer this question, it is necessary to take a similar perspective to that used in judging functional conflict. Two situations represent dysfunctional conflict: (1) when duplication of effort exists, and (2) when channel members dissipate their resources

[37] Kenneth E. Boulding, "The Economics of Human Conflict," in *The Nature of Human Conflict*, ed. Elton B. McNeil (Englewood Cliffs, N.J.: Prentice-Hall, Inc., 1965), pp. 174–175.

[38] Robert F. Lusch, "Channel Conflict: Its Impact on Retailer Operating Performance," *Journal of Retailing* (Summer 1976), p. 3. See also: Michael Pearson, "The Conflict-Performance Assumption," *Journal of Purchasing* (February 1973), pp. 57–69.

[39] Alderson, op. cit., p. 252.

[40] Stern and Gorman, op. cit., p. 171.

in prolonging and heightening the conflict rather than seeking constructive solutions.

Duplication of Effort   The duplication of effort resulting from channel conflict is illustrated in the following series of relationships:[41]

1   The higher the level of perceived vertical conflict among channel members within any given channel system, the lower the probability of functional cooperation among members.
2   The lower the probability of functional cooperation, the greater the duplication of effort among channel members.
3   The greater the duplication of effort, the lower the performance of the channel system.

If, for example, the conflicting channel members remained in a buying-selling relationship but chose not to cooperate in performance of other marketing functions, it is quite likely that duplication, or at least unnecessary performance of functions at some levels in the channel, could develop. The reduction in efficiency would be dysfunctional from the consumer's viewpoint. In addition, the increased cost resulting from duplication would probably impair the system's ability to compete effectively. The result could be an inability of channel members to achieve their goals and a heightened level of frustration among channel members.

Resource Dissipation   Conflict which wastes the resources of all channel members and fails to result in formation of a more effective distribution system is dysfunctional.[42] Boulding termed such conflict as pathological because, in attempting to injure or thwart the competitor in goal attainment, one's own resources are expended and self-attainment of goals is thwarted.[43] In such situations the conflicting parties lose sight of the original issues and allow such emotions as revenge, distrust, or insecurity to proliferate and escalate the conflict. Conflict with these characteristics is not only dysfunctional for each party in the channel but also causes inefficiency in the total system.

The aim of the marketing manager involved with channel strategy is not necessarily to avoid all conflict, but rather to avoid conflict which will have dysfunctional system consequences. A level of tension which drives channel members to seek better solutions to common problems may not only lead to more satisfactory attainment of individual organizational goals but also will improve the competitive posture of the overall distribution channel. Thus, the major interest of the channel strategist is conflict management rather than conflict avoidance.

[41] Stern and Heskett, op. cit., p. 293. Copyright © 1969 by L. W. Stern. Reprinted by permission of Houghton Mifflin Co.
[42] Larry J. Rosenberg and Louis W. Stern, "Toward the Analysis of Conflict in Distribution Channels: A Descriptive Model," *Journal of Marketing* (October 1970), p. 42.
[43] Kenneth E. Boulding, "The Economics of Human Conflict," in *The Nature of Human Conflict,* ed. Elton B. McNeil (Englewood Cliffs, N.J.: Prentice-Hall, Inc., 1965), p. 175.

SUMMARY

At the beginning of this chapter an overall framework for viewing interorganizational behavior was presented and illustrated in Figure 3-1. Businesses differ in their abilities and desires to perform marketing functions. Therefore, through the process of specialization, they often align themselves with other firms into organized marketing channels. As a result of this combination, each firm becomes dependent upon others in the channel system to accomplish its objectives. This mutual dependence lays the foundation for three types of behavior: conflict, power utilization, and cooperation. This chapter has concentrated on conflict.

Channel conflict occurs in three forms. The first is horizontal conflict, or competition, which takes place among firms on the same level of distribution. For example, two drugstores competing for the same group of customers are involved in horizontal conflict. The second form of conflict, intertype, takes place between two competing or alternative channel systems. Of particular interest to us is the third form of hostility, vertical conflict, which occurs among different levels of a marketing channel.

Although the seeds of vertical conflict lie in mutual dependence, several primary causes of this behavior have been identified. When the goals of individual firms are incompatible with each other or with channel goals, conflict may develop. Poor specification or performance in positions, roles, or domains may lead to hostile behavior. Differing perceptions among firms, communications breakdowns, and differing ideologies may also precipitate conflict.

Vertical conflict can have important ramifications upon the performance of firms within the system as well as on the system itself. A low level of tension among firms may lead to better performance but, as conflict escalates, the system is disrupted. Nevertheless, system disruption is not necessarily dysfunctional. If disruption results in changes or new alignments of firms which perform marketing functions more effectively or efficiently, the conflict is functional from a total system perspective. Conflict is dysfunctional when the organizations waste resources in the conflict process or when system adaptations result in new channels which cannot perform marketing functions as efficiently or effectively as the original system. The discussion of interorganizational behavior is continued in Chapter 4, which deals with power, leadership, and conflict resolution.

QUESTIONS

1   Why is intertype competition considered a means by which industries remain efficient in their response to changing market conditions?
2   Explain why mutual dependence is considered the basis for channel conflict.
3   Why do you believe the authors feel that conflict which results in disintegration of a channel is not necessarily dysfunctional? Give a real or hypothetical example to support this contention.

4 Explain in your own words the interorganizational behavior framework illustrated in Figure 3-1.
5 Explain the concepts of position, role, and domain. Draw upon your knowledge of the channels for automobiles to illustrate each concept.
6 How might development of advanced point-of-sale (POS) systems for retail stores help reduce communication breakdowns in channels of distribution? Can you think of circumstances in which conflict might be increased due to these systems?
7 If conflict may have functional consequences for channel members, why do you suppose attempts to identify a functional level of conflict have been unsuccessful?
8 "Since each business firm desires to maximize its own profits, there must necessarily be conflict among channel members concerning the distribution of total channel profits." Discuss this statement.
9 Why should a formal definition of conflict rely on the perceptions of the involved parties rather than focus only on overt instances of hostile behavior?
10 If cooperation is more prevalent in distribution channels, why should so much attention be focused upon conflict and its causes?

CASE 3-1: Riverview Distributing Company, Incorporated (A)

In August 1977, David Rose, president and owner of Riverview Distributing Company, became concerned about expanding his company's sales. As a rack jobber of housewares, batteries, light bulbs, and home entertainment equipment based in Lansing, Michigan, Rose felt that opportunities for continued sales growth in his current lines were very limited. For the past few years he had been considering opening a retail outlet in the Lansing area which would specialize in electronic and home entertainment equipment. Before proceeding, he approached a friend who taught at the local university and arranged to have a group of students conduct a feasibility study on the proposed expansion as a class project.

BACKGROUND

Rose opened Riverview Distributing Company in 1965 when he realized that his earning potential as a ski instructor was low. The first product lines handled by his firm were light bulbs and electrical hardware equipment. His initial success appeared to be due to development of specialized display equipment which presented to customers many different bulbs and hardware items at one time. Previously, most retailers had purchased these products from cash-and-carry wholesalers, but Rose was successful in placing his display units in variety, drug, and grocery stores on a consignment basis. Although Riverview's prices were slightly higher than those of other wholesalers, the display units and service provided by his firm were attractive to many retailers. The stores using Riverview's display units greatly increased their sales of those products.

As the firm continued to grow, several new product lines were added. Because of its success with light bulbs, the firm added a photolamp product line which ultimately led to the inclusion of batteries for the photography market. The tremendous growth of transistorized radios and tape recorders further increased demand for batteries. The firm also expanded into the household products field. Kitchen utensils and supplies provided a steady, but not spectacular, source of income.

During 1973 and 1974, Rose decided that his firm would distribute radios and tape recorders since it was currently selling batteries for those products. These two products were successful and other home entertainment equipment was added. By 1977, Riverview's product lines in the home entertainment field included radios, tape recorders, tape players, and stereo components such as speakers, amplifiers, and tuners. The addition of these "brown goods" brought about some changes in the firm's operations. Although each sale had a higher per-unit value than other products, customer financing was required for a longer period of time. Since this merchandise represented the company's fastest-growing product line, accounts receivable tripled between 1974 and 1976.

The gross profit margins for products distributed by Rose varied considerably. Although houseware items carried only a 16 percent margin, batteries and related items contributed a much higher margin of about 40 percent. Rose believed that with increases in sales his profit margins would also increase because his firm would qualify for volume discounts from suppliers. An examination of Riverview's income statements in Table 1 shows that the gross margins in 1974, 1975, and 1976 were 27 percent, 27 percent, and 19 percent. Table 2 contains balance sheets for the three most recent years.

Table 1
Riverview Distributing Company, Inc.
Statement of Income and Retained Earnings

	For the year ending:		
	1/31/75	1/31/76	1/31/77
Sales	$195,702	$298,683	$385,070
Cost of sales:			
Opening inventory	48,713	76,186	125,600
Purchases	170,500	266,159	352,400
	219,213	342,345	478,000
Closing inventory	76,186	125,600	165,537
	143,027	216,745	312,463
Gross margin	52,675	81,938	72,607
Operating expenses:			
Advertising, travel, and promotion	2,375	4,450	6,158
Truck expenses	4,121	4,587	7,201
Bad and doubtful accounts	249	272	1,892
Bank charges and interest	1,035	1,418	2,406
Depreciation	4,083	4,097	5,510
Insurance	105	770	966
Legal and audit	620	791	2,702
Light, heat, and power	923	1,069	1,254
Municipal taxes	1,300	1,628	2,102
Office supplies	1,221	2,292	4,156
Repairs	551	895	406
Salaries—executive	10,500	10,500	10,500
—other	12,940	22,840	35,496
Telephone	639	672	1,058
	40,662	56,281	81,807
	12,013	25,657	(9,200)
Cash discounts earned	1,098	3,215	3,686
Net income before taxes	13,101	28,872	(5,514)
Income taxes	3,275	7,218	——
Net income	9,826	21,654	(5,514)
Retained earnings, beginning of year	28,850	38,676	60,330
Retained earnings, end of year	$ 38,678	$ 60,330	$ 54,816

Table 2
Riverview Distributing Company, Inc.
Comparative Balance Sheets

	For the year ending:		
	1/31/75	1/31/76	1/31/77
Assets			
Current:			
Cash	$ 300	$ 4,300	$ 200
Accounts receivable, less allowance			
for doubtful accounts	16,876	33,706	58,405
Inventory, valued at the lower of cost			
or market	76,186	125,600	165,537
	93,362	163,606	224,142
Fixed:			
Display racks, building improvements, automotive			
and office equipment, at cost less accumulated			
depreciation	28,506	28,553	34,330
Total assets	$121,868	$192,159	$258,472
Liabilities			
Current:			
Bank loans, secured	$ 5,000	$ 10,000	$ 15,000
Accounts payable and accrued	31,224	70,608	139,052
Income and other taxes payable	1,252	2,607	990
	37,476	83,215	155,042
Long-term:			
Loans due to directors	44,716	47,614	47,614
Shareholders' equity:			
Capital stock:			
Authorized—3,600 7% redeemable preference			
shares, par value $10 each			
—4,000 common shares without			
par value			
Issued —1,000 common shares	1,000	1,000	1,000
Retained earnings	38,676	60,330	54,816
Total liabilities	$121,868	$192,159	$258,472

SALES REPRESENTATIVES AND CUSTOMERS

Riverview operated in three sales territories, each of which was covered by a single sales representative. The three territories were designated North, West, and South, with the major cities in each being Lansing, Grand Rapids, and Jackson. Each sales representative had full responsibility for maintaining established accounts and opening new accounts in these territories. The sales representatives carried merchandise in a truck, made sales calls, and replenished stock on the spot. They were also responsible for inventory control in the

Table 3   Riverview Distributing Company, Inc.: Analysis of Active Accounts by Type and by Route

Type of account	South route	West route	North route (includes Lansing)	All accounts
Variety stores	62 Accounts 21 with sales of over $1,000 1 with sales of less than $100	41 Accounts 10 with sales of over $1,000 4 with sales of less than $100	93 Accounts 26 with sales of over $1,000 6 with sales of less than $100	195 Accounts 57 with sales of over $1,000 11 with sales of less than $100
Grocery stores	18 6 over $1,000	12	20 0	50 6 over $1,000
Drugstores	10 6 over $1,000	7 2 over $1,000	8 1 over $1,000	25 9 over $1,000
Hardware stores	4	1	13 1 over $1,000	18 1 over $1,000
Discount stores	1	8 5 over $1,000	10 7 over $1,000	19 12 over $1,000
Camera shops	9 7 over $1,000*	4 2 over $1,000	6 5 over $1,000†	19 14 over $1,000
Department stores	5	5 1 over $1,000	4	14
Radio/TV/appliance	10 5 over $1,000	14 3 over $1,000	19 6 over $1,000	43 14 over $1,000
Gas stations/auto supply	9 2 over $1,000	10 4 over $1,000	34 4 over $1,000	53 10 over $1,000
Miscellaneous	14 3 over $1,000 4 less than $100	16 5 over $1,000 5 less than $100	35 1 over $1,000 8 less than $100	65 9 over $1,000 17 less than $100

* Includes company's second largest account—$5,575.
† Includes company's largest account—$5,653.

Table 4   Riverview Distributing Company, Inc.: Analysis of Accounts by Type of Account for the Year Ended December 30, 1977

Type of Account	All routes		
	Number of accounts	Cumulative sales	Percent of total sales
Variety stores	6	$ 22,040	5.0
	13	39,206	10.0
	24	58,068	15.0
	38	77,416	20.0
	54	96,578	25.0
	77	116,217	30.0
	107	134,870	35.0
	163	154,144	40.0
	195	158,050	41.0
Grocery stores	25	19,379	5.03
	50	22,520	5.8
Drugstores	18	19,465	5.05
	25	20,584	5.34
Hardware stores	18	8,100	2.10
Discount stores	8	20,320	5.27
	19	31,033	8.04
Camera shops	4	18,235	4.90
	19	38,464	9.98
Department stores	14	9,403	2.44
Radio/TV/appliance	8	19,198	4.98
	43	36,560	9.49
Gas stations/auto supply	13	19,798	5.14
	53	32,009	8.31
Miscellaneous	7	18,842	5.01
	65	28,347	7.36

trucks and for accounts receivable. Sales representatives replenished their inventories from Riverview's office-warehouse location in Lansing. They were compensated on a straight commission basis, 7.5 percent of their net collected sales.

Sales representatives were given complete discretion to call on accounts they felt would be potential customers. Informal meetings were held periodically in which Rose discussed the company's plans and encouraged the sales force to discuss problems they had with products and/or customers. Through such meetings and with many sales contests, he emphasized the importance of increased sales volume.

An analysis of the company's active customers by type and route is shown in Table 3. Table 4 shows the sales breakdown by type of account.

COMPANY GROWTH

Rose and his wife initially assumed all management responsibility for the firm. Mrs. Rose handled office duties until the job became so complex that another person was hired to handle all record-keeping. The firm had moved from the basement of the Rose home to an office-warehouse location in Lansing in 1970. As product lines and sales volume grew, Rose hired a warehouse manager who also did some selling in the company's showroom attached to the office.

OBJECTIVES

Rose wanted to increase sales because he wanted the firm to make more money. Until 1965 he had been interested primarily in skiing and enjoying life. But, after Rose married, his father-in-law began to pressure him to build a career. The other members of Mrs. Rose's family had successful professional careers, and Rose was determined to show his father-in-law that he could be just as successful. His objective for Riverview Distributing Company was to achieve a sales volume of $1,000,000 by 1980.

PLANNED RETAIL EXPANSION

Although approximately 45 percent of the accounts in the North territory were located in Lansing, 90 percent of its battery and transistor sales were outside the Lansing area. For this reason, Rose did not think his wholesale business would be jeopardized if a retail store were opened in Lansing. From his point of view, the competition for his store would be limited. He realized that there were department stores with stereo departments and local television and radio shops. However, he felt that no existing store emphasized the listening needs of the so-called professional listener, for whom quality stereo components were more important than fancy furniture and cabinetry.

Rose was unable to project sales volume for such a store but he hoped that sales might be as high as $200,000. Since he would be purchasing at distributor prices and selling at retail, his margin would be much higher than on his current wholesale operation. He believed a 40 to 45 percent margin was possible. As far as other costs were concerned, he guessed that inventories would increase and that it would be necessary to hire one additional person to act as manager and salesclerk of the retail outlet.

THE STUDENTS' REPORT

Rose noted that the students' analysis of the competitive situation differed sharply from his own:

> The Lansing market appears to be saturated with stores selling stereo equipment. Lansing has two large department stores; eight mass merchandisers such as Woolco and K-Mart; two catalog showroom stores; five large specialty stores; 20 smaller specialty shops; and five television and furniture stores. In short, there are over 40 stores in the Lansing market selling stereo components.

Table 5
Riverview Distributing Company, Inc.
Pro Forma Income Statement for Proposed Retail Outlet
for the Year Ended July 31, 197–

Revenues: Sales[1]		$272,160
Cost of goods sold:		
Beginning inventory—August 31, 197–	$ 51,300	
Add: Purchases	164,030	
	215,330	
Less: Ending inventory	28,900	
		186,430
Gross profit on sales:		$ 85,730
Expenses		
Advertising	$ 4,950	
Amortization expense[2]	25	
Bad Debt expense[3]	5,443	
Depreciation—building[4]	3,000	
Depreciation—equipment[5]	950	
Depreciation—paving[6]	320	
Heat, light, and power[7]	1,750	
Insurance[8]	1,200	
Accrued interest (long-term)[9]	5,700	
Interest (short-term)[10]	1,166	
Legal and auditing[11]	1,000	
Licensing (retail)	25	
Municipal taxes	2,288	
Business taxes	686	
Office supplies	2,500	
Salaries[12]	8,000	
Telephones	250	
Miscellaneous	1,000	
		40,253
Net profit on sales:		$ 45,477
Income taxes[13]		11,638
Net profit:		$ 33,839

Notes:
[1] Based on 10 percent market share at wholesale prices.
[2] Building permit, amortized over 15 years.
[3] Two percent of gross sales.
[4] Depreciated over 20 years straight-line.
[5] Depreciated over 5 years straight-line.
[6] Depreciated over 5 years straight-line.
[7] Based on current figures for Riverview's warehouse-office complex.
[8] $100 per month.
[9] 9½ percent on principal of $60,000.
[10] 10 percent on forecasted cash.
[11] Assumed to increase by $1,000.
[12] Salary for one additional sales clerk.
[13] Calculated on the basis of past Riverview figures at a rate of 25½ percent.

Table 6
Riverview Distributing Company, Inc.
Pro Forma Balance Sheet for Proposed Retail Outlet
as of July 31, 197–

Assets

Current:

Cash		$ 14,657
Accounts receivable	$11,000	
Less: Uncollectable accounts	454	
		10,546
Inventory		28,900
Total current assets		$ 54,103

Plant and equipment:

Building	$60,000	
Less: Accumulated depreciation	3,000	
		57,000
Equipment	4,750	
Less: Accumulated depreciation	950	
		3,800
Paving	1,600	
Less: Accumulated depreciation	320	
		1,280
Total plant and equipment		$ 62,080

Other:

Building permit	$ 125	
Less: Amortization	25	
		100
Total assets		$116,283

Liabilities

Current:

Accounts payable		$ 22,625
Income taxes payable		5,819
Total current liabilities		$ 28,444

Long-term:

Long-term note (building)	$66,000	
Less: Principal repaid	6,000	
		54,000

Equity:

Retained earnings		33,839
Total liabilities		$116,283

The report pointed out that large specialty stores carried stereo components ranging from economy lines in the $100-to-$250 price bracket, to medium-
priced and quality lines in the $250-to-$600 range, to very good quality lines
which retailed for more than $600. The best sets frequently sold for prices in
excess of $2,000. These large outlets usually had one favorite line, but stocked
a broad selection of three or more brands.

Smaller specialty outlets were found in shopping centers, department stores, and television and furniture stores, and were usually a department of a larger store. Normally these stores sold just one product line which was secondary to major products such as televisions, furniture, records, or musical instruments. Products carried were in the medium- and low-price range. Only a small selection of components was stocked.

In a survey of 230 Lansing area consumers, the student researchers found that 43 percent of the respondents would purchase from a wholesale outlet if one were available, and an additional 34 percent said they might do so. Sixty-six percent said they would be willing to drive 6 miles or more to shop at such an outlet, and 43 percent said they would be willing to drive 10 or more miles.

Quality was judged to be the most important criterion in brand selection, followed by service, warranty, price, and store. Eighty-eight percent of the respondents said they would compare brands and prices in three or more stores before making a decision.

Based on these data and a projected annual market in the Lansing area in excess of $3 million, the students recommended that Rose "open a wholesale sound specialty store in Lansing, paying particular attention to service, warranty, and quality." Since the most price-sensitive group of consumers desired medium-priced components ($200–$700), this price range was recommended. The report also included consumer attitudes toward various brands of components.

It was recommended that the wholesale image be reinforced by construction of a 5,000-square-foot building adjacent to the existing warehouse office complex. A first-year net profit of $33,839 after taxes was projected based on an expected 10 percent market share (see pro forma financial statements, Tables 5 and 6).

CASE 3-1: QUESTIONS

1 What potential channel conflicts may arise with Riverside Distributing Company?
2 If you were Rose, what would you do?

CASE 3-2: Oakville Mall

In the fall of 1977, Ms. Roberta Brent, president of E. L. Lint Company, a department store firm with branches in three mid-Michigan cities, was concerned about reports that another major department store chain, well-known in several states, was considering opening branch stores in Lint's market areas. In December, Ms. Brent's fears were confirmed when it was announced that the firm, Deming Stores, planned to open two branches in Lint's major market. One of the branches was to be located in a new mall to be developed and built by Deming's Properties. Brent realized that this new mall would present substantial competition for all area retailers, but there was little that could be done to prevent entry by this source of competition. She was extremely concerned, however, about the announcement that Deming's also planned to open a store in Oakville Mall, an existing shopping center in which Lint's maintained a large branch store.

OAKVILLE MALL

Oakville Mall opened in 1969. The developer of this shopping center project was Cal Martin Properties, Incorporated. Oakville was the first enclosed regional shopping center in its market, a standard metropolitan statistical area (SMSA) with a population of over 250,000. The original development contained gross leasable area of 300,000 square feet. Besides the Lint's store, which was the largest in the shopping center, there were two other large general merchandise stores in the mall as well as a number of smaller specialty stores. In the original development, however, Cal Martin had considered Lint's the primary traffic generator for the project. Lint's was in the center of the mall; the other two major tenants were at opposite ends.

As in most shopping centers, lease arrangements between Cal Martin and the tenants of Oakville Mall varied. Lint's contract contained the most favorable rental rates for any tenant, with the store paying a guaranteed minimum rent of $1.25 per square foot of area occupied. Thus, Lint's minimum rent during a year was $112,500. The contract also called for Lint's to pay 3 percent of its net sales as rent, if that figure exceeded the $112,500 minimum. The highest

Table 1
Oakville Mall—Selected Operating Analyses

	1976	1973	1969
Income:			
Minimum rents collected	$1,081,000	$1,050,000	$951,000
Miscellaneous income			
(rides, public telephones, etc.)	10,000	8,000	3,000
Percentage rentals collected	321,000	157,000	21,000
Total income	$1,412,000	$1,216,000	$975,000
Expenses:			
Taxes	$ 165,000	$ 125,000	$105,000
Insurance	54,000	46,000	30,000
Promotion (does not include promotional			
efforts of the merchants' association)	35,000	30,000	25,000
Legal and auditing	45,000	42,000	26,000
Miscellaneous	66,000	55,000	48,000
Total expenses	$ 365,000	$ 298,000	$234,000
Cash available for debt service	$1,047,000	$ 918,000	$741,000
Debt service:			
Mortgage (principal and interest)	$ 637,000	$ 637,000	$637,000
Land contract	182,000	182,000	182,000
Total debt service	$ 819,000	$ 819,000	$819,000
Cash throwoff	$ 232,000	$ 99,000	$ (78,000)

rental paid by any of the tenants in Oakville Mall called for a $12 per square foot minimum or 16 percent of net sales. The candy shop which signed this lease had a prime location in the center of the main aisle.

After a poor first-year start, Oakville Mall became quite profitable for Cal Martin Properties. Sales volume for most tenants has grown steadily, and very few tenants have gone out of business because of poor performance in the shopping center. However, one of the large general merchandise stores closed in early 1977. Although this store was paying rent above its minimum, indicating a satisfactory sales volume, the national chain of which it was only one unit filed for bankruptcy in 1977 and closed all its stores in the United States. The closing of this branch, therefore, was not due to any problems with the Oakville Mall unit. Table 1 presents operating analyses from three selected years for Oakville Mall.

Roberta Brent was particularly pleased with the performance of the Lint store in Oakville Mall. Although sales volume in 1969 had not been great enough to require that the percentage rental clause be in effect, Lint paid a total of $158,600 in rent to Cal Martin in 1976. Ms. Brent considered the Oakville Mall branch of Lint's one of the most successful units operated by the firm.

PROPOSED EXPANSION OF OAKVILLE MALL

The proposal to expand Oakville Mall with the addition of Deming's would also add many new specialty stores. As a result, the total size of Oakville Mall would be increased to 578,000 square feet, with Deming's occupying 103,000 square feet. The expansion was to be constructed on vacant land on the westernmost portion of the Oakville Mall site, the only vacant land available. Figure 1 contains a site plan of the 1977 Oakville Mall as well as the proposed addition.

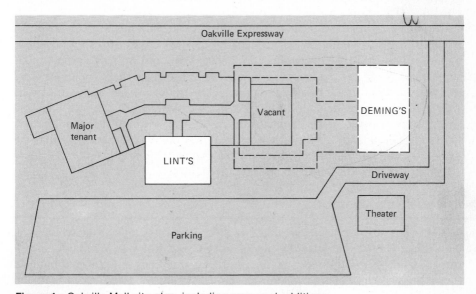

Figure 1   Oakville Mall site plan, including proposed additions.

LINT'S POSITION

Brent commented that she was not pleased that Deming's had decided to enter the market. She knew that the competition would be very strong. Deming's was well known as a retailer of fashion-oriented, quality merchandise. With Deming's having tremendous resources at the disposal of the regional firm, Lint's would probably have a difficult time maintaining its dominant position in the local market. Brent did say, however, that the competition could force Lint management out of its complacency and into a new era of aggressiveness. The firm had never been challenged in its dominant position.

Although concerned about the new competition, she was also very angry about the proposed changes at Oakville Mall: "I want to make it very clear to everyone that we think competition will be beneficial to area consumers and we therefore welcome Deming's to the market," Ms. Brent said in a newspaper interview. "We even think that their coming to Oakville Mall will be good for all parties concerned. As long as they are going to locate in this area we would rather see them in Oakville than any other shopping center. However, we do not think that there is any need to destroy the present configuration of the mall just to get them into the location. They could move into the recently vacated store which contains 50,000 square feet and begin operations immediately. This would be good for all parties concerned. Cal Martin would have its vacant store leased, Deming's could open its doors sooner, and the present mall configuration would be preserved."

"The major problem with the proposed expansion is that it totally changes the site plan. Whereas our Lint store is presently in the center of the mall, after the expansion we will be at the east end. We contend that this change would greatly inconvenience our customers and would ultimately result in a decline in our sales. Therefore, we must be opposed to this proposal."

In a later conversation, Ms. Brent continued her thoughts: "You know, it is interesting how conditions change. In 1967, when Cal Martin approached us about Oakville Mall, he needed us very badly. Without Lint's as a tenant in his project, he could not get mortgage financing to build the mall. Since we were the major retailer in the market, no financial institution would agree to a mortgage unless we were included. We saw it as a worthwhile project, however, and agreed to lease space once the mall was under way. With our promise, he was able to obtain financing, find other tenants, and build Oakville. Now that the mall is a tremendous success, he wants to expand. We are in favor of expansion, but not if it will put us in an inferior position."

CAL MARTIN'S POSITION

Cal Martin said that he really didn't understand Lint's objections to the mall expansion. He felt that since Deming's entry to the area was inevitable, his efforts to have them locate in Oakville Mall were good not only for him but also for all the Oakville tenants: "After all, with Deming's located in our mall and the tremendous increase in the number of other stores, we should draw many more customers than ever before. Why, instead of a decline in sales, I expect to see everyone's sales climb after the expansion is completed."

Martin agreed with Brent's contention that Oakville Mall would not have become a reality in the late 1960s without Lint's agreement to locate in the shopping center. He went on to say, however, that the original development had always been considered only the first phase of a major commercial development which was planned ultimately to include office and residential areas as well as the shopping center itself. He said the final project would include 2 million square feet of leased space. Martin claimed that the development was always envisioned as including the area of the proposed expansion and that it should have been obvious to anyone that the acreage west of the mall was intended to be part of the mall someday. "Why else," he asked, "would I have built the driveway where it is and located the movie theater so far from the mall itself? It was general knowledge that I planned to expand the mall as soon as I became financially able to do so."

To summarize his position, Martin said: "I don't know what all the fuss is about. Everyone is going to be better off when I finish this project."

DEMING'S POSITION

A representative of Deming's commented that Deming's entry to this new market represented the first time the firm had planned to open two stores at one time in a new area. It was felt that such an opening thrust would allow the firm to penetrate the market rapidly. The representative also commented that the firm definitely intended to develop its own mall on the opposite side of town from Oakville Mall, approximately 20 minutes' driving time away.

CASE 3-2: QUESTIONS

1 What elements of shopping center development can be considered analogous to distribution channels?
2 What interorganizational principles can be observed in the Oakville Mall case?
3 What should Ms. Brent and Mr. Martin do to resolve their disagreement?

Interorganizational Behavior: Power, Leadership, and Conflict Resolution

For many years, marketing literature has been concerned with power in channels of distribution. The concept of channel leadership, in terms of an organization which directs the efforts of the system, is often discussed in introductory marketing textbooks. The objective of this chapter is to extend our discussion of interorganizational behavior to include power and the role of leadership in conflict resolution. Our attention focuses first upon the concept of power—how it is obtained and how it is utilized in a marketing channel as a leadership effort. We will then investigate the complex and interrelated nature of power and conflict behavior. Next, attention is directed to methods of conflict resolution. Finally, Chapters 3 and 4 on interorganizational behavior are completed with a discussion of cooperation—the prevailing behavior among channel members.

POWER

Many definitions exist regarding the concept of power. In the social sciences, power is usually defined as the ability to get someone to do something that would not otherwise be done.[1] An alternative is to view power as the ability to

---

[1] Robert A. Dahl, "The Concept of Power," *Behavioral Science* (July 1957), p. 202.

induce change.[2] For our purposes, power in a distribution channel is defined as the ability of one channel member to influence or alter the decisions of other channel members.[3] For example, a manufacturer has power over wholesalers and retailers to the extent that the decisions of those firms can be influenced. If the retailer changes a product's shelf position in response to a manufacturer's request, power has been exercised. It is important for the marketing manager to understand the forces which cause a specific firm to have power.

Power-Dependence Relationships

In Chapter 3 a model of interorganizational behavior was presented which illustrated the importance of mutual dependence. The analysis of power in channel situations depends upon the degree of dependence that exists among members. The concept of mutual dependence implies that, to some degree, each channel member is in a position to facilitate or to hinder the goal attainment of one or more members.[4] This mutual dependence is clearly stated by Richard Emerson, a noted sociologist, in the following:[5]

> The dependence of actor A upon actor B is (1) directly related to A's motivational investment in goals mediated by B, and (2) inversely proportional to the availability of those goals to A outside of the A–B relation.

A very broad meaning can be attached to the term "goal." Goals may be either tangible gratifications which are consciously sought or they may be unconscious psychological satisfactions which are obtained in the relationship. By "mediation," Emerson is referring to the ability of one party to affect the ability of the other to satisfy goals. "Motivational investment" refers to the strength of the desire to achieve a goal.

The above definitions are useful in understanding functioning of a marketing channel. Channel members enter into a relationship because they are unable to perform efficiently all the functions which must be completed to accomplish their goals. To the extent that a firm has established its goals, and a limited number of alternatives exist by which these goals can be achieved, that channel member is extremely dependent upon other firms. As a result, other channel members will be able to influence and perhaps change the decisions and behavior of the dependent firm. For example, in the retail industry it is common for each geographic market area to contain a few large brokers who have well-established ties with discount and department store buyers in the area. A new manufacturer desiring a high degree of market penetration in the area would be well advised to obtain the representation of one of these established brokers. For the manu-

---

[2] James G. March, "An Introduction to the Theory and Measurement of Influence," *American Political Science Review* (1955), p. 434.

[3] Robert A. Robicheaux and Adel I. El-Ansary, "A General Model for Understanding Channel Member Behavior," *Journal of Retailing* (Winter 1975–1976), p. 19.

[4] Richard Emerson, "Power-Dependence Relations," *American Sociological Review* (February 1962), p. 32.

[5] Ibid.

facturer, the alternatives are few and the goal is important. Because of the manufacturer's dependence, brokers may be able to exert considerable influence upon the relationship. Conversely, a large, well-known manufacturer may exert considerable influence over a broker due to its ability to help the broker achieve goals.

A number of important concepts emerge from the perception that power is a function of dependence in a channel system. The first is the idea of power advantage. From the beginning of our discussion of interorganizational behavior we have stressed that *mutual* dependence exists in a channel system. Each channel member possesses some degree of power over the others. Rarely, if ever, does one party enjoy complete power. When examining channel relationships, it is important to focus upon the degree of power held by each firm and to determine if anyone holds an advantage.

The second important concept concerns the perception of power by various channel members. Power is not necessarily observable in all interactions among channel members. It often exists only as a potential force to be utilized when and where needed by the channel member who possesses it. The effectiveness of this potential power, however, depends upon how it is perceived by others. A wholesaler may not perceive the power advantage held by the manufacturer and therefore may not respond to a manufacturer's program or direction. The result could be a serious conflict in the relationship. On the other hand, it is quite possible to perceive that a firm holds more power than it actually does. In such situations, the firm perceived to hold power will be able to influence the decisions of the others. The perceptions and attributions become, in a sense, self-fulfilling prophecies. If a retailer *thinks* a manufacturer is powerful, the retailer will act as if the manufacturer *does* have that power. The importance of these perceptions will become more apparent when we discuss negotiations in Chapter 6.

The third important concept is that power is limited both in scope and in domain.[6] By limited scope, we mean that the issues or decisions which a channel member can influence are limited. A manufacturer may be able to exert considerable influence over the retailer's advertising copy but will have little influence on store locations. The scope of power depends upon relative advantages among channel members and circumstances of a particular situation. A retailer may be susceptible to the manufacturer's attempts to regulate pricing, but government regulations may prevent any direct effort on the part of the manufacturer. Recently, General Electric tried to encourage dealers to offer $50 off on specific appliances. In national television advertising, GE stated that the discount would be offered only by "participating dealers." In this case, GE could not force dealer participation but, as the manufacturer, it was clearly using a power play by announcing the discount to the general public.

The concept of limited domain refers to the fact that power is restricted in

---

[6] For a discussion of scope and domain in social sciences, see: Dorwin Cartwright, "Influence, Leadership, and Control," in *Handbook of Organization,* ed. James G. March (Chicago: Rand McNally & Company, 1965), pp. 22–23.

the number of parties over whom it may be exercised. In a distribution channel, the manufacturer may exert control over retailers but not over wholesalers. Or, some retailers in the system may be influenced by the manufacturer while others are not. Domain, then, may be considered to include those firms over which a power advantage is enjoyed. Notice the similarity of the concept of domain in a power context and the concept of organizational domain in a conflict context. The primary difference in the two is that a power advantage may not, and most likely does not, exist relative to all firms within a channel member's organizational domain.

Sources of Power

The foundation for channel power is mutual dependence, which aids or hinders members in meeting their goals. Firms in a distribution channel can influence each others' goal attainment in many ways. Each gives rise to a source of power which may be utilized to influence the behavior of other channel members. Five types of power particularly applicable to distribution channels have been identified by sociologists: reward power, coercive power, legitimate power, referent power, and expert power.[7] Each type is based on its source or origin. The following sections develop each source in detail.

Reward Power   Reward power lies in a channel member's ability to give other members something of value which will facilitate their goal satisfaction. Thus, all channel members maintain some degree of reward power. Retailers possess rewards such as preferred shelf space, feature space in advertising, and sales support. All these may be desired by manufacturers to promote sales. In such situations, retailers may be able to influence manufacturers' decisions by promising that rewards will be forthcoming. Similarly, manufacturers can provide rewards desired by other channel members. These rewards include cooperative advertising money, expedited shipments, discounts, allowances, and lower prices. Retailers may be inclined to change their behavior if such rewards are thought to be forthcoming. In all cases, the strength of rewards as a source of power depends upon the perceived probability that the desired benefits will be received if the appropriate behavior is undertaken. A firm's ability to use rewards effectively as a source of power may increase after rewards have actually been employed, because the perceived probability of the promise to deliver is intensified.[8] In other words, if a channel member promises a reward and then fulfills that promise, future promises are likely to be perceived as truthful. On the other hand, failure to fulfill a promise will reduce the potential of rewards as a source of power.

An excellent example of reward power is the development of the Universal Product Code (UPC) in the retail food industry. Retailers desired the UPC be-

---

[7] John R. P. French, Jr., and Bertram Raven, "Bases of Social Power," in *Studies in Social Power,* ed. Dorwin Cartwright (Ann Arbor: University of Michigan Press, 1959), pp. 154–155.
   [8] Cartwright, op. cit., p. 28.

cause of the perceived benefits of faster customer transactions, fewer errors in customer billing, less labor in the checkout process, and improved inventory control information. Food suppliers were influenced to proceed with the development of product symbol marking (the thick and thin vertical lines on product packages) by the promise of retail executives that they would be allowed to share in the benefits of the system. Specifically, manufacturers were led to believe that retailers would make available to them the vast market data provided by the retail scanning devices. These data include market share information, product preferences, and product trends on almost a real-time basis. Manufacturers proceeded to develop the symbols, labels, and packaging needed to implement the scanning concept. In some special cases where UPC was implemented, certain retailers decided that the information provided was so valuable that manufacturers should pay for it. In this instance, failure to deliver the promised reward seriously hindered future attempts by these retailers to use the promise of rewards.

Coercive Power   Coercive power is similar to reward power in that it is based on a channel member's control of resources or ability to facilitate other channel members' goal achievement. Coercion, however, relies on channel members' beliefs that punishments will be forthcoming unless they cooperate. Although punishments may only consist of revoking rewards which were previously delivered (for example, a retailer devoting less shelf space to a manufacturer's products), any threat to remove a desired resource may be considered coercive. As with reward power, actual exercise of the punishment may enhance the coercive source of power in future incidents.

Because of the similarities in reward and coercive power, it is tempting to group them under the heading of "sanctions."[9] However, the implications of rewards or punishments on the cooperative nature of channel relationships differ considerably. Consistent use of punishments or threats may encourage members to change or dissolve the channel relationship entirely, whereas exercise of reward power may strengthen the situation.[10] A retailer who is consistently threatened with the loss of rights to distribute a product may decide to seek out an alternative source of supply. Because of this aspect of coercive power, it is normally employed only when the power advantage is clear and the influenced party's alternatives are limited. Even then, coercive power can be expected to lead ultimately to channel conflict because of the natural tendency to resist force.

Legitimate Power   Legitimate power is the most complex source of power. Essentially, it is based on the belief by one party that another has the "right" to prescribe behavior.[11] In marketing channels, legitimate power arises from a

[9] French and Raven, op. cit., p. 157.
[10] Ibid.
[11] John R. P. French, "A Formal Theory of Social Power," *Psychological Review* (1956), p. 184.

channel member's reputation, position, and role. For example, manufacturers may be considered to have the right to make certain decisions simply because they produce products. In reality, there is little reason for such "rights" to be accepted as inviolable. Legitimate power results from a channel member's value system, which more or less grants power automatically. In other words, legitimate power exists in a firm or channel position because of values of other channel members. Legitimate power may, of course, be enhanced and given formal recognition through legal actions such as brand name registration, patent rights, or contractual (franchising) arrangements. On the other hand, repeal of fair trade laws gave formal recognition to the retailer's legitimate right to determine selling prices.

Referent Power Referent power results from one channel member's identification with, or attraction to, another channel member. Thus, the roots of referent power are psychological. The following two situations illustrate referent power.

The first example is a situation where channel members believe that it is consistent with the desired image to identify with certain other firms or organizations. For example, motel owners who want their motels to be identified as high-quality establishments may join a well-known national chain organization.

Referent power may also be in operation when channel members in long-term satisfactory relationships respond to influence attempts to preserve the stability of the system.[12] Thus, a distributor who has been associated with a supplier for a long period of time may respond to the supplier's influence in order to maintain harmony and cooperation, realizing that resistance could lead to disruption. In this instance, the supplier would be drawing upon a base of referent power to induce the desired changes in the distributor's actions.

Expert Power Expert power is based on a channel member's superior knowledge or information, which is desired or needed by other members. Although knowledge or information can sometimes be used as part of a channel member's rewards, it differs from rewards in that it is potentially self-defeating.[13] Knowledge or information, once given, is no longer a source of power. It is a resource which, if used as a reward and given to someone else, cannot be taken away. As a result, the recipient of the information becomes an expert.

Expert power in distribution channels is common. In many industries the primary role of the manufacturer's sales force is to provide information and advice to distributors in order to assist them in merchandising. The distributors may turn to the sales force as a source of information, not only about products but also about such diverse topics as market trends, inventory control, promotional techniques, and store planning. In such situations, the manufacturer has

---

[12] Frederick J. Beier and Louis W. Stern, "Power in the Channel of Distribution," in *Distribution Channels: Behaviorial Dimensions,* ed. Louis W. Stern (Boston: Houghton Mifflin Company, 1969), p. 104.

[13] Beier and Stern, op. cit., p. 101.

a strong power position based on superior industry knowledge. This form of expert power is common in the appliance industry.

A very visible form of expert power evolves from the information and communication network of the channel.[14] If a channel member becomes established as the permanent source of information or as the communications center for the system, that firm's expert power is enhanced. In this context, the process of uncertainty absorption becomes important. Uncertainty absorption occurs when inferences are drawn from a body of evidence which is then passed to others in the channel.[15] A firm which establishes itself as the absorber of uncertainty in a channel system is in a unique power position. Of course, decisions of others in the system could be drastically altered by passing on incomplete information or by distorted communications. In such situations, however, the firm's position as uncertainty absorber would be short-lived.

The preceding discussion of power sources presents a typology which is widely accepted in marketing literature. It would be rare for any particular attempt to influence behavior to be limited to one basic power source. In most instances, a power position results from a combination of several bases.[16] A manufacturer attempting to influence a retailer to order larger quantities may use information concerning high costs of hand-to-mouth buying and the cost savings possible from improved ordering techniques. If this approach fails, quantity discounts may be offered as a reward for compliance. If the reward fails, the manufacturer may threaten to refuse small orders or to place a special handling charge on them. In such instances, reliance upon several power sources may be effective since each reinforces the other to obtain compliance.

LEADERSHIP

We have noted that channel power is limited in scope to specific issues. All members of a channel maintain a degree of power because of mutual dependence. However, power is not equal among all channel members and those members possessing power advantages may assume a position of channel leadership. Firms assume the leadership role so that they can intentionally influence decisions and behavior of other channel members. The goal of leadership is to contribute to a better level of performance for either the leader or the overall channel.[17] In other words, attempts to exercise power in a distribution channel may be viewed as attempts to assume leadership. The purpose of such leadership generally is to improve performance and coordinate efforts of the channel members. Although the leadership position depends to some extent on the possession of power advantage, it also relates to the tolerance of other members.

[14] Ibid.
[15] James G. March and Herbert A. Simon, *Organizations* (New York: John Wiley & Sons, Inc., 1958), p. 165.
[16] French, op. cit., p. 184.
[17] Robicheaux and El-Ansary, op. cit., p. 20.

Tolerance

A firm's tolerance for control is based on a number of factors concerning its relationships with other channel members. It is directly related to the firm's dependence upon other channel members and the degree to which performance can be improved by submitting to control.[18] If a firm is highly dependent upon others, by definition it is in an extremely poor relative power position. Such a firm may have no choice but to tolerate leadership. A rural retail grocery store may have only one wholesaler willing to make deliveries. As a result of the strong dependence and lack of available alternatives, the retailer would tolerate almost any decision or behavior of the wholesaler.

The second factor that would lead a firm to tolerate leadership would be an expectation of improved performance. This could be true even when firms enjoy relatively equal power positions. If a firm perceives that total channel performance will be improved or, more specifically, its own performance will be enhanced by submitting to leadership, it is likely to be tolerant. Although tolerance is related to reward power, a difference exists. Tolerance based on the expectation of improved performance does not necessarily have to derive from rewards at the disposal of the leader. A retailer may decide to follow a manufacturer's dictates because it expects the result to be higher profits. Many retailers cooperate with manufacturers' suggested resale price policies for no other reason than their belief that higher retail prices and profits will result. Of course, this perception may differ among retail firms. Others may follow the suggested price policy because they fear that, if they do not, the manufacturer may discontinue distribution.

Like power, tolerance is issue-specific.[19] It can be expected to change over time and with circumstances. When a firm realizes a level of profit which management considers sufficient, it may suddenly become less tolerant of control even though the expectation of higher profits exists. This situation is similar to the "big business" versus "small business" conflict discussed in the previous chapter. The small business which reaches a satisfactory income level may reject a larger firm's attempts to exercise control simply because the managers of the small business resent intrusion upon their independence. Many people who are engaged in small business have chosen to do so primarily because of their desire to control their own activities. In such instances, tolerance for control from others will be very low unless expected performance improvements are great.

The Leadership Process

Leadership is derived from a channel member's possession of power and from the tolerance of other firms in accepting direction. By exercising leadership and influencing the decisions of others, the channel leader is better able to predict

---

[18] Louis P. Bucklin, "A Theory of Channel Control," *Journal of Marketing*, (January 1973), pp. 39–47.

[19] Robicheaux and El-Ansary, loc. cit.

with accuracy the performance of other channel members. This allows the leader to undertake activities which will maintain or enhance overall system performance. The fundamental purpose of leadership is to use power in improving not only system, but also individual performance as well. We leave it to others to debate the merits of each institution's claims upon the role of channel leader. Indeed, strong cases may be constructed to support almost any type of institution in its effort to achieve the leadership position.[20] We believe that different circumstances coupled with different environmental influences make it impossible to generalize as to any one type of institution's ability to lead a channel system effectively. In any case, the firm assuming leadership should be the channel member best able to utilize power effectively to stimulate the channel toward more efficient performance. Those marketing managers who desire to elevate their firm into the leadership role must examine the applicable sources of available power, the relative power position of channel members, and the tolerance level each member will exhibit toward leadership attempts.

RELATIONSHIP BETWEEN POWER AND CONFLICT

It is obvious by now that power and conflict have close ties. The fact that both patterns arise from mutual dependence in a channel system is in itself an indicator of the similarities. The preceding discussion of channel member tolerance toward leadership efforts provides further evidence that the two concepts are closely related. At this point we will examine more precisely the nature of this relationship.

A clear statement of the relationship between power and conflict follows:[21]

> It is apparent that a principal factor differentiating vertical conflict from horizontal and intertype competition is that it is so directly a power conflict. Power relationships among horizontal competitors occasionally are significant, but this power usually is narrowly limited. . . . This latter type of competition [intertype] is almost devoid of power relationships. . . . In the plane of vertical conflict, however, power relationships are direct, obvious, and important to the extent that the market is imperfect.

From the above it appears that attempts to utilize power may actually precipitate conflict episodes. If a channel member has a low level of control tolerance and another system member attempts to exercise leadership, a situation of stress and conflict will develop. It is important to note that the conflict will surface over the issue of attempted leadership, but the underlying cause of conflict may be more difficult to identify. It could stem from such basic causes as goal

---

[20] See for example: Bruce Mallen, "A Theory of Retailer-Supplier Conflict, Control, and Co-operation," *Journal of Retailing* (Summer 1963), p. 31; or Robert W. Little, "The Marketing Channel: Who Should Lead This Extra-Corporate Organization," *Journal of Marketing* (January 1970), p. 38.

[21] Joseph C. Palamountain, Jr., *The Politics of Distribution* (Cambridge, Mass.: Harvard University Press, 1955), pp. 51–52.

incompatibility or dissatisfaction over reward distribution. But it is important to understand that when an attempt to control a channel member's decisions or behavior exceeds that firm's tolerance, conflict will result.

Conflict may also develop from a firm's attempt to gain more power. In instances where power can be enhanced through acquisition of a scarce resource, hostility is likely to emerge.[22] What is not clear in such instances, however, is whether the attempt to gain the resource is undertaken to develop power or to satisfy the firm's goals. A retailer who undertakes a market study to gain information may simply desire better knowledge so that internal decisions can be formulated more effectively. However, the information will most likely also serve to increase the retailer's base of expert power.

The nature of the power structure may itself result in conflict. A relationship in which one party maintains a distinct power advantage may be considered an unstable relationship because it encourages the use of power.[23] The implication is that the more powerful channel member may become insensitive to the tolerance level of the other firms.

Although power can precipitate conflict, it is also the means by which conflict or hostility between members is resolved. The following section deals with methods of conflict resolution. Our concern, of course, will be with those methods which have consequences for the channel as a whole. Each method of resolution discussed involves, to a greater or lesser extent, power relationships among conflicting channel members. A marketing manager must be sensitive to how power is directly or indirectly related to attempts among channel members to maintain cooperative relationships.

CONFLICT RESOLUTION

Once an established channel experiences conflict, a natural tendency exists to seek a satisfactory solution. Four basic processes by which conflict may be resolved have been identified in the field of *organizational behavior*. These four methods are:[24]

Problem solving. It is assumed in problem solving that conflicting parties share mutual objectives and that the problem is to find a solution which satisfies those shared goals.
Persuasion. In persuasion, it is assumed that the goals of the conflicting parties differ, but that these goals are not necessarily fixed. A basic agreement exists regarding objectives, and conflict over subgoals can be resolved by reference to common objectives.
Bargaining. In bargaining, or negotiation, disagreement over goals is taken as fixed. An end to conflict is sought by development of new agreements with no attempt to refer to common objectives.

[22] Raymond Mack and Richard Snyder, "The Analysis of Social Conflict: Toward an Overview and Synthesis," *Journal of Conflict Resolution* (June 1957), p. 220.
[23] Emerson, op. cit., pp. 31–41.
[24] Adapted from March and Simon, pp. 129–130.

Politics. Politics is similar to bargaining with the exception that participants attempt to increase the number of parties involved in the resolution process.

The following section develops these four processes for conflict resolution in greater detail as they relate to channel management.

Problem Solving

A number of problem-solving techniques exist within distribution channels. The two most important are the development and emphasis of superordinate goals, and improvement of the communications process among channel members.

Superordinate Goals Since each member in the channel has joined with the other firms to achieve goals which could not be obtained otherwise, a basis for problem solving exists. Essentially, a superordinate goal is one which all channel members desire but which cannot be achieved by any one firm acting alone.[25] All channel members have a stake in the operating efficiency of the channel system and most likely have as an overriding goal a desire to increase the total output (sales volume or profits) of the system. By increasing total output, all firms may be better off than if they allow conflict to limit or restrict the system's ability to produce. In such instances, appeals to the superordinate goal may aid in ending a conflict episode.

The development of superordinate goals becomes most pronounced when the channel is confronted with an external threat. Only a few years ago conflict between gasoline service station operators and oil refineries was common. In recent years, however, this conflict has been reduced as the overall petroleum distribution system has been confronted with numerous threats, such as supply shortages and potential congressional actions. Similarly, conflicts among members of a channel seem to dissipate when an alternative channel system arises. The development of superordinate goals and reduction of conflict in the above situations may be only temporary. When the outside threat is removed, internal stress and conflict is likely to occur again.

Communication Processes A number of methods exist to alleviate communication noise in distribution channels. More efficient flow of information and/or communications in the channel will permit channel members to find solutions to their conflict based on common objectives.

Many industries have established trade organizations which invite mem-

[25] See Muzafer Sherif, O. J. Harvey, B. Jack White, William R. Hood, and Carolyn W. Sherif, *Intergroup Conflict and Cooperation: The Robbers Cave Experiment* (Norman, Okla.: University of Oklahoma Press, 1961), p. 208. See also Louis W. Stern and J. L. Heskett, "Conflict Management in Interorganizational Relations: A Conceptual Framework," in Louis W. Stern, ed. *Distribution Channels: Behavioral Dimensions,* (Boston: Houghton Mifflin Company, 1969), pp. 294–295.

bership from all levels of the distribution channel. The International Foodservice Manufacturers Association (IFMA) is a trade group dealing in distribution of food to the away-from-home market. The membership of the IFMA includes not only food processors, but also equipment manufacturers, food brokers, and hotel and restaurant chains. Through their meetings and trade publications, the channel members are able to share information and improve communications. In addition, meetings permit member firms an opportunity to develop solutions to common problems and thus reinforce prevailing channel relationships.

Communications may be enhanced through the uncertainty absorption process discussed earlier. While uncertainty absorption gives rise to a source of power for a channel member performing the service, it will also reduce the amount of information which other channel members must consider. When many different channel members are required to decode the same data, differing perceptions will result. Through the uncertainty absorption mechanism, fewer firms are required to decode data and translate them into useful information. The result should be a more congruent perception of reality among channel members.[26] For example, IFMA hires one consulting firm to conduct marketing research studies, gather market trend information, and prepare yearly forecasts. The study conclusions are presented at a joint meeting of all members early each year. Thus, all firms have access to the same information and should perceive important market trends in a similar fashion. The result should be fewer conflicts among channel members concerning market conditions. Of course, uncertainty absorption may increase channel conflicts if incomplete or inaccurate inferences are communicated to the other channel members.

To some extent, all channel communications are efforts to decrease or avoid conflict. The use of sales representatives by a manufacturer to convey information to and from wholesalers and/or retailers implies that the manufacturer is attempting to encourage attainment of individual as well as common goals. The sales representative's function for a manufacturer has often been described as that of a problem solver.

Similar arguments can be developed which support advertising as a communication process. When communication exists simply for the purpose of delivering information, it constitutes a problem-solving effort. Advertising normally goes beyond information dissemination to include persuasion.

Persuasion

Persuasion as a means of resolving conflict implies that the involved institutions draw upon their power resources or leadership potential. By its very nature, persuasion involves communication between conflicting parties. The emphasis is upon influencing behavior through persuasion rather than through sharing information. Specifically, the purpose of persuasion in resolving conflicts lies primarily in attempts to avoid or reduce conflict concerning domain.

In the previous chapter we discussed disagreement or overlap in domains as a primary cause of channel conflict. Since channel members may agree upon

[26] Stern and Heskett, op. cit., p. 296.

superordinate goals, persuasion may be employed to help members resolve differences concerning territories, functions, or customers. The important point concerning persuasion as a means of reaching domain consensus is that the persuading member appeals to the conflicting channel member's commitment to superordinate goals of the channel. Agreement which is reached through the process of persuasion alleviates or reduces stress. It also usually results in a new understanding among channel members regarding domain. Persuasion allows channel members to reach a consensus concerning relevant domains and results in agreement without formal bargaining.

Bargaining or Negotiation

Bargaining, or negotiation, is similar to persuasion except that stress may continue to exist in the system even after agreement is reached. Because of widespread use of the term *bargaining* in labor-management relations, we will use the term *negotiation* when referring to the process in a channel context. Negotiation is a vital aspect of the functioning of new as well as mature channel systems, and the topic is developed fully in Chapter 6. In this section, attention is limited to a general review of negotiation as a source of conflict resolution.

In negotiation, no attempt is made to fully satisfy a channel member. Instead, the negotiation objective is an accommodation halting a conflict episode among firms. Such compromise may resolve the episode but not necessarily the fundamental stress over which the conflict erupted. If stress continues in the channel, it is likely that some issue or another will precipitate conflict again at some later time.

Compromise is one means by which bargains can be reached among channel members. In compromise situations, each party gives up something it desires in order to prevent or to end conflict. Often, compromise is necessary to reach domain consensus in instances when persuasion is ineffective.

Both persuasion and negotiation draw upon abilities of the involved parties to communicate. In fact, resolving conflicts by utilizing either of these processes requires that each party develop a strategy in order to ensure a favorable resolution. To reach a satisfactory agreement, it is important that both parties reach a solution which does not increase hostility. It is extremely important for the marketing manager to understand how effective negotiation strategies are developed.

Politics

Politics refers to resolution of conflict by involving new organizations or parties in the process of reaching agreement. Examples of such solutions are coalition formation, arbitration or mediation, and lobbying or judicial appeal.

Coalitions The formation of coalitions among channel members is, in effect, an attempt to alter the power structure within the channel.[27] The National

---

[27] Louis W. Stern and Ronald H. Gorman, "Conflict in Distribution Channels: An Exploration," in Louis W. Stern, ed. *Distribution Channels: Behavioral Dimensions* (Boston: Houghton Mifflin Company, 1969), p. 162.

Automobile Dealer's Association offers dealers the capability of dealing effectively with auto manufacturers. Voluntary and cooperative retail chains allow smaller retailers to negotiate with food processors on an equal basis with large supermarket chains. The formation of such coalitions represents a political move by channel members. Once formed, however, the conflict resolution process may be achieved through problem solving, persuasion, or negotiation. In addition, coalitions may become involved in additional forms of political activity which are discussed below.

Mediation and Arbitration   Both mediation and arbitration involve a third party in the conflict resolution process. In mediation, the third party may suggest a solution to the conflict but channel members are not required to accept that solution. In arbitration, the solution suggested by the intermediary is binding upon the conflicting parties. Although there are many reasons to submit to mediation or arbitration to resolve distribution conflicts, actual examples of such solutions are rare. Perhaps the major reason for the failure to use these mechanisms is the inability to find a neutral third party whose decision would be acceptable to the conflicting channel members.

It is often suggested that trade associations undertake the mediator or arbitrator function. At least two factors usually preclude trade association involvement. The first is the fact that trade associations normally have predominant membership from one channel level, thus their views will most likely be biased and unacceptable to one or more of the conflicting parties. The second factor concerns the nature of the arbitration or mediation process, which may require that proprietary information be revealed. Neither channel member is likely to want to share this information with other trade members.

Lobbying and Judicial Appeal   Channel members may resort to the governmental process in order to resolve conflicts. Attempts to influence the legislative process through lobbying activities are frequent. Court litigation is also a popular means to resolve conflict by drawing outside parties into the relationship. Further discussion of the government's role in conflict resolution is reserved until Chapter 5, which discusses the legal environment in which channel members operate.

Withdrawal

An additional method for terminating conflict is the withdrawal of one firm from the relationship in order to avoid the hostile behavior existing in the channel. Withdrawal is a relatively common method of resolving conflict. A firm which decides to terminate its existing channel relationship should have an alternative available or must be willing to change the nature of its business and goals if such alternatives are not available.

If a firm decides to continue in the same business, alternatives must exist which can supply the same assistance as the existing channel. Implied is either that the cost of the alternative will be no greater than the cost of the existing system, or that the firm is willing to incur higher costs to avoid the hostility of the existing channel system. A retailer may choose to end a relationship with a current supplier due to some activity on the part of that supplier (a price increase, for instance). The retailer can easily do so as long as alternative sources of supply exist and can provide essentially the same services as the current supplier.

A firm may choose to withdraw from a channel if it decides to alter its mission. In this case, benefits gained from the existing channel are reduced in importance or at least the goals of the firm have altered so that they are less important than the avoidance of confrontation in the channel. A manufacturer, for example, may terminate relationships with an entire retail chain or group because the profits obtained from a specific line of private label merchandise are not sufficient to compensate for the psychological (or real) costs involved in conflict resolution.

If a firm has alternatives or a changing mission, then its withdrawal from the system is likely to have functional consequences. Otherwise, as we observed in Chapter 3, the result will be a reduction in efficiency.

COOPERATIVE BEHAVIOR

Attention is now directed to cooperation among channel members. Appropriately, treatment of cooperation has been delayed until the end of our discussion of interorganizational behavior since we want to reemphasize that cooperation among channel members is far more prevalent than any other behavioral pattern. It should also be evident that the primary purpose of an in-depth discussion of conflict and power is to uncover the means by which cooperation can be maintained in a channel system. Although the theory of cooperation is less formal than other theories of behavior, an understanding of the basic nature of cooperation is important.

Two fundamental human drives exert opposite forces on an individual. The first is *monostasy,* the desire to be independent, and the second is *systasy,* the drive to stand together.[28] The urge to stand together normally arises from the realization that more can be accomplished by working together than by working individually. When systasy predominates, cooperation will result. When monostasy predominates, conflict may be expected. In channels of distribution, the drive for systasy typically outweighs monostasy due to recognition that the welfare of all parties is enhanced and superordinate goals can be accomplished. During periods of little or no stress, channel members will cooperate to achieve the system objectives which also result in attainment of their individual objectives.[29] In such a situation, channel members voluntarily cooperate with one another to achieve mutual objectives.[30] Nevertheless, stress

[28] Wroe Alderson, "Cooperation and Conflict in Marketing Channels," in Louis W. Stern, ed. *Distribution Channels: Behavioral Dimensions* (Boston: Houghton Mifflin Company, 1969), pp. 195–196.

[29] Robicheaux and El-Ansary, op. cit., p. 24.

[30] The notion of voluntary versus enforced cooperation is further developed in Bruce Mallen, "Conflict and Cooperation in Marketing Channels," in L. George Smith, ed. *Progress in Marketing* (American Marketing Association, 1964), pp. 65–84.

may arise for any of the reasons discussed previously. When it does, the system may develop conflict, during which time the drive to be independent will temporarily overtake the urge to cooperate. Usually, however, channel members desire a return to harmonious relations so that organizational objectives can be fulfilled. The processes of conflict resolution may emerge to eliminate or subordinate the cause of stress. Interestingly, most methods of conflict resolution involve utilization of power or leadership to return the system to equilibrium. Channel members draw upon their arsenal of power resources to solve problems, persuade, bargain, or politic in order to resolve a conflict episode and continue normal system functioning. In fact, the means by which channel members attempt to dominate or lead the system's activities are nothing more than methods by which cooperation is enforced.

SUMMARY

We began this chapter by investigating the fundamental nature of channel power—the ability to influence or change decisions or behavior of channel members. Power arises from mutual dependence in a channel system and exists as a potentially disruptive or cohesive force. Specifically, power arises from five sources: reward, coercion, legitimacy, reference, and expertness.

Leadership develops from a firm's power position relative to others in the channel system. Of fundamental importance to the leadership position is the tolerance of channel members to efforts to change their behavior or decisions.

A direct relationship can be observed between power and conflict. First, attempts to gain or utilize power may precipitate a conflict episode. Second, power is also observed in many of the processes which resolve conflict episodes. Power may be employed in problem-solving behavior which seeks to develop and emphasize superordinate goals, and in more effective channel communications. Power is a key element in persuasion and negotiation. Political moves by channel members are nothing more than attempts to change existing power structure. Of course, if all other attempts to resolve conflict fail, channel members may select to withdraw from the relationship.

Cooperation, which stems from the desire to work with others as a means of achieving goals, is the most commonly observed form of behavior in distribution channels. Cooperation exists on a voluntary basis or as a result of conflict resolution by the channel leader.

The total economic and behavioral actions of a channel take place within the legal environment of the society. To complete our review of the basic concepts of marketing channels, in Chapter 5 attention will be directed to a review of the contemporary legal environment.

QUESTIONS

1   Using the concepts developed in this chapter, how can you explain the fact that it is not always the largest firm in the channel which has the greatest power? What exam-

ples can you develop which demonstrate that power advantages may lie with a smaller channel member?

2   Over which manufacturers do you suppose Sears might enjoy a power advantage? What are the sources of this power? Might some manufacturers have a power advantage over Sears? Why or why not?

3   In your opinion, which type of marketing institution is best suited to assume the position of channel captain?

4   In your own words, describe the complex relationships between the concepts of power and conflict.

5   What is the major difference between persuasion and negotiation as means of resolving conflict? Is this difference important in actual practice?

6   What would be desirable characteristics for a mediator or arbitrator of channel conflicts?

7   Explain the process of uncertainty absorption. How might a business use this concept to enhance its own power position?

8   The text uses the example of the oil industry to demonstrate adoption of superordinate goals in response to an external threat. Can you think of other recent examples? What were the existing conflicts? What was the threat?

9   How can the concept of tolerance be used to explain the difference between rewards and coercion as alternative bases of power?

10   Can you explain why a theory of cooperation is less formalized than the theories of other behavior patterns? In your own words, describe the theory of cooperation.

CASE 4-1: Williams Institutional Food Company

In July 1977, Jack Jones and Bill Williams were discussing the latest computer printout of sales results for Williams Institutional Food Company. After some time, Jack said: "Bill, the Vacation Motel restaurants are still keeping our total gross margin too low. Even though we need an average gross margin of about 15 percent to break even, we get only about 10 percent on our sales to their restaurants. If you look at the sales of products under the Vacation brand name, we are in even worse shape. We get only about 8 percent margin on those items. Now that they are pressuring us to expand our territory and service more of their restaurants, I think it's time we seriously evaluate the entire Vacation Motel program."

COMPANY BACKGROUND

Although Williams was founded in the 1930s as a meat processor catering to the retail grocery trade, many changes had occurred by 1977. Williams no longer processed any meat items, having phased this aspect of the business out of operation in 1964. In addition, the retail grocery trade in its market area had become so dominated by national and regional chains and local cooperatives that the firm shifted its customer focus to institutional and industrial markets. Recognition of this shift in customers was formalized in 1965 when the name of the firm was officially changed from Williams Sausage Company to Williams Institutional Food Company (WIFCO). By 1976, WIFCO was the second largest institutional food distributor in its market with a sales volume of approximately $3,500,000 in that year.

As an institutional food distributor, WIFCO's customer base included such outlets as restaurants, cafeterias, hospitals, schools, colleges, and industrial plants with in-house feeding facilities. The company carried a complete product line of dry, canned, refrigerated, and frozen food items to meet the needs of these customers. The product line consisted of approximately 2,500 items. The only items not carried by WIFCO which customers normally needed were fresh produce and paper products. These items were not sold by most other institutional distributors but were available to customers from several special-line wholesalers.

WIFCO management felt that the company had an excellent reputation among the institutional trade, based on its quality products, honesty and fairness in dealing with customers and competitors, and emphasis on customer service. WIFCO sales personnel were expected to be more than simply order-takers. They were expected to acquire sufficient product knowledge to advise their customers on which particular product would be best for use in a particular situation. They were also expected to learn the customer's business to be able to make suggestions concerning changes in the menu and new items which might be appropriate for use. Sales personnel were expected to handle any problems in serving the customer and any complaints which arose.

WIFCO also undertook other methods to increase its customer service. The company made every effort to avoid stockouts of any item in inventory. Whenever stockouts did occur, employees who loaded the trucks were instructed to substitute, whenever possible, an item which could best serve the customer's intentions. If the substituted product was higher in price, the customer was charged only for the product originally ordered. Efforts had also been made to upgrade service by improving the efficiency of truck drivers. For a short period of time, drivers had been offered an incentive plan by which the customer was allowed to judge the quality of the driver's service and conduct. Sales personnel distributed cards to selected customers (whose identity was unknown to the drivers), and when the customer felt the driver had performed adequately and demonstrated a desire to serve the customer, the card would be given to the driver. The driver returned this card to the company and received $5.00. In addition, a list was kept showing how many cards each driver had received and this became a matter of great pride to the drivers.

COMPETITIVE SITUATION

There were several institutional distributors in the area, two of which were members of controlled-label cooperatives. Most of their products were purchased through a cooperative which was responsible for having the products manufactured under the appropriate label. These two distributors handled the Nugget and Pleezing brand products. Several distributors in the area were, like WIFCO, independent distributors. These independent distributors sold products packed under their own brand names. All the distributors, both independent and controlled-label, also sold national brand items. WIFCO, for example, carried a complete line of Hunt-Wesson and Pillsbury products. WIFCO was the second largest distributor in the area; another independent distributor was the largest. However, WIFCO executives felt that their recent growth rate had closed the gap between the two considerably and they hoped to be the largest soon. They felt that their reputation which had been developed in recent years would be instrumental to this growth.

Competition was also entering from another source. Amalgamated Grocers of Alabama had recently established an institutional division. Within a few months this firm had been able to establish a strong position in the institutional market. Amalgamated Grocers had not made an attempt to compete in service with other distributors, but its strong financial position in the retail market had allowed the company to compete by selling at very low prices.

The 1960s and 1970s saw the failure of several small food distributors in the area. As these companies failed, the other distributors had taken their customers and increased their own sales. It looked as if this trend would continue until there would be only two or three major distributors left in the area.

THE VACATION MOTEL PROGRAM

In the summer of 1973, the Vacation Motel Food Sales Division of the Vacation Motel Corporation (VM) had been looking for a new food distributor in central Alabama. Under its proposal, Vacation Motel would give the distributor exclusive rights to distribute merchandise under the VM label to all restaurants owned by Vacation Motel in the distributor's area. Approximately half of all Vacation Motel restaurants were company-owned, while the rest were franchised to independent operators. The managers of the company-owned restaurants were required to buy all merchandise available under the VM label from the VM distributor in the area. For example, the managers had to purchase VM catsup only; they could not purchase other brands. It was estimated that merchandise under the VM label would account for 60 percent of a restaurant's food purchases. The distributor, on the other hand, was expected to maintain a complete inventory of VM merchandise which was purchased through the Vacation Motel Food Sales Division. Vacation Motel Food Sales issued a price list each month for all products. This price list showed the distributor's cost and the price at which to sell to the restaurants. The distributor had no discretion in this area. Products under the VM label included many meats, frozen and canned fruits and vegetables, seafood, poultry, desserts, prepared entrées, and portion-packed dry products. If the restaurant manager desired an item which was not included on the price list, he was free to deal with any distributor.

WIFCO decided to accept this program for distribution to the five company-owned inns in Birmingham. It was estimated that sales to these inns would be approximately $20,000 per month in Vacation Motel products. Vacation Motel also asked that WIFCO take over distribution to inns located in Hattiesburg, Mississippi; Dauphin Island, Alabama; and Destin, Florida. These represented sales of $15,000–$20,000 per month in VM products. Although WIFCO did not operate in those areas at that time, there had previously been much discussion about the feasibility of hiring sales personnel to develop those territories. It was decided that WIFCO could use the Vacation Motels as a sales base to justify hiring a new person to further develop the territories. The management therefore decided to serve these inns.

Adoption of the Vacation Motel program also created some problems for WIFCO. First of all, Bill Williams wondered about the inventory which would be necessary to fully serve the inns. Although there was enough space at that time to accommodate the inventory, it was expected that within a few years normal growth of the company would utilize this space. Especially critical was room in the 10,000-square-foot freezer. The program necessitated that the company duplicate many products under the VM label which were already available under the WIFCO or some other label. The initial inventory required to begin deliveries to the restaurants required an investment of approximately $75,000, which was about one-half the company's present inventory.

During the next two years the Vacation Motel program was revised many times, with most changes involving minor additions and deletions from the product line. In April 1975, however, the program underwent an extensive modification. Vacation Motel Food Services decided to eliminate almost one-half of the products under the VM label. These products were primarily the canned and frozen fruits and vegetables which accounted for a great deal of the physical space which had been used. However, the products accounting for the largest dollar volume, the meat items, were retained.

MARGIN ON THE SALES

Table 1 shows a breakdown of margins allowed on Vacation Motel products by product group versus the margins obtained by WIFCO on similar items with other brand names. Although the VM program guaranteed the distributor a large volume of sales, the gross margin allowed was very low. When the management of WIFCO accepted the program, it had hoped that the company would also be able to distribute noncompeting products to these inns. The margin on these products varied considerably, but averaged from 16 to 18 percent. Thus, Williams believed that the overall margin on total sales to the inns could be raised to approximately 14 percent. However, competitive pressures had not allowed this. Competitors were cutting their prices to get a share of the Vacation Motel business. Also, restaurant managers who were required to purchase over half their merchandise from WIFCO were reluctant to concentrate the remainder of their business with this one supplier. There was some resentment on their part that they had no discretion in purchasing many of their items. Thus, although WIFCO's total sales to Vacation Motels were $50,000–$60,000 per month, over 80 percent of these sales were in VM products, which had a very low margin (see Table 2).

SALES COSTS

WIFCO sales personnel were compensated on the basis of their gross margin on sales. Although they had a guaranteed salary per month, they were ex-

Table 1 Average Margins Allowed on Vacation Motel Products Versus Normal Distributor Margins

Product category	Margin allowed (Percent)	Normal distributor margins (Percent)
Processed meats	6	18
Red meats	5	20
Frozen foods	12	18
Seafood	12	18
Desserts	12	16
Frozen entrees	10	18
Nonfrozen foods	10	14
Coffee and tea	6	14

Table 2 Sample of Vacation Motel Invoices during a Typical Week

Invoice number	VM amount	Other	Total	Percent VM
10765	$320.68	$ 70.70	$ 391.38	81.9
10766	417.89	55.14	473.03	88.3
10875	236.76	43.31	280.07	84.5
10901	297.00	58.20	355.20	83.6
10922	344.20	76.11	420.31	81.9
10934	152.67	17.60	170.27	89.7
10956	373.53	75.65	449.18	83.2
10974	498.20	566.18	1,064.38	46.8
11002	407.18	57.91	465.09	87.5
11015	709.73	197.19	906.92	78.3
11036	842.95	258.38	1,101.33	76.5
11051	557.45	44.90	602.35	92.6
11078	365.22	—	365.22	100.0
11079	546.63	—	546.63	100.0
11091	776.90	131.87	908.77	85.5
11094	407.02	95.06	502.08	81.1

pected, and usually were able, to earn more by their commissions. Sales personnel were guaranteed $800 per month. Each month the company received a computer report showing each salesperson's gross margin for the month. The company took 25 percent of this gross margin and deducted one dollar for each delivery the salesperson had accounted for during that month. If the result was greater than $800, sales personnel received the difference as additional pay to their guaranteed salary. Otherwise, they received the $800.

DELIVERY EXPENSE

WIFCO leased all its delivery trucks from one company. The leasing firm charged a flat fee of $110 per week, plus $0.50 per hour on the refrigeration unit for each hour it was running, plus $0.14 per mile. The drivers and other hourly personnel were paid an average of $3.25 an hour.

DISTRIBUTION TO VACATION MOTELS

After the acceptance of the Vacation Motel program, WIFCO decided to hire a salesperson to work in the northeastern Florida and southern Mississippi areas. By June 1975, this territory developed to the point that sales were approximately $40,000 per month. About half these sales were to Vacation Motels in the area. Deliveries were made to this territory three times per week, and total mileage required for the trucks was approximately 1,900 miles. Deliveries to Mississippi covered 700 miles and the driver was expected to make the trip in 1 day. The trip usually required that the driver be paid for 24 hours. The delivery into the Mobile area required 550 miles and took about 20 hours. The trucks were usually empty on the return trip, which accounted for 40 percent of the time involved, and the refrigeration units were shut off.

Between 1973 and 1977, Vacation Motel Food Sales had added several inns to WIFCO's area of coverage. Although these inns could be covered with existing drivers and sales personnel, they did add to the inventory problem. By June 1977, WIFCO had an inventory of about $100,000 tied up in VM products, in spite of the fact that the number of products had been reduced considerably. The program had thus far necessitated addition of one new truck to serve the new territories. The plant manager estimated that the increased work load had accounted for the hiring of two hourly workers—one to unload shipments from manufacturers during the day and one to load WIFCO trucks on the night shift.

PROPOSAL TO SERVE GEORGIA

In July 1977, the Vacation Motel Food Service requested that WIFCO take over deliveries to four restaurants in Georgia. At that time WIFCO was not operating in that territory. The four inns represented a combined sales potential of approximately $10,000 per month on VM products. It would be necessary to make deliveries to these inns once each week. The estimated round-trip distance on the route was 650 miles and would be 24 hours' time for the driver. It was believed that WIFCO's sales supervisor could call on these accounts periodically but that, in most cases, the orders would be taken by telephone. The divisional vice president of Vacation Motel's Food Sales Division indicated that if WIFCO refused to deliver to the restaurants in Georgia, VM might look for another distributor to undertake the entire program for its restaurants in Alabama, Florida, Mississippi, and Georgia.

Since the adoption of the Vacation Motel program, WIFCO executives had questioned the profitability of delivering to the inns. However, no one had ever undertaken an in-depth analysis of the program. The proposal to take the four inns in Georgia caused them to seriously reconsider the entire Vacation Motel program. They knew that the program had provided several benefits to WIFCO. In addition to providing increased sales to Vacation Motels, the fact that the firm was a distributor for Vacation Motel had been a successful selling tool in approaching other customers. The sales base provided by Vacation Motels had also been very useful in opening new territories, especially in the case of the Florida–Mississippi route. However, the low margins, increased inventory, and other operating expenses caused WIFCO executives to question the desirability of the program. They had considered alternatives such as pressuring Vacation Motel Food Sales to increase distributor margins or to require that restaurant managers purchase non-VM items from WIFCO. Finally, WIFCO management wondered how to respond to the threat by Vacation Motels to terminate its program if WIFCO refused to open the Georgia territory.

CASE 4-1: QUESTIONS

1   Diagram the distribution channel for Vacation Motel food products. What elements of this channel make it different from distribution channels for other institutional food products?
2   Assess relationships among Vacation Motel Food Sales, WIFCO, and Vacation Motel restaurants in terms of the interorganizational behavior concepts discussed in Chapters 3 and 4.
3   If you were Bill Williams, how would you respond to the request to serve the restaurants in Georgia?

CASE 4-2: Ace Brokerage Company

John Kline is concerned about his recent conversation with Bob Morreaux, vice president of marketing and distribution for the Morreaux Sugar Company. Kline is president of the Ace Brokerage Company, a large food broker located in Steel City, Alabama. During their conversation, Morreaux told Kline that his firm wanted Kline to put more emphasis on developing an institutional trade for sugar. In the past, he had done an excellent job of developing the retail grocery market for Morreaux. As a matter of fact, almost 70 percent of all sugar purchased in Steel City area supermarkets is Morreaux brand. However, the rapid growth in away-from-home eating had caused Morreaux's sales to level off in the Steel City area. Ace Brokerage had concentrated its efforts on supermarkets in Steel City and had never attempted to obtain institutional distribution for the principals it represented. Kline wondered if he should consider hiring new personnel to begin developing the institutional business in response to the request by Morreaux.

BACKGROUND

Steel City is a unique market area for the supermarket industry, particularly food processors and manufacturers, since over 80 percent of all retail grocery sales are made through locally owned chains or local cooperatives. Although the metropolitan area contains over 600,000 people, only one national chain has more than four outlets and that chain captures only about 10 percent of total retail volume. In contrast, Table 1 presents data concerning the major local chains and cooperatives in Steel City. Thus, food processors depend upon Steel City food brokers to present their lines to supermarket buyers since they cannot rely on their contacts with the national supermarket chains to obtain penetration in the market.

There are more than twenty food brokers in the Steel City area. Ace Brokerage is one of the three largest, with brokerage commissions of approximately $500,000 per year. Ace represents twenty-five noncompeting grocery and household supply manufacturers. Although Ace's contracts with its princi-

Table 1   Major Supermarket Outlets in Steel City

Firm name	Type	Number of stores	Approximate market share (Percent)
Freedom Grocers	Local chain	3	13
Bear Stores	Local chain	18	22
Southern Supermarkets	Cooperative	18	18
Bigg's Super Stores	Cooperative	16	16

pals (suppliers) specify commission rates varying from 1 to 5 percent, average commissions are slightly less than 3 percent. Thus, Ace accounts for about $18 million in sales for its principals.

To earn the commissions, Ace performs several services for the principals as well as for the supermarket buyers. Ace representatives visit buyers periodically to present new products, take orders, and inform them of possible market changes. In this capacity, the firm acts much as the manufacturer's own sales force might. Ace also employs ten field personnel who visit individual stores to help with counting stock, replenishing shelf stock, delivering manufacturer point-of-purchase displays, and attempting to make sure that Ace principals are receiving adequate support in the stores. Ace also maintains a small warehouse with some inventory (provided on consignment by the principals) to meet any emergency needs of its customers.

Although Ace represents twenty-five principals, Morreaux Sugar Company is one of the largest. Over $80,000 of Ace's brokerage commissions come from Morreaux. The other major account for Ace is a large tuna and canned fish processor which, like Morreaux, has a 70 percent market share in Steel City and generates about $80,000 per year brokerage fee for Ace. The remainder of Ace's revenues is spread over the other principals, with yearly commissions ranging from less than $1,000 to $35,000.

Kline believes that his firm has an excellent reputation with supermarket buyers due to the quality of service offered by his firm as well as the principals represented by Ace. As one example of Kline's emphasis on quality products and service, he had recently withdrawn from a brokerage agreement with a processor of fruits and pie fillings due to some indications of quality control problems in the processor's plant. Two supermarket buyers had asked Kline to remove a few cases of the product from their shelves and arrange reshipment and credit due to poor quality. Although both buyers indicated that they would reorder from the same manufacturer (specifying different canning dates from those of the off-quality goods), Kline felt that quality problems caused his field personnel too much trouble and might, in the long run, damage the reputation of Ace Brokerage. Even though this principal had paid brokerage commissions of over $30,000 to Ace in the previous year, Kline terminated his relationship with the processor and found another fruit packer desiring representation in the Steel City market. While the lost revenues have not been totally replaced by the new principal, Kline is satisfied that his firm has been able to generate commissions of $12,000 from a principal who is new to the Steel City market.

Kline admits that his lack of concern over the lost commission may be partially due to the fact that Ace Brokerage Company will report a net profit of $85,000 for the year. As owner of 60 percent of the shares in the firm (the remainder is held by three other employees), he seems satisfied with his salary as president and the dividends paid from the firm's earnings.

ACE–MORREAUX RELATIONSHIP

Ace Brokerage Company has represented the Morreaux Sugar Company in the Steel City market for four years. Prior to this arrangement, Morreaux utilized the services of Underwood Brokers, Inc., whereas Ace represented Provincial Sugar. Underwood Brokers is another of the three largest firms in Steel City. Four years ago, Morreaux was unhappy with the performance of Underwood, as their brand had only one-third of the total market at that time. Bob Morreaux felt that stronger effort by the broker would result in higher market share. Underwood was unwilling to devote more effort to Morreaux and expressed the belief that sugar was such a competitive commodity that a market share of more than 30 to 35 percent was unreasonable. At that same time, John Kline and Ace Brokerage had become disenchanted with Provincial Sugar because of that firm's refusal to commit more money to advertising and promotion in Steel City. Kline felt he could increase Provincial's penetration considerably greater than its 25 percent market share with more promotional effort by the firm. It was under these conditions that Kline and Morreaux met and decided that the two firms seemed compatible in their goals. In effect, a swap was arranged, with Morreaux being represented by Ace and Provincial handled by Underwood. Morreaux is very pleased that he was correct about the potential to increase market share in the retail grocery business. On the other hand, he knows that Provincial Sugar still has 20 percent of the retail market for sugar and that Underwood Brokers has actively solicited wholesale distributors in the institutional field to carry the Provincial brand. As a result, Provincial controls about 30 percent of the institutional sugar sales. Morreaux, on the other hand, obtains very little of this business since it has no active representation in the field.

PRIMARY CONCERNS OF MORREAUX SUGAR COMPANY

Morreaux is concerned about the failure of Ace Brokerage Company to solicit wholesale institutional distribution for several reasons. Obviously, the lost sales potential is a major concern. Although the institutional food business is not as large as the retail grocery field in sales volume, it still represents a major opportunity for food processors and manufacturers. The growth of the away-from-home eating market is a particular concern to everyone in the food industry. Morreaux had read reports which estimate that approximately one-third of all meals consumed in the United States during 1975 were consumed away from home. He is particularly interested in projections estimating that, by the mid-1980s, one-half of all meals will be consumed away from home.

The growth of the institutional business may explain Morreaux's second concern, which is the leveling off of sales in the Steel City area. With a 70 percent share of a market which expects little real growth, he believes it will be very difficult to increase sales substantially unless alternative forms of distribution are developed. Incremental gains to be realized from capturing further market share points would, in his opinion, be outweighed by the costs involved.

Morreaux is also concerned because he has recently concluded meetings with several major restaurant, fast-food, and institutional feeding companies, all of which have outlets in the Steel City area. Some of these firms wanted to sign contracts with Morreaux which would specify that Morreaux Sugar be used in their outlets. In return, Morreaux would package the sugar in individual serving envelopes imprinted with messages specified by the customers. Morreaux's major problem lies in promising distribution capability to these companies. While two of the feeding institutions maintain their own distribution centers in Steel City and could be supplied directly, the others utilize Steel City wholesalers and would need to have the product available from at least one of them.

Morreaux believes he could find time himself to call on a distributor in Steel City and find the means to fulfill these contracts. Most distributors would be willing to handle the product, since its sale is essentially guaranteed by the contract and because it would immediately give the distributor a means to develop sales of other products to the outlets. However, Morreaux knows that this action would not solve the basic problem of Ace's failure to cultivate the institutional market.

ALTERNATIVES

Both Ace Brokerage Company and Morreaux Sugar Company have several possible solutions to their problem. Kline may simply refuse to open an institutional sales division and wait to see the reaction of Morreaux to this decision. He knows that if he makes this decision, Morreaux can do one of two things. First, Morreaux may decide to forgo the lost opportunity in the institutional field and be satisfied with the retail grocery trade. Second, Morreaux may cancel its relationship with Ace and look for a broker with capability in both retail and institutional sales. Kline hopes that since the other large brokers already have principals for sugar, Morreaux will be afraid to cancel their agreement since dealing with a small brokerage firm would be somewhat risky for Morreaux. Of course, Morreaux could also find a broker to handle its products for the institutional business only. Kline is afraid that if Morreaux took this course and other principals followed, a fourth large brokerage firm might emerge in the Steel City market. Still, Kline knows that developing an institutional division would require addition of at least two new staff members and would create a new set of customers and problems with which he would have to deal. He also knows that Morreaux has to be concerned about Ace's reaction to any of Morreaux Sugar Company's decisions since, after all, Ace has been largely responsible for Morreaux's market dominance in Steel City.

CASE 4-2: QUESTIONS

1 How would you assess the relative power positions of these two firms? What power bases can each draw upon? Be specific. In your opinion, who has the power advantage?
2 In reference to the alternatives discussed in the text, how might the conflict between these two firms be resolved?
3 If you were John Kline, what would you do? Why?
4 If you were Bob Morreaux, what would you do? Why?

Chapter 5

The Legal Environment

While scholars debate the future direction of law, the business community is being overwhelmed by the number of and contradictions in regulatory compliance requirements, overlapping jurisdictions, legality of actions and, more recently, executive liability. In a recent survey of twenty-eight marketing leaders, 82.1 percent felt that government legislation regulating consumer and marketing practices would increase further by 1985.[1] The potential ramifications of this so-called "legal age" influence decision making among all firms in a marketing channel, regardless of size or activity. Regulation is particularly applicable to the interorganizational relationships which are of primary concern in the study of marketing channels.

In this chapter we examine first the foundations of the regulatory activities of federal, state, and local governments. Attention is then focused on the changing perspectives in legal regulation, ways in which specific legislation affects institutional marketing practices and channel participant behavior, and public policy issues regarding channels of distribution and the law. This chapter completes our macro treatment of channels of distribution.

[1] Gene R. Laczniak, Robert F. Lusch, and Jon G. Udell, "Marketing in 1985: A View From the Ivory Tower," *Journal of Marketing* (October 1977), p. 48.

FOUNDATIONS OF PUBLIC REGULATION

The power of the federal government to regulate business activity is found in the commerce clause of the Constitution. Article I, Section 8 states that "Congress shall have the power . . . to regulate commerce with foreign nations, and among the several states, and with Indian tribes. . . ." Over the years, the courts have found it difficult to define what the terms "foreign" and "among the several states" mean. Nevertheless, the federal right to regulate foreign commerce is considered to be supreme since any foreign commerce, even that entering a single state, has implications for all other states. Thus, individual states may not regulate foreign commerce. "Among the several states" has been broadly interpreted and referred to as "interstate commerce," which means any commerce involving more than one state. Importation of raw materials or parts from one state for manufacture and sale within another state is considered interstate commerce.

Regulation by state and local governments derives from the "police power" guaranteed by the Constitution. It is interpreted as the power to control persons and property for purposes of promoting the general welfare. The states, in turn, delegate portions of this power to local governments. State governments are frequently tougher than federal regulators and local bodies occasionally try to outdo both.

If interstate commerce is in any way affected, federal regulations most often supercede state and local regulations. However, some recent examples (stringent automobile emission control standards in California and throwaway-container bans in several states) have been either not challenged by the federal government or have withstood the test of legality.

Based upon the commerce clause and the police power of the states as granted in the Constitution, a framework has developed regarding legal regulation of business. We now examine some of its more recent developments.

Changing Perspectives in Legal Regulation

This section reviews three aspects of the legal framework implementing the constitutional right to regulate commerce: judicial law, legislative law, and administrative law.[2]

Judicial Law

Judicial law in the United States has its roots in English common law. Under common law the courts "make the law" as they decide controversies brought before them. The doctrine of *stare decisis,* whereby prior decisions provide precedents for subsequent cases involving similar legal questions, has been adopted in this country. If no similar case has been adjudicated, the court ren-

[2] Much of the material in this section was taken from Marshall C. Howard, *Legal Aspects of Marketing,* (New York: McGraw-Hill Book Co., 1964); and Robert M. Corley, Robert L. Black, and O. Lee Reed, *The Legal Environment of Business,* 4th ed. (New York: McGraw-Hill Book Co., 1977), Chapters 5, 6, 7, 10, 11, and 12.

ders its decision and a precedent is established for future cases. Common law is thus used to interpret legislation and to create legislation when none exists.

In preparing for court under judicial law, an attorney spends a great deal of time reviewing past cases, searching for legal precedents which the court will follow in rendering a decision. A single court decision is usually not sufficient to establish a rule of law. Rather, a precedent is established when a rule of law is cited by the courts over years in many different cases.

Judicial law attempts to provide an element of certainty. It is *retrospective* in that it looks to the past for a solution to disagreements among litigants. However, the sheer number of judicial decisions in federal courts coupled with an equally large number in state courts renders judicial law anything but certain. Any decision ultimately depends on which set of legal precedents put forth by the plaintiff and the defendant is determined applicable by the judge.

Legislative Law

Legislative law is the method by which society sets forth rules of conduct for the functioning of that society. Legislative law is tied to judicial law and an understanding of the relationship is important.

Relationship to Judicial Law   In an effort to add an element of certainty to judicial law, federal and state governments have passed legislation attempting to spell out those practices considered illegal. Most business litigation, particularly that involving participants in a channel, requires interpretation of the applicable legislation by the courts. Legislative law is general and *prospective,* in contrast to judicial law, which is specific and *retrospective.* Legislative law attempts to anticipate events which, if allowed, would result in ineffective functioning of society. The legislative branch of government makes laws and the judicial system interprets those laws. In this chapter, we focus primarily on federal legislation, but we do not imply that the impact of state legislation on business practice is less important.

Applicable Legislation   Since they affect channel relationships, the federal statutes of importance in business regulation are the Sherman Antitrust Act, the Clayton Antitrust Act, the Federal Trade Commission Act, the Robinson–Patman Act, and the Celler–Kefauver Act. Other statutes regulating business are more concerned with regulation of business enterprises rather than with relationships between enterprises. A review of the major provisions of each act follows.

The Sherman Antitrust Act, 1890   Often referred to as the antitrust law, this act is aimed at protecting the public from monopoly. It is grounded in the belief that competition is the only form of economic activity which can stimulate growth through innovation, lead to efficiency in operation, and result in low prices to the consumer. Section 1 of the Sherman Act prohibits contracts, combinations, and conspiracies in restraint of trade or commerce. A contract or a conspiracy is either a written instrument or an implied agreement which may be legal in itself but which may be illegal under the Sherman Act if the effect is to restrain commerce or trade. Section 2 attempts to prevent any action which results in monopolizing any part of interstate or foreign commerce. Whenever an excessive concentration of market power appears to be vested in a single firm, the courts may order dissolution and divestiture.

The Sherman Act was intended to cover all restraints of commerce but it soon became apparent that clarification was necessary if all possible abuses were to be covered.

The Clayton Antitrust Act, 1914   This act was designed to prevent situations which *tend* to lessen competition or create a monopoly. The Sherman Antitrust Act was inadequate in such cases. Under the Clayton Act proof of violation is easier since it prohibits those situations which *tend* to lessen competition or create a monopoly. Under the Sherman Act it was necessary to prove that the action actually *did* lessen competition or create a monopoly. The Clayton Act prohibits interlocking directorates, price discrimination, tying contracts, and exclusive dealing. At the same time that the Clayton Act was passed, the Federal Trade Commission (FTC) was established to enforce the Clayton Act and other laws.

The Federal Trade Commission Act, 1914   In addition to creating the Federal Trade Commission, this act specified that all "unfair methods of competition" were unlawful. Congress did not specify which unfair methods it meant but left that determination in the hands of the Federal Trade Commission. The law was passed in an attempt to stop those acts which were not illegal under the Sherman Act or the Clayton Act. As we shall see later, an act by a business may fall short of violation in a judicial proceeding but can be stopped by a "cease and desist" order from the Federal Trade Commission.

The Robinson–Patman Act, 1936   The Clayton Antitrust Act, although designed to prohibit price discrimination, was inadequate since it allowed for discrimination in price "on account of difference in the grade, quality, or quantity of the commodity sold, or that make only due allowance for difference in the cost of selling or transportation." This provision allowed many large retailers to use their buying power to negotiate for discriminatory prices. The Robinson–Patman Act was passed as an amendment to the Clayton Act in an effort to specify illegal price discrimination.

Major provisions of the Robinson–Patman Act are as follows. Section 2(a) defines an illegal price discrimination. An illegal price discrimination exists when different prices are charged for goods of "like grade and quality . . . where the effect of such discrimination may be substantially to lessen competition or tend to create a monopoly in any line of commerce, or to injure, destroy, or prevent competition with any person who either grants or knowingly receives the benefit of such discrimination, or with customers of either of them." The section then grants two important exclusions: (1) "differentials which make only due allowance for differences in cost of manufacture, sale, or delivery resulting from the differing methods or quantities . . . sold or delivered," and, (2) differentials "in response to changing conditions affecting the market . . . such as . . . actual or imminent deterioration of perishable goods, obsolescence or seasonal goods, distress sale under court process or sales in good faith in discontinuance of business in the goods concerned." Section 2(a) provides three defenses to charges of price discrimination. First, a cost savings defense is implied in the act but the courts have not been willing to accept a standard for measuring cost. Second, sale of goods is legal under changing conditions such as deterioration, obsolescence, or seasonal goods, or distress sale under court order, or discontinuance of the goods. Finally, price discrimination is legal when there is no injury to competition.

Section 2(b) states that "the burden of rebutting the *prima facie* case of discrimination thus made by showing justification shall be upon the person charged. . . ." Thus, the burden of proof in price discrimination cases is placed on the defendant. Another allowable defense is "showing that his lower price or the furnishing of service or facilities to any purchaser or purchasers was made in good faith to meet an equally low price of a competitor, or the services of facilities furnished by a competitor."

In the 1920s and early 1930s, large retailers were able to extract lower prices by billing the seller for brokerage services provided by a brokerage subsidiary of the buyer. The payments by the seller amounted to a reduction in the sale price and were interpreted as price discrimination. Therefore, Section 2(c) of the Robinson–Patman Act attempts to prevent price discriminations arising through payment of unearned brokerage fees to a buyer. It states that "it shall be unlawful for any person engaged in commerce . . . to pay or grant, or to receive or accept, anything of value as a commission, brokerage, or other compensation, or any allowance or discount in lieu thereof . . . either to the other party to such transaction or to an agent, representative or other intermediary . . . where such intermediary is acting in fact for or in behalf, or is subject to the direct or indirect control, of any party to such transaction other than the person by whom such compensation is so granted or paid."

Another common practice at that time was for larger buyers to extract promotional allowances from sellers for cooperative advertising. To the extent that these allowances were not offered to all sellers or were never used for promoting, they were a way of granting a discriminating price. Section 2(d) was inserted to prevent discrimination in price arising from payment of such promotional allowances by the seller to some customers. It states "that it shall be unlawful . . . to pay or contract for the payment of anything of value . . . in connection with the processing, handling, sale or offering for sale . . . unless such payment . . . is available in proportionately equal terms to all other customers competing in the distribution of such products or commodities."

Rather than promotional allowances, a seller may have made the services of a demonstrator available to a retailer. Such arrangements were common in the cosmetic industry. The demonstrator acted as a salesperson and, in effect, provided a service at no cost to the buyer. Since the buyer did not incur the cost of providing this service, it amounted to a discrimination in price. Section 2(e) makes this practice illegal if offered "upon terms not accorded to all purchasers on proportionately equal terms."

The activities described in Sections 2(d) and 2(e) of the Robinson–Patman

Act were considered legal discriminations if they were made in "proportionately equal terms" to all customers. However, the Federal Trade Commission and the courts have had a difficult time interpreting "proportionately equal terms." For example, a manufacturer's offer of a 5 percent cooperative advertising allowance may be meaningful for a large retailer who often advertises but meaningless to a small retailer who rarely uses advertising.

Section 2(f) makes it illegal "knowingly to induce or receive a discrimination in price which is prohibited by this section." Thus, a buyer who receives the benefit of price discrimination may be subject to the same penalties as the supplier who grants the price differentials. Enforcement of the Robinson–Patman Act was delegated to the Federal Trade Commission. The enforcement procedure is described in the section dealing with administrative law.

The Celler–Kefauver Act, 1950   Section 7 of the Clayton Antitrust Act, which prohibits acquisitions or mergers tending to lessen competition or create a monopoly, was inadequate to scrutinize the large number of acquisitions occurring in the 1940s and 1950s. That act required proof that the acquisition of stock had a reasonable probability of lessening competition. The Celler–Kefauver Act of 1950 was passed as an amendment to Section 7 of the Clayton Antitrust Act to slow the tide of acquisitions and mergers. It prohibits acquisition of stock or assets if the result is a tendency to lessen competition or create a monopoly. It further changed the wording of the Clayton Antitrust Act which originally stated that there must be a tendency to lessen competition between the corporation whose stock is being acquired and the acquiring corporation. This wording implied that horizontal mergers were prohibited but vertical mergers were not. The Celler–Kefauver amendment simply states "where the effect may be to lessen competition substantially in any line of commerce in any section of the country."

Table 5-1 diagrams the major legislative acts applicable to interorganizational relationships found in a channel of distribution. Other acts, such as the Lanham Act (trademarks), the Consumer Product Safety Act, the Hazardous Substances Act, and the National Environmental Policy Act, can be relevant since they regulate institutions in the channel but they influence channel relationships only incidentally.

Administrative Law

The increasing complexity of our society—the result of new technology and rapid growth, changing social goals, and conflicting objectives—has placed a heavy burden on the legislative, executive, and judicial branches of government. Legislators do not have time to legislate all facets of our lives; the judicial branch is inundated with cases and the backlog of court cases is enormous. Furthermore, neither legislator nor judge can be an expert in all areas needing regulation. To ease the burden, the legislature has delegated part of the task to federal agencies and has conferred on them a quasi-judicial capacity. Some of these agencies at the federal level are the Justice Department, the National Labor Relations Board, the Occupational Safety and Health Administration,

Table 5-1 Applicable Federal Legislation Affecting Channel Relationships

Act	Year	Provisions	Applicable defenses	Maximum penalty Individual	Maximum penalty Corporate
Sherman Antitrust Act	1890	**1** Prohibits contracts, combinations, and conspiracies on restraint of trade or commerce **2** Prohibits any action which results in monopolizing any part of interstate or foreign commerce	**1** Prove the action did not lessen competition or create a monopoly	Up to $100,000 and/or up to 3 years in prison; a felony	Up to $1,000,000, injunction, divestiture, triple damages to injured party
Clayton Antitrust Act	1914	**1** If the result is to *tend* to lessen competition or create a monopoly, it prohibits: **a** Interlocking directorates **b** Price discrimination **c** Tying contracts **d** Exclusive dealing	**1** Prove the action would not tend to lessen competition or create a monopoly	Criminal sanction for directors or agents; $5,000 and/or 1 year	Injunction, triple damages to injured party, fine, civil penalty
Federal Trade Commission Act	1914	**1** In enforcing the Clayton Antitrust Act and enforcing other acts, it prohibits: **a** All unfair methods of competition	**1** Prove the action would not tend to lessen competition or create a monopoly	Restitution, injunction, fine up to $5,000 or up to 3 years	Restitution, injunction, divestiture, $10,000/day for violation of rules or orders; for each violation —a civil penalty
Robinson–Patman Act	1936	**1** Prohibits price discrimination where the effect may be to substantially lessen competition or tend to create a monopoly, such as: **a** Unearned brokerage fees **b** Promotional allowances under some circumstances **c** Promotional services under some circumstances	**1** Prove no injury to competition **2** Cost/savings to justify discrimination **3** Sale under changing market conditions **4** Discrimination made in good faith to meet the equally low price or service or facilities furnished by a competitor **5** Promotional allowances made on proportionately equal terms for all buyers **6** Promotional services made on proportionately equal terms to all customers	Same as Clayton Antitrust Act	Same as Clayton Antitrust Act
Celler–Kefauver Act (amendment to Clayton Antitrust Act)	1950	**1** Prohibits both horizontal and vertical acquisitions or mergers through purchase of stock or assets if the effect is to tend to lessen competition or create a monopoly	**1** Prove the action would not tend to lessen competition or create a monopoly	Same as Clayton Antitrust Act	Same as Clayton Antitrust Act

the Consumer Product Safety Commission, the Food and Drug Administration, the Department of Transportation, the Securities and Exchange Commission and, as we have already seen, the Federal Trade Commission.[3]

Enabling legislation is passed by Congress to create both the agency and the legislation it is to oversee. As other legislation is passed, it is sometimes delegated to an existing agency for administration.

Agency Rule Making The role of an agency is to hear complaints, investigate what appear to be violations of law, and issue restraining orders. For example, the Federal Trade Commission, created in 1914, now administers the Export Trade Act, the Lanham Trademark Act, the Wool Products Labeling Act, the Fur Products Labeling Act, the Textile Fiber Products Identification Act, the Fair Packaging and Labeling Act, the Consumer Credit Protection Act, the Clayton Antitrust Act, the Federal Trade Commission Act, and the Robinson–Patman Act.

Under any of these acts a violation may be charged by either an injured party, a government agency, or the Federal Trade Commission itself. If cause is discovered after an investigation, a complaint is issued to the company in the name of the FTC. If the firm consents to the complaint, the investigation ceases. The company can, however, file an answer. A hearing examiner who functions somewhat as a trial judge then hears the case and issues an order. If the company charged disagrees with the order, it can go to the full FTC for a hearing. If the FTC determines that a violation is present, it will issue a cease and desist order. The company must then petition the U.S. Circuit Court of Appeals within 60 days if it disagrees with this order. If the court upholds the FTC, the cease and desist order becomes an injunction followed by contempt of court proceedings if the company charged does not comply. At any time throughout this procedure, the firm may agree to settle and a consent order will be issued by the commission.

The Federal Trade Commission also offers advisory opinions to inquiring companies, issues trade regulation rules which have the force of law and, in cooperation with entire industries, drafts and issues trade practice rules and guides.

All federal agencies function in a similar way, relieving the burden on the legislative and executive branches. Due process is preserved and a place exists for judicial review of agency rules. On the other hand, the proliferation of agencies with rule-making authority and their wide investigative authority has caused a nightmare for business managers. Robert J. Brotje, Jr., vice president and treasurer of Champion Spark Plug Company in Toledo, reports that the company now files more than 500 reports to some fifteen bureaus and agencies of the federal government, and 2,500 other reports to local and state agencies across the country.[4] Often, agency regulations conflict: "Heinz U.S.A. cites

---

[3] Corley, Black, and Reed, op. cit., p. 155.
[4] "The Law Closes In On Managers," *Business Week* (May 10, 1976), p. 114–115.

one instance when the company followed a Federal Power Commission (FPC) order to 'turn down the lights; you're using too much power,' only to be told by OSHA, 'Turn up the lights; you are creating a safety hazard'.''[5] These problems, coupled with increasing executive liability for managers at all levels, require some executives to spend up to 25 percent of their time on regulatory matters.

In this section we have reviewed the legislative and administrative framework which has emerged for regulation of business. In the next section the legality of specific actions and types of interorganizational behavior is discussed.

LEGAL ASPECTS OF INTERORGANIZATIONAL BEHAVIOR

In Chapters 3 and 4 of this text we developed three behavioral concepts often observed in a channel of distribution: conflict, power, and cooperation. The United States legal system has evolved as a set of parameters and restraints on the behavior of firms with the purpose of defining more precisely the specific behavior which firms can exhibit toward one another. Many business actions and practices have been specifically prohibited or severely limited by legislation, regulation, and/or judicial decision.

The fundamental objective of these legal restraints is to ensure the competitive character of marketing operations.[6] It would appear that the government does not wish to check growth of business firms unless that growth interferes with the rights of other firms through unfair competition, abusive practices, or attempts to gain monopoly.[7] Essentially, the legal system operates to preserve the most important elements of free competition by (1) prohibiting undue uses of power which might in the long run destroy competitive relationships; (2) prohibiting certain cooperative relationships which might injure competition; and (3) providing a means of recourse to those who need or desire an outside party to resolve conflict. We will now discuss specific business practices which involve attempts to utilize power and which have been prohibited or restrained by the legal system, specific methods of cooperation deemed questionable or illegal due to their potential for competitive harm, and the relationship of the legal system to methods of conflict resolution.

Power Restraints

Although many actions and decisions made by a firm are intended to influence behavior of other channel members and may therefore be considered attempts to utilize power, the majority of these activities can be considered normal business activity. A few of these actions, however, involve attempts to restrict or harm competition to such an extent that they have been deemed illegal. Four

[5] Ibid., p. 116.
[6] Howard, op. cit., p. 2.
[7] Harry A. Lipson and John R. Darling, *Marketing Fundamentals: Text and Cases,* (New York: John Wiley & Sons, Inc., 1974), p. 162.

important activities which are either illegal in themselves or which may be illegal under certain circumstances are (1) exclusive territories and exclusive dealing, (2) use of discounts and allowances, (3) tying contracts, and (4) reciprocity. When these policies involve either the attempt to gain market power or to utilize market power so that an unfair competitive advantage exists or is created, the courts and regulatory agencies have tended to interpret the applicable legislation to preserve competition. The following discussion focuses on the manner in which these interpretations have been made.

Exclusive Territories and Exclusive Dealing Exclusive territorial arrangements and exclusive dealing often occur together within a distribution channel. In utilizing exclusive territories for distributors a supplier will either agree to sell to only one distributor within a given geographic region or will require that distributors restrict their selling activities to one specific region. Such arrangements may be desirable for manufacturers of certain types of goods requiring strong reseller support since the purpose of the policy is to encourage resellers to develop their regions without fear of being raided by another reseller of the same brand. Exclusive territories have been used in the soft drink industry where high capital investment and strong effort by local bottlers are necessary to ensure effective market penetration for a brand. Fear of competition by another bottler offering the same brand might discourage such efforts.

The legality of exclusive territorial agreements has been an on-again, off-again situation. In 1967 the U.S. Supreme Court determined that exclusive territorial arrangements are violations per se of Section 1 of the Sherman Antitrust Act if legal title to the goods has passed from seller to buyer. In that decision concerning the Arnold Schwinn Company, the court reasoned that such arrangements are, in effect, nothing more than attempts to divide the market and, therefore, represent contracts which restrict competition. The court determined that they were violators of the law. However, in a 1977 case involving GTE Sylvania, the same court overturned the Schwinn decision and determined that territorial restrictions may be legal, and the "rule of reason" should be utilized in determining the legality of such arrangements. The court ruled that, since exclusive territorial agreements can have positive benefits such as promoting interbrand competition, inducing retailers to be more aggressive, helping smaller retailers to compete against larger ones, and encouraging marketing efficiency, the extent to which intrabrand competition is restricted should be balanced against the extent to which potential interbrand competition is enhanced.[8] The net result of these decisions is that the power of a supplier to restrict dealers to specific geographic territories, or to reward dealers with a geographic monopoly, has been severely limited. At this time, such uses of power must be carefully evaluated in terms of their effects on inter- as well as intrabrand competition.

---

[8] For a discussion of the Schwinn and GTE Sylvania cases see *Journal of Marketing* (January 1978), pp. 106–107.

In an exclusive dealing agreement, a buyer agrees to handle the products of only one seller. Although exclusive dealing can exist without territorial restrictions, the two arrangements are closely related since originally manufacturers offered exclusive territories in return for the reseller's promise not to deal in a competitor's goods. Under the Clayton Antitrust Act, exclusive dealing is illegal if it results in substantial lessening of competition or encourages a tendency toward monopoly. The major issue in determining the legality of a particular exclusive dealing agreement concerns the extent of competitive harm. In order to establish that substantial competitive harm has occurred, the courts must attempt to determine both the total size of the relevant market and the portion of that market from which the exclusive dealing arrangement excludes competition. Two classic court cases can be cited to demonstrate the nature of this problem. In the first case, the Standard Fashion Company, a producer of dress patterns, prohibited its retailers from using competitors' patterns. Since the firm had a 40 percent share of the market for dress patterns, the court determined that exclusive dealing would lead to further concentration in the industry and result in substantial lessening of competition.[9] However, in another case involving J. I. Case Company, a manufacturer of farm implements, the court determined that exclusive dealing was not illegal because other manufacturers were able to find dealers to distribute their products and that many manufacturers were represented in most geographic regions.[10] Thus, for J. I. Case, there was no substantial reduction in competition nor any tendency toward monopoly.

Discounts and Allowances Granting of various types of discounts and allowances by manufacturers may be considered attempts to utilize power over wholesalers and/or retailers. For example, the offering of a quantity discount, either cumulative or noncumulative, is essentially an attempt to influence the buyer's decisions on whether to purchase a product and how much of that product to purchase. Similarly, cooperative advertising allowances are designed to influence the retailer's advertising policies. These attempts to utilize power are legal as long as they do not result in price discrimination as defined by the Robinson–Patman Act. As noted earlier in the chapter buyers may not use their size or market power advantage over the manufacturer to coerce granting of discounts or allowances which would result in price discrimination. This provision of Robinson–Patman has rarely been invoked. Recently, however, Thrifty Drug Stores of California was ordered by the FTC to stop seeking advantageous prices and promotional aid from suppliers.

Tying In a tying arrangement, a seller refuses to sell one product unless the potential buyer agrees to purchase other products. Since such arrangements often result in the buyer's inability to deal with other suppliers, the effect

[9] Howard, op. cit., p. 97.
[10] Ibid., p. 98.

of tying may be exclusive dealing. Tie-in agreements are not necessarily illegal but will usually be judged so if the supplier is large enough to force a restraint of trade. To determine if tying is illegal, three conditions must be met: (1) two distinct products or services must be involved, (2) the seller must have economic power sufficient to impose restriction in the tied market, and (3) the amount of commerce involved must be substantial.[11] Thus, International Salt Company, which had developed a salt dispensing machine, was not allowed to tie the lease of this machine to the sale of salt since the amount of business involved was quite substantial.[12]

The growth of franchising as a means of conducting business has spawned considerable litigation because franchisees are often required or strongly encouraged to purchase numerous products and/or services from the franchisor. The fear exists that the franchisor may charge exorbitant prices for supplies and that other suppliers will be excluded from the market. On the other hand, franchisors claim that such practices are necessary to protect the image and quality of the franchise.[13] In a decision concerning Kentucky Fried Chicken, the opinion of the courts was essentially summarized with the statement that if the gain in quality resulting from such tie-ins is greater than the detriment to competition, such arrangements are legal.[14]

A special form of illegal tie-in arrangement is known as full-line forcing. A manufacturer who attempts to utilize this practice refuses to sell one item to a middleman unless that middleman agrees to handle the manufacturer's full line of merchandise. For example, Levi Strauss was charged by the Federal Trade Commission with forcing retailers to handle several types of clothing if they desired to sell Levi jeans.

Reciprocity Reciprocity is an agreement between firms to become customers of each other. Although reciprocity could be considered a form of cooperative behavior, it is included here because it becomes an illegal form of behavior when the agreement results from unequal power of the parties. If one firm threatens or coerces the other firm into the reciprocal buying arrangement, this use of power will be interpreted as an unfair trade practice under the Federal Trade Commission Act. Thus, when General Motors routed its rail shipments to railroads using General Motors locomotives but did not ship with railroads which purchased locomotives manufactured by other firms, illegal reciprocity was charged by the government.[15]

Reciprocal buying arrangements can be quite complex, involving a number

[11] These conditions were outlined in *Arlie Mack Moore, et. al. v. Jas. H. Matthews & Co., Rest Haven Memorial Association, et al.* For discussion, see *Journal of Marketing* (October 1977), p. 108.

[12] Howard, op. cit., p. 102.

[13] For an excellent discussion of these issues see Shelby D. Hunt and John R. Nevin, "Tying Agreements In Franchising," *Journal of Marketing* (July 1975), pp. 20–26.

[14] For a discussion of *Kentucky Fried Chicken Corp. v. Diversified Packaging Corp., et al.* see *Journal of Marketing* (October 1977), pp. 107–108.

[15] Howard, op. cit., p. 94.

of participants. For example, du Pont was charged with attempting to increase sales of explosives in an arrangement whereby pressure was exerted on Curtis Publishing Company. Du Pont wanted Curtis to pressure one of its subsidiaries, a paper producer, to require its coal supplier to purchase Du Pont explosives. Although reciprocal buying is not per se a violation of the law, it seems very clear that the FTC will look more closely at such arrangements in the future to determine any coercive aspects of the agreement and to weigh possible restraints of trade which might arise.

Cooperative-Behavior Restraints

Just as certain uses of power are restrained by the legal system, many forms of cooperation are also limited or restrained because of their potential impact on competitive relationships. We are specifically concerned with collusive practices and mergers.

Collusive Practices The ways in which collusion can be practiced in business are almost limitless. In general, the Sherman and Clayton Antitrust Acts can be invoked against any collusion involving an attempt by several people or firms to restrain trade. Perhaps the most important form of prohibited collusion is price-fixing. Under no circumstances may competitors form any agreement concerning prices to be charged for products. In addition, since April 1976 a manufacturer is no longer able to agree with retailers on "fair trade" prices and require all other retailers within a given territory to abide by those prices. Such agreements, allowed under the Miller–Tydings and McGuire Acts in states which had established fair trade laws, are now illegal.

Mergers When two or more business firms agree to merge (a form of cooperation), the potential impact upon competition must be evaluated carefully. Regardless of whether the agreed-upon merger occurs through acquisition of stock or of assets, possible violations of either the Clayton or Celler–Kefauver Acts and their provisions concerning anticompetitive mergers are critical.

When mergers occur among firms at the same level of competition, many factors must be considered to determine potential impact on competition. These factors include the relevant geographic market, number of sellers in the market, size of the companies and their relative market positions, economies of scale in the industry, and the products being sold and their substitutability.[16] Thus, Lever Brothers' acquisition of All detergent was judged to be legal when the relevant market was defined by the court as "low-sudsing heavy duty detergents" in which the firm had no product offering at the time of the acquisition, rather than simply the "detergent" market in which Lever had several products. On the other hand, Procter & Gamble was forced to divest itself of the Clorox Chemical Company even though acquisition of that firm represented Procter & Gamble's first entrance into the bleach market. The court ruled that

[16] Ibid, p. 79.

Procter & Gamble was so large and had such vast resources that it should have developed its own brand of bleach rather than acquire an existing brand.[17]

If a merger involves vertical integration, competitors may be foreclosed from the opportunity to do business with the acquired buyer. If the industry is highly concentrated, such mergers may be illegal. In a recent case, Work Wear Corporation, a major manufacturer of work clothes and uniforms, was determined to be in violation of antimerger statutes with its acquisition of eleven laundry-leasing companies. The government argued that the acquired firms provided a captive market for Work Wear's clothing production and that the amount of business foreclosed to other uniform producers was substantial enough to require that the firm divest itself of the laundry-leasing facilities.[18]

Conflict Resolution

Methods by which conflict is resolved in disputes between business firms have been given a set of parameters by the legal system. Although any of the practices discussed above may result in conflict between channel members, the United States legal system becomes involved with the manner in which this conflict is resolved in two particular situations. The first is an instance in which the manufacturer decides to end the conflict by refusing to deal with the resellers. The second situation concerns initiation of litigation by one of the channel members to determine the legality of the specific circumstances, including circumstances surrounding a manufacturer's refusal to deal with resellers.

Refusal to Deal It is a well-established principle that sellers have the right to select customers according to any reasonable criteria they may choose to establish and announce. If a seller believes that exclusive dealing is necessary to ensure proper support for products, then the seller may refuse to deal with those resellers who fail to devote proper attention to the products.[19] Similarly, in order to maintain control over resale prices now that legal sanction of fair trade has been abolished, manufacturers may still legitimately refuse to deal with retailers who insist on discounting their products. The manufacturer's right to refuse to deal was established in 1919 with the "Colgate Doctrine" in a case involving Colgate.[20] Thus, when a manufacturer is in conflict with a middleman concerning these issues, the manufacturer has the right to terminate the relationship to end the conflict.

However, the manufacturer's right to utilize this form of conflict resolution has been severely restricted. Two conditions must be met. First, the threat of refusal to deal cannot be used in an attempt to force a reseller's compliance with any of these policies. Second, refusal to deal must result from a unilateral action by the seller and may not be part of any collusive action on the part of

---

[17] Ibid., pp. 82–83.
[18] See "Work Wear Tries to be No. 1 Again," *Business Week* (November 7, 1977), p. 84.
[19] Howard, op. cit., p. 98.
[20] Ibid., p. 41.

the seller or a group of resellers. The following examples may clarify situations in which refusal to deal is a legal response to conflict.

Farah Manufacturing Company is a leading manufacturer of men's clothing. The firm refuses to deal with any retailer who sells below its suggested retail prices. In addition, Farah sales personnel are prohibited from discussing prices with retailers but are told to report discounting to headquarters. Thus, when the local Farah sales representative reported that Garrett's, Incorporated, a retailer, was selling below suggested prices, the representative was told to discontinue solicitation of orders from that firm. When Garrett's sued, alleging a violation of the Sherman Antitrust Act, Farah was found not guilty because there was no attempt to persuade Garrett's to maintain prices and because the facts which led to Garrett's loss of the right to sell Farah products came only from Farah employees.[21]

Another set of circumstances led to a different ruling with Nissan Motors Corporation, an automobile manufacturer. In this case, the manufacturer had a stated policy of discouraging advertising which suggested price-cutting. In addition, Nissan employees strongly recommended that dealers maintain factory list prices and other dealers were encouraged to report any discount advertising. The court determined that the manufacturer's policies went beyond legal limits, that coercion existed, and collusion with other dealers was present to implement the refusal to deal.[22] The facts of this and other similar cases in which refusal to deal has been prohibited center on the conspiracy clauses of the Sherman and Clayton Antitrust Acts rather than on any infringement of the manufacturer's right to choose which dealers will be utilized as representatives in the marketplace.

Thus, refusal to deal can be used as a means of resolving conflict with resellers if it is an action undertaken unilaterally and without threats or coercion by the manufacturer. If the threat of refusal to deal is used as a form of power in order to obtain compliance with desired policies, however, such behavior will not be allowed. In addition, other resellers may not be used to police and report violations of such policies due to the potential charge of illegal conspiracy in restraint of trade.

Litigation   As discussed in Chapter 4, any channel member may attempt to resolve conflicts with other channel members by resorting to the legal system. Indeed, a primary function of the courts and many regulatory agencies is to weigh the facts of any particular disagreement between channel members, to decide whether the disagreements involve potential illegal actions, and to determine the most equitable resolution of conflict between channel members. The legal principles discussed above have evolved from existing legislation modified by many court and agency interpretations in order to regulate interor-

[21] See *Garrett's, Inc. v. Farah Manufacturing Co., Inc.* in *Journal of Marketing* (October 1976), p. 113.
[22] *Garrett's v. Farah,* pp. 113–114.

ganizational behavior. However, these principles are subject to even further modification or interpretation. The Supreme Court reversed itself within a period of 10 years on the question of exclusive territorial agreements. Other changes are possible.

PUBLIC POLICY ISSUES AND CHANNEL MANAGEMENT

The preceding sections of this chapter have dealt primarily with the legal environment and its relationship to the protection of a free competitive market. A second major objective of legislation and regulation is to protect consumers from harm by business practices. The amount of such consumer-oriented activity is staggering. Many administrative agencies discussed earlier are more directly concerned with this type of business regulation than with attempts to maintain competition. Some agencies, such as the FTC, are involved in both activities. Although it is not possible to catalog all agencies, rules, and regulations here, it is important to understand the effects of such agencies upon channel performance and relationships. Thus, we will use the Consumer Product Safety Commission (CPSC) as one example.

During the 1960s a key issue in the consumer movement was product safety. Many hazardous products were exposed by consumer advocates, including faulty automobiles, dangerous food and drug products, defective children's toys, and color televisions with high levels of radiation. As a result, several pieces of legislation were passed for the protection of consumers. The Consumer Product Safety Act of 1972 established the CPSC and gave the commission authority to require manufacturers to recall, repair, replace, and/or refund defective products.

The CPSC has been extremely active. Many manufacturers, especially in the toy and appliance industries, have been required to recall defective products. These recalls ultimately involve major channel issues since the manufacturer must depend upon the cooperation of wholesalers and retailers to ensure compliance with the commission's rulings. Retailers are also required by law to inform the CPSC of any product which fails to comply with product safety rules or which contains a defect leading to a substantial product hazard.[23] Thus, product recalls can substantially affect channel relationships. Retailers must expend considerable time and effort in locating recalled products and arrangements must be made for disposition of those goods. One study of recall problems revealed that manufacturers are often reluctant to reimburse retailers for their expenses.[24] The potential for conflict is obvious.

The CPSC is just one agency responsible for consumer protection. Many

[23] Mary C. Harrison and M. Bixby Cooper, "An Analysis of Retailer Participation in Product Recalls," *Proceedings of the Southern Marketing Association 1976 Conference,* p. 89.
[24] Harrison and Cooper, op. cit., p. 90.

other public policy rules exist at the federal, state, and local levels. Although business relationships are not the primary focus of these activities, their impact on channel member interaction is extremely important.

LEGAL REMEDIES

Violations of the laws and regulations discussed can carry very strong penalties. A conviction under the Sherman Antitrust Act is a federal crime punishable by a corporate fine of up to $1 million for each offense. In addition, victims of antitrust action under the act can collect triple damages, plus court costs and legal fees. Legal cases under this act may be initiated by an individual or by the federal government, usually the Justice Department, which can request that the courts issue an injunction to stop the alleged violation. If the violator does not obey, contempt of court can be charged. In any event, the violator must work out a compromise or fight the issue in court.

Although violations of most federal legislation and agency rulings have always allowed penalties against individuals, the courts were traditionally very reluctant to impose those sanctions against executives of business firms. This condition appears to have changed considerably in recent years. Fifteen executives from paperboard box companies, including the president of Container Corporation of America who drew a 2-month sentence, were sentenced to jail in a price-fixing case. All the executives were also fined.[25] In another case six executives of Velsicol Chemical Corporation were indicted for withholding test data concerning hazards of the company's leading pesticides.[26]

It is important to note that top-level executives are not immune and are being held responsible for subordinates' activities. In forcing the Wilson Sporting Goods Company to comply with safety standards for baseball bats, the CPSC also named the chairman of Wilson's parent firm, Pepsico, Inc.[27] In a 1975 case involving the president of American Stores, a major food company, the Supreme Court ruled that a firm's chief executive officer is responsible for failure of subordinates to comply with federal laws. This case, which involved unsanitary conditions in one of the firm's warehouses, established a precedent which has seen several executives fined by the courts. As yet, however, no person has been sentenced to jail under this executive accountability rule.[28] Earlier in this chapter, Table 5-1 summarized various penalties which may be imposed against corporations and individuals under many of the more significant laws and agency rulings. Evidently the courts feel they will ensure compliance with the law by imposing penalties upon individuals. Whether or not this is true, a new dimension has been added to executive decision making.

[25] "Marketing Briefs," *Business Week* (December 13, 1976), p. 38.
[26] "Marketing Briefs," *Business Week* (December 26, 1977), p. 44.
[27] "Marketing Briefs," *Business Week* (May 10, 1976), p. 113.
[28] Jack Moore, "Protection of Small Firms Has Been Keystone of U. S. Regulatory Efforts," *Supermarket News* (October 24, 1977), pp. 58–59.

SUMMARY

The purpose of this chapter has been to provide an understanding of the legal framework which affects the business community in making decisions concerning channels of distribution. Federal, state, and local governments have authority to regulate business activities. Three types of law provide this framework. The first, judicial law, derives from the court system and its adjudication of disputes between businesses. The second type, legislative law, sets forth rules of conduct which are then interpreted by the courts in litigation. The Sherman, Clayton, Federal Trade Commission, Robinson–Patman and Celler–Kefauver acts provide the primary structure for regulating relationships among business firms. The third type, administrative law, is relatively new and has evolved to relieve the burdens on other branches of government. Many administrative agencies have quasi-judicial powers to regulate business.

One of the basic objectives of the legal system is to preserve free competition by regulating behavior of business firms. This objective is accomplished by preventing undue uses of power such as exclusive territorial and dealership arrangements, improper utilization of discounts and allowances to ensure compliance, forced tying, and forced reciprocity. The objective is also accomplished by preventing forms of cooperation such as collusion and mergers which would harm competitive relationships. Finally, the legal framework establishes allowable means of resolving conflicts among business firms by establishing conditions under which firms may refuse to deal with one another, and by providing recourse to the court system as an ultimate solution to disputes.

Another objective of the legal system is consumer protection. Although consumer protection laws and regulations are not directly concerned with relationships between channel members, they indirectly affect channel power, conflict, and cooperation.

The chapter concluded with a discussion of penalties for failure to comply with the law. The recent trend toward individual liability for corporate activities is an important concern for those individuals responsible for making channel decisions.

QUESTIONS

1   What are the philosophical foundations for federal and state government regulation of commerce and business activity?
2   Compare and contrast the nature of judicial and legislative law. How do these two aspects of the legal framework relate to each other?
3   Trace the development of major federal legislation affecting channel relationships.
4   Why has administrative law become so prevalent in recent years? From what sources do administrative agencies derive their rule-making powers?
5   What are the legal system's basic objectives with respect to channel relationships? Discuss the potential contradictions which may be faced in attempting to fulfill these objectives.

6 What is exclusive dealing? Under what conditions might exclusive dealing arrangements be judged illegal?

7 Why is the legal system of the United States concerned about reciprocal buying arrangements?

8 Using the factors listed in the text, discuss the potential legality of an acquisition of Bic pens by the Cross Pen Company.

9 Under what circumstances might a manufacturer's refusal to deal with a retailer be judged illegal? Compare the facts of the cases involving Farah and Nissan Motor Company.

10 Why do you suppose the courts have become more willing to impose penalties against individuals as well as corporations for violations of federal legislation?

CASES: Legal Situations

In this chapter we depart from the case approach used in other chapters. Instead, we have developed six vignettes which present potential legal situations. Although names of companies and products are disguised in most cases, each vignette represents an authentic legal situation. Our purpose is to acquaint you with the pervasiveness of the law and its influence on both strategic and daily operational decisions within a channel.

CASE 5-1: Global Manufacturing, Incorporated

Global manufactured a line of road building and light construction equipment. Their primary product was the road scraper, an item which had gained a world-wide reputation for durability and reliability. As export sales began to increase in the mid-1960s, Global established a system of dealers in thirty-four major world capitals. In the early 1970s, the U. S. government, looking for ways to encourage export sales, allowed the charter of Domestic International Sales Corporations (DISC). Ninety-five percent of DISC's gross receipts were to come from qualified exports. Profits were limited to 4 percent of export sales. No income taxes were assessed on profits. However, 50 percent of income was required to be received by shareholders and taxed as part of their income. Global chartered a DISC under the name of the Lance Corporation in 1973. From that time forward all export sales were administered by Lance.

From its inception Lance Corporation had found it difficult to realize rapid parts distribution to customers. In export marketing of industrial equipment ability to provide rapid parts service is a major consideration in the original equipment sale. In 1977 the parts distribution problem became very serious. The market area having the most difficulty was the Near East. Sensing the opportunity, an enterprising Lance dealer in Manila established a company in San Francisco. This company purchased parts from the central parts distribution of Global, inventoried them in San Francisco, and provided speedy service to all Lance customers in the Near East. The dealer charged 40 percent over the domestic purchase price and customers were willing to pay the premium price for rapid service. However, they became increasingly antagonized by Lance Corporation's inability to provide adequate service at Global's basic price.

Toward the end of 1977 the situation reached serious proportions and Lance was losing the reputation it had established in the Near East. The president of Lance Corporation decided to deal boldly with the problem. He ordered the Manila dealer to stop doing business with the San Francisco operation. The implication was that the Manila franchise would be canceled if the dealer did not comply. The dealer indicated no intention of closing the San Francisco operation. The dealer's response was that if Lance Corporation carried out its threat a court case would result, charging Lance with unfair competition.

Lance executives were not sure whether such a move would be considered an unfair competitive practice; however, the threat was sufficient to force them to consider other alternatives. The alternative given the most serious consideration was for Lance to make an offer to purchase the San Francisco parts warehouse outright and operate it as a division of Lance.

Is there a valid unfair competition case against Lance? In your answer elaborate on the presence or absence of any lessening of competition in the distribution of Global parts. Do you think the alternative solution is legal? Why or why not? To what extent is Global liable for the actions of Lance?

CASE 5-2: Winston Iron Works

A division of Winston Iron Works in Portland, Oregon, developed a substantial sales volume in wood-burning stoves. These stoves were sold as supplementary residential heating units. During the energy crisis of 1973 Winston engineers developed a supplemental wood-burning unit which could be tied into an existing gas or oil furnace. The unit was thermostatically controlled in such a way that when it was fired with wood the oil or gas burners of the furnace shut off. If the add-on unit was unattended, the gas or oil burners would take over automatically.

This new product, which retailed at about $595, had great market potential. Management was very enthusiastic about market growth and profitability estimates. The marketing department was asked to develop a complete marketing program. A review of the present distribution system indicated that greater control would be needed to market the add-on unit. In order for the device to be installed properly and safely, it was decided that only selected dealers could adequately provide installation in strict conformance with local building codes. The marketing department had long been dissatisfied with haphazard distribution of other products in the line and planned to use the new product as a means of exercising more control over the marketing channel. It embarked on the development of a system of exclusive dealerships and promised territorial protection in return. The first stage of the plan called for 123 exclusive dealerships.

When the plan was presented, top management praised the new approach and congratulated the marketing group. For years there had been a general awareness that more control over distribution was essential if Winston products were to be represented properly. At the end of the meeting, one member of top management indicated support for the plan but suggested its legality should be reviewed.

The planning group immediately contacted the company attorney and asked for an opinion on such a controlled distribution system. The attorney replied that until 1967 the Supreme Court had enunciated a "rule of reason" doctrine for evaluating territorial or customer restrictions in exclusive dealer arrangements. That is, the reasonableness of the restriction would be used by the court to determine if any restraint of trade had occurred. In 1967 the Schwinn decision declared that all control techniques involving territorial allocation or restriction were violations per se of the Sherman Antitrust Act if title to the product had passed to the dealer. However, between 1967 and 1973 some decisions followed the per se violation of the Schwinn case and some followed the older "rule of reason" doctrine. The attorney pointed out that, in his opinion, the cases following the "rule of reason" doctrine involved four situations:

1 The manufacturer was not resolute in refusing to deal with dealers who did not adhere to the territorial restrictions.
2 Products in which improper use would endanger the user.
3 Cases in which areas of primary responsibility were spelled out in the agreement, and the dealer must first make a primary sales effort before selling out of the territory.
4 Sale of a service rather than a good.

In 1974 the Circuit Court of Appeals returned to the per se violation in the Coors case. Coors Brewery argued that its beer (1) was more costly to produce, (2) needed refrigeration at the distribution level, and (3) had a limited shelf life. Therefore, it was mandatory that Coors select distributors willing to make the necessary investment in equipment to ensure proper distribution of the product. In return, Coors was obligated to give territorial protection to its distributors. The argument was not accepted, and the Supreme Court denied an appeal.

The Winston attorney suggested that one way to avoid the problem was to ship all products to the dealers on consignment, and not pass title until the product was sold for installation.

What should Winston do concerning its controlled distribution plan? Can Winston develop a valid argument for a "rule of reason" doctrine decision in the event of litigation? How workable is the attorney's suggestion to ship on consignment? Can a manufacturer be held responsible for faulty representation and installation by a dealer?

CASE 5-3: Belmont Corporation

Belmont manufactured a line of in-plant conveyer systems for use in manufacturing operations. It had been very successful and had a 1977 sales volume of $600 million, about 20 percent of which was export sales to foreign countries. In June 1977 the export division heard that the Franklin Corporation of Atlanta, Georgia, was building a new plant in Porto Alegre, Brazil. Franklin was familiar with Belmont's systems since they were used in many of Franklin's United States plants. From information assembled on the size of the new plant the Belmont export sales group estimated that the equipment order would amount to about $2.5 million.

Belmont began to work closely with its exclusive distributor in Brazil to obtain the equipment order for the new plant. Belmont felt it had a good chance since Franklin was familiar with the product and Belmont could offer a competitive price. Export sales discounts given to foreign distributors were much larger than those given to United States distributors. Foreign distributors normally needed a wider margin to allow for negotiation.

Through careful coordination with its Brazil distributor, Belmont was successful in closing the Franklin order in March 1978. At the same time that negotiations were being conducted by the export sales group, the Belmont distributor in Brazil, and Franklin, another Belmont distributor located in Atlanta was negotiating with Franklin's United States headquarters to purchase the necessary equipment in Atlanta. This was unknown to the export sales group of Belmont. When the Belmont domestic distributor found that the order went to the Brazilian distributor, a quiet search was started. Through friends at Franklin, it was discovered that the Atlanta distributor lost the order because the price offered by the Brazilian distributor was considerably below the domestic price. The loss in profit was substantial for the Atlanta distributor and, after discussions with legal counsel, the situation was interpreted as outright discrimination on the part of Belmont. The Atlanta distributor was advised to sue for triple damages.

What should Belmont's position be if the suit is filed? Is there anything Belmont can or should do to pacify the Atlanta distributor and avoid being sued?

CASE 5-4: Newton Incorporated

Newton Incorporated manufactured a line of indoor cleaning equipment that enjoyed a very favorable reputation among users. Newton products were more expensive than competitive products, but the price was justified by the quality reputation. Newton had achieved a very respectable share of the market through a system of controlled distribution. Sales were made directly by the company's own sales force to a network of 142 exclusive dealers across the country. Dealer sales were restricted to exclusive territories arranged to provide complete market coverage.

In 1974 dealers began complaining that Newton's high prices made it almost impossible for them to bid successfully on large purchases made by institutional buyers such as school districts and municipal, county, and state governments. Those institutions were required to purchase from the lowest bidder unless justifiable cause could be demonstrated for a higher price. On indoor cleaning equipment, the sale usually went to the lowest bidder.

Newton marketing people investigated the dealer complaints and found most cases to be true. Among alternative solutions lowering the price was rejected because of discriminatory implications and the fact that the quality reputation had been responsible for an increasing market share over the years. Newton desired to preserve the quality image at all costs. One acceptable solution was to develop a second, lower quality, lower price line of products. In order to preserve the image of the higher priced line, Newton decided to disassociate the two lines completely and establish a different brand name and dealer organization for the new lower priced line. The same controlled distribution system would be used for the new line with the added advantage of doubling dealer representation for supplemental Newton products.

The plan was implemented in 1977 much to the displeasure of many older dealers. Several of them had requested the opportunity to carry the new product line but Newton management, fearful of damaging the quality reputation of the older line, steadfastly refused such requests. Some of the more antagonized dealers reviewed their exclusive territory dealer agreements and hinted at a violation of those agreements.

Is there a legal issue involved in this situation? How might the problem have been avoided?

CASE 5-5: Heinz versus Campbell

In September 1976 H. J. Heinz and Company sued the Campbell Soup Company for $315 million in damages. Heinz charged that Campbell was guilty of illegal monopoly since it held 75 percent of the market. Heinz contended that Campbell used manipulated prices, deceptive advertising, and brand proliferation in order to force supermarket retailers to allocate a disproportionate share of shelf space to Campbell products. This left little shelf space for other brands. Although Heinz had discontinued marketing soup under its own brand name, it was still a major producer of private label soups. In its defense, Campbell Soup Company filed a countersuit against Heinz charging that Heinz held 80 percent of ketchup sales. Campbell contended that not only was this monopolistic, but Heinz consistently forced retail operators to purchase other Heinz products if they wished to continue stocking the ketchup. Campbell also accused Heinz of giving discounts to preferred food service customers.

Both Heinz and Campbell distribute their products to retail and to institutional food markets (hotels, restaurants, hospitals, schools, in-plant feeding establishments, etc.).

Is there any illegality involved in the actions of either Heinz or Campbell in this situation? Is there any possibility of a charge of an illegal practice by one of the customers of either company?

CASE 5-6: Danhoff Brothers

In 1967 Danhoff Brothers operated two very successful coffee shop restaurants in Macon, Georgia. Both outlets were located near expressway interchanges and had developed an excellent reputation for a diverse menu, quality products, medium prices, good service, and excellent sanitary conditions. In 1969 two additional outlets were opened on the outskirts of Atlanta, both near expressway interchanges. The same high standards were maintained. In 1970 another restaurant following the same pattern of operation was opened in Valdosta, Georgia.

Along with opening the fifth restaurant, Danhoff also opened a food preparation center in Macon. This center handled all purchasing, advanced food preparation, and portion control. The center also had a small research laboratory in which new menu items were developed and tested. It was felt that the center would be an important part of the total operation when additional expansion occurred. In its first months of operation the center proved to be a very important part of the business. Not only were costs reduced but the quality and attractiveness of food served improved over an already acceptable level.

At a meeting of the two Danhoff brothers data were reviewed on the traffic flow along Interstate I-75, the major route from the northern Midwest states to Florida. Potential customer traffic was large, but competition from many other restaurants along the route was enormous. At that meeting it was decided to revise and distribute the presently used table customer questionnaire to get some idea of how transient customers ranked Danhoff among other restaurants along the route. Danhoff invariably came out superior to others on the questionnaire. The brothers also knew that they had a very enviable reputation among restaurant operators in Georgia, Tennessee, and north Florida.

The Danhoff brothers wanted to expand their operations but could not see how they could finance the investment in additional units along the route. On the other hand, they had become a model for restaurant operations in the area and many restaurant operators from as far away as Tennessee and Florida had visited them to gain a better insight into their operations.

It was decided to approach other restaurants on the feasibility of accepting a franchise from Danhoff. The franchise offered the use of the Danhoff name, management standards, and inspection to ensure the same high-quality operation as the Danhoff-owned restaurants. The franchisees were requested to purchase 80 percent of their food from the Danhoff Food Preparation Center.

At least eight family-owned restaurants along I-75 showed some interest. Legal franchise agreements were drawn up and within 10 months the eight restaurants were signed as Danhoff franchisees. The arrangement appeared to be profitable for the franchisees and sales increased substantially. In fact, sales increased so much that those franchisees became prime targets for other institutional food service suppliers. Those suppliers began offering price discounts which made their products attractive to the Danhoff franchisees.

In time, some of the franchisees began to purchase products from suppliers other than the Danhoff Food Preparation Center to such an extent that their purchases dropped below the agreed-upon 80 percent level. Two franchisees were particularly notorious offenders. After much discussion in an effort by Danhoff to persuade compliance, the two franchisees were informed in writing that if they did not abide by the agreement the franchises would be canceled.

The franchisees in turn held firm on their interpretation of the franchise agreement, contending that the 80 percent clause was illegal and that Danhoff could not refuse to sell them food.

Is the tying clause in the franchise agreement legal? If the tying clause is violated, does Danhoff have the right to cancel the agreement and refuse to sell?

Chapter 6

Enterprise Positioning
and Negotiation Strategy

The first five chapters have developed the economic, behavioral, and legal settings within which channel arrangements are formulated. Although every firm may desire to be self-sufficient, none is. Even the largest industrial and marketing organizations must develop working alliances with customers, suppliers, and vendors. The management process by which distribution channels are created and dissolved is *interorganizational negotiation.*[1]

Interorganizational negotiation is defined as *the management process of reaching agreement regarding commitment to roles and rewards in joint marketing channel performance.* Thus, negotiation is a form of cooperative behavior in which participants identify what they will do and what they will receive before they perform specified marketing functions. For example, when a retailer agrees to stock a specific manufacturer's product line, interorganizational negotiation will usually precede any final commitment on such important matters as transfer price, discount, delivery terms, promotional plans, cooperative advertising, and other elements of the marketing mix.

---

[1] The concept and structure of this chapter draw a great deal upon Richard E. Walton and Robert B. McKersie, *A Behavioral Theory of Labor Negotiations* (New York: McGraw-Hill Book Co., 1965).

Negotiation in marketing is a key managerial process. In this chapter a comprehensive review of the negotiation process serves as a bridge from broad treatment of basic channel concepts to specifics of managerial planning. The initial section of this chapter introduces the nature of negotiation in marketing. Next, attention is directed to the strategy of negotiation. The final section examines specific objectives in channel negotiation.

NEGOTIATION IN MARKETING

Alderson has pointed out the interesting origins of the term "negotiation" and its application to business:[2]

> The word "negotiation" has an interesting history in relation to business. The term for business in the Latin language is *negocio*. This word is related in its original significance to the word "negation." In classical times anyone who was in government or the army, in philosophy or the arts, had a recognized occupation. Businessmen were not engaged in any of these recognized occupations, so they were regarded as occupied with negotiating—in other words, doing nothing.

Negotiation—the occupation of doing nothing—is now viewed as the main process by which the resources of two or more organizations are aligned into a marketing channel. It is the process by which economic values are specified and structure is identified through the exercise of relative power. Through the negotiation process a specific firm positions itself in one or more channel arrangements. Thus, negotiation is viewed as the key strategic process in channel management.

Within limits, each firm in the overall marketing system is free to choose the specific channel arrangements it seeks to develop and perpetuate. The prerogative to initiate negotiation can rest with any firm in the overall marketing channel regardless of size or relative power. However, all firms have the right *not* to negotiate. Over the course of a year thousands of business organizations may seek to establish marketing arrangements with Sears. Even without examining specifics, Sears' management may reject attempts to negotiate with the majority of firms. Similarly, a small manufacturer may reject an offer from Sears to negotiate contract manufacturing through fear of overcommitment to one organization and potential loss of autonomy.

With interorganizational negotiation, it is important to realize at the outset that participation is a form of *self-resolution* for each firm involved. Once the negotiation process begins and as it is repeated the position of self-resolution is clouded by the history of commitments and performance.

The Negotiation Perspective

The need to negotiate results from the high degree of mutual dependence characteristic of channel members as they seek to exploit joint opportunity. The

---

[2] Wroe Alderson, *Marketing Behavior and Executive Action* (Homewood, Ill.: Richard D. Irwin, Inc., 1957), p. 130.

economic origins of the fundamental need to cooperate with other organizations were developed in Chapter 2. From an overall viewpoint interorganizational negotiation can be divided into processes which involve new channel situations and those which involve mature or established situations. Each is discussed.

New Channel Negotiation　A new channel negotiation is characterized by lack of experience—that is, no track record exists between two organizations. The objective of the negotiation may be formulation of either a onetime transaction or an enduring relationship. In either case both parties to a new negotiation have no history of commitments and performance to draw upon in evaluating alternative agreements.

In free-flow channels negotiation will likely be transaction oriented. For example, in the unprecedented 1976 wheat deal with the U.S.S.R. and the United States, the pretransaction negotiation took several months and covered such subjects as terms of payment and relative percentage of the tonnage to be shipped by each nation's flag vessel. In a single negotiation as complicated as the wheat deal, transfer price may well be the least difficult aspect of the negotiated agreement.

In contrast, when two parties negotiate a franchise, the process may be rather simple with respect to variations in the standard agreement. If an individual wishes to franchise and operate a McDonald's restaurant, terms and conditions under which the agreement will be concluded are specified far in advance of formal negotiation. McDonald's, like most organizations offering a strong franchise, insists upon a standard agreement regarding almost every phase of the proposed operation. The primary subject of negotiation in such situations is the financial and managerial qualification of the potential franchisee.

In the above two illustrations the commitments range from a one-time deal, the wheat negotiation, to a long-term agreement, the McDonald's franchise. Naturally, a new negotiation could involve several intermediate degrees of commitment depending upon the specifics of the individual situation. If the new channel negotiation results in an ongoing situation, from that time forward the discussions fall into the category of mature negotiations. If the negotiation is for a single transaction the deal is ended once all terms and conditions are satisfied. Of course, future negotiations between the involved parties will be framed in terms of previous experience but they will be classified as new channel negotiations.

The significant advantage of a new channel negotiation is that the interruption in operations provides the opportunity to establish a new agreement without obligation to previous arrangements. In essence, the firm is once again in the position of self-resolution with respect to future negotiations.

Mature Channel Negotiation　Mature channel negotiation occurs between organizations that have an ongoing agreement which requires modification. In certain situations contracts will call for renegotiation at a specified expiration date. For example, a tool and die shop may have a contract with Oldsmobile for the 1980 model year. Both Oldsmobile and the tool shop may expect to renew contracts for future years, but each year's arrangement is based on a new negotiation.

In addition to renewal negotiations, the three most common types of mature negotiation in marketing channels are (1) changing balance of power, (2) conflict resolutions, and (3) termination settlements. Each is discussed and illustrated.

It can be expected that members of a channel of distribution will experience a relative change in power over time. Thus, the first form of mature negotiation is adjustment of an ongoing business arrangement. A prime example has been the rapid growth of large retailers. Because of size and market power, suppliers dealing with retailing giants such as K-Mart have been required to make substantial modifications in their methods of operation from year to year. At one time a supplier may have shipped directly to individual K-Mart stores. Today, however, larger shipments made directly to distribution warehouses may be the only way that K-Mart will do business with selected suppliers. The switch from direct store delivery to distribution warehouse shipment required renegotiation of such items as price, delivery schedule, freight payment terms, discounts, and many other important aspects of the total transaction. Accommodation of changing relative position within an existing channel is the most common form of mature negotiation. Both parties to the negotiation plan to continue the channel relationship unless the day-to-day adjustments become matters of substantial conflict.

The second major form of mature channel negotiation is required when overt conflict develops. Conflict resolution negotiation is only a matter of degree in comparison to the routine power adjustments discussed above. When conflict erupts, continuation of the channel may be in jeopardy. As discussed in Chapters 3 and 4, the event leading to the conflict may or may not be the real issue. Nevertheless, one party is seeking a major realignment of the channel relationship without the full cooperation of the other party. Depending upon the propensity of the parties to negotiate and compromise their existing positions, the channel arrangement may be either modified or terminated.

The third major form of mature channel negotiation involves the termination of an existing arrangement. In most termination situations the conflict between channel members has become dysfunctional. In any event one or both parties wish to terminate the buy-sell arrangement. John R. Commons has discussed the typical nature of termination disputes.[3] Specifically, four related issues may require settlement:[4]

> *First,* is the issue of *competition,* as to whether the competitors have acted fairly toward each other.

[3] John R. Commons, *Institutional Economics* (New York: The Macmillan Company, 1934), p. 62.
[4] Ibid., pp. 62–64.

Second, is the issue of *equal opportunity,* as to whether the actual buyer discriminates unfairly between the sellers or the actual seller discriminates unfairly between the buyers, by charging or paying different prices under similar circumstances.

Third, is the issue of bargaining power, as to whether the price, or consideration agreed upon by the actual buyer and seller was determined with or without duress, coercion, unfair competition, or unequal opportunity, known as a *fair or reasonable price or value.* These, . . . , are treated technically as the law of fair and unfair competition.

Fourth, is the constitutional issue of *"due process of law,"* which might be named the due "operation of law," as to whether the trial court, the executive, or legislature, unjustifiably deprived any one of the participants of his liberty or property.

It is clear that a termination negotiation can range from a relatively peaceful settlement to a full legal battle, depending upon each party's perception of the other party's obligation. The negotiability of a termination will vary with each situation. One common feature is that most terminations involve a considerable period of time and, in some cases, there will be extended time lapses before full settlement is reached. An extreme example of elapsed time to fully terminate an agreement occurred when A&P stopped distributing Plaid Stamps provided by the E. F. MacDonald Stamp Company. Over 10 years elapsed from the time of A&P's decision to discontinue issuing stamps to full settlement of all claims. It is interesting to note that no legal conflicts were involved in the A&P–E. F. MacDonald settlement. Terminations involving legal settlements can extend for many years and may reach the U.S. Supreme Court before final settlement.[5]

Negotiation Perspective—Conclusion

It should be clear from the above discussion that many different negotiations can develop within the arena of marketing channels. The fact that most business agreements are performed in a channel context makes almost all negotiation a matter of concern in the formulation of distribution arrangements. From a strategic viewpoint, a clear distinction can be made between new and mature channel negotiations. The stake involved in each situation is substantially different. The next section deals with the strategy of channel negotiation.

NEGOTIATION STRATEGY

When approaching a channel negotiation, each party has at least a vague idea of what would constitute an ideal arrangement. The fundamental objective of negotiation is to reap the benefits of joint opportunity. In situations other than single transaction negotiations, the expectation is that the agreement will result in a form of routinized behavior by all parties.[6] Thus, the uncertainty inherent

---

[5] For a discussion of the typical legal resolution procedure see Chapter 5, pp. 142–143.
[6] Alderson, op. cit., pp. 296–304.

in a typical marketing situation is replaced, to a degree, by an articulation of each party's expectations. Strategic negotiation is a form of cooperative behavior wherein participants first prescribe each individual's share in the output of the economic activity and then decide what is required from each.[7] Thus, negotiation leads to agreement reducing the anticipatory nature and related risk of the distribution process. Despite the cooperative foundations of negotiation, the process of arriving at agreement involves all parties' directed efforts to "negotiate" the best arrangement possible for their own organizations. In this section we review the range of negotiable actions, state the prerequisites to successful negotiation, and examine the basis upon which strategies are formulated.

Scope of Channel Negotiation

Labor negotiations have identified five actions which describe the range of bargaining activities:[8]

> *Share bargaining.* The process by which opponents share or ration the settlement range between themselves. If one gets more, the other gets less.
> *Problem solving.* The process by which both parties work together to solve each other's problems. In this process both gain at the same time.
> *Attitudinal bargaining.* The process by which a mutually workable attitudinal relationship is developed to facilitate negotiation.
> *In-Group bargaining.* The process by which a negotiator bargains with members of his own team and decision-making group to derive workable organizational objectives.
> *Personal bargaining.* The process by which a negotiator makes a behavioral choice involving conflicting personal needs and goals.

All the above types of negotiation are important in the formulation of channel relationships. The ideal situation would be a negotiation environment dominated by problem-solving solutions, which were discussed in Chapter 4. As will be noted later in this chapter, many negotiated channel arrangements do in fact involve efforts toward synergism. However, an equal number of situations are characterized by share bargaining. As a general rule new channel negotiation will be characterized by share bargaining while more mature situations, short of termination, will be characterized by joint problem solving.

While reviewing the scope of channel negotiations it is important to remember that the basic process is an attempt to identify and establish an operating structure. Unlike labor bargaining, the parties involved are not necessarily cast in adversary roles. Nevertheless, the process must also include attitudinal, in-group, and personal aspects of negotiation if an effective arrangement is to result.

---

[7] Wroe Alderson, *Dynamic Marketing Behavior* (Homewood, Ill.: Richard D. Irwin, Inc., 1965), pp. 244–251.

[8] Chester L. Karrass, *The Negotiating Game* (New York: World Publishing Company/Times Mirror, 1970), chap. 11 and Walton and McKersie, op. cit.

Prerequisites for Negotiation

Four characteristics are necessary for successful channel negotiation. Unless the following characteristics are part of the negotiation process, a satisfactory compromise is unlikely.

    1 The parties to the negotiation must have alternative courses of action. Availability of alternatives is important in both new and mature channel negotiations. Unless alternatives exist, no effective balance of power will be available to the negotiating parties.

    2 To arrive at an effective agreement the involved parties must establish credible rules or procedures to guide negotiation. In essence, this form of pre-negotiation agreement constitutes attitudinal bargaining. Unless each party fully understands the ground rules, negotiation will be difficult to conduct.

    3 To engage in effective negotiation the parties must be in a position to exchange benefits or rewards. If a retailer wants a drug wholesaler to preprice selected merchandise the retailer must be willing to offer some form of counter-balance incentive. The incentive offered by the retailer in such a situation could range from direct payment for the service to simply continuing to purchase from the wholesaler. Regardless of the exact composition, the capability of both parties to grant some form of reward is essential to the negotiation process.

    4 Each party to a negotiation must be willing to make a clear commitment. In many ways the entire process is founded upon the willingness of the negotiating parties to take a position. Because negotiation rests upon a predetermination of each party's stake prior to actual performance, the agreement can only be as good as the commitment which backs it up.

The four prerequisites—alternatives, rules and procedures, reward capability, and commitment—are essential to good faith negotiation. In single transaction or free-flow negotiations, many of the prerequisites are being tested by the parties involved. If each party is satisfied, the free-flow arrangement may evolve into a routinized relationship in which each party has expectations and confidence that the other party will perform according to the predetermined agreement. From this foundation of expectation and confidence mature channel negotiation begins. Regardless of whether negotiation is centered on a new or mature situation, each party must formulate a negotiation strategy.

Strategy Formulation

In a successful negotiation both parties must feel they have gained and are better off as a result of the agreement. However, the usual result is that one party benefits more than the other.[9] The strategic objective of any negotiation is to be the party that enjoys the maximum advantage once agreement is reached.

    The sources of channel power were identified in Chapter 4. From a strategic viewpoint power assessment is a critical aspect of negotiation. Power is de-

[9] Karrass, op. cit., p. 4.

fined as the ability of one party to influence the behavior of another party.[10] The primary purpose of power application in a channel situation is to shape the outcome of the negotiation process. This is not to imply that all agreements are power solutions. On the contrary, the best application of power may simply result from the fact that both parties are aware that it exists and they understand their relative positions. For example, if a manufacturer is aware that a given retailer has adequate market acceptance to get by without stocking the manufacturer's brand of products, attitudes and willingness to compromise will be considerably different in the negotiation procedure. In such situations the retailer need not demonstrate power to gain negotiation benefits. Thus, any negotiation is influenced by each party's real as well as perceived power.

An interesting paradox is that in selected channel situations power exists simply from the fact that one party to the negotiation has no power.[11] In a vertically administered channel situation some members may be at the mercy of the dominant organization. A large organization such as Ford Motor Company can and does dominate a vast number of organizations by virtue of its power to ensure survival by granting contracts. In these unique situations prerequisites to successful negotiation exist, but the balance is so much in favor of the dominant firm that an almost protective atmosphere surrounds the negotiation process.

Four characteristics of power are of particular interest in formulating a negotiation strategy. Before continuing with this discussion of the particular aspects of power, the reader may wish to review the more general treatment of power in Chapter 4.[12]

1 All power involved in channel negotiation is relative and is thus limited. New negotiations are particularly vulnerable to power violations. One party may perceive its power as being greater than the other party is willing to concede. The result can be a premature conclusion to negotiation simply because one party went too far or demanded too much. Although channel negotiations are not usually balanced or countervailing power situations, the relative power difference between two parties may be slim. A situation close to countervailing power is often found in merger situations. In most channel negotiations a power advantage exists and the art of framing a negotiation consists of a proper assessment of the relative balance of power.

2 Another characteristic of negotiation power is that it need not be exercised to be effective. In mature channel situations the most cohesive force preventing dysfunctional conflict is often a realization on the part of all concerned that a balance of power does exist. The mere recognition of the power potential that one firm enjoys relative to the other can expedite resolution of the process.

3 Negotiation power must be real. In many other bargaining situations, brinkmanship may be important in realizing the best possible settlement.[13] But in channel negotiations that extend beyond a single transaction, bluffing can be

---

[10] See Chapter 4, pp. 99–100.
[11] Karrass, op. cit., p. 68.
[12] See Chapter 4, pp. 99–105.
[13] Karrass, op. cit., p. 68–69.

a costly tactic. Parties to channel negotiations have every reason to believe their counterparts are acting in good faith since all will be engaged in the resulting arrangement for an indefinite time period.

4 Negotiation power can be expected to change over time. This shifting power base was noted earlier as one of the prime reasons that negotiation is a continual process in mature channels. To maintain a viable channel relationship over time, all parties must acknowledge and adapt to the power shifts inherent in the competitive system.

From the above discussion we can conclude that relative power assessment is an important aspect of channel negotiation and that the foundation of negotiation strategy is power.

NEGOTIATION OBJECTIVES

The basic objective of negotiation is to establish, maintain, or alter a channel arrangement. Specific channel negotiations are described as either transactional or operational in this section. Although this delineation is convenient for discussion purposes, it should be remembered that in practice both combine to identify a firm's domain and marketing channel strategy.

Transaction Negotiation

The most fundamental negotiation involves terms and conditions related to ownership transfer of goods and related services. From the viewpoint of channel members negotiations regarding transactions incorporate all aspects of the marketing mix. The marketing mix of each channel member represents the way a firm differentiates its competitive activities.[14] The overall marketing mix of manufacturers, wholesalers, and retailers is composed of four subcombinations: the product mix, the distribution mix, the communication mix, and the price mix. The mixes are briefly discussed and illustrated since they create negotiation interfaces among firms engaged in channel arrangements.

Product Mix Negotiation   A primary focus of all marketing activity is the assortment of products and related services offered to consumers and customers as a result of the combined efforts of all channel members. Economic foundations of channel product sorting were discussed in Chapter 2.[15] At the individual firm level, selection of the product-market target is one of the firm's primary strategic commitments. Similarly, the established product strategy is one of the fundamental forces leading to establishment of specific channel arrangements.[16]

[14] Thomas A. Staudt, Donald A. Taylor, and Donald J. Bowersox, *A Managerial Introduction to Marketing* (Englewood Cliffs, N.J.: Prentice-Hall, Inc., 1976), pp. 464–481.

[15] See Chapter 2, pp. 36–39.

[16] Donald J. Bowersox and E. Jerome McCarthy, "Strategic Development of Planned Vertical Marketing Systems," in Louis P. Bucklin (ed.), *Vertical Marketing Systems* (Glenview, Ill.: Scott, Foresman and Co., 1970), pp. 52–72.

Channel design from the manufacturer's perspective is developed in Chapter 8. Chapter 9 presents similar coverage from the retailer, wholesaler, and franchise viewpoints. As would be expected, the relative power of different institutions in various industries is a prime determinant of prevailing industry channel structures.

The primary negotiation between channel members regarding product mix is the decision to stock or not to stock a product line. In many industries specific negotiations may aim at developing customized product modifications to ease marketing or to reduce costs. Examples ranging from minor packaging to private label packing will illustrate the scope of product mix negotiations.

For many years Johnson & Johnson (J&J) has followed the practice of applying customer stockkeeping numbers to its products for major retailers at the manufacturer level of the channel. Applying the retailer's own stock identification number facilitates identification and handling of J&J's products throughout the marketing channel and improves overall inventory control. The practice provides a convenience for the retailer. Like most negotiations, however, this particular agreement is both a cost and a benefit to J&J. The benefit is a close and repetitive purchasing arrangement. The cost is the labor required to place each involved retailer's stock number on cases and commitment of specific inventory to the account on an exclusive basis.

A second example of product negotiation is contract preparation of private label or generic label merchandise by manufacturers and processors for specific retailers. As a result of negotiated agreements a manufacturer may produce an inventory under the label of a particular retailer. Once produced, such private labels have value only to the retailer involved in the negotiation. In this situation both the retailer and the manufacturer make commitments and assume risk.

Distribution Mix Negotiation One of the primary functions performed through collective effort by marketing channel members is transportation and warehousing of merchandise. Terms and conditions of physical distribution are an important part of the overall transaction process. In many cases specialists such as public warehouses and transportation companies are used by one or more members of the channel to facilitate the physical distribution process. Each arrangement of this kind within the marketing channel requires negotiation.

In recent years many innovations have been introduced to the channel in an effort to improve physical distribution efficiency. The operations established often result in less than traditional arrangements. For example, Super Value Stores' warehouse provides physical distribution support for Jewel Stores outside the Chicago metropolitan area and for A&P in the Birmingham and Milwaukee areas. The supporting logic is simply that the physical distribution functions must be performed regardless of whether Super Value is involved. This form of negotiation among traditional competitors increases efficiency which works to the benefit of all concerned.

Another example of distribution negotiation between channel members is the practice of using joint inventories to satisfy market demand. For appliances or TV sets the most effective distribution system may be one in which consolidated inventories are held at public warehouses rather than one which ships in advance to local dealers. This cooperative behavior allows all dealers to draw upon the centralized inventory with two beneficial results. First, dealers do not have to assume the risk of in-depth inventory stocking of all items in the product line since they can obtain rapid delivery of needed products. Second, the overall effectiveness of the distribution channel is improved because inventory is not shipped to dealers in anticipation of sales that may not materialize. Thus, inventory is more apt to be available at the public warehouse when needed by a specific dealer.

Beyond negotiation of particular distribution arrangements, agreements must be reached regarding such matters as point of shipment, size of order, elapsed time for delivery, freight payment responsibility, transportation consolidation arrangements, and a host of other operational matters before a marketing channel can routinize transactions. At some point during transactional negotiation these details must be discussed and agreed upon.

Communication Mix Negotiation   The communication mix consists of the advertising, promotion, and personal selling efforts of firms engaged in a channel arrangement. The communication mix is unique in that a great deal of an individual channel member's effort is directed toward influencing the behavior of other firms in the same channel. For example, a substantial portion of a manufacturer's communications may be aimed at encouraging retailers or wholesalers to participate fully in a marketing program.

In addition to the persuasive aspect, a great deal of marketing communication consists of a joint effort by retailers, wholesalers, and manufacturers to stimulate consumer purchases. The details of all such programs must be negotiated. A significant form of interorganizational joint communication is cooperative advertising programs. A cooperative advertising program may be offered wherein retailer expenditures will be matched or partially reimbursed by the manufacturer provided specific products are featured in the ads.

One of the most common forms of interorganizational communication effort is the manufacturer's cents-off coupon. The manufacturer provides consumers with coupons entitling them to discounts on specific products purchased at the retailers' stores. The coupons are usually distributed in newspaper ads or by direct mail. However, it is also common for coupons to be distributed by the retailers as part of their weekly promotional effort. When the consumer purchases the product the retailer provides the discount off the market price. The retailer is then reimbursed for the discount amount plus an agreed-to handling charge by the sponsoring manufacturer.

Some of the most complex transactional negotiations involve the joint communication efforts of a channel toward ultimate consumers of a product. In many situations such programs involve product modifications which must be accommodated through the distribution portion of the channel. For example, special promotional packages which will be marketed only for a limited period of time must be stocked and distributed to the point of sale prior to the promotional period. Following the promotion, unsold special packages must be liquidated or removed from the channel some other way.

The process of negotiating joint channel communication effort is complicated by the fact that not all promotions are limited to vertical arrangements. In certain cases two manufacturers will jointly promote their products at the retail level. Such joint promotions usually develop around products with complementary demand, such as soft drinks and snacks sold during holiday periods.

The variety of potential communication negotiations is substantial. The significant point is that all channel members have a stake in the sale of products to ultimate users. In industrial marketing the communication negotiation may center on joint personal selling efforts between manufacturers and their agents in cooperation with dealers and distributors. In consumer marketing the selling effort is often complicated by joint advertising and promotional programs. Details of all such joint efforts must be agreed to beforehand as an integral part of the communication effort of transaction negotiation.

Price Mix Negotiation   Negotiation of price is critical in arriving at a transactional agreement. Price is properly viewed as the value placed on the combination of product, distribution, and communication functions that each firm will perform in a channel arrangement. As noted earlier in this chapter negotiation is a form of cooperative behavior in which participants identify what they will do and who will get what *prior to* performance of specified marketing functions. Specification of an agreed-to transfer price places performance of marketing functions into a cost-revenue perspective.

Negotiation of price involves more than identification of transfer value. Important aspects of price negotiations are discount structures, credit limits, return allowances, and terms of payment that will prevail in the channel arrangement. A closely related matter is the negotiation of who is responsible for payment of freight and associated claims.

Price negotiations bring the total channel arrangement into focus. As would be expected, all other aspects of transactional negotiation become meaningful only within the perspective of a fully negotiated price agreement.

Operational Negotiation

Whereas transaction negotiation is aimed at arriving at an agreement to do business, operational negotiation is the process through which mature channel arrangements are maintained or modified. For purposes of discussion operational negotiation is divided into functional, performance, and performance postponement categories.

Functional Negotiation   In effect, establishment of a channel arrangement means that agreement has been reached regarding which members will perform which functions. From the beginning of operations a continuous modification of functional performance agreements can be observed. Individual firms are engaged in a constant process of functional spin-off or absorption, depending upon the relative economics and power balance of the channel.

Functional spin-off occurs when one firm transfers a function to another firm. The spin-off may or may not be desired by the receiving firm. Functional spin-off is usually chosen when a firm finds it economically advantageous to subcontract or delegate specific functions to specialist firms.[17] Two common forms of spin-off are the use of for-hire transportation or public warehousing in physical distribution operations, and manufacturers subcontracting packaging of specific products to a processor or some other firm. In both cases the assumption is that the firm accepting the spun-off function will benefit from a lower average cost curve.[18] In reality, however, often the firm receiving the spun-off function takes on the added work only because it fears repercussions if it does not cooperate. Thus, a manufacturer may agree to extend credit terms or perform a specific packaging function if the alternative is losing the retailer's business.

In many ways functional absorption is the opposite of spin-off. It is true that one firm must absorb a function for another firm to be able to spin it off. However, situations may develop wherein a firm desires to take over performance of a function when the firm currently performing the function does not want to alter the existing situation. The firm wishing to absorb a function may enjoy a lower average cost curve or may be seeking greater control over the marketing situation. A prime example of functional absorption is shipment of appliances direct to dealers from manufacturers' warehouses. In this situation the wholesale distributor no longer performs the traditional physical distribution function. Appliances are transported direct to dealers with the distributor performing sales but not physical distribution functions. The incentive for establishing such programs is reduced per-unit physical distribution cost for all parties concerned. However, the scope of distributor function and control is reduced despite the fact that the total channel is rendered more efficient by eliminating duplicate functions.

Functional negotiation is critical to mature channel situations. From time to time a channel must be reviewed and may need to adjust its functional assignments in order to remain effective. The prime justification for functional realignment is improved efficiency, but both functional spin-off and absorption may also result from disproportionate countervailing power.

Performance Negotiation   Performance negotiation deals with the nature of day-to-day operations in a mature channel arrangement. Once a channel has been established and functional assignments agreed to, many situations will arise that require clarification regarding operational performance. An area of constant operational adjustment is service and warranty of products. In the au-

---

[17] Bruce Mallen, "Functional Spin-Off: A Key to Anticipating Change in Distribution Structure," *Journal of Marketing* (July 1973), pp. 18–25; and George J. Stigler, "The Division of Labor Is Limited by the Extent of the Market," *The Journal of Political Economy* (June 1951), pp. 185–193.

[18] Stigler, op. cit., p. 187.

tomobile industry, for example, terms of reimbursement for dealer warranty service have changed several times in recent years. In certain situations, such as some franchise operations, performance agreements exist regarding purchase of supplies and materials. However, from time to time such agreements may require renegotiation due to shortages or lower local prices.

The range of potential performance negotiations within a mature channel is unlimited. For the most part adjustments are minor and participants do not view their revised agreements as negotiations. However, the importance of a channel mechanism to accomplish performance negotiation cannot be overemphasized. Most legal disputes within mature channels originate with what initially appeared to be a minor operational adjustment.

Performance Postponement Negotiation   The concept of postponement has received considerable attention in recent marketing literature.[19] Over the past few years negotiating postponement into channel arrangements has gained wider managerial acceptance.[20]

In traditional marketing emphasis has been placed on movement of products in anticipation of future transactions. Anticipatory action is characteristic of all aspects of manufacturing, wholesaling, and retailing. Generally, products are produced, transported, stored, handled, bought, and sold several times before arriving at a location where they are offered for final sale.

Postponement is a risk-reducing device. To the extent that agreements can be negotiated which postpone final manufacturing or physical distribution of a product until final customer commitment is obtained, anticipatory action is reduced, resulting in little or no risk of error.

The attributes of postponement may be incorporated into a logistical system on the basis of *form* and/or *time*. Form postponement consists of holding the final manufacturing, assembly, or packaging until customer preference is identified. The classic example is mixing paints to customer specification at retail stores. Time postponement consists of delaying product movement until customer orders are received. Sears' new program of direct delivery of appliances from regional distribution centers to consumers rather than stocking inventory at retail stores is an example of time postponement.

Introduction of postponement into a marketing channel involves a special type of innovation. In essence, postponement negotiation is an agreement to centralize operations which may or may not involve functional realignment.

Negotiation—Conclusion

The process of "agreeing to do business" means that channel members must negotiate all aspects of a transaction before performing as an interorganizational

[19] Wroe Alderson, "Marketing Efficiency and the Principle of Postponement," *Cost and Profit Outlook* (September 1950); and Louis P. Bucklin, "Postponement, Speculation, and the Structure of Distribution Channels," *Journal of Marketing Research* (February 1965), pp. 26–31.

[20] Donald J. Bowersox, "The Need for Innovative Distribution Management," *Distribution Worldwide* (December 1977), pp. 27–30.

unit. The extent of pretransaction negotiation will vary between new and mature channel situations. The nature of the channel arrangement will also influence the nature and magnitude of transaction negotiation. Regardless, the focus of negotiation will be the activities that constitute combined marketing efforts of all channel members. Thus, we illustrated specific aspects of transaction negotiations by referring to the marketing mix. Although the examples were not exhaustive or comprehensive, they are typical of the many facets of transactional negotiation.

Operational negotiation deals with maintaining or modifying existing arrangements. Three types of operational negotiation were discussed: functional, performance, and performance postponement. Although the categories may overlap, each is unique and may be critical to maintaining channel efficiency and effectiveness.

The objective of channel negotiation is to achieve profitable working arrangements. Although specific channel negotiations were discussed as either transactional or operational, we stressed that in practice all forms of negotiation combine to identify a firm's domain and marketing channel strategy.

SUMMARY

In this chapter we have dealt with the scope and strategy of interorganizational negotiation. Negotiation in a channel context was defined as *the management process of reaching agreement regarding commitment to roles and rewards in joint marketing channel performance*. Negotiation was identified as a form of cooperative behavior in which participants agree in advance on efforts and rewards.

Negotiation is the process by which channel structure and function is identified. All firms have the right to initiate negotiations as well as the right not to negotiate. Thus, it is important to keep in mind that participation in initial negotiation is a form of self-resolution for all firms involved. Once agreement has been reached, future negotiations can become clouded by the performance track record.

From a managerial perspective, channel negotiations can be viewed as new or mature. The reason for new negotiations is to seek effective channel arrangements. Mature channel negotiations result from (1) a changing balance of power, (2) conflict resolution, and/or (3) termination settlements.

Considerable attention was directed to the strategy of negotiation. Prerequisites for negotiation are (1) alternatives, (2) procedures, (3) reward potential, and (4) willingness to commit. The capability to direct negotiation strategy is related to a firm's relative power position. Power was defined as the ability of one party to influence the behavior of another party.

The basic goal of channel negotiation is to establish, maintain, or alter a channel arrangement. Depending upon the situation, specific negotiations may be focused on transactional or operational matters. In total, all forms of negotiation combine to identify a firm's domain and marketing channel strategy.

QUESTIONS

1 What is interorganizational negotiation? Why is it important to channel management?
2 What are the distinguishing characteristics of new channel negotiations?
3 What are the primary similarities and differences among the three types of mature channel negotiations?
4 What are the four characteristics necessary for channel negotiations to be successful? Explain in your own words why each is necessary.
5 Compare and contrast transaction and operational negotiations.
6 What are the four types of transaction negotiations? Develop examples other than those described in the text.
7 Alpha Dog Food Company, a large regional producer of dry dog food, is considering a special promotion which consists of a 50¢ off coupon for consumers who purchase a six-pack of canned dog food introduced especially for the promotional period. Describe the types of channel negotiations necessary before the promotion can be introduced to consumers.
8 What is functional spin-off? How does it differ from functional absorption? Which, do you suppose, has greater potential for overt conflict?
9 Recently, automobile manufacturers have been involved in a number of major product recalls to repair defects or safety hazards resulting from faulty design. What types of channel negotiations do you think would arise as a result of these recall activities?
10 Describe the process of performance postponement. Why is it necessary to negotiate postponement activities?

CASE 6-1: Happy Grove Dairy

INTRODUCTION

Reflecting on the call he received last Friday from Joe Martin, president of Good's Supermarket, Jack Rowland, president of Happy Grove Dairy, realized he should not have been surprised. But he was.

His secretary informed him that Joe was on the line just as Jack was starting his daily inspection trip through the milk processing plant. Jack picked up the phone and had the following conversation:

Joe: Good morning, Jack—hope you've been well.

Jack: Can't complain too much, Joe. What's happening?

Joe: Well, Jack, all our retailers were together for the monthly meeting yesterday. Our new member from Stockville once again got on the subject of milk cost. Seems he was buying milk from Farmer's Cooperative Dairy at a price much less than ours from Happy Grove. He's sure putting pressure on our gang to shift to Farmer's.

Jack: Joe, we've been over this before . . .

Joe: I know, Jack, but it looks like I can't keep the troops happy with talk. Despite the fact that we can only get gallons and half-gallons and not the rest of the line from Farmer's, some of our store owners feel we should go for the lower price. I can't . . .

Jack: I'm sorry to interrupt, Joe, but you know we sell to you now for $1.49 a gallon and our costs are almost $1.48. You can't squeeze blood out of a turnip. What the hell is Farmer's offering now?

Joe: Well, I'll tell you because we've been together a long time. Farmer's is offering $1.45 per gallon as well as a price 3¢ lower than yours on half-gallons. Looks like they've got you coming and going on price. The only difference is that they plan to deliver by semivan twice a week to each store.

Jack: Well, Joe, even if you can live with twice a week delivery, how about specials and weekend deliveries? We've been over all this before. Full distribution service is worth something.

Joe: Jack, I hope we can work it out, but I need facts and a presentation for our store owners. They're ready to switch to Farmer's if Happy Grove can't improve over our present deal. We would like you to come over next Thursday and let us know what you can do. As much as I hate to say it, Jack, things don't look too good. You had better take a good look at every angle and get close to Farmer's offer or it will be out of my hands.

Jack: I'll do the best I can. What time Thursday?

Joe: How's 9:00 A.M. at our board room?

Jack: Fine. See you then, Joe.

BACKGROUND

Happy Grove Dairy was founded in 1936 by the combining of three smaller dairy operations. Two retail store groups split off their farms and milk processing plants and merged with a local milk wholesaler and home delivery operator who also operated farms and dairy herds. The new organization became known as Happy Grove Dairy and was operated by Allen Rowland, Jack's father. The operation of Happy Grove consisted of the dairy farms plus a retail home delivery distribution system that serviced a medium-sized metropolitan area in northeastern Michigan. In addition to home delivery Happy Grove operated a wholesale delivery route to a small number of retail stores. The two retail groups that were partial owners of Happy Grove operated thirty stores. In addition, approximately seventy-five other retailers were served on a daily basis. The typical wholesale delivery consisted of stocking the milk cooler each day with a full line of dairy products. During the early years wholesale delivery was on a daily basis, six days a week, while home delivery was on an every-other-day basis.

Business was good for Happy Grove from its inception. Despite the constraints of World War II, Happy Grove continued to grow and was profitable every year of its operation until 1950 when Allen Rowland retired and turned the operation over to his son, Jack. By 1950 several major changes had taken place in Happy Grove. The most significant are listed below:

In 1946 the dairy farms were sold to raise cash to buy out the two retail groups that helped form Happy Grove. This action was justified by two events. First, dairy ingredients could be purchased on the open market as cheap or cheaper than produced on Happy Grove's own farms. Second, the fact that Happy Grove was partially owned by two retailers created some conflict with other retail stores who felt they were helping their competition if they purchased from Happy Grove. After the farm sale and repurchase of the original stock of the two retailers who participated in founding Happy Grove, the dairy became wholly owned by the Rowland family.

By 1948 it became clear that the trend in shopping was toward supermarkets. Beginning in 1946 home delivery customers rapidly began to discontinue Happy Grove in favor of buying milk products at a lower price from retail stores. Thus, the nature of Happy Grove's volume was rapidly shifting from retail to wholesale. In 1950 Happy Grove's business was 80 percent wholesale and 20 percent retail. In 1940 the split had been 70 percent retail and 30 percent wholesale.

By 1950 the concentration of Happy Grove's wholesale business had shifted from a number of individual stores to several different groups of supermarkets. This change of customer pattern reflected the normal growth of supermarket chains throughout the United States.

Happy Grove's business continued to grow at a profitable rate during the 1950s and until the mid-1960s. In 1965 the dairy had both record sales and profits. The management was very proud of the 1965 figures since sales topped $10 million for the first time and profits just exceeded $1 million.

By 1965 the retail portion of Happy Grove's business had been completely phased out. The dairy became fully wholesale, serving 637 individual retail stores. Although Happy Grove had 637 retail delivery shops, the customer count was somewhat lower because of chains and cooperative groups. Table 1 provides the distribution of Happy Grove's 1965 business. Jack Rowland was not happy with the fact that 14 percent of his customer's stores accounted for 53 percent of his total milk volume.

From 1966 to 1978 Happy Grove Dairy began to feel the pressure of "bigness" in both retail and dairy operations. At the wholesale level the dairy business became more and more concentrated as national dairies such as Sealtest and Borden's purchased a great many local dairies. In addition, farmer cooperatives became a major force in the wholesale dairy business. These cooperatives had the main objective of supporting farm level prices. As such, they were difficult to compete with on a price basis.

At the retail level a great many changes occurred during the period from 1966 to 1978. Most large regional supermarket chains went extensively into private label milk. More and more small stores were forced out of business or, if their size was sufficient, they became affiliated with cooperative buying groups. In addition, small stores were being replaced by the rapidly growing number of convenience stores. The convenience store concept consisted of limited-line multiple outlets owned and operated like a minisupermarket chain.

The combined changes over the 12-year period had a significant impact on Happy Grove operations. Although volume was maintained at around the $10 to $12 million range, aftertax profits dropped to an average of $300,000 per year. The period was characterized by constant changes in business as customers were either gained from or lost to competition. During this period, Happy Grove lost its two largest customers, Smudt's Supermarkets and Kroger. Both instituted private label milk programs. The distribution of Happy Grove's business on January 1, 1978, is illustrated in Table 2.

As Table 2 shows, Happy Grove's total retail count had dropped by over 200 stores. In terms of distribution, 28 percent of the large customer stores accounted for 77 percent of total milk volume. What is perhaps even more significant is the fact that one customer, Good's Supermarkets, provided 28 percent of Happy Grove's total dairy volume.

In 1977 dairy operations had a gross volume of $11.2 million and profits were $265,000, or 2.4 percent of sales. The nature of operation was for the most

Table 1   Happy Grove Dairy 1965 Sales Distribution

Customer	Stores	Percent total business
Smudt's Supermarkets	22	16
Kroger Supermarkets	10	12
Good's Supermarkets	15	10
Jones Markets	12	8
Ready Convenience Stores	31	7
All others	547	47
Totals	637	100

Table 2   Happy Grove Dairy 1978 Sales Distribution

Customer	Stores	Percent total business
Good's Supermarkets	38	28
Jones Markets	20	18
Ready Convenience Stores	50	16
ABC Convenience Stores	16	15
All Others	307	23
Totals	431	100

part to deliver direct to retail stores on an every-other-day basis. With few exceptions dairy products were delivered to a back room storage area. Retail stocking was the responsibility of retail store personnel. However, Happy Grove did maintain a detail sales force to ensure that retail store managers in larger stores displayed their product properly in the dairy cases. A significant problem Happy Grove experienced in the late 1970s was a sharp increase in accounts receivable. On January 1, 1978, overall accounts receivable amounted to $589,916 compared to a total of $319,400 on January 1, 1977. For the most part the increase of $270,516 was concentrated in large accounts who generally paid on the 1st and 15th of each month regardless of volume purchases.

THE GOOD'S SUPERMARKETS NEGOTIATION

In review of the Good's situation, Jack Rowland was well aware that 28 percent of Happy Grove's total milk volume was sold to the thirty-eight member stores of the retail cooperative. Happy Grove's specific volume to Good's stores in 1977 was $3.136 million. The total sales consisted of a full line of dairy products. However, the majority of the volume was in one-gallon and half-gallon cartons of various milk products.

As a standard practice Happy Grove delivered milk to thirty stores on an every-other-day basis. The remaining stores were larger, and delivery was required on a daily basis. While Happy Grove felt such frequent delivery constituted outstanding customer service, the managers of Good's Supermarkets felt the frequency of delivery created unnecessary work for store personnel. However, all Good's managers were aware of the special shipments and weekend deliveries provided by Happy Grove. Storage capacity was adequate at each store to handle larger milk shipments. However, Happy Grove trucks were not sufficiently large to handle such shipment sizes. Despite the difference of opinion regarding desired frequency and size of shipment, all agreed that Happy Grove's current practice resulted in a consistently fresh supply of all dairy products.

In terms of Happy Grove's accounts receivable balance, Good's account represented 50 percent of all accounts outstanding, or just under $300,000. This year-end balance was close to Good's average outstanding accounts receivable total over the year. However, the balance had not changed out of

Table 3   Happy Grove Dairy Cost and Selling Price to Good's Supermarkets

	Total processing	Ingredients	Total dock	Delivery	Sales	Total	Price
Gallons	$.361	$.913	$1.274	$.163	$.036	$1.473	$1.49
Half-gallons	$.175	$.456	$ .631	$.081	$.018	$ .730	$ .75

proportion to Good's purchases over the past few years. Jack figured it cost Happy Grove approximately $30,000 per year to finance Good's accounts receivable.

Because of purchase volume Good's stores were buying at the lowest delivered price offered by Happy Grove Dairies. Table 3 provides Happy Grove's cost and selling price to Good's.

As Jack reviewed the figures, it was clear that Happy Grove had little if any margin to offer Good's in the form of a straight price reduction. Based upon Joe's call, he was aware that Farmer's Cooperative was offering Good's a price of $1.45 per gallon and $.72 per half-gallon. Jack was sure that Joe was not bluffing regarding Farmer's offer. Jack and Joe had done business for a number of years without a formal contract. The relationship had always been on a good and fair basis.

As Jack planned for the Thursday meeting, he was well aware he couldn't meet Farmer's prices if Happy Grove continued to perform all services in the current manner. He reviewed the deal being offered by Farmer's Cooperative Dairy and tried to appraise his alternatives and the relative power of Happy Grove's negotiating position.

CASE 6-1: QUESTIONS

1   What are the specifics of Farmer's deal? How does it compare to Happy Grove's programming besides being lower in price?
2   What options does Jack have to formulate a new deal for Good's?
3   Which plan would you recommend that Jack offer and why?
4   What negotiating strategy would you recommend that Jack follow in presenting the plan to counteract Farmer's Cooperative?

CASE 6-2: Kramer Company

Feldon Kramer, founder, owner, and president of Kramer Company, was disturbed by the latest report from Ernie Roberts, his manager of auto accessory sales: "One more instance of slow delivery to the West Coast would wreck the distribution network we've established there, and news of trouble on the West Coast would spread across the country and create customer resistance in other important market areas," claimed Ernie Roberts.

The Kramer Company is a small Detroit firm organized as a design job shop. Kramer handles electronic design problems for several smaller manufacturers supplying the auto industry and is also involved in complex engineering projects through subcontracts with other design job shops.

While working on an automobile accessory project in 1974, Fel Kramer observed that the two fastest growing accessory items were headrests and in-car stereo systems. In his spare time Kramer developed a stereo headrest which he regarded as a "perfect marriage" of the two accessory items.

Since the company's past experience was as a supplier of engineering services the marketing of a tangible product caused considerable change and trouble for the company. At first Kramer tried to sell his stereo headrest to automobile manufacturers, and then to their suppliers. When he received unfavorable responses in the original equipment market, he explored the automotive aftermarket. He found that many headrests and stereo systems were *not* sold by the car dealer but were purchased by the car owner *after* the car left the dealer's hands.

Kramer established a separate department to sell his stereo headrest to the auto accessory market. Arrangements were made for a Pennsylvania electronics firm, Penntron Products Company, to manufacture the stereo unit and to ship the product directly to distributor or dealer customers in the accessory market. Ernie Roberts, formerly a manufacturer representative in the auto electronics market, was hired as manager of the new department. He felt his principal concern was rapid promotion of sales of the new product and he quickly developed a network of manufacturer representatives which covered the country.

Even before launching the sales campaign in early September 1975, Fel Kramer spent over $26,000 promoting the stereo headrest. (As a small service business, Kramer Company found that almost all its operating expenses were out of pocket. Thus the expenditures for stereo promotion put a pinch on the firm's working capital.) Kramer authorized another $20,000 for promotion of the product in the last 4 months of 1975. The break-even figure for the project was only 1,500 per month, and it was felt that sales of 2,000 units per month were readily attainable in a period of 3 months. Sales were expected to increase at the rate of 500 units a month through the first 4 months of promotion, and then to climb more slowly until spring when displays at regional accessory shows would push the monthly sales to over 3,000 units per month.

Penntron stated that it could produce at least 300 units per week in September, 500 units per week by November, and 1,000 per week by January of 1975. On the basis of these production estimates the Kramer Company issued a purchase order of 600 units for September, 1,200 for October, 2,000 for November, and 2,000 for December. Shipments were to be made either directly to customers or to a specified warehouse in the Detroit area.

The order handling process, as Ernie Roberts saw it, should be as uncomplicated as possible. The manufacturer representatives (MRs) took the order from a distributor or dealer customer and sent the order to Kramer in Detroit.

Kramer Company would check the customer's credit and, if credit was approved, would telephone shipping instructions to Penntron Products. Documents followed by mail. Kramer handled billing and collection. It was expected that a small stock of stereo headrest parts would build up in a Detroit warehouse but could be managed easily. Since orders came into the Kramer office first, Roberts could either ship from the Detroit location or advise Penntron to make shipment. The fact that only one model of the product was being offered simplified distribution.

The sales campaign began in early September. In the Los Angeles and Detroit areas response was immediate and warm. By the middle of the month orders for 720 units had been received and transmitted to Penntron Products. Ernie Roberts immediately asked for a change in the production schedule and was assured by Penntron that they would manufacture 1,200 units in September. To play safe, Ernie Roberts contacted the Kramer MRs and advised them: "Although the auto accessory market expects delivery in 10 to 14 days, please remind your customers that we are just going into production of a new item and ask them to be understanding if our first shipments don't arrive within 2 weeks. However, you may rest assured that this is only a *temporary* situation and that Kramer's deliveries will be in keeping with industry practices after we overcome start-up problems."

Total orders for September (1,152 units) were considerably in excess of the forecast of 500. October orders were 1,584 units and, again, considerably in excess of the 1,000 units forecast. Other developments in October were not as pleasant. It was the middle of October before any shipments were made by Penntron to the Kramer customers and by the end of October only 576 units had been shipped against the 2,736 units ordered. Fel Kramer, elated by the sales performance, was concerned about the back-order situation and about working capital. He applied as much pressure as he could to Penntron and placed orders for 1,000 units to be shipped to Detroit as soon as customer orders had been satisfied. Although he had spent over $41,000 on promotion through October, he had not yet received his first payment from his customers. (The credit terms of the industry were 2 percent discount with payments made before the tenth day of the following month; payment to be made without discount by the end of the month following delivery.)

November orders of 1,872 were slightly in excess of October. However, the backlog of orders at Penntron increased to 2,304 units and dissatisfaction arose among both customers and MRs. Cancellations of back orders were received on November 10 for 432 units. Shortly after, manufacturer representatives in Los Angeles and San Francisco threatened to drop the line. Only a rapid visit to the West Coast by Ernie Roberts prevented the loss of the representatives and other back orders.

Fel Kramer looked upon December with mixed emotions. December orders dropped to 1,296 units, but Penntron had reduced back orders to 720 units. Tables 1 and 2 summarize customer order data from September–December, 1975. Renewed market interest arose for the stereo headrest but dealer

Table 1 Customer Order Data
(By Time Period)

	Units ordered	Units shipped	Units on back order
September 1975	1,152	—	1,152
October 1975	1,584*	576	2,160
November 1975	1,872	1,496†	2,304
December 1975	1,296	2,880	720
Totals	5,904	4,952	—

* Does not include the 996 units ordered by Kramer for delivery to Detroit.
† In addition to these shipments, orders for 432 units were canceled.

customers were demanding that the product be made available in a variety of colors—red, white, brown, blue, green, and silver, in addition to black. Continued sales growth appeared to hinge upon this product adjustment. Inquiries were arriving from catalog wholesalers and retail chain operations. They expressed an interest in private label possibilities, particularly if the product were

Table 2 Customer Order Data, September–December 1975
(By Areas or Origin)

Area	Number of orders	Average time lapse in days (between order placement and delivery)
West Coast		
Los Angeles	89*	45.5
San Francisco	66*	43.5
Midwest		
Detroit–Toledo	83*	20.5
Cleveland	28*	17.5
Chicago	19	16.0
Pittsburgh	17	16.5
East Coast		
Philadelphia	19	10.5
New York City	8	12.5
Baltimore	5	13.5
Southwest		
Phoenix	13*	59.5
Dallas	6	38.5
Gulf Coast		
Houston	19	29.5
Southeast		
Miami	4†	—
Total	366	—

* Some orders from customers in these areas are still on back order.
† No order from Miami has been filled as of December 31, 1975. Orders on file were dated December 14 and 15.

offered in a broad range of colors. Frequently Kramer questioned keeping the project. Because of the favorable market response to the product and his heavy financial involvement, he decided to "ride with the project" if he could iron out the problems of supply by April 1976.

Fel Kramer and Ernie Roberts met frequently in early January to define their problems and determine what alternatives existed. They concluded that (1) Penntron Products Company would not be an adequate supply source since it seemed capable of manufacturing only 2,000 to 3,000 units per month and had not proved highly reliable, (2) the addition of a warehouse facility had to be considered for the operation, and (3) the order processing needed examination. Kramer accepted the assignments of finding new or additional sources of supply and of examining warehouse facilities. Roberts took on the assignment of analyzing the ordering system.

A NEW SUPPLY SOURCE

Finding another manufacturer capable of and interested in making the stereo headrest turned out to be a delightfully easy task for Fel Kramer. In the first week he had discussions with seven firms and settled on Olympian Auto Products as the best prospect. Although Penntron Products had experience in electronics, their lack of experience in headrest manufacturing had caused problems. On the other hand, Olympian manufactured headrests for the three major U.S. car makers and convinced Fel Kramer that it would have no trouble incorporating stereo units into the headrests.

Two other factors made Olympian an appealing source of supply for Kramer. First, Olympian was located in the Detroit area and, therefore, would be much easier to contact than Penntron. Second, most of their production was directed to the major auto producers. Olympian had expressed interest in selling the stereo headrests to the "Big Three" auto producers as optional equipment. Fel Kramer felt that Olympian would provide sales assistance in the next 2 years as well as a reliable supply in the near future.

Olympian would begin to manufacture the stereo headrest units in early April. Once set up for production, Olympian could manufacture as many as 3,000 units per week. Each shift was capable of producing 200 units, and Olympian was willing to use as many as three shifts and 5 working days per week to meet Kramer demands. The stereo headrest could be run on parallel production lines with the other headrest products made by Olympian.

Olympian asked that purchase orders be given at least 6 weeks ahead of expected deliveries. Olympian would allow cutbacks in scheduled production as long as the cutback notice was received at least 2 weeks ahead of a scheduled production run.

As a supplier to the major auto companies, Olympian was accustomed to releasing shipments against a blanket purchase order. To smooth out the production load and to maintain customer satisfaction, Olympian carried substantial quantities of parts in its own warehouse. Storage space at Olympian was in excess of 38,000 square feet and it was estimated that seldom was more than 60

Table 3   Cost Data Estimates* for Kramer Stereo Headrests by Penntron Products

Selling price per unit (FOB, factory)†	$15.80
Less factory selling price to Kramer	8.10
Gross Margin	$ 7.70
Less compensation for manufacturer representatives	2.40
Contribution to overhead/profit	$ 5.30

Expenses:		
Sales salaries	$18,000	
Travel and entertainment (for sales manager)	24,000	
Additional office salaries (includes fringe expenses)	9,000	
Special office supplies	180	
Brochures, mailers, catalogs, price sheets	2,800	
Sales kit (for MRs)	5,600	
Dealer demonstrator units	8,300	
National advertising	9,600	
Cooperative advertising	13,000	
Telephone expenses	1,600‡	
Mail and miscellaneous	1,400	
	$95,480	

* Based on estimates for the year as developed in August 1975.

† Transportation of units to Kramer warehouse will cost 0.38 per unit from Penntron. (These are approximate charges. Actual amounts will vary with number of units in shipments.)

‡ About 90% of $784 expense was incurred by telephone calls to Penntron offices, August–December 1975.

percent of the storage space occupied. Olympian was willing to carry some stereo headrest units in the warehouse as a buffer for Kramer and its own production scheduling requirements.

Olympian was also willing to ship orders of forty-eight units or more directly to Kramer customers out of their warehouse operation. The master carton was to carry six stereo units of the same color. Olympian agreed to produce any of the seven colors in multiples of six. However, Olympian's production cost would be about 10 percent higher than Penntron's due to the number of colors to be handled. Therefore, the price to Kramer would be higher. Tables 3 and 4 present cost data from Penntron and Olympian.

The Kramer sales forecast for 1976 was for 37,500 units. Orders in early 1976 were expected at around the 2,000 unit per month level with steady increases starting in the spring (Table 5). Black and red were expected to be the

Table 4   Cost Data Estimates for Stereo Headrest Supplied by Olympian

Selling price per unit (FOB factory)*	$15.80
Less: Factory selling price to gross margin	9.20
Less: Compensation for manufacturer's representatives	2.40
Contribution to overhead/profit	$ 4.20

* Transportation of units to warehouse will cost 0.12 per unit from Olympian.

Table 5   Sales Forecast for Stereo Headrests by Units

Models by color	January	February	March	April	May	June	July	August	September	October	November	December	Totals
Black	1,800	2,000	2,200	600	740	850	880	1,000	1,100	1,200	1,320	1,440	15,130
Red	*	*	*	780	900	1,000	1,000	1,100	1,200	1,220	1,340	1,440	9,980
White	*	*	*	240	270	300	310	340	370	400	440	480	3,150
Blue	*	*	*	200	210	240	260	280	300	330	360	390	2,570
Green	*	*	*	200	200	220	230	250	270	310	340	370	2,890
Silver	*	*	*	190	190	200	220	230	240	280	310	350	2,210
Brown	*	*	*	190	190	190	200	200	220	260	290	330	2,070
Totals	1,800	2,000	2,200	2,400	2,700	3,000	3,100	3,400	3,700	4,000	4,400	4,800	37,500

* Not available for shipment in this period.

183

most popular colors, each accounting for 30 percent of the units ordered. Dealer surveys indicated that white, the next most popular color, would account for approximately 10 percent of the units ordered. Blue, green, silver, and brown were expected to have about equal popularity, accounting for 7 to 8 percent of total units each. Since color units would be supplied solely by Olympian, Kramer would be unable to take orders for anything except black before the middle of March.

Kramer believed that Olympian might be persuaded to maintain at least a week's supply of black and red models if asked to do so, particularly if production runs could be for a month's supply. However, he feared that Olympian would not stock the other color models in quantities large enough to fill all orders between production runs.

WAREHOUSE FACILITIES

Ernie Roberts, searching for low-cost warehouse facilities near his offices, found four buildings that met these qualifications (Table 6). He also looked at public warehouses but discounted them as inappropriate. He believed Kramer Company should have close control over shipment and handling of the electronic headrest units. He feared public warehouses lacked such control.

The headrests were packaged in individual cartons which in turn were boxed in a master carton of six. The master carton was $19 \times 23 \times 30$ inches and weighed thirty pounds. Roberts felt that while only one person would be re-

Table 6   Data on the Facilities under Consideration as Warehouses

	A	B	C	D
Construction type	Brick, concrete block	Concrete block	Brick	Brick
Date of construction	1967	1971	1964	1958
Original intended use	Light manufacturing	Pattern work shop	Light manufacturing	Light manufacturing
Loading/unloading facilities	Raised dock	Raised dock	Raised dock	Ground level dock
Floor dimensions of storage areas	36×44	32×38	36×46	22×34
Shipping door (width and height)	16×12	12×10	12×10	10×10
Ceiling height	12	12	12	10

Restrooms, telephone, heat, and small office facilities are at each location. Telephone charges at any of the locations would be approximately $8.50 per month. All require one-year leasing agreements.

Lease conditions:

A—$250 per month, includes heat and water; $500 deposit (forfeit if lease broken); insurance, $57 per year.

B—$150 per month, utilities not included; $450 deposit (forfeit if lease broken); heat averages $45 per month; water, $5 per month; insurance, $50.50 per year.

C—$200 per month, utilities not included; $600 deposit (forfeit if lease broken); heat averages $52 per month; water, $5 per month; insurance, $37 per year.

D—$125 per month, utilities not included; $250 deposit (forfeit if lease broken); heat averages $55 per month; water averages $5 per month; insurance, $61 per year.

quired for the warehousing operation, the activities of the warehouse were so critical to the Kramer sales program that someone highly reliable and intelligent was necessary. This meant the cost of the one-person warehouse force would probably range from $500 to $700 a month for wages plus 25 percent for payroll tax and fringe benefit expenses. Roberts felt that the company should be willing to accept a $10,000 total yearly payroll for a modest warehousing operation.

Roberts visualized that the warehouse operation would handle only sealed master cartons of six. No inspection of the units would be performed unless the exterior of the master carton suggested hidden damage. Principal functions in the warehouse would be to:

1   Receive shipments from Penntron or Olympian.
2   Stack shipments according to color models.
3   Do whatever was required to protect the units from damage and theft.
4   Maintain accurate records of inventory stocks.
5   Label the cartons and prepare them for shipment.
6   Obtain the fastest, most reliable transportation to the customer.
7   Maintain transportation cost and reliability records on both incoming and outgoing shipments.

While waiting for Olympian to start production, Kramer planned to build up stocks of units manufactured by Penntron. As soon as Olympian production permitted, Kramer would phase out Penntron as a source of supply. Customer relations made it imperative that Kramer be able to supply its customers with at least the black model while Olympian geared up for production.

By the middle of January Fel Kramer and Ernie Roberts felt that the distribution program for 1976 was beginning to take shape. Kramer believed that Olympian would be able to handle most of the customer orders on a drop shipment basis. Ernie Roberts still pushed for a Kramer Company distribution center that would prevent the possibility of slow delivery and customer order cancellations. Fel Kramer, who claimed he now had about $60,000 of his money at stake in the stereo headrests, was willing but wanted the warehouse investment minimized. He felt, however, that Kramer should have a well-conceived inventory program which would specify the stocking levels needed throughout 1976. If he knew what the inventory requirements would be for 1976, Kramer said he could make a better choice of low-cost warehousing. It was Fel Kramer's opinion, however, that the warehouse facility alone would not ensure satisfactory customer service.

THE MEETING WITH OLYMPIAN

With this background Fel Kramer was ready to negotiate a final contract with Olympian. Although Olympian's strengths were obvious, several details remained to be finalized: the number of colors to be produced, Olympian's price to Kramer, and inventory warehousing responsibility.

CASE 6-2: QUESTIONS

1   Assess the overall negotiating strength of both Kramer and Olympian.
2   If you were Kramer, what negotiating strategy would you employ?
3   If you were Kramer, what is the least favorable settlement to which you would agree?
4   What further knowledge about Olympian would you desire in order to assess more completely the relative negotiating positions of the two firms?

Chapter 7

Channel Structure and Design

Effective and efficient market performance is directly related to the structure of the distribution channel. Channel structure differs based upon functional assignments and responsibilities of member firms. Some intermediaries perform a single marketing function such as transportation or storage while others perform multiple functions. Channel structure affects (1) control over functional performance, (2) speed of product delivery and communications, and (3) operational cost.[1] The most desirable channel relationship for any member is one that achieves corporate and marketing objectives in terms of the firm's operating philosophy, identifiable strengths and weaknesses, and in cooperation with available channel partners.

This chapter is the first in a series of four devoted to channel structure design and performance evaluation. In this chapter basic design considerations are presented in a way that should be useful to any managerial team concerned with channel development or redesign. Chapter 8 deals specifically with design considerations from the manufacturer's viewpoint. Chapter 9 presents parallel

---

[1] Louis W. Stern, "Channel Control and Interorganization Management," in Peter D. Bennett (ed.) *Marketing and Economic Development* (Chicago: American Marketing Association, 1965), pp. 655–665.

coverage from the perspective of retailers, wholesalers, and firms engaged in franchise agreements. Chapter 10 is devoted to performance measurement.

Chapter 7 provides a framework to guide the channel design process. In the first section of the chapter the difference between channel evolution and planning is described. While historical data suggest a traditional failure to plan channel arrangements, contemporary competitive pressures have placed greater emphasis on channel planning. The second section identifies the critical role of customer orientation and considers the design process as it applies to sale of consumer products, industrial products, and services. The third section develops the concept of structural separation. The theory supporting separation in structural design is that unique treatment of transaction-related and physical distribution-related functions offers the potential for greater specialization. The fourth section treats transaction-related functions and the fifth section explores physical distribution functions in greater depth. The chapter concludes with a managerial model to guide channel design. The model presented is developed further in Chapters 8 and 9.

CHANNEL EVOLUTION OR DESIGN

As a starting point it is useful to appraise the extent to which channels traditionally have been designed. Although the literature commonly reflects a design orientation, considerable evidence exists to support the view that the majority of channels are not designed but evolve over time.[2] A recent study of eighteen manufacturers supports this conclusion. Typical responses to the question, "How was your current channel structure determined?" were:[3]

"This channel has been in use for as long as our product has been distributed nationally."

"Our distribution channels have never changed at least as far as I'm aware of."

"Hit and miss . . . trial and error. It is the kind of thing that happened over time."

"Do not know for sure but the channel we are using now is the one that we have always used. . . ."

"The current channel has evolved over time."

"Changes in physical distribution have been in response to competition."

"The company's major channel has been using company-owned retail outlets and this policy was adopted many years ago."

"There was a time when every salesman had a warehouse. We had to show sales how we could reduce total costs and provide the desired service without the facility."

[2] Phillip McVey, "Are Channels of Distribution What the Textbooks Say," *Journal of Marketing* (January 1960), pp. 61–65.

[3] Douglas M. Lambert, *The Distribution Channel Decision,* (New York: National Association of Accountants; and Hamilton, Ontario: The Society of Management Accountants of Canada, 1978), pp. 56–59.

"Basically when we started some 70 years ago we chose to sell through the five-and-dime stores. We have never totally moved away from being a direct house. How was it selected? It started that way and I think that it kind of happened. I think that we might be victims of one of those situations where business has run us and maybe we didn't run it."

Even though current practice reveals a lack of planning in channel design, benefits of careful design are timely given recent developments of interorganizational behavior and negotiational procedures. In most situations not all channel alternatives are known when structural arrangements are negotiated. Consequently, decisions may later prove to be less than adequate and pressure for change may develop. Even if the best channel is selected at a particular point in time, unanticipated changes may require future reconsideration. For example, when Westinghouse Corporation decided to withdraw from the appliance industry, many competent dealers and distributors became available as channel members for the remaining firms in the industry.

Channel design may take many different forms based upon events that lead to a review. First, the objective may be to replace an existing channel. Second, the objective may be to modify the existing channel by replacing one or more members. Third, the revised design may result in development of a multichannel or dual distribution structure.[4] Although it is conceivable that a total channel could be replaced, one would expect channel modification to be more likely. The significant point is that planned change is prevalent now and will become more so in the future. The nature of such planning will depend upon the design strategy of the dominant firm and is discussed in Chapter 11.

CHANNEL DESIGN STRATEGY

Channel design strategy is closely related to a firm's corporate and marketing objectives. Thus, if channels are to function effectively, goals must be stated in operational terms such as (1) expected sales and profitability by period, (2) desired market coverage, (3) required sales and service support, and (4) desired return on investment. The channel strategy comprises decisions regarding intensity of distribution, appropriateness of direct or indirect channels, plans for gaining desired intermediaries in each geographic area and, finally, implementation of those decisions.

Channel design is the planning process which takes place when a firm decides either to market a new product or service or to modify existing arrangements. Walters has referred to the former as channel adoption and the latter as channel creation:[5]

---

[4] See A. L. McDonald, Jr., "Do Your Distribution Channels Need Reshaping?" *Business Horizons* (Summer 1964), pp. 29–38.

[5] C. Glenn Walters, *Marketing Channels* (New York: The Ronald Press Company, 1974), p. 149.

Channel adoption typically occurs only once in a product's life, but may occur often in an innovative firm that frequently adds products . . . channel creation typically involves designing new institutions or using existing institutions in a new manner.

An example of channel adoption is the manufacturer that sells a new product to consumer markets using wholesalers while selling all other products through traditional institutional channels. An illustration of channel creation is the recent trend toward selling automotive parts and accessories in supermarkets.

The channel design process consists of seven distinct steps:

1 Formulate channel objectives.
2 Develop channel strategy.
3 Determine channel structure alternatives.
4 Evaluate channel structure alternatives.
5 Select channel structure.
6 Generate alternatives with regard to specific channel members.
7 Evaluate and select individual channel members.

Once channel design is implemented, two additional steps remain to be performed on a continuous basis:

8 Measure and evaluate channel performance.
9 Modify channel arrangements if and when necessary.

At the conclusion of this chapter, a model is presented as a general guide to channel design. To a large extent, specific design strategy will depend upon the end objectives the channel is expected to satisfy, and the resulting structure will vary depending upon the marketing situation confronted. Design of a channel for consumer goods will differ substantially from an industrial product or service channel. Some general strategic considerations related to each design situation are elaborated in the following sections.

Customer Focus

As indicated earlier, the customer is the focus of all marketing activities. Channel design is no exception. Thus, channels are designed to meet specific objectives in selected target markets.

Figure 7-1 illustrates one possible framework for customer analysis. The first step is to define meaningful customer groups or segments. Figure 7-2 summarizes the most common bases for market segmentation: demographics, consumption patterns; personality traits and life-styles; and attitudes, perceptions and preferences.[6] An often overlooked basis for market segmentation is cus-

[6] For a comprehensive treatment of market segmentation see Ronald Frank, William Massy, and Yoram Wind, *Market Segmentation* (Englewood Cliffs, New Jersey: Prentice-Hall, Inc., 1972).

Information categories \ Customer groups	A	B	C	D
Who buys?				
Why do they buy?				
Where do they buy?				
When do they buy?				
What do they buy?				
How do they buy?				
Competitive environment				

Figure 7-1 A framework for customer analysis.

tomer needs. What unmet needs does the product satisfy? What problem does it solve?

Regardless of which basis is chosen for market segmentation, it should satisfy the following evaluative criteria:

1 The variables should divide the market into homogeneous groups that respond differently to marketing efforts.
2 The variables should be measurable.
3 The variables should be accessible.
4 The variables should reveal a segment(s) that offers significant profit potential.

The method of segmentation should be selected so that the remaining questions from Figure 7-1 can be answered in a meaningful fashion. These questions include:

1 Who buys?
2 Why do they buy?

Measures \ Customer characteristics	General	Specific
Objective	Demographics (age, sex)	Consumption patterns (brand loyalty, shopping patterns)
Inferred	Personality traits Life styles	Attitudes Perceptions Preferences

Figure 7-2 Bases for market segmentation.

3   Where do they buy?
4   When do they buy?
5   What do they buy?
6   How do they buy?
7   What is the competitive environment in each segment?

Based on such an analysis, management should identify a segment or segments which appear to be promising targets for further cost revenue analysis. If financial analyses for selected target markets meet predetermined profitability and return on investment criteria, information gathered in the customer analysis forms the basis for designing the overall marketing mix *including the desired channel structure*.

Consumer Products Channels

A large number of specialized intermediaries form consumer product channels. A variety of possible channel structures is illustrated in Figure 7-3. However, Figure 7-3 is somewhat misleading in that it does not include all institutions typically involved in marketing. For example, common carriers and public warehouses, which perform basic marketing functions, and specialized institutions, which provide market information and finance market risks, are not included. You will recall from the W. T. Grant case in Chapter 1 that the American Credit Indemnity Company played a critical role in the demise of this large retailer.[7] By canceling Grant's credit insurance policy, American Credit Indemnity Company in effect told the retailer's suppliers that Grant was unlikely to pay its bills. As a result, Grant's found it difficult and, in some cases, impossible to secure merchandise for Christmas in 1974.

Channel design may be undertaken by the manufacturer, wholesaler, or retailer. The degree of freedom a specific firm will have in channel design depends upon relative market power, financial strength, and availability of desired channel partners.

The Manufacturer's Perspective   In the case of the manufacturer, market power is derived from customer brand preference. If customers are inclined to demand a particular brand, retailers and, consequently, wholesalers will be anxious to participate in marketing new products because of potential benefits. On the other hand a small manufacturer of a new product may find it difficult to attract potential channel partners because the manufacturer cannot offer market power as an incentive in channel negotiation. Financial resources determine the extent to which a manufacturer can afford to perform marketing functions internally. Small manufacturers usually must rely on wholesalers for product distribution. Another factor that limits channel design is that acceptable middlemen may not be available in every geographic area or line of trade. For example, "In a product line such as fashion apparel,

---

[7] See Case 1-1, p. 16.

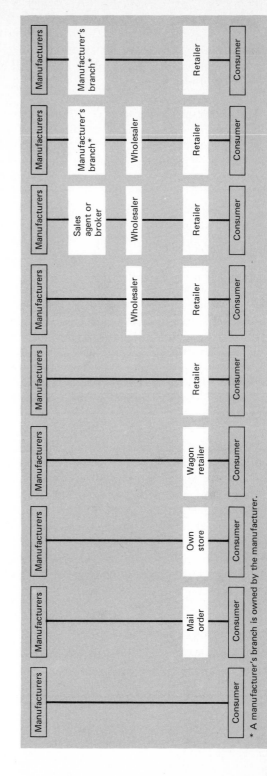

Figure 7-3 Traditional marketing channels for consumer products.

* A manufacturer's branch is owned by the manufacturer.

a garment maker may have an extremely limited choice of type of middlemen: the selling agent, the broker, the direct-buying retailer, or the chain store buying office.''[8]

The Wholesaler's Perspective Wholesalers emerged in distribution because they offered an efficient way to develop an assortment of products for distribution between producers and retailers.[9] The justification for wholesalers is their ability to improve distribution efficiency. They reduce the discrepancy of assortment by "breaking bulk" and sorting goods for retailers or industrial customers.

Wholesaler market power is the greatest when the value per retailer order of an individual manufacturer's products is relatively small and/or suppliers represented by the wholesaler have limited financial resources. Manufacturers with high-value products may have sufficient margin per unit to justify sales directly to the retailer even when the number of items sold to each retailer is small. An example is high-fashion dresses. In contrast, the manufacturer of budget glassware may be able to market profitably only by using a wholesaler, even though a large number of items is sold to each retailer.

Financial strength in relation to profit opportunity assessment determines the marketing functions a wholesaler can be expected to perform in a channel arrangement. Each function performed represents a profit opportunity as well as its associated risk. The presence or absence of other firms offering similar services will contribute to or detract from the market power of an individual wholesaler.

The Retailer's Perspective Retailers exist in channel arrangements because they provide convenient product assortments for their customers. Retailer power is derived from location, assortment, price, and image within the geographic market served. The degree of customer preference a retailer enjoys in a specific area will have a direct bearing upon channel negotiation. The retailer's financial capability and size can be expected to influence the degree of vertical integration desired in channel design.

The above generalizations concerning relative power of manufacturers, wholesalers, and retailers in the channel design process are explained in subsequent chapters. Some generalized comments concerning industrial products and service channels follow.

Industrial Products Channels

Industrial marketing is concerned with the supply of goods and services to firms for use in the manufacturing process. Channels for industrial products include some of or all the following groups: (1) industrial users who consume the product or service, (2) original equipment manufacturers (OEMs) who use the

---

[8] McVey, op. cit., p. 62.
[9] For elaboration see p. 33.

product as a component in their product, (3) dealers and distributors who resell the product in the same form to industrial users and OEMs, and (4) agents or brokers who perform the sales function for the manufacturer but do not take title to the goods. A few possible industrial channel structures are shown in Figure 7-4. Similar to Figure 7-3, institutions involved in finance, selected communication, transportation, and storage are not illustrated.

In many industrial markets differentiating a firm's product is difficult because many ingredients are produced to standard specifications. In such cases channel selection can be a major factor in success. When deciding between a direct or an indirect channel, the industrial marketer must consider the customer, the product line, geographic area, the nature of the selling job, and the cost and revenue considerations associated with each alternative.

The cost of direct distribution selling may be prohibitive for a manufacturer who offers a narrow product line to geographically scattered customers purchasing small quantities. Conversely, the manufacturer of a full line of products with large and geographically concentrated customers may find that direct selling is the most profitable distribution alternative.

Service Channels

The marketing concept can be applied in marketing a wide range of services for profit, nonprofit, and publicly financed organizations. The distribution functions for educational services, tourism, recreation, insurance, home maintenance, security systems, child care services, nursing homes, health care services, family planning services, and accident prevention services require effective channel design. The service channel used by the National Safety Council for its Defensive Driving Course is illustrated in Figure 7-5.

Since this text focuses on the management of channels for economic goods, service channels are not discussed in depth. However, the concepts discussed throughout this text can be applied to service channel management.[10]

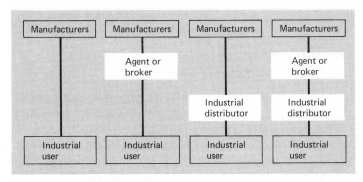

Figure 7-4 Traditional marketing channels for industrial products.

---

[10] The interested reader should refer to Philip Kotler, *Marketing For Nonprofit Organizations* (Englewood Cliffs, N.J.: Prentice-Hall, Inc., 1975).

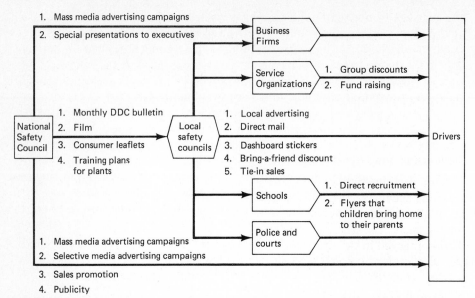

Figure 7-5   An example of a service channel. [*Philip Kotler, Marketing for Nonprofit Organizations (Englewood Cliffs, N.J.: Prentice-Hall, Inc., 1975), p. 299.*]

Summary—Design Strategy

This section has defined the strategic perspective that should guide planned channel designs and modifications. The appropriate orientation will vary between consumer, industrial, and service channels. In addition, all channel members will have a different vantage point from which to approach the design process. One common feature is that all channels must be designed to meet specific goals in terms of selected customer requirements.

The next section introduces the concept of channel structure separation, which increases the opportunity for functional specialization and operational postponement.[11]

STRUCTURAL SEPARATION

The separation of marketing into demand creation and demand supply activities has received considerable attention in the literature.[12] Although both physical distribution and legal exchange of ownership must take place if the marketing channel is to satisfy its mission, there is no reason why these two efforts must transpire simultaneously or within the same network of intermediaries. A product may change ownership one or more times without physically moving, or it may be transported across the nation without changing ownership.

[11] For elaboration see p. 5.
[12] The discussion in this section draws upon Donald J. Bowersox, *Logistical Management*, rev. ed. (New York: The Macmillan Company, 1978), pp. 36–40.

The Logic of Separation

Activities involved in the physical movement of products are not directly related to transaction-creating efforts such as advertising, pricing, credit, and personal selling, and therefore offer unique opportunities for functional specialization. In fact, the most effective network for achieving profitable sales may not be the most efficient arrangement for physical distribution. Based on specialization in primary flow, the marketing channel may be separated into transaction and physical distribution channels.

Transaction and Physical Distribution Channels

The transaction channel consists of specialized intermediaries such as manufacturing agents, sales personnel, jobbers, wholesalers, and retailers engaged in negotiation, contracting, and posttransaction administration of sales on a continuing basis. The physical distribution channel contains a network of intermediaries engaged in the functions of physical movement. Participants are physical distribution specialists concerned with solving problems involved in product transfer. The physical distribution channel provides time and place utility at a cost consistent with marketing objectives.

Examples of Channel Separation

Figure 7-6 illustrates potential separation of the overall distribution channel for color television. The only times the transaction and physical distribution channels merge formally is at the manufacturer's factory and the consumer's home. Two sets of intermediaries are deployed in the overall channel, offering maxi-

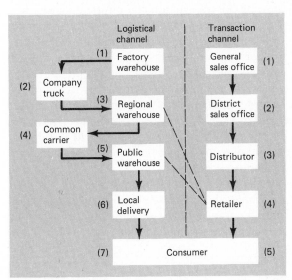

Figure 7-6 Marketing channel exchange and transaction separation. [*Reprinted with permission from Donald J. Bowersox, Logistical Management, rev. ed. (New York: The Macmillan Company, 1978), p. 38.*]

mum opportunity for specialization. Three specialists are employed in the physical distribution channel: a common carrier, a public warehouse, and a specialized local delivery firm. In addition, three levels of physical distribution are performed by the producing firm. Television sets are stored in the company's factory warehouse, transported in company trucks, and stored in the company's regional warehouse before specialized intermediaries begin to participate in the physical distribution channel.

Although the distributor holds legal title to the television sets from the time they leave the manufacturer's regional warehouse, retailers are served from a public warehouse and the distributor never physically handles the television sets. When sales are made by the retailer, delivery is made to the consumer from the distributor's stock in the public warehouse. The retailer has limited stocks for model display, and sales are negotiated with a commitment to deliver the specified model and color to the consumer's residence. Direct customer shipment is made from a strategically located warehouse which may be many miles from the point of transaction.

Another example of channel separation is the factory branch sales office that does not carry inventory. This office exists exclusively for transaction creation. The method of physical distribution between buyer and seller is determined by such factors as value, size, weight, and perishability of the shipment. The network of branch offices is selected to give the manufacturer greatest market impact in terms of transaction creation. The exchange intermediaries are selected in order to achieve the most efficient physical distribution given specified performance levels.

At this point it may be useful to illustrate inefficiencies that can be introduced into the channel by not viewing the transaction and physical distribution flows separately. Consider, for example, the wholesaler who obtains a truckload order from a retail chain, places the order with the manufacturer, and receives a full truckload of the product which moves into the wholesaler's warehouse, only to be reloaded onto another carrier for shipment to the chain distribution center. The inefficiencies are apparent. Contrast this to the policy employed by another wholesaler and manufacturer whose truckload orders are shipped directly to the customer. On such orders the manufacturer pays the wholesaler a smaller margin, but the manufacturer pays the freight to the customer. Since the increased transportation cost is less than the savings in margin paid to the wholesaler, the manufacturer earns more on the sale. Likewise, the reduction in margin to the wholesaler is less in total dollars than the cost that would have been incurred by the wholesaler if the wholesaler had participated in the physical flow associated with the transaction. Consequently, both parties share savings realized by removing system inefficiencies.[13]

The concept of separation should not be interpreted to mean that either the transaction channel or physical distribution channel can stand alone. Such a conclusion could be drawn from the emphasis placed on the transaction chan-

[13] Lambert, op. cit., pp. 120–121.

nel in recent marketing literature. But both channels must function to realize a profitable sale and both are essential to the marketing process.[14]

Separation should be encouraged only to the extent that it offers improved performance through functional specialization or functional spin-off.[15] Separation does not require separate legal entities since the same intermediary may be capable of performing both transaction and physical distribution flows. Many wholesalers successfully combine the performance of both flows.

Cost reductions are not the only benefits possible from efficient channel design. By providing dependable delivery when and where desired by customers, overall marketing effort can be enhanced. We will now consider the design of transaction and physical distribution channels.

TRANSACTION CHANNEL DESIGN CONSIDERATIONS

A number of factors must be considered in the design of the transaction channel. Transaction channel design is influenced by market coverage of the firm, product characteristics, and availability of channel partners. The purpose of transaction channel design is to determine, given those constraints, which channel intermediaries can get the product either to where the customer expects to purchase it or where the customer will go to purchase it, and which intermediaries can provide the services required by the customer.

Market Coverage Objectives

Market coverage objectives should be established only after giving full consideration to customer requirements, distribution intensity, market control, and outlet selection.

Customer Requirements   Once potential customer segments have been determined (from the analysis outlined in Figure 7-2), patronage motives of customers must be determined to select appropriate intermediaries who will perform the selling function to target markets.

Bucklin has constructed a product-patronage matrix which provides the marketer with a framework for considering alternative strategies at the retail level.[16] Figure 7-7 presents nine types of buying behavior which might characterize the purchase behavior of the target market toward a product. Generally, three or four cells would represent the behavior of a specific target group, with the remaining cells left empty. Using this analysis, the channel designer is now in a position to determine the retail segment or segments that should be em-

---

[14] Transportation and storage have been recognized as marketing functions from the early conception of marketing as a discipline to the present time. See Fred E. Clark, *Principles of Marketing* (New York: The Macmillan Company, 1923), p. 11; and Robert Bartels, *Marketing Theory and Metatheory* (Homewood, Ill.: Richard D. Irwin, Inc., 1970), pp. 166–175.

[15] For a discussion of functional spin-off see Bruce Mallen, "Functional Spin-off—A Key to Anticipating Change in Distribution Structure," *Journal of Marketing* (July 1973), pp. 18–25.

[16] Louis P. Bucklin, "Retail Strategy and the Classification of Consumer Goods," *Journal of Marketing* (January 1963), pp. 51–56.

Categorization of goods / Categorization of stores	Convenience	Shopping	Specialty
Convenience	Consumer prefers to buy the most readily available brand of product at the most accessible store.	Consumer selects purchase from among the assortment carried by the most accessible store.	Consumer purchases a favorite brand from the most accessible store that has the item in stock.
Shopping	Consumer is indifferent to the brand of product to be purchased but shops among different stores in order to secure better retail service and/or lower retail prices.	Consumer makes comparisons among both retail-controlled factors and factors associated with the product (brand).	Consumer has a strong preference for a particular brand but shops among a number of stores to secure the best retail service and/or price for this brand.
Specialty	Consumer prefers to trade at a specific store but is indifferent to the brand of product purchased.	Consumer prefers to trade at a certain store but is uncertain as to which product to purchase and examines the store's assortment for the best buy.	Consumer has a preference for both a particular store and a specific brand.

Figure 7-7   The product-patronage mix. [*Adapted from Louis P. Bucklin, "Retail Strategy and the Classification of Consumer Goods," Journal of Marketing (January 1963), pp. 53–54. Reprinted by permission of the American Marketing Association.*]

ployed to reach the target market or markets. Industrial marketers must also identify potential users and determine how each type of user buys. The industrial buyer's behavior will be shaped by whether the firm is a user, an OEM, or a distributor. The industrial buyer is usually a technically qualified person and, through purchasing power and product knowledge, is in a strong position to bargain with regard to price, product specifications, delivery schedules, and maintenance contracts and service. Depending on the product's value, frequent or infrequent purchase, and degree of technical support required, the industrial customer may prefer to deal direct or to purchase from a distributor.

Distribution Intensity   Distribution intensity refers to the degree of market exposure desired by the firm. Three types of market exposure exist: (1) intensive distribution, (2) exclusive distribution, and (3) selective distribution.

Intensive distribution refers to the sale of a product to as many appropriate retailers or wholesalers as possible, because convenience is the primary factor influencing the customer. Consider such consumer products as chewing gum, pencils, candy bars, and cigarettes. All these items would fall into the convenience goods/convenience stores category in the product-patronage matrix illustrated in Figure 7-7 and would require the most intensive distribution possible. Industrial products which may also require intensive distribution include pencils, paper clips, carbon paper, file folders, typing paper, screws, and nails.

Exclusive distribution occurs when a single outlet is given an exclusive franchise to sell the product in a geographic area. Products such as new automobiles, some major appliances, some brands of furniture, and certain lines of clothing which enjoy a high degree of brand loyalty are more likely to be distributed in this manner, particularly if the consumer is willing to overcome the inconvenience of traveling out of the way to obtain the product. Exclusive distribution is usually undertaken when the producer desires more agressive selling on the part of the intermediary, or when increased control over distribution is deemed to be important. Exclusive distribution may also enhance the product's image so that higher retail prices can be charged. The specialty goods/specialty store combination is the ultimate in exclusive distribution. However, exclusive dealing might be chosen for certain shopping goods, such as women's apparel and some brands of men's shoes, when sales to specialty stores or shopping stores would enhance the product's image and provide sufficient margins to retailers.

Manufacturers sometimes use multiple brands to offer exclusive distribution to more than one retailer or distributor. Exclusive distribution generally occurs more frequently at the wholesale level. However, many wholesalers who demand exclusive representation in a territory sell to retail accounts on an intensive or selective basis.

Selective distribution involves limiting the number of outlets that may carry a product, but not to the extent of exclusive dealing. It is used primarily for shopping goods by companies with established reputations and by new companies and/or new products as a method of gaining distribution. By carefully selecting intermediaries, the manufacturer can concentrate on potentially profitable accounts and can develop solid working relationships to ensure that the product is displayed and sold in the desired manner. Also, the number of outlets may be restricted if the product requires specialized servicing or sales support. Examples of products lending themselves to selective distribution include clothing, appliances, televisions, stereo equipment, home furnishings, and sports equipment.

In general, exclusive distribution lends itself to direct channels (manufacturer-retailer), while intensive distribution is more likely to involve indirect channels with two or more intermediaries between manufacturer and consumer.

Outlet Selection   With customer requirements and distribution intensity determined, institutions that should carry the product must be selected. Increased use of scrambled merchandising complicates this task. For example, Safeway Stores Incorporated, a California-based retailer of grocery products, has begun to sell nongrocery items such as $380 Sony television sets and $22 slow cookers in an effort to improve margins and profitability.[17]

---

[17] "Safeway: Selling Nongrocery Items to Cure the Supermarket Blahs," *Business Week* (March 7, 1977), pp. 52–58.

In addition to customer requirements and distribution intensity, a number of factors may restrict the availability of outlets, including (1) the financial strength of the middleman, since this will influence the ability to provide desired inventory levels and consumer credit; (2) the need for specialized service facilities; (3) market coverage of the middleman; (4) product lines carried and the degree of support that will be given to the product; (5) the middleman's physical distribution capabilities; and (6) the middleman's ability to grow with the business.

Market Control In many cases the manufacturer will want to exercise a measure of control over the distribution channel to ensure product quality and/or postpurchase services. The need for control can be explained in terms of the manufacturer's desire to protect the long-range profitability of the firm. For example, a manufacturer of premium confectionery products distributes the line nationally through a chain of company-owned retail outlets and selected department stores, drugstores, and specialty outlets. The marketing manager stated that the company would not sell to wholesalers because it wished to avoid the mass market in order to maintain control over margins and product quality.[18] If the company sold its products to a wholesaler, it could not control the selling policies of that wholesaler and, consequently, the wholesaler might sell to a mass merchandiser in order to increase sales volume. No doubt the mass merchandiser would discount this nationally recognized brand and thus destroy the market for the very profitable company stores and other channels of distribution which rely on the substantial margins allowed by the premium price.

Product Characteristics

Those product characteristics that will influence transaction channel design must be considered. Four of the more important product characteristics that should be analyzed by the channel designer are (1) the value of the product, (2) the technicality of the product, (3) the degree of market acceptance, and (4) the degree of substitutability of the product. It should be recognized that this review of product characteristics is related to the previous discussion on market coverage and, in fact, the two may take place simultaneously.

Value The higher the per-unit cost of the product, the larger the investment required to stage inventories in the field. This usually means that manufacturers with limited resources will seek middlemen in order to shift some of the burden. High per-unit value also tends to limit availability of middlemen, and often leads to direct distribution because the high dollars-per-unit margin is sufficient to cover the cost of direct sales and physical distribution.

When the unit value is low, channels tend to be indirect unless volume is

---

[18] Lambert, op. cit., p. 56.

high enough to generate the dollar margins required to support direct channels. In general, low-value products tend toward intensive distribution.

Technicality   For highly technical products a technically competent salesperson is usually necessary to demonstrate the product for the customer. Also, prepurchase and postpurchase sales service often requires stocking repair parts. Technical products might include high-priced stereo components, major household appliances, sewing machines, imported sports cars, and a multitude of industrial products. Generally, firms marketing highly complex products tend toward direct channels and selective or exclusive distribution policies.

Market Acceptance   The degree of market acceptance will determine the amount of selling effort required to sell the product. If the product is a new offering of a recognized brand-name manufacturer and significant introductory advertising is planned, customer acceptance will most likely be high and middlemen will be eager to add the new product. However, for new products with little market acceptance and low brand identification, aggressive selling at each level of the channel will be necessary. Middlemen will be reluctant to provide special treatment for the line and the manufacturer may be required to employ "missionary salespeople" or "detail people" to call on various channel members and promote the line.

Substitutability   The degree of product substitutability is closely related to brand loyalty. Brand loyalty is lowest for convenience goods and highest for specialty goods. When brand loyalty is low, substitution takes place readily and intensive distribution is required. This places a premium on point-of-purchase displays in high-traffic areas requiring the aggressive selling discussed previously. In order to gain support for products that are easily substituted, higher than normal margins may be offered to wholesalers and/or retail outlets in the shopping and specialty categories. The use of selective or exclusive distribution makes it easier for the producer to provide necessary channel support.

PHYSICAL DISTRIBUTION CHANNEL DESIGN CONSIDERATIONS

In this section we will discuss how the channel designer should develop the network of specialized institutions to perform the functions of transportation, storage, inventory management, order processing, and material handling. Although successful performance of these functions has always been required to achieve closure between producer and customer, in recent years the emphasis has been on viewing these activities as an integrated system.[19]

[19] For a historical review of the development of the physical distribution concept, see Donald J. Bowersox, "Physical Distribution Development, Current Status and Potential," *Journal of Marketing,* (January 1969), p. 63–70.

The four causes for increased management attention to integrated distribution during the 1950s and 1960s were:[20]

1 A more scientific approach to business management.
2 Advances in computer technology.
3 Importance of distribution in providing increased levels of customer satisfaction.
4 The "profit squeeze" and consequent potential of "profit leverage" from increased efficiency in distribution.

Design of the physical distribution channel must include development of customer service objectives, consideration of product characteristics, and total cost integration of physical distribution activities.

Customer Service Objectives

Customer service represents physical distribution's interface with the demand criterion portion of marketing. Thus, customer service is a critical input in the marketing mix decision. This is true not only in terms of the *place* component of the marketing mix, but also in the case of *price*. Customer service can be used to differentiate the product and may influence the market price if customers are willing to pay more for better service. In addition, distribution costs add to product costs and may affect the selling price set by the company.

Customer service is a complex subject and means different things to different people.[21] It is usually measured in terms of (1) the percentage of product availability relative to some time standard, (2) the speed and consistency associated with the order cycle, and (3) the quality of reporting that takes place between seller and customer. Customer service levels should be set only after a careful study of customers' needs.

Availability The most critical measure of customer service is inventory availability for servicing orders. Inventory availability is measured with respect to some time standard and may be expressed in terms of (1) the number of items out of stock compared to the total number of items in inventory, (2) the items shipped calculated as a percentage of the number of items ordered, (3) the value of items shipped as a percentage of the value of items ordered, and (4) the number of orders shipped complete as a percentage of total orders received.

The first measure is deficient in that, unless items are categorized based on profit contribution to the firm using an ABC approach, a stockout on a fast-moving item is treated the same as a stockout on a slow-moving item even though customer reactions may be very different. The second measure

[20] Bernard J. LaLonde, John R. Grabner and James F. Robeson, "Integrated Distribution Systems: A Management Perspective," *International Journal of Physical Distribution* (October 1970), p. 136.

[21] The interested reader should refer to Bernard J. LaLonde and Paul H. Zinszer, *Customer Service: Meaning and Measurement,* (Chicago, Ill.: National Council of Physical Distribution Management, 1976).

is weak since it fails to recognize that some items are more important to the customer than others. Also, some items have a higher selling price, and losing the sale of those items may result in a larger lost contribution to the supplier. The third measure, based on the value of items ordered, eliminates the weakness of the second measure but does not necessarily eliminate the weakness of the first measure. The fourth measure is most likely to reflect the customer's view of customer service.

The best measure of customer service reflects both the importance of the product to the customer and the importance of the customer to the company. Consider the manufacturer of farm implements who received an emergency order from a farmer whose combine suffered a breakdown just before harvest. If twenty items were ordered and nineteen were shipped, customer service could be recorded as 95 percent. Similarly, if the total value of the order was $100 and the value of the item out of stock was $1, customer service could be recorded as 99 percent, which is indeed impressive. However, if all twenty parts were required in order to repair the combine, from the farmer's viewpoint the manufacturer has achieved a zero service level.

Speed and Consistency Speed and consistency[22] refer to the time required from order placement to receipt of the products, and the ability of the supplier to meet the targeted order cycle time consistently. The typical order cycle between a supplier and a customer in a single-echelon system consists of (1) order transmittal, (2) order processing, (3) order fill, (4) order transport, and (5) customer delivery. The speed and consistency with which such activities can be performed by channel intermediaries is of prime importance to the channel designer. It is generally believed that most customers prefer consistent service to fast service, since the former allows them to plan inventory levels to a much greater extent than is possible with a fast but highly variable order cycle.

A third factor, error rate, might be added to speed and accuracy. Errors in shipping, picking, packing, labeling, and documentation are an expensive inconvenience to the customer and should be measured. Damage rates experienced by carriers, public warehouses, and distributors should also be measured.

Quality Quality refers to the firm's ability to supply timely information to the customer regarding such factors as order status, order tracing, back-order status, order confirmation, product substitution, order shortages, and product information requests. The ability of channel members to cooperate in this regard is also a major factor in channel design. For example, a large manufacturer of paper products has reached an agreement with a common carrier enabling the manufacturer to access the carrier's computer to trace a shipment and determine its current status.

In general, "customer service standards should (1) reflect the customer's

---

[22] This discussion draws upon Bowersox, *Logistical Management*, pp. 264–269.

point of view, (2) provide an operational and objective measure of service performance, and (3) provide management information for corrective action.''[23]

Product Characteristics

As with the transaction channel, product characteristics play an important role in the design of the physical distribution channel. By analyzing the product the designer can determine if special transportation, storage, or handling is required. The product characteristics most relevant in physical distribution channel design are (1) value, (2) bulk, (3) perishability, (4) geographic concentration, (5) seasonality, and (6) width and depth of the product line.

Value   The product's value will influence its inventory carrying costs and will therefore determine the desirability of premium transportation. Low-value grocery products will most likely be shipped by rail car and stored in field warehouses. High-value component parts and products such as high-fashion merchandise are often shipped air freight to reduce inventory carrying costs, and to minimize in-transit inventories by holding inventory at a central location.

Bulk   Bulk is closely related to value, with low-value–high-weight products generally restricted to local markets close to the point of production. Special materials handling skills may also be required. With small weight and cube, more units can be shipped in a truck, rail car, or air container, thereby reducing the per-unit cost of transportation. Shipment of orange juice concentrate from Florida to northern markets by tank truck is an example of the principle of postponement, whereby product adjustments are moved closer to the point of consumption to overcome value and bulk restrictions.

Perishability   Perishability may refer to physical deterioration, or to product obsolescence caused by changing customer taste or technological change. When goods are subject to physical deterioration the channel designer must find intermediaries capable of minimizing product losses in transportation and storage. Perishable products are usually sold on a direct basis to hasten product movement through the channel and reduce the potential for inventory loss.

Geographic Concentration   The cost of reaching customers is generally less when the market is concentrated in a geographic area. In such cases direct channels may be the most effective and efficient. However, when markets are widely dispersed, specialized middlemen are necessary to realize efficiencies associated with moving larger quantities. This is precisely the reason many food processors utilize a network of brokers throughout the country to market their products. It also helps explain the development of pooling agencies which aggregate many small shipments into truckload or carload units for movement to distant points.

---

[23] LaLonde and Zinszer, op. cit., p. 180.

Seasonality Seasonality is a primary concern for manufacturers who experience larger than normal sales at certain times of the year or who have raw materials available for production only at specific times during the year. An example of the former is toy sales at Christmas and an example of the latter is canning of fresh fruits and vegetables. Consequently, out-of-season storage is required and manufacturers must either invest in storage facilities or provide economic incentives to middlemen to encourage them to perform the storage function. For example, toy manufacturers might offer a seasonal discount to retailers who agree to take delivery in early summer rather than wait until the customary fall selling period.

Width and Depth The width and depth of a supplier's product line influence the channel design decision. Even a manufacturer of low per-unit value products may be able to enjoy intensive distribution with short channels (direct sales) if the product line is broad enough to result in a relatively large average sale. Food products manufacturers such as Kellogg's or General Foods are an example. However, a manufacturer of a very limited line of products will typically find the cost of direct sales prohibitive and will have to use indirect channels to achieve adequate market coverage.

Total Cost Integration

The integrated distribution management concept requires that the total cost associated with performance of physical distribution activities be measured so that the least-cost alternative for satisfying customer needs may be chosen.[24] This process is referred to as distribution cost trade-off analysis.

Cost categories which must be considered and measured if distribution cost trade-off analysis is to be implemented are customer service levels (cost of lost sales), transportation costs, warehousing costs, lot quantity costs, and inventory carrying costs (Figure 7-8).

Customer Service Costs The cost associated with customer service levels is the cost of lost sales—not only the margin lost by not meeting current sales demand, but the present value of all future contributions to profit forfeited when a customer is lost due to poor availability—which is indeed difficult, if not impossible, to measure, at least at the consumer level.

The objective becomes one of minimizing total costs given a level of customer service. With this information management can make a knowledgeable judgment concerning the likelihood of recovering, through increased sales, the increase in total system costs brought about by an increase in customer service levels. Another possibility, of course, would be to reduce spending in some other component of the marketing mix (promotion, for example) in order to

[24] This section draws heavily on Douglas M. Lambert, *The Development of an Inventory Costing Methodology: A Study of the Costs Associated with Holding Inventory* (Chicago, Ill.: National Council of Physical Distribution Management, 1976), pp. 6–15.

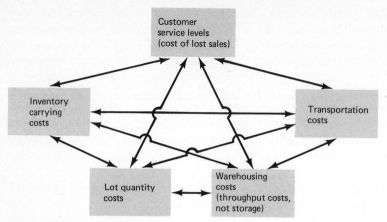

Objective: Minimize total costs.

Total costs = Inventory carrying costs + lot quantity costs +
warehousing costs + transportation costs + cost of
lost sales.

Figure 7-8 Cost trade-offs required in the logistics system. [*Douglas M. Lambert, The Development of an Inventory Costing Methodology: A Study of the Costs Associated with Holding Inventory (Chicago, Ill.: National Council of Physical Distribution Management, 1976), p. 7.*]

maintain profits with similar sales volume. Likewise, with decreases in customer service levels, profitability can be improved or other components of the marketing mix may receive increased expenditures in an effort to maintain or improve market position.

It is apparent that, even though costs associated with customer service are elusive, intelligent management decisions are possible if good cost data are available for the other four cost categories shown in Figure 7-8. (It is reasonable to expect that similar customer service objectives would be assumed when making a comparison of alternative physical distribution channels.)

Transportation Costs The next category of costs is associated with the transportation function. These costs can be dealt with either in total or on an incremental basis. Transportation costs, if not currently available in any other form, can be determined by a statistical audit of freight bills.

Warehousing Costs Warehousing costs include all expenses that can be eliminated or must be increased as the result of a change in the number of warehousing facilities. There has been a great deal of confusion in the literature about these costs. Many authors have included warehousing costs in inventory carrying costs. This is a misconception, however, since most of these costs will change not with the level of inventory stocked but with the number of stocking locations. Nevertheless, the converse is true—the number of warehouses employed within the distribution system will have an impact on inventory safety stocks. In addition, in the case of leased or owned facilities these costs take the form of step-functions. Thus, their inclusion in inventory carrying costs necessitates a recalculation of the carrying cost percentage each time a decision involves the possibility of opening or closing a warehouse. The most straightforward method is to separate warehousing costs into two distinct categories, those related to throughput and those related to storage. Throughput costs are those associated with selling a product in a given market by moving it into and out of a warehouse. Examples of throughput costs are charges that public warehousers assess for handling-in and handling-out of their facilities. These charges are related to how much product is sold in that market and are distinct from storage space costs public warehousers assign to their customers based on the amount of inventory stored in the facility. The former group of costs should be included in warehousing costs so that increments can be added or subtracted easily with changes in distribution system configuration.

Lot Quantity Costs   Lot quantity costs are those costs that change as a result of a change in the distribution system and usually include some or all of the following costs:

1   Cost of issuing and closing orders.
2   Related costs of handling.
3   Production preparation costs.
   a   Set-up time.
   b   Inspection.
   c   Set-up scrap.
   d   Inefficiency of beginning operation.
4   Lost capacity due to changeover.
5   Materials handling, scheduling, and expediting.

The production preparation and lost capacity costs are usually available since they are used as inputs to production planning. The other costs can be approximated by taking the incremental total costs incurred from one year to the next and dividing by the increment in volume or by using regression analysis. The number obtained can be used as an input to logistics system design.

Inventory Carrying Costs   Inventory carrying costs should include only those costs that vary with the level of inventory stored. They can be categorized into the following groups: (1) capital costs, (2) inventory service costs, (3) storage space costs, and (4) inventory risk costs.

Capital Costs on Inventory Investment   Holding inventory ties up money that could be used for other investments. This reasoning holds for both internally generated funds and funds obtained from outside sources. Consequently, the company's opportunity cost of capital (the hurdle rate, the minimum acceptable rate of return on new investments) should be used to reflect accurately the true cost involved. It should be used by companies experiencing capital rationing, which is the rule rather than the exception. Where capital rationing does not exist, the capital invested in inventory is expected to earn a rate competitive with marketable securities and/or other liquid investments of the firm. In some special circumstances such as in the fruit canning industry, short-term financing may be used to finance the seasonal buildup of inventories. In these situations the actual cost of borrowing is the acceptable cost of money.

Many managers think that inventory is a relatively liquid and riskless investment and that a somewhat lower return can be justified on inventory investments. However, inventory requires capital that could be used in other corporate investments. By investing funds in inventory a firm forgoes the rate of return that could be obtained on alternate investments. Therefore, the company's opportunity cost of capital should be applied to the investment in inventory. This cost of capital should be applied only to the out-of-pocket investment in inventory. Although most manufacturers use some variation of absorption costing for inventory valuation, only variable manufacturing costs are relevant. That is, the cost of capital, the company's minimum acceptable rate of return, should be applied to only the variable costs directly associated with inventory.

Inventory Service Costs   Inventory service costs are comprised of taxes and insurance. Depending on the state in which inventories are held, tax rates can range from zero in states where inventories are exempt to 19.8 percent of the assessed value in Indiana. In general, taxes vary directly with inventory levels. Although *insurance* rates are not strictly proportional to inventory levels and since insurance is usually purchased for a specified time period, the insurance coverage will be revised periodically based on inventory policy. In some instances reporting form insurance policies may be used where premiums are based on the monthly amounts insured. Insurance rates vary depending on materials used in construction of the building, its age, and other considerations such as the type of fire prevention equipment installed.

Storage Space Costs   In general, four types of facilities should be considered: (1) plant warehouses, (2) public warehouses, (3) rented (leased) warehouses, and (4) privately owned warehouses.

The costs associated with plant warehouses are usually fixed in nature, although some variable costs, such as the cost of taking a physical inventory or other expenses that change with inventory level, should be included in inventory carrying costs. Fixed charges and allocated costs are not relevant for inventory policy decisions. If the warehouse space could be rented or used for some other productive purpose, then the associated opportunity costs are relevant. In such cases, if the opportunity costs are not readily available to the manager, the appropriate fixed or allocated costs may be substituted.

Space in public warehouses is usually billed on either a dollar per hundredweight or a volume occupied basis. Use of public warehouses involves a design decision, which results because the public warehouse is the most economical way to provide the desired level of customer service without incurring excessive transportation costs. For this reason the majority of costs related to public warehouses should be considered as throughput costs. Only charges for recurring storage that are explicitly or implicitly included in the rental cost should be considered a component of carrying costs. Of course, capital costs associated with holding inventory in public warehouses must be included in inventory carrying costs.

A rented (leased) warehouse is normally contracted for a specific length of time. The amount of space rented is constant for the period of the contract. Thus, the rate of incurring warehouse rental charges does not fluctuate from day to day with changes in the inventory level, although the rental rates can vary from month to month or year to year when a new contract is negotiated. Most operating costs are fixed for a period of time, but some vary with inventory level. Only those costs that will vary with inventory levels should be included in inventory carrying costs. The other costs belong in the warehousing cost category (see Figure 7-8). Their inclusion in inventory carrying costs would cloud the issue and force an unnecessary recalculation of the inventory carrying cost percentage each time a decision has to be made.

All operating costs that could be eliminated by closing a company-owned warehouse, or the net savings that would result from a change to public warehouses, should be included in warehousing costs.

Inventory Risk Costs   These costs vary from company to company and include charges for (1) obsolescence, (2) damage, (3) pilferage, and (4) relocation of inventory.

The cost of obsolescence is the cost of each unit which must be disposed of at a loss because it becomes obsolete. This cost is the difference between the original cost of the unit and its salvage value. This figure may or may not show up on the profit and loss statement as a separate item. Usually obsolescence results in an overstatement of the cost of goods manufactured account or the cost of goods sold account. Consequently, arriving at this figure may be difficult.

The cost of damage should be included only for the portion of damage that is variable with the amount of inventory held. Damage incurred during shipping should be considered a throughput cost since it will continue regardless of inventory levels. Often this figure is identified as the net amount after claims.

Pilferage has become an increasingly important problem for American business. In the opinion of many authorities inventory theft is a more serious problem than cash embezzlement. It is far more common, involves more employees, and is harder to control. Although this cost may be more closely related to company security measures than inventory levels, it will definitely vary with the number of warehouse locations. Thus, in many companies it may be more appropriate to assign some or all the pilferage costs to the warehousing cost category.

Relocation costs are associated with movement of inventory from one stocking location to another. These costs are usually the result of decisions involving trade-offs between transportation and warehousing costs and are not relevant for classification as inventory holding costs unless they were incurred to avoid product obsolescence.

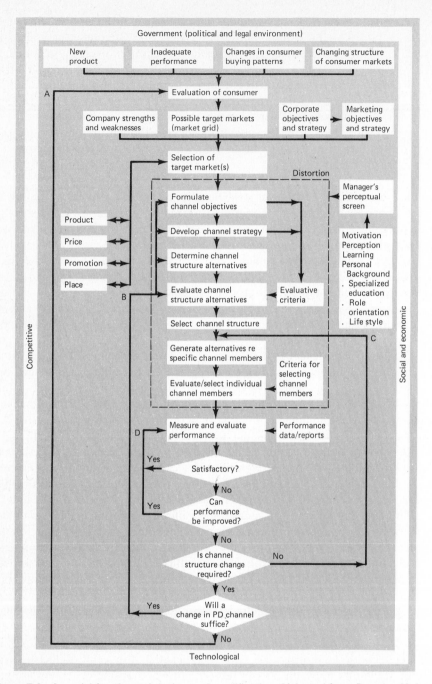

Figure 7-9 A model for channel design and modification. [*Adapted from Douglas M. Lambert, The Distribution Channels Decision (New York: National Association of Accountants; and Hamilton, Ontario: The Society of Management Accountants of Canada, 1978), pp. 44–45, and pp. 112–113.*]

Total Cost and Channel Integration

Arguments used in support of a systems integration of physical distribution can be extended to include a systems integration of transaction and physical distribution channels. The cost of performing many physical distribution functions can be spun off to intermediaries such as full-service wholesalers who will absorb many of the associated costs in exchange for a margin on the sale of the product. Also, the manufacturer may increase market exposure by such a spin-off and total corporate profitability may be improved. Total channel cost integration will be elaborated in Chapter 10, which deals with channel performance measurement and channel profitability analysis.

A MODEL FOR CHANNEL DESIGN

Based upon the material developed thus far, a model to guide channel change and modification is presented in Figure 7-9. Nine steps of the design and modification process were listed on page 192. The model permits the overall planning process to be viewed in a managerial context and within a framework of overall corporate and marketing objectives. Specific aspects of performing the design process are covered in depth in the following three chapters.

The model outlines a decision process that, if followed, will lead to the evolution of a normative channel. Bucklin has defined the normative channel as that group of channel institutions that generates maximum profits and consumer satisfaction per dollar of product cost.[25]

Channels may not gravitate to or obtain the normative structure specified by Bucklin due to the influence of social, cultural, political, competitive, and economic variables. Reasons for the existence of uneconomic channels will be discussed in Chapter 11 in the section entitled "Resistance to Change." In any case, the framework provided in Figure 7-9 should lead to the best possible channel configuration given all external constraints.

SUMMARY

Current practice reveals that many channels of distribution were not designed but evolved over time in response to problems in the marketplace. In most instances in which the channel of distribution undergoes change, the manager must start with an existing channel arrangement and work toward an ideal or more suitable system.

The strategy of channel design can be considered from the viewpoint of the manufacturer, wholesaler, and the retailer but, as with all marketing situations, the customer must be the primary focus in channel planning. Channel design, the planning process that occurs directly or indirectly at least once in the life of an organization, product, or service, will vary somewhat among consumer, industrial, and service channels. Also, specified channel members may vary in

[25] Louis P. Bucklin, *A Theory of Distribution Channel Structure,* (Berkeley, California: Institute of Business and Economic Research, University of California, 1966).

their approach to the design process but all must consider the needs of the target market to which the product or service is aimed.

Separating ownership from physical flow can lead to many efficiencies such as cost reductions and improvements in customer service. Transaction channel design is constrained by market coverage objectives and product characteristics. The goal is to select channel intermediaries that can best satisfy consumer needs and expectations in terms of product availability and services performed. Customer service objectives and product characteristics present similar constraints to design of the physical distribution channel. Another major factor in design of the physical distribution channel is total cost integration which requires that the total of the following costs be minimized: customer service levels (the cost of lost sales), transportation costs, warehousing costs, lot quantity costs, and inventory carrying costs.

A model of channel design and modification illustrates the importance of performance evaluation in the evolution of marketing channels. With this background you are now prepared to study channel management from the perspective of manufacturers and intermediaries.

QUESTIONS

1 At the beginning of this chapter nine responses of business people were given to the question, "How was your current channel structure determined?" Would you have anticipated those responses? Why or why not?
2 What is the customer's role in the channel design process?
3 What are some of the constraints affecting the options available to the channel designer?
4 Explain the concept of structural separation within the channel of distribution. What are the implications of structural separation for the design of an efficient channel system?
5 Discuss intensive distribution, exclusive distribution, and selective distribution and give examples of situations when each one would be an acceptable strategy.
6 How might product characteristics influence the channel of distribution chosen by a manufacturer?
7 Customer service has been described as "physical distribution's interface with the demand creation portion of marketing." Explain what customer service is and why the previous statement is true.
8 Explain how product characteristics influence the design of the physical distribution channel.
9 What are the cost trade-offs required in the logistics system? How is this cost trade-off analysis operationalized?
10 A model for channel design was introduced at the end of this chapter. Which steps in the design process do you believe are the most important? Why?

Case 7-1: Smith Chemical Company

This case involves an evaluation of the customer service and cost of an agricultural chemical physical distribution system. Because of the industry's highly competitive nature, management decided to review its existing physical distribution system structure and operating practices.

Figure 1 outlines the existing Smith Chemical Company physical distribution system. Three types of facilities make up the system: (1) two continuous-process manufacturing plants, (2) six in-transit warehouses, and (3) twenty-three full-line distribution centers. For the review, management has excluded any relocation of the manufacturing plants and associated material management operations. The review's scope is limited to the physical distribution of packaged dry and liquid chemicals.

Smith distributes ninety-four different products, or stock-keeping units (SKUs), on a national basis. For distribution considerations, the products can be grouped into two categories. Category A consists of ten SKUs of a product called "Prevention." The sales of Prevention are highly seasonal and account for 75 percent of Smith's total revenue. The eighty-four category B products (called "Support") sell throughout the year but also have a seasonal pattern similar to that of Prevention's sales. Although the sales volume of category B is only 25 percent of Smith's total revenue, this group of products contributes approximately 40 percent of total before-tax profits. The typical end user of Smith's products buys a variety of both A and B products. In many cases, the products are used jointly in agricultural applications.

Smith's total product line is marketed through a network of agricultural dealers. Smith sells to the dealers, who resell products to farmers. The typical dealer provides farmers with a broad line of products, including those that are directly competitive with Smith products. Farmers tend to purchase both Prevention and Support products 1 to 2 weeks before field application. Application occurs at different times in different parts of the country and is directly related to the intensity of rainfall. Thus, Smith's products must be available when the farmers need them. Likewise, the quantity needed per acre

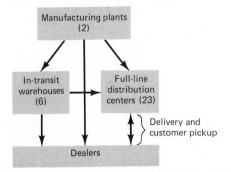

Figure 1   Smith Chemical Company existing physical distribution system.

varies depending on the rainfall an area receives. Therefore, although Smith produces Prevention and Support all year, sales to farmers take place during a very short time period. Farmers' requirements vary in time and duration of use throughout the country.

To even out physical distribution across the year to dealers, Smith offers an early-order program. For those dealers who purchase at least 90 days in advance of estimated application dates, Smith offers a warehouse allowance. The allowance is based on two features. First, the earlier the dealer commitment before the 90-day cut-off, the larger the discount. Second, the larger the quantity of the early order, the greater the discount. The application date is forecast by Smith's planning department. Even though the date has not been historically accurate, its specification has not caused conflicts between Smith and its dealers. In past years, the size of early-order discounts has ranged from 2 to 10 percent off normal dealer prices. The early-order program accounts for 65 to 75 percent of the total annual sales of Prevention and Support.

For the dealer, placing an early order means taking an inventory position on Prevention in advance of farmer purchases. However, since both Prevention and Support products are available, in effect the early-order warehouse allowance means a special discount on the Support products that sell all year. To avoid abuse of the program, Smith requires that at least 50 percent of each order consist of Prevention products. Smith also agrees to accept returns up to 15 percent of the total quantity of early-ordered Prevention products. The return policy is a refund of the full purchase price providing dealers prepay the return freight to a Smith warehouse.

In actual operation, the early-order program uses two physical distribution patterns. First, early-order shipments are scheduled at Smith's convenience to achieve the lowest possible transportation cost, which usually means full carload or truckload shipments direct to dealers. Second, the early-order program offers an added incentive to dealers to use their own transportation equipment to pick up early orders. These dealers are given an additional discount which is less than the transportation paid by Smith. Thus, to some degree, both parties benefit from dealer pickup. Analysis of past early-order programs indicates that approximately 30 percent of the dealers participate in the early-order program. Because of their desire to obtain both Prevention and Support products, dealers are allowed pickups only at the twenty-three full-line distribution centers.

Dealer sales not included in the early-order program—that is, those within 90 days of estimated application dates—are referred to as "seasonal sales." Most seasonal sales to dealers occur within a few days of field application. Thus, to a significant degree, the quantity of seasonal sales depends on Smith's ability to deliver products rapidly. During the seasonal period, dealers expect Prevention and Support to be available for pickup at distribution centers within a few hours of the time of order. During this period, approximately 50 percent of the dealers pick up products. If transportation is arranged by Smith, dealers expect overnight delivery. Although the service level required during the seasonal period is high, these sales are very profitable for the dealers because the farmers who purchase the products are willing to pay the full dealer price. The capability to provide products during the application period is one of the most important criteria dealers use when selecting the chemical firms they will do business with.

Historically, sales have concentrated in ten Midwestern states that account for 70 percent of annual revenue. A summary of 1978 sales data is presented in Table 1.

The existing Smith distribution pattern is as follows. The two manufacturing plants are located in Houston and in New Orleans. The Houston facility produces Prevention, and all Support products are processed at New Orleans. Both facilities are continuous-process plants, and their location at deep-water ports facilitates economical inbound raw material movement.

The six in-transit warehouses are utilized because the manufacturing plants have only enough storage space for two or three days' production. Table 2 lists the in-transit facility locations and the Smith products stored at each.

In terms of the total system, the in-transit warehouses have three functions: (1) storage is provided until forward shipments are required, (2) the close proximity of the in-transit warehouses to manufacturing plants postpones the risk of advance shipment, and (3) the use of in-transit warehouses provides a combination of transportation rates that is lower to field distribution centers than the sum of published rates into and out of the in-transit warehouse. In a sense, the in-transit warehouses are economically supported by special transportation rates. All warehouses and distribution centers in the Smith system are public facilities. Therefore, Smith's costs are based on volume throughput and duration of storage.

The twenty-three full line distribution centers are the primary facilities from which dealers are served. Although some early orders are shipped directly from plants and in-transit warehouses to dealers, those orders are limited to either Prevention or Support products, because the plants and in-transit warehouses lack full-line availability. The only in-transit warehouse that can make mixed shipments directly to customers is the one in Mobile. In total, less than 10 percent of the annual tonnage is shipped directly to dealers from plants or in-transit warehouses. Thus, 90 percent of all tonnage is either shipped from or picked up by dealers at the full-line distribution centers. Table 3 provides a list of distribution center locations. Replenishment of distribution center inventories is primarily on an allocation (push) basis controlled by central inventory planning.

All orders are processed on a daily batch basis at the central office after

Table 1   Annual Sales, 1978

Dollars	$338,511,000
Weight (lbs.)	300,274,000
Ft^3	17,331,000
Cases	4,880,000
Lines	51,000
Orders	27,000

Table 2   In-transit Warehouse Locations

Location	Product
Baton Rouge, Louisiana	Prevention
Houston, Texas	Prevention
Lake Charles, Louisiana	Support
Mobile, Alabama	Prevention and Support
New Orleans, Louisiana	Support
Shreveport, Louisiana	Prevention

they are received over a telecommunication network. The elapsed time from order entry to shipment release from the distribution center is less than 24 hours. During the early-order period this rapid processing is important, because it provides maximum time to consolidate dealer orders and realize transportation savings. During the seasonal application period, the system speed of order processing can be increased by short-interval order batching. During busy periods, two or three order batches are often processed in a single day. Usually, early orders that are picked up by dealers are processed using the normal system. However, during the application period, the distribution centers can release products on the telephone to dealers who want a same-day pickup. In these situations, the released quantity is transmitted from the distribution center to central order processing following the dealer pickup.

The primary method of shipment from plants to in-transit warehouses and distribution centers is rail carload. Shipment from in-transit warehouses to distribution centers is also normally by rail. However, when inventory is needed quickly, the in-transit opportunity is bypassed and distribution center replenishment is made by common carrier truck. Dealer shipments from distribution centers are made by truck. Transportation accounts for approximately 51 percent of total distribution cost.

A primary objective of the physical distribution system review is to evaluate the cost and service of the existing program in comparison with alternative methods of operation. Despite relatively smooth operations, the fact remains that at the end of each application season, many dealer requirements have not

Table 3   Full-line Field Distribution Center Locations

Baltimore, Maryland	Little Rock, Arkansas
Boise, Idaho	Louisville, Kentucky
Chicago, Illinois	Minneapolis, Minnesota
Columbus, Ohio	Morgantown, West Virginia
Dallas, Texas	Omaha, Nebraska
Des Moines, Iowa	Portland, Oregon
Fort Wayne, Indiana	Reno, Nevada
Grand Rapids, Michigan	Riverside, California
Greensboro, North Carolina	St. Louis, Missouri
Indianapolis, Indiana	San Jose, California
Iowa City, Iowa	Syracuse, New York
	Tulsa, Oklahoma

Table 4   Annual Distribution Costs, 1978

Transportation to warehouses	$6,868,000	
Transportation transfers between distribution centers	2,107,000	
Transportation to dealers	6,801,000	
Total transportation		$15,776,000
Storage		2,863,000
Handling		1,010,000
Ordering		843,000
Inventory		10,301,000
Total		$30,793,000

been satisfied, while other dealers have returned inventory. Thus, sales are lost that could have been enjoyed if products had been available to the dealers in need. A critical element of customer service is forward inventory availability to accommodate customer pickup.

Before deciding to undertake the study, management asked the accounting department to provide standard costs. The following standards were developed:

1   Order processing at a standard fixed cost per month with a variable cost per order.
2   Inventory at before-tax cost of 18 percent per annum of average inventory per field warehouse location.
3   Handling and storage at actual local cost for each existing and potential facility. Appropriate storage rate applicable at in-transit warehouses.
4   Inbound transportation from plants and in-transit warehouses to field warehouses based on point-to-point rates.
5   Transportation rates to customers based on a combination of point-to-point and regression equation rates.

The costs for the reference year of 1978 are contained in Table 4.

CASE 7-1: QUESTIONS

1   To what extent does the existing design of Smith's physical distribution system incorporate the concept of structural separation?
2   The existing physical distribution system has twenty-three full-line field warehouses. If these warehouses are reduced in number, management expects that total distribution costs will be reduced. (a) Do you agree? (b) Why or why not? (c) Assuming the above expectation is correct, how could customer service be improved by reducing the number of warehouses, rather than having all benefits realized in the form of total cost reduction?
3   If Smith were to reduce its number of total warehouses, do you feel conflict would develop regarding reduced availability of dealer pickup opportunities? Assuming it would, how would you suggest Smith prevent the development of such conflict?
4   Do you see justification for the development of an exclusive distribution system by Smith?

CASE 7-2: Pop Shoppes of Canada Ltd. (C)

In September of 1969, the management of Pop Shoppes of Canada Ltd. faced the problem of determining the best way for their new company to expand its operations, or indeed, if the company should expand at all. At that time, the company had only one outlet open and that had been in operation for just three months. Consequently, management felt that a thorough review of the company's history, taking careful note of both good and bad decisions, would be essential. In addition, a detailed analysis of the various opportunities for expansion would be required.

HISTORY OF THE COMPANY

In 1968, Mr. John Barber approached Mr. Roger Burd, a partner in the London-based advertising agency, Thompson and Burd Ltd., with the idea of marketing a five-cent soft drink in the London area. Mr. Burd was intrigued with the idea but was skeptical of the profitability of such a venture. Mr. Barber assured him it could be profitable to sell a case of 24 10-ounce bottles or 12 30-ounce bottles for $1.20 plus deposits of $1.20 for the bottles and $.40 for the case itself. Once the proposition had been explained in detail, Mr. Burd became very enthusiastic about the idea. As a result, both Mr. Burd and his partner Mr. Ray Thompson decided to each purchase an interest in the company, as did Messrs. Scott Gordon and Bob Sinclair, owners of a large retail store in London.

Mr. Barber invested $35,000 and each of the other men invested $7,500 and the company, Pop Shoppes of Canada Ltd., was formed in February of 1969.

The company had rented a building on Trafalgar Street just off Highbury Avenue, a main north-south traffic artery in the eastern part of the city. A red sign with a green bottle was fixed to the front of the building which had been painted white [Exhibit 1 (a)]. Red and white plastic cases [Exhibit 1 (b)] were also purchased. In addition, the Pop Shoppe purchased used bottling equipment from a nearby bottler [Exhibit 1 (c)].

Advertisements such as the one shown in Exhibit 2 were run in the *London Free Press* just prior to the opening of the Pop Shoppe and later as part of a follow-up campaign.

In addition to the newspaper campaign, radio stations CFPL, CKSL and CJOE in London, and radio station CHLO in St. Thomas were used to promote the Pop Shoppe. A large sign showing the flavours available and the prices was hung in the centre of the factory [Exhibit 3 (a)].

The plant layout was arranged so that when the customer entered the Pop Shoppe she would select a four-wheel cart and as many empty cases as she re-

Exhibit 1 (a) Front view of Pop Shoppe. (b) Examples of Pop Shoppe cases and bottles. (c) and (d) Pop Shoppe equipment in operation.

quired. She would then proceed down one of the two aisles and make her selection of flavours from the bottles stacked on either side of the aisles [Exhibit 3 (b)]. After the selection was complete, she would pay for the soft drinks at one of the two check-outs at the front of the factory [Exhibit 3 (c)].

FIRST THREE MONTHS OF OPERATION

A number of unforeseen difficulties arose during the first three months of operation which resulted in departures from the *pro forma* profit and loss statement shown in Exhibit 4.

First of all, the company was forced to delay the opening until June because of delivery delays from the plastic case supplier and the bottle manufacturer. In fact, the 10-ounce bottles did not arrive until early in July. All sales for

Exhibit 2   Typical Pop Shoppes Advertisement

Exhibit 3 (a) Point of purchase advertising. (b) View of carts and one of the two aisles with soft drinks stacked on each side according to flavour. (c) One of the two check-outs in operation. (d) The competition reacts.

June and the first week of July were in 30-ounce bottles. *Pro forma* figures had been based on 60% of the company's sales being in the 10-ounce bottles. A continued shortage of cases during June meant that the company was unable to sell 30-ounce bottles of many popular flavours. In spite of these difficulties, sales for this early period exceeded projections: July temperatures were unusually high for London.

Projected labour costs turned out to be low because sales volume had been heavier than predicted and additional staff was required to manufacture the soft drinks. Additionally, original estimates with regard to the efficiency of the production equipment had been over-optimistic with regard to the amount of labour required to operate it.

In considering the difficulties, results for the first three months of opera-

Exhibit 4 Pop Shoppes of Canada Limited Projected Statement of Income
(For the Period May 1, 1969 to April 30, 1969)

	1969								1970				Total
	May	June	July	August	September	October	November	December	January	February	March	April	
Sales	$3,300	$13,200	$16,500	$16,500	$8,800	$6,600	$5,500	$22,000	$11,000	$6,600	$8,800	$11,000	$129,800
Cost of sales:													
Ingredients	1,237	4,950	6,188	6,188	3,300	2,475	2,062	8,250	4,125	2,475	3,300	4,125	48,675
Labour	600	2,400	2,400	3,000	2,400	3,000	2,400	2,400	3,000	2,400	2,400	2,400	28,800
Bottle and case allowance	240	960	1,200	1,200	640	480	400	1,600	800	480	640	800	9,440
	2,077	8,310	9,788	10,388	6,340	5,955	4,862	12,250	7,925	5355	6,340	7,325	86,915
Gross income	1,223	4,890	6,712	6,112	2,460	645	638	9,750	3,075	1,245	2,460	3,675	42,885
Expenses:													
Depreciation and amortization	450	450	450	450	450	450	450	450	450	450	450	450	5,400
Utilities	210	840	1,050	1,050	560	420	350	1,400	700	420	560	700	8,260
Advertising	500	2,500	1,500	500	500	500	500	1,500	500	500	500	500	10,000
Write-off of pre-opening expenses	750	750	750	750	750	750	750	750	750	750	750	750	9,000
Rent	100	350	350	350	350	350	350	350	350	350	350	350	3,950
Sundry	100	300	300	300	300	300	300	300	300	300	300	300	3,400
	2,110	5,190	4,400	3,400	2,910	2,770	2,700	4,750	3,050	2,770	2,910	3,050	40,010
Net income (loss)	$(887)	$(300)	$ 2,712	$ 2,712	$(450)	$(2,125)	$(2,062)	$ 5,000	$ 25	$(1,525)	$(450)	$ 625	$ 2,875

Exhibit 4 (Continued) Pop Shoppes of Canada Limited Projected Statement of Cash Flow
(For the Period May 1, 1969 to April 30, 1969)

	1969								1970			
	May	June	July	August	September	October	November	December	January	February	March	April
Bank balance, beginning of month	$21,997	$22,542	$ 6,642	$18,154	$ 334	$ 34	$ 809	$ 781	$ 6,461	$ 5,066	$ 181	$ (19)
Add:												
Cash flow from operations consisting of—												
Net income (loss)	(887)	(300)	2,312	2,712	(450)	(2,125)	(2,062)	5,000	25	(1,525)	(450)	625
Depreciation and amortization	450	450	450	450	450	450	450	450	450	450	450	450
Write-off of pre-opening expenses	750	750	750	750	750	750	750	750	750	750	750	750
	345	900	3,512	3,912	750	925	862	6,200	1,225	(325)	750	1,825
Deposits from customers	4,800	19,200	24,000	24,000	12,800	9,600	8,000	32,000	16,000	9,600	12,800	16,000
Proceeds of bank loans					7,000	6,000	3,000			5,000		
	5,145	20,100	27,512	27,912	20,550	14,675	10,138	38,200	17,225	14,275	13,550	17,825
Deduct:												
Pre-opening expenses	3,000											
Bottle and case purchases		28,000		24,000								
Refunds of deposits to customers	1,600	8,000	16,000	22,400	20,250	15,450	10,110	16,520	18,620	19,160	12,750	12,750
Repayment of bank loans								16,000			1,000	4,000
	4,600	36,000	16,000	46,400	20,250	15,450	10,110	32,520	18,620	19,160	13,750	16,750
Bank balance, end of month	$22,542	$ 6,642	$18,154	$ 334	$ 34	$ 809	$ 781	$ 6,461	$ 5,066	$ 181	$ (19)	$ 1,056

tion left Mr. Barber confident that the company would exceed the projected annual net profit before taxes of $2,875.00. Actual net income for July and August was roughly $2,600.00 and $2,800.00 compared with projected income of $2,312.00, and $2,712.00 respectively. The unit sales volume was 19,500 cases for July and 22,000 cases for August. All opening expenses were being written off over 12 months, leasehold improvements over 36 months and the equipment on a straight line basis of 20% annually. Because the machines just could not keep production up to sales without working a second shift and due to the other difficulties previously mentioned, management made the decision to do no advertising after July.

In an interview on September 10, 1969, Mr. Barber stated that the company had not found it necessary to purchase new bottles or cases in over a month and that management estimated that 75% of the company's sales were in the form of repeat purchases.

In summary, then, the company expected to exceed its planned sales and profit figures for the first year's operation in spite of all the difficulties encountered in the first three months of business and without the planned advertising expenditures.

COMPETITION

The least expensive 30-ounce bottles of soft drinks on the market when the Pop Shoppe opened its door for the first time were the A&P Company's "Yukon Club" brand. These bottles retailed at 6 for $.89 plus deposit (Appendix A). Yukon Club in 10-ounce cans sold at 6 for $.49 and the Food City private brand sold at 4 for $.29. Most brands, however, retailed at 6 for $.69.

Since the Pop Shoppe sold its beverages at $.10 per 30-ounce bottle and $.05 per 10-ounce bottle, its prices were well below those of the lowest-priced competitors and less than half the price of the major brands.

Only one competitor reacted to the pricing strategy introduced by the Pop Shoppe. The Shaw's Dairy store next door to the Pop Shoppe reduced the price on its Farmer Jack's soft drinks to 12 30-ounce bottles for $1.20 plus deposit and promoted the line by placing large signs in front of the store [Exhibit 3 (d)].

When asked about the possibility of some type of retaliation by soft-drink bottlers, Mr. Barber responded:

"We don't expect to be a threat to the Coca-Cola company. They are selling half of all the soft drinks in North America. . . . I don't think that Pepsi Cola is going to be affected either. The people that might be affected are the small bottlers, with products that are only known locally. They may decide to pave their lawns and turn into factory-to-you operations, but Coca-Cola and Pepsi, which are the two giants, would be unlikely to turn their plants into factory-to-you, because of their investment in trucks, and the fact that the retailers would all turn on them. . . . Now I suppose there are men at Coca-Cola for instance who might say I know all about the soft drink business. . . . I've been running this Coca-Cola plant for the past 22 years and I'm going to open up a factory-to-you soft drink plant. We, of course, are selling only the home market and not at all affecting on-premise consumption. I would guess the main impact we'd have on the total market would be one of increasing per-capita consumption.''

ALTERNATIVES FOR EXPANSION

As of August 1969, the executives of the Pop Shoppe had raised the possibility of expansion of their company and a number of ideas had been given consideration.

Mr. Barber felt that the alternatives for future expansion of the company should be limited to the following:

1   Selling through depots,
2   Selling to retail outlets,
3   Using home delivery service,
4   Selling a larger volume from the existing plant by advertising heavily,
5   Opening additional company-owned outlets across Canada by going public, or
6   Franchising Pop Shoppes across Canada.

With any of the first three possibilities the company would be required to use second or third shifts in the existing plant or to build a new plant in London at a cost of approximately $250,000. The new machinery would be completely automatic and would produce 6,000 cases of soft drinks per day on one shift. The old equipment could be sold or perhaps moved to a smaller city and the old Pop Shoppe location on Trafalgar Street could perhaps be used as a depot or sub-leased.

1   *Depots.* Mr. Barber related some of the latest thinking of the management group regarding the use of depots.

"Depots would offer many potential customers more convenient locations rather than having to drive all the way to the Pop Shoppe. We'd be offering more convenience, the same red plastic case, which seems to take people's fancy, and a low price, say $1.30 plus deposit. However, we would be missing the fact that a depot isn't the factory, it's a retail outlet. Management are split in their opinions on the importance of the plant being part of an outlet. Some feel that buying at the plant is not that important. They believe most people are buying our products because they want to save money, and if they can save that same amount of money in a local shopping plaza, they'll go there. Others regard the plant contact as an important part of our customer appeal."

One member of the management group thought that the company should open depots and, in order to make them as inexpensive as possible for the soft-drink operation, gasoline pumps should be added. He felt that the gasoline business would not only help to pay the expenses of the depot, but would attract more customers. With this kind of arrangement the customer could charge both gas and soft drinks on his gasoline credit card.

The estimated cost of operating a depot, including trucking, salaries and rent, was $500 per month or approximately $.30 per case based on estimated monthly sales volumes of about 1,700 cases per depot.

2 *Retail Sales.* Mr. Barber was in favour of selling to retail outlets in order to increase sales volume. He felt that some kind of discount should be offered to the retail trade and was considering $1.10 per case plus deposit. Mr. Burd was opposed to this concept if the retailers were going to be selling the soft drinks by the bottle rather than by the case. He believed that selling the bottles individually would reduce the probability of the bottles being returned and thus increase bottle losses. Mr. Barber knew that because of the company's limited resources it was important not to tie up too much capital in bottles and cases. It was this belief that had originally led to the company's desire to sell 12 30-ounce bottles or 24 10-ounce bottles to each customer. It was hoped that this would create a situation where the consumer had a substantial investment in bottles and for this reason would return them even if a repeat purchase would not occur. If the retailer sold the 10-ounce bottles individually for $.15 plus $.10 deposit this commitment would be reduced.

3 *Home Delivery.* Management thought that home delivery was another possibility and cited as an example the Home Juice Company which had been very successful in delivering juice in Canada from 1966 to 1969. However, the Pop Shoppe would not be able to maintain the $.10 price for 30-ounce bottles if home delivery was used. Mr. Barber reflected:

> "We would need a fleet of trucks and also drivers, etc. . . . The price would have to be almost as high as that in the chain stores . . ."

4 *Advertising.* Another alternative was to increase the traffic and sales at the Trafalgar Street location by increasing the company's advertising budget. Rates for the local newspaper, radio stations and television are summarized in Exhibit 3 of Pop Shoppes (B).

5 *Company-owned Outlets.* The company could proceed along the lines of raising money from the public and opening company-owned Pop Shoppes in major Canadian cities.

Management felt that the big potential for their company was to sell the concept across North America. However, in order to expand this way it would be necessary to raise "millions of dollars."

In an attempt to raise capital, the company's executives approached a local bank but the maximum loan available to them was $25,000. They also approached Roynat, a term lender, but any money received from that source would be at a 12% rate of interest.

The other method of raising capital would be to go public but management would be required to give up too much of the company at this point in time. Mr. Barber reflected:

> "We could go public—that's a very popular thing these days—but we wouldn't have nearly as much to offer in the form of past earnings and future potential as we

will if we wait for six months or a year. . . . By waiting we could sell shares for much more money and the Ontario Securities Commission would not prevent us from selling our personal holdings if we so desired."

6 *Franchise Pop Shoppes.* The final possibility was franchising. If franchising was chosen two broad courses of action would be open to the company. They could require that the franchisee put up a large amount of capital for the franchise or demand small capital investment and a share of the on-going business.

The main advantage of demanding a high initial deposit from the franchisee was that it would result in immediate working capital which could be used to open company-owned outlets.

One of the members of the management group felt that the franchise fee should be determined by the potential market in the area being purchased. For example, if a Pop Shoppe was to be built in a community of 300,000 people the franchisee would be required to sign a note for one dollar per potential customer or $300,000. The Pop Shoppe could use these notes as collateral for a loan and the franchisee would pay this note out of the profits of his operation. Mr. Barber added:

"We could have the franchisee pay us a down payment of, say $45,000, and then we could go and borrow the remainder and construct this plant. Harvey's are apparently doing it in this fashion, as is Red Barn.[1]

In this case, the franchisee rents the building and property from the franchisor.

Another alternative was to sell a franchise for $10,000.

"We could ask for $10,000 and give him the franchise for a city or a portion of it. . . . For example the city could be Kitchener–Waterloo. The area has about 200,000 people living in and around it. He would receive this territory for $10,000 and he would be given a map showing how far he could go with depots, direct-selling, door to door or, if he preferred, he could have a one-factory outlet. In any case, he would be told how far he could go out to reach customers, and what media he would be allowed to use to attract these customers. In other words, he would not be allowed to go on CFPL in London to attract people to the Kitchener Pop Shoppe. He would have to use Kitchener media. He would be given advice as to where to locate, but location would be his decision. He would buy our sign, our bottles, our cases and he would be required to spend a certain per cent of his sales in advertising and buy his syrup from us."

In this alternative, the franchisee would be required to pay Pop Shoppes of Canada Ltd. $.10 per person living in the city for which he wanted the franchise. This would be payable in ten equal annual installments. For his flavours,

[1] Harvey's and Red Barn are two well-known fast-food chains in Canada.

the franchisee would pay the franchisor $.10 per case, over and above the factory cost. He would also pay $.10 per case for advertising and promotion which would be done for him by Pop Shoppes of Canada Ltd. This cost would be added to the per gallon price of the syrup. If this alternative was chosen the cost of the soft drinks would have to be raised to $1.38 plus deposit in order to assure that the venture would be profitable for the franchisee.

The latest estimates of the investment required to open a Pop Shoppe were in the neighbourhood of $125,000 but this figure would vary somewhat with the size of the community being serviced. This estimate included bottles, cases, ingredients, working capital and the leasing of machinery. The machinery being considered would cost $135,000 if it was purchased new and would be capable of producing 500 cases of soft drinks per hour. Second-hand machinery of this type could be purchased for about $75,000.

Mr. Barber felt that it was imperative that they decide on a course of action within the next few weeks so that Pop Shoppes of Canada Ltd. would not miss out on the 1970 summer sales period.

Chapter 8

Channel Management: Manufacturing Enterprises

The typical situation confronted by manufacturers is that they must rely upon wholesalers, retailers, and other intermediaries to assist in the performance of selected marketing functions.[1] The goal of a manufacturing operation in channel design is to achieve effective performance of all marketing functions at the minimum total cost expenditure. The model to guide channel design or modification, presented in Figure 7-9, provides the framework for development of this chapter. In this chapter we build upon the material presented in Chapter 7 and customize it from the vantage point of channel design by manufacturers.

The initial section examines the formulation of channel objectives and associated strategies. What a manufacturer wants to achieve and the selected methods of accomplishment are primary determinants of channel structure. The next section discusses the process of identification and selection from among channel structure alternatives. Considerations related to identification and selection of specific channel members are then examined. The final section reviews feedback and control of channel performance.

This chapter follows a logical progression: objectives and strategy determine structure which, in turn, identifies alternative channel members. The dy-

[1] The treatment of basic marketing functions was presented in Chapter 2.

namic nature of the business environment makes it necessary for a firm to monitor and evaluate channel performance continually. When goals are not satisfied, most manufacturers will need to find ways to improve performance of existing channels or will need to reevaluate channel alternatives and institute a program of change. Even though the above progression is basic, distribution channels have been singled out as "one of the least managed areas of marketing" within manufacturing concerns.[2]

FORMULATION OF CHANNEL OBJECTIVES AND STRATEGY

Objectives to be achieved in a distribution channel arrangement are an extension of the organization's marketing objectives. Thus, channel strategy, structure, and membership selection are an integral part of the firm's marketing mix strategy.[3] Channel strategy is the basic plan for achieving channel objectives. Selected aspects of channel objectives and strategy are discussed in this section.

Channel Objectives

Assume that a manufacturing firm's marketing objective is to maintain or increase market share while realizing a 20 percent return on investment. The corresponding channel objectives necessary to realize this goal must be stated in specific operational terms which can be used to identify and select among alternative channel structures. For example, the following specifications will assist in achieving the basic objective:

1　Planned sales and profitability by time periods.
2　Desired market coverage.
3　Required sales and service support.
4　Desired physical distribution support.
5　Desired return on investment by individual channel function.

In the final analysis, the process of implementing channel objectives involves determining which functions the manufacturer desires to perform. Performance of the remainder becomes the subject of negotiation with potential channel members.

Channel Strategies

Channel strategy is the specific plan which guides achievement of channel objectives. Strategy has been defined as "the schemes (or key concepts) whereby a firm's resources and advantages are managed (or deployed) in order to sur-

---

[2] Reavis Cox and Thomas F. Schutte, "A Look at Channel Management," in Philip McDonald (ed.), *Marketing Involvement in Society and the Economy* (Chicago, Ill.: American Marketing Association, 1969), p. 105.
[3] See Chapter 6.

prise and surpass competitors or to exploit opportunities."[4] Thus, channel strategy is the heart of the manufacturer's program for gaining and maintaining a competitive differential advantage.

A variety of alternative strategies may be employed simultaneously to achieve the channel objective. Although many alternative strategies exist to guide channel performance, four deserve special mention: (1) pull, (2) push, (3) functional spin-off and/or absorption, and (4) distribution expansion.

Pull   One outstanding example of a channel pull strategy is the marketing practice followed by breakfast cereal processors. Major cereal companies utilize all forms of mass communication to create a brand preference among consumers. The objective of a pull strategy is to stimulate sufficient consumer desire for the brand to encourage or force retailers to stock that as well as other products sold by the same manufacturer. The manufacturer's expectation is that both retailers and wholesalers will stock the products because of the ease with which they can be sold. Thus, while per-unit profit margins for channel members may be lower when a pull strategy is employed, so will the associated cost of retail and wholesale marketing.

The most obvious examples of pull strategies are found in the consumer goods industry. However, the same concept can be effectively applied to market products to industrial or agricultural buyers. Ciba-Geigy Corporation utilizes extensive television advertising each spring to stimulate farmer preference for its agricultural products. Likewise, many jobbers advertise their products on radio and television in the Detroit area to attract purchasing and design managers of the automotive manufacturers.

The intent of a pull strategy is development of a strong brand preference on the part of the ultimate buyer. To the extent the product is pre-positioned in the marketplace, the manufacturer gains negotiating power with potential channel members.

Push   A push strategy receives its name from the fact that the manufacturer's sales force uses aggressive selling to encourage wholesalers and retailers to handle the product. Wholesalers will "push" the product to retailers, who will promote it to consumers. The manufacturer may encourage channel members to carry the product by offering high margins, free cases, "buy five, get one free," trade promotions such as retail displays and cooperative advertising allowances, and sales-force training and aids. The push strategy is most effective for products of high quality that require personal selling but this is not always the case. A small manufacturer of consumer-packaged goods may be unable to finance a pull strategy and may have to "push" a product into the market by providing high margins and other incentives for middlemen.

The competitive situation, availability of suitable channel members, con-

---

[4] David J. Luck and Arthur A. Prell, *Marketing Strategy* (New York: Appleton-Century-Crofts, 1968), p. 2.

sumer attitudes and perceptions, product characteristics, and overall channel objectives will influence whether a push or pull strategy or a combination of both should be used. The producer of Lestoil household cleaner, a relatively small manufacturer, was unsuccessful in attempting to gain market position by utilizing a push strategy. But heavy advertising combined with a program of cents-off coupons mailed to households developed consumer demand. This pull strategy ultimately led to trade acceptance of the product.

Functional Spin-Off and Absorption Functional spin-off and absorption were discussed in terms of channel negotiation in Chapter 6. These concepts are important to manufacturers because of the various potential strategies implied. However, the same potential strategies are also available to powerful retailers and wholesalers.

To illustrate, a manufacturer may decide to spin off small and unprofitable accounts to distributors or wholesalers. Union Carbide maintains a policy of utilizing distributors for all chemical and plastic orders under a specific weight or dollar value. Larger orders are marketed and distributed directly from corporate facilities.

Functional absorption provides for a manufacturer's forward extension of marketing activities. An example is replacing a wholesaler's selling effort with the manufacturer's own sales force, or establishing a private truck fleet to replace common carrier delivery to wholesalers.

Distribution Expansion A final channel strategy is a concentrated effort by manufacturers to introduce products into retail outlets that do not or traditionally have not stocked a specific product. This trend to expand the sales base of a product is described as *scrambled merchandising*. The supporting concept is that profitable volume can be added if products can be exposed to any point-of-sale location patronized by the desired target market clientele.

A second way to expand sales is with more effective merchandising of products within existing outlets. This battle for shelf space or display space is constant among manufacturers selling products within the same retail outlet. As we noted at the outset, a manufacturer seldom utilizes a single strategy to gain channel objectives. Gillette's introduction of Ultra-Max Hairspray combined a $17 million media pull with extensive push incentives. The objective was to simultaneously launch a new product successfully and expand distribution of Gillette products in existing retail outlets. Efforts to expand distribution either within existing channel arrangements or to new outlets can be expected to be implemented in concert with a push or pull strategy.

Conclusion—Channel Objectives and Strategy

Overall marketing objectives are operationalized in channel design. Channel objectives and related strategies provide specifications for identification and selection of the desired channel structure. The channel strategy is a specific plan for guiding resources allocated to gain a competitive differential advantage. Attention is now directed to identification and selection of the basic channel structure.

IDENTIFICATION AND SELECTION OF CHANNEL STRUCTURE

Once channel objectives and strategy have been established, the manufacturer must identify the most desirable channel structure. For example, the manufacturer may sell direct or use agents, brokers, jobbers, wholesalers, and/or retailers. The desired number and location of intermediaries must be determined. Availability of physical distribution intermediaries will also influence final channel structure. All marketing functions must be accomplished but they will be performed in different ways depending on the institutions selected to form the channel structure. Since the manufacturer is required to shoulder more economic risk when fewer intermediaries are used, financial strength may limit available options.[5] Within such constraints the manufacturer must decide where and how products can be sold most profitably. Arrangements must then be made to gain the cooperation of final selling units such as retailers or industrial distributors. The final sales outlets selected will determine whether wholesalers can or must be used to reach those markets. In the final analysis matching the number, size, and location of customers with product characteristics is the primary determinant of channel structure.

Although channel structure options are restricted, it would be unusual for a firm to be limited to only one way to distribute its product. Consequently, it is necessary for the manufacturer to determine the sales potential, growth rates, and relative profitability of each channel alternative. To complete such an analysis, operational requirements and performance analysis considerations must be reviewed. Each is discussed below.

Operational Requirements

The primary operational considerations are (1) the importance of captive and independent outlets, (2) geographic differentiation, and (3) product differentiation. Each influences channel structure selection.

Captive or Independent Outlets Captive outlets are wholly owned by the manufacturer. SCOA Industries is an example of a vertically integrated corporate channel system. The company owns shoe manufacturing facilities in New England and distributes its own production as well as imported items throughout the United States. In total, over 850 outlets are utilized including company-owned Gallenkamp and Schiff family shoe stores and leased departments in discount department stores. The financial resources required to establish a corporate channel are substantial and may preclude this option. In addition, a

---

[5] Eugene W. Lambert, Jr., "Financial Considerations in Choosing a Marketing Channel," *MSU Business Topics* (Winter 1966), p. 17–26.

rather extensive product line is required to justify a specialized retail outlet. For example, Singer is able to combine the sale of sewing machines, materials, patterns, and related items into a specialized retail offering.

Many manufacturers have successfully combined captive and independent outlets. The Sherwin-Williams Company uses three types of retail outlets to distribute its paint products. The first type is a chain of company-owned decorating centers which carry the Sherwin-Williams name and sell paints, wallcoverings, and carpeting. The second channel is comprised of independent retail outlets supplied either by independent wholesalers or on a direct sales basis. Finally, the company sells private label paints to co-op retailers and national chains on a direct sales basis.

The majority of manufacturers use independent outlets exclusively. For example, most manufacturers of grocery products sell to wholesalers, chain stores, co-ops and/or the military. Manufacturers such as International Harvester reach the industrial market by using independent dealers. Although some of International Harvester's competitors have used company-owned dealers, the current trend seems to be away from such a practice. In contrast, the appliance industry for the most part uses independent dealers for retail sales. However, the method of servicing dealers consists of direct sale, independent distributors, and company branches. Some firms use a combination of all three channel structures.

Geographic Differentiation Alternative channel structures may be necessary to realize distribution objectives in different geographic areas. In densely populated areas such as the Northeast and Midwest, a manufacturer may be able to serve customers most profitably using a direct sales force and company-operated distribution warehouses. However, in less populated areas wholesalers may be the preferred channel. When volume is less concentrated, wholesalers often can achieve transportation economies by consolidated delivery to individual customers. In such situations the wholesaler typically absorbs the inventory risk and selling functions.

Assignment of orders based on size to different channels is a form of geographic differentiation in that the manufacturer is aware of inefficiencies associated with small-volume special orders. Steel service centers have created a specialized channel for steel based upon their capabilities to fabricate small quantities of products.

Product Differentiation Finally, the manufacturer may desire to participate in product differentiation and to utilize more than one channel. This operational posture is commonly called dual distribution. To illustrate, for many years Spalding has sold certain brands of golf equipment only to professional shops on golf courses. While the Elite brand represented the top of the line in golf clubs at the pro shops, the Robert T. Jones, Jr. brand represented the top of the line in other retail outlets. This was done primarily to protect professional shops from direct price competition from mass merchandisers. The policy allowed the manufacturer to participate actively in more than one market with essentially the same product.

The same result can be accomplished by developing private label business. Engaged in this distribution practice are manufacturers of tires, clothing, food products, personal hygiene products, liquor, and paints, to name a few. Referring to the Sherwin-Williams example discussed earlier, the company manufactured private label paints for sale to co-op retailers and national chains. This practice allows the company to compete in more than one market without confusing consumers or destroying business in the more profitable captive channel.

Performance Considerations

Each of the channel options available to the manufacturer has associated advantages and disadvantages. Consequently, a method for systematically comparing the alternatives is required. Three methods of dealing with channel selection in an organized manner are presented. The first is a ranked preference method whereby channel alternatives are eliminated for failure to meet performance goals. The second method is estimated cost-revenue analysis, and the third method utilizes computer simulation.

Ranked Preference Method The ranked preference method requires that factors critical to channel success be listed in order of importance to the firm.[6] In addition, the minimum or maximum acceptable level of performance must be established for each factor. For example, the most important consideration may be the investment required. Assume a firm is limited to a maximum channel investment of $5 million. If the company is considering five alternative channels, the first step in the comparative analysis is to estimate the investment for each channel. The format for conducting a rank preference analysis is illustrated in Table 8-1. Assume that channel alternative 5 would require an investment greater than $5 million and the other four alternatives are under the maximum. Alternative 5 would be eliminated from further consideration because it failed to meet the factor identified as most critical to success. The procedure is repeated through successively less important criteria until one alternative remains.

Many weaknesses are associated with this method. First, it is necessary to rank selection criteria. Second, because of the elimination factor, it is necessary to drop a channel without considering the relative advantage of one alternative over another when judged by multiple factors. Finally, the method fails to consider such critical items as profitability and return on investment.

---

[6] This method is based on the hierarchical preference ordering method described in Philip Kotler, *Marketing Decision Making: A Model Building Approach* (New York: Holt, Rinehart and Winston, Inc., 1971), pp. 294–296.

Table 8-1   A Ranked Preference Method for Selecting Channel Structure

Critical success factors	Minimum or maximum acceptable level of performance	Most likely (expected) level of performance Channel alternative				
		1	2	3	4	5
1 Required investment	Maximum investment that firm can afford					
2 Percent of investment recoverable if product fails	Minimum percentage acceptable					
3 Sales	Minimum sales volume acceptable					
4 Growth potential (expressed as an annualized percentage)	Minimum percentage acceptable					
5 Market coverage	Minimum percentage acceptable					
6 Relative advantage gained by company's present strengths (rate on scale of 1 to 10)	Minimum accepted level (i.e., 7)					

Source: Adapted from Philip Kotler, *Marketing Decision Making: A Model Building Approach* (New York: Holt, Rinehart and Winston, 1971), p. 295.

Cost-Revenue Analysis   Judging alternative channel structures on the basis of estimated cost and revenue analysis overcomes many problems associated with the ranked preference method. Table 8-2 illustrates the framework recommended for this form of analysis. Market research can be used to formulate revenue estimates for each alternative channel structure. Next, manufacturing costs are estimated for various levels of activity. Variable marketing and physical distribution costs such as sales commissions, transportation, warehousing, and order processing must be projected along with inventory requirements and accounts receivable. The corporate cost of money should be applied to accounts receivable, and inventory carrying costs added to inventory investment. Assignable nonvariable costs incurred for each segment should be added to each alternative. Finally, the corporate opportunity cost of money should be used as a charge for all other assets required by each channel structure alternative. The size of the net segment margin will determine which structural alternative is the best option from a financial performance standpoint. This information combined with estimates of future growth for each structural alternative permits the channel designer to select the most desirable alternative.

Computer Simulation   Computer simulation is a more comprehensive method of achieving results similar to those possible using cost and revenue analysis. Simulation also has the advantage of allowing the channel manager to

Table 8-2   Channel Cost/Revenue Analysis—Contribution Approach with a Charge for Assets Employed

	Channel alternative				
	1	**2**	**3**	**4**	**5**
Net sales					
Cost of goods sold (variable manufacturing cost)	—	—	—	—	—
Manufacturing contribution	—	—	—	—	—
Marketing and physical distribution costs					
Variable					
Sales commissions					
Transportation					
Warehousing (handling in and out)					
Order processing					
Inventory carrying costs					
Charge for investment in accounts receivable	—	—	—	—	—
Segment contribution margin	—	—	—	—	—
Assignable nonvariable costs (costs incurred specifically for the segment during the period):					
Salaries					
Segment related advertising					
Bad debts					
Other	—	—	—	—	—
Segment controllable margin	—	—	—	—	—
Charge for assets used by segment	—	—	—	—	—
Net segment margin	—	—	—	—	—
Assumptions:					
Public warehouses are used for field inventories					

project profitability and investment requirements for a number of years into the future and under varying assumptions.[7] Simulation has been defined as[8]

> . . . the use of a model to represent over time essential characteristics of a system or process under study. The model may be manipulated in ways impossible or impractical to perform on the system being represented. The dynamics of the behavior of the system represented may be inferred by the operation of the model.

The best way to view a channel simulation is as a computer program that replicates or quantifies the projected performance of a proposed channel. This capability to quantify system performance permits managerial evaluation of channel performance before negotiations are finalized and resources committed to a specific program.

Although simulation models may be the best method of channel analysis, they are costly to develop. Likewise, results are only as good as the assump-

[7] For a detailed example of simulation in a channel context see Donald J. Bowersox, et. al., *Simulated Product Sales Forecasting* (East Lansing: Michigan State University Business Research Bureau), 1979.

[8] Robert C. Meier, William F. Newell, and Harold L. Pazer, *Simulation in Business and Economics* (Englewood Cliffs, N.J.: Prentice-Hall, Inc., 1969), p. 2.

tions and data used in their development. The simulation method has the advantage of integrating the marketing and physical distribution aspects of channel design. Thus, the specialization benefits of structural separation can be analyzed without the danger of suboptimization. Channel performance, using simulation, can be evaluated on a total channel basis rather than viewing marketing or physical distribution arrangements in isolation.

A combination of all three methods may be the most desirable framework for making the channel structure decision. That is, the ranked preference method and/or cost and revenue analysis can be used to reduce the number of alternatives to two or three which can then be analyzed further using simulation.

IDENTIFICATION AND SELECTION OF CHANNEL MEMBERS

The channel structure selected identifies specific types of intermediaries eligible for consideration as members. A number of possible sources of information may be used to identify alternative channel members. For example, customers or potential customers may be able to provide names of middlemen they would prefer to deal with. Trade directories, editors of trade publications, members and officials of trade associations, business associates, suppliers, and educational institutions are all potential sources of information.

James R. Stock found that the following sources were used to gain information about modes of transportation: past experience with the mode (83.4 percent of the respondents), carriers' sales calls (61.1 percent), trade directories/routing guides (49.8 percent), present users of the mode (47.2 percent), other distribution and traffic managers (46.9 percent), present or potential customers of the firm (44.1 percent), and other information sources with lower ratings such as marketing and sales departments, traffic clubs, and outside consultants.[9]

Once identified, potential channel members must be evaluated to ascertain which best fit the manufacturer's objectives. Table 8-3 provides a list of general criteria which can be used to evaluate wholesalers and retailers. General criteria must be supplemented by specific statements concerning what the manufacturer desires to achieve regarding each aspect of the intermediaries' performance.

FEEDBACK AND CONTROL

Channel management is not completed with the design of the distribution system. It is necessary to implement an information system and to establish standards so that channel performance can be measured and evaluated. On a con-

---

[9] James R. Stock, "How Shippers Judge Carriers," *Distribution Worldwide* (August 1976), pp. 32–35.

Table 8-3 Criteria for Selecting a Channel Member

1 Size of prospective channel member—sales, financial strength
2 Sales strength
   Number of sales personnel
   Sales and technical competence
3 Product lines
   Competitive products
   Compatible products
   Complementary products
   Quality of lines carried
4 Reputation
   Leadership
   Well-established
5 Market coverage
   Geographic coverage—outlets per market area
   Industry coverage
   Call frequency or intensity of coverage
6 Sales performance
   Performance with related lines
   General sales performance
   Growth prospects
7 Management
8 Advertising and sales promotion
9 Sales compensation
10 Acceptance of training assistance
11 Transportation savings
12 Inventory
   Kind and size
   Inventory minimums—safety stocks
   Reductions in manufacturer inventories
   Extent of postponement—speculation
13 Warehousing—supplied in field
              —ability to handle shipments efficiently
14 Lot quantity costs—willingness to accept our ordering policies

Source: Douglas M. Lambert, *The Distribution Channels Decision* (New York: National Association of Accountants; and Hamilton, Ontario: The Society of Management Accountants of Canada, 1978), p. 37.

tinuous basis management must determine (1) if the entire channel performance is adequate, (2) whether a change in channel structure will lead to improved performance, and (3) if existing channel members can improve their performance. Chapter 10 provides a comprehensive treatment of channel performance measurement.

CHANNEL DESIGN AND CURRENT INDUSTRY PRACTICE

The preceding discussion has followed a logical progression from statement of objectives to final selection of channel partners. The question remains: To what extent do manufacturers in fact follow such a procedure when selecting and implementing a channel design?[10] A recent study of eighteen manufacturers with annual sales from $9 million to over $1 billion provides considerable evidence that manufacturers do not follow a formal procedure when making channel decisions.

Only six of the studied firms reported that potential new products were screened in advance on the basis of whether or not they were compatible with the firm's existing channel or channels. Seven manufacturers indicated a strong preference for the existing channel or channels but would not rule out a new product opportunity because it did not fit an existing channel:

> Normally we would not attempt to market a product that did not fit one of our existing channels. However, it is conceivable that a potential new product would be so attractive that the new product development committee (comprised of top management and heads of the functional areas) would investigate alternative channels.

The remaining five firms exhibited varying degrees of sophistication when selecting channel structure. A manufacturer of consumer-packaged goods used the following criteria:

1 Who would likely purchase the product?
2 How can we reach them effectively?
3 Who is selling to this market now?
4 How is the market growing?
5 Are there segments of the market not being served by the most common channel?

An executive with a manufacturer of nonconsumer durables commented on how channels of distribution for new products were determined in his company:

> In the past, each functional area handled its own problems with regard to new products. Now, the functions get together and work on the new product introduction. Recently the channel was changed to accommodate a new product and a new market.

However, this integrated approach was not always used. A manager whose firm marketed industrial chemical products replied:

> Within our company top management asks the financial management people for a decision which they will make without consulting distribution even though they do not understand the distribution function.

In general, the study found that management of the total channel by manufacturers was not a reality.

---

[10] This section is based upon Douglas M. Lambert, *The Distribution Channels Decision* (New York: The National Association of Accountants; and Hamilton, Ontario: The Society of Management Accountants of Canada, 1978), pp. 51–115.

SUMMARY

Channel design at the manufacturer's level must begin with a clear statement of objectives and strategy. Channel objectives—the targets that are set for the systems—must be based on corporate and marketing objectives. Channel strategy can take the form of pull strategies, push strategies, functional spin-off and absorption, and distribution expansion.

Once objectives and strategy have been determined, channel structure alternatives must be identified. Selection of channel structure can be made on the basis of operational requirements or performance considerations. Operational considerations include evaluation of captive or independent outlets, geographic differentiation, and product differentiation. Performance of alternative structures can be judged on the basis of critical success factors (the ranked preference model), cost and revenue analysis, and/or computer simulation.

When the channel structure decision has been made, management must identify and select individual channel members. Decisions made with respect to structure identify specific types of intermediaries eligible for channel membership. However, specific criteria must be developed to guide selection of channel members.

Finally, a system of feedback and control is necessary to monitor channel performance and determine if objectives are being achieved. If performance is not satisfactory, modifications may be required in order to improve corporate profitability.

In reality, most manufacturers do not follow channel decision procedures such as those we have detailed. However, available evidence suggests that the "flying by the seat of the pants" era is rapidly ending among progressive manufacturers.

QUESTIONS

1 Distribution channels have been singled out as "one of the least managed areas of marketing." Why do you suppose that this is the case?
2 Give an example of how channel objectives might be operationalized.
3 Compare and contrast pull and push marketing strategies. How would selection of one or the other of these strategies influence the distribution channels chosen?
4 Explain the concept of functional spin-off and its implications for channel design.
5 How has scrambled merchandising influenced design of channel structures?
6 How do operational considerations such as (a) captive and independent outlets, (b) geographic differentiation, and (c) product differentiation influence selection of channel structure?
7 What are the relative advantages and disadvantages of the following methods of comparing channel alternatives: (a) ranked preference method, (b) cost-revenue analysis, and (c) computer simulation?
8 Why is the feedback loop important for management of the distribution channel?
9 What are the pro's and con's of adopting a policy of screening out new product opportunities based upon whether or not they fit the firm's existing channels of distribution?

10 One executive gave the following explanation for how channels of distribution were
    determined in his firm:

    "In the past, each functional area handled its own problems with regard to new
    products. Now the functions get together and work on the new product introduc-
    tion. Recently the channel was changed to accommodate a new product and a new
    market."

    What problems may be associated with the lack of an integrated approach to the
    selection of channels of distribution for new products?

CASE 8-1: Associated Carpet Manufacturers, Incorporated

In the spring of 1978 John C. Bishop, president of the newly formed Associated Carpet Manufacturers, Inc. (ACM), was faced with the problem of determining how the company's products were to be distributed.

BACKGROUND

The association was formed in January 1978 by six manufacturers of quality floor coverings in northwestern Georgia. Each of the companies manufactured quality floor coverings and each supplied carpets for a particular segment of the household market. The largest and oldest of the six firms, The Carpet Factory, was founded in Dalton, Georgia, in 1905. The company specialized in a few major carpet weaves and concentrated its main effort on production. The narrowness of its line brought it into contact with the Smith Company, one of the industry's leaders. Smith manufactured and distributed a complementary carpet line and both companies saw the opportunity for a mutually beneficial arrangement. Consequently, a sales agency agreement was entered into in the late 1930s, with Smith offering the product through about 5,000 of its 12,000 retail dealers. This agreement enabled the Dalton manufacturer to ignore the total distribution process while permitting Smith to market a line without a capital investment. This arrangement continued until 1977.

In June 1977 John Bishop became president of The Carpet Factory. Bishop was an MBA graduate from a well-known midwest business school and had been marketing manager for a large carpet manufacturer in Pennsylvania.

The dependence of The Carpet Factory on Smith Company and a history of conflict resolution in favor of Smith led Bishop to consider alternative marketing strategies. He was aware of five other firms who were somewhat smaller in sales but who were facing similar problems with their sales agents. After months of negotiating, these six firms dropped their sales agents and merged to form the new company, Associated Carpet Manufacturers, Incorporated. Bishop was retained as president of the new organization.

THE BUSINESS PROBLEM

With annual sales in excess of $50 million, ACM was considered a relatively large firm in the industry. Although ACM was not a challenge to the top three manufacturers, it was certainly well above the lower group. Bishop's responsibility was to determine if the new organization should use wholesaler middlemen or sell on a direct basis.

Although direct sale would provide the company with better control over retail outlets and offer the advantages of a hard-core aggressive sales force, wholesalers performed some worthy functions, not the least of which were maintaining warehouses, extending credit, and providing rapid delivery service. Moreover, wholesalers carried a complete line and could support a more extensive sales force and warehousing system than could a limited-line manufacturer. Thus, the immediate consideration was a trade-off between the 20 percent of sales that would be paid to wholesalers and increased costs (and sales and control) through direct selling.

Bishop realized the importance of warehousing and transportation, since retailers desired quick delivery on orders. It was also possible to reduce shipping costs on orders, an important consideration for carpets, by shipping in carload lots to strategically located warehouses rather than shipping small orders direct from the mill to the retailer. In this regard ACM's new traffic manager, Casey Jones, was respected throughout the industry as a magician in obtaining the best route structure at the minimum rates available. In fact, his efforts on behalf of his former employer considerably decreased that company's transportation costs. A new mixing warehouse in Dalton would allow consolidation of products to take advantage of lower transportation costs.

Direct Sales

Bishop realized that ACM would need to maintain an active sales force of approximately 100 to ensure adequate sales coverage on a national basis. He estimated the annual cost to the company for each salesperson at $25,000.

With a direct sales approach ACM would have to consider how to warehouse inventory in the field most efficiently. Since warehousing arrangements were paramount, Bishop set out to determine the required number and locations. Based on a review of competitors' current locations and his experience in his former position, Bishop determined that $4 million in sales was necessary to support a warehouse economically. This represented an annual cost of $500,-000 per facility.

Another aspect of the warehousing problem, however, was to minimize freight rates as much as possible. Under industry pricing, retail outlets bore the burden of freight charges from either the mill or the warehouse, whichever was closer. Within the area served by one warehouse, prices to retailers would vary according to the distance of the retailer from the warehouse. Prices at each warehouse would be identical, however, reflecting "equal freight charges" from Dalton to each warehouse. Consequently, more warehouses meant that retailers would be closer and would thus enjoy lesser charges.

Bishop estimated that it would be necessary to establish facilities in seven selected cities: San Francisco, Chicago, Dallas, Atlanta, New York, Cleveland, and Philadelphia. Most of these cities were supporting competitors' requirements successfully and the markets were centers of population and high-income groups. Also, in all but Dallas and Atlanta, existing structures were available at a lower cost than if they had to be built. A large sales branch could be established in each warehouse serving a major area.

Sales personnel perform varied functions such as taking orders, checking inventory, arranging displays, accepting and processing complaints, and other general selling activities. One recent company estimate by a competitor had shown that sales personnel place an average of five calls per day and spend an average of 54 minutes with each customer. Half that time is spent verifying inventory and the remainder is divided among the above-mentioned areas. Two items of note were that 13 minutes per call were spent on general chatting, while 9 minutes were spent on actual selling. Bishop felt that the company's ability to increase its sales would depend on an extensive and aggressive sales force operation.

Order Handling

John Bishop reflected on the order handling procedure used by his previous employer. Sales personnel normally tried to obtain the order personally from the customer. If this was not possible, the customer mailed or phoned the order into the regional sales office. Company orders averaged 100 per day. Generally, the sales office would consolidate orders until a carload was indicated and then forward the order to headquarters. The order was then screened for detail and passed to both the sales and traffic departments for appropriate action on service and routing. Orders were then teletyped to the plant and delivery was accomplished. The total reorder cycle varied from 4 to 20 days depending on the amount, urgency, and nature of the request. This central control was considered a progressive step toward directing company efforts and effecting cost economies.

The costs of order handling were estimated as follows:

Order processing	$ 40,000
Headquarters administration	80,000
Field administration	130,000
Credit	40,000
Accounting	10,000
Total costs	$300,000
Orders processed	50,000
Cost per order	$6.00

Bishop believed that the costs of order processing at ACM would be similar. He also believed that inventory levels would be about 20 percent of sales.

THE ENVIRONMENT

The industry was experiencing a business boom and increasing competition. The recent trend was toward discount houses, mail-order operations, and large carpet retailer specialists, and away from department stores and specialty shops. Industry statistics suggested that 40 percent of the retail outlets accounted for 95 percent of the sales volume. Moreover, several large retailers maintained swatches of each carpet variation available, but carried only a limited amount of inventory in each line. When a customer decided on an item that was not carried, the retailer placed the order and requested next-day delivery.

Because of increasing competition, expanded sales operations, increased retail outlets, shifting inventory burdens by retailers, and spiraling costs, ACM must review its traditional methods of doing business. In order to grow, ACM has to increase service and curtail costs. The evolution of current industry practice must be reviewed to discover the pitfalls to be avoided in the design of a distribution network. ACM's preliminary review indicated a need for a more integrated system of operation from production to delivery.

CASE 8-1: QUESTIONS

1 Which method of distribution should Associated Carpet Manufacturers, Incorporated, use?
2 Is there additional information Bishop would find useful when making this decision? Explain.

CASE 8-2: Fisher-Price Toys, Incorporated

Early in 1969, Mr. H. Fisher, Chairman of the Board, and Mr. H. H. Coords, President and Chief Executive Officer of Fisher-Price Toys, Inc., were evaluating three alternative proposals for modification of the company's sales and service force. They were prepared either to accept any one of the proposals or to provide guidelines for the development of a different plan, which might include portions of the current proposals. Both men recognized that their decision would be influenced to a significant extent by changes in the wholesale and retail distribution of toys.

Mr. Coords had initiated a review of the company's selling and service activities in anticipation of increased competitive activity in the markets served by Fisher-Price. He believed that competitors, some of whom had recently been strenghtened financially by mergers, might attempt to erode the company's market position by providing retailers with extensive merchandising and service support, rather than by attempting to compete head-on with Fisher-Price's traditionally strong product line. Mr. Coords reasoned that even a product line well accepted by consumers could not maintain its share of market without adequate retail distribution and retailer support.

At the same time as he was considering proposals for changes in the sales and service force, Mr. Coords was discussing with other company executives

This case was made possible through the cooperation of Fisher-Price Toys, Inc. The case was prepared by Associate Professor Richard N. Cardozo and James E. Haefner, Teaching Associate, as the basis for class discussion, rather than to illustrate appropriate or inappropriate handling of administrative problems.
Copyright © 1970, University of Minnesota. Reprinted with permission.

increasing the company's use of national television advertising for its products. Company officials were aware that other toy manufacturers spent millions of dollars on television advertising and were likely to increase their expenditures. Heavy use of television advertising would represent a departure from Fisher-Price's traditional promotion policies, which emphasized retailer support and modest expenditures on magazine advertising.

THE COMPANY

Fisher-Price sold through major retail toy outlets a line of 70 different educational toys designed for children from six months of age to school age. The principal products in the line were pull and push toys, which were used by children during the period when they were learning the basic motor skills of walking, running, and elementary manual dexterity. The company also fabricated a large number of musical toys. Each year 25 percent of the company's product line was comprised of items which were wholly new or substantially revised.

Retail prices of Fisher-Price toys ranged from $1 to more than $15. Most of the company's sales came from toys with suggested retail prices between $2 and $5.

In 1968, Fisher-Price was one of the 10 largest toy manufacturers in the United States. The company's sales had increased at a rate of more than 15 percent per year during the past 20 years. Management noted that during the past decade Fisher-Price sales had increased nearly twice as fast as industry sales, despite a decline in the number of pre-school children. Company officials attributed Fisher-Price growth to the design and quality of the company's products, on whose design and development the company was thought to spend

Exhibit 1   Fisher-Price Toys, Inc.
Statement of Consolidated Income

	Year ended January 31	
	1969	1968
Net sales	$32,398,294	$30,274,836
Cost of goods sold	23,434,432	21,663,767
Gross margin	8,963,862	8,611,069
Selling, administrative and general expenses	3,156,253	2,952,828
Operating income	5,807,609	5,658,241
Other expenses (net)	367,665	205,848
Income before profit-sharing and taxes on income	5,496,842	5,452,393
Provision for employees' profit-sharing plan	1,272,485	1,194,731
Income before taxes on income	4,224,384	4,257,662
Taxes on income:		
Current	2,295,000	2,208,154
Deferred	(8,000)	(79,000)
Net income	$ 1,937,384	$ 2,128,508

Source: Annual Report.

Exhibit 2   Fisher-Price Toys, Inc.
Consolidated Balance Sheet

	January 31	
	1969	1968
Assets		
Current assets:		
Cash	$ 257,408	$ 670,822
United States treasury obligations, at cost	300,000	2,000,000
Accounts receivable, less allowance for doubtful accounts		
of $560,985 and $490,966 respectively	3,836,930	1,657,215
Inventories, at lower of cost or market—Raw materials,		
including process goods	2,719,865	2,346,838
Finished goods	1,558,064	1,755,700
Prepayments, principally insurance and taxes	184,889	170,715
Total current assets	8,857,156	8,601,290
Accumulated income tax prepayments	192,500	184,500
Investments and other assets	209,080	78,030
Properties, plants and equipment, net	6,870,263	5,544,440
	$16,128,999	$14,408,260
Liabilities and shareholder's equity		
Current liabilities:		
Accounts payable	$ 1,082,268	$ 816,068
Employees' retirement and savings		
profit-sharing	793,215	782,565
Taxes on income	443,448	903,819
Accrued salaries, wages and vacation pay	471,192	206,430
Total current liabilities	2,790,483	2,708,882
Shareholders' equity		
Common, Class A stock (voting) par value $5 a share		
—authorized and issued 18,000 shares	90,000	90,000
Common, Class B stock (nonvoting) par value		
$5 a share—authorized 522,000 shares; issued		
415,071 shares	2,075,355	2,070,655
Capital in excess of par value	32,566	7,701
Income reinvested in the business	11,402,543	9,772,470
Less common stock held in treasury, at cost—Class A,		
1,772 shares; Class B, 47,160 shares	261,948	241,448
	13,338,516	11,699,378
	$16,128,999	$14,408,260

Source: Annual Reports.

more than its competitors. Fisher-Price toys were popular with consumers and were considered a "staple" by the retail trade. Recent operating statements appear in Exhibits 1 and 2.

In 1968, Fisher-Price had sales in excess of $30 million on approximately 24 million toys. Company officials forecast sales in the early 1970s of more than

$50 million a year, and production of 35 million toys per year. Some officials expected that, by 1980, Fisher-Price would be producing 70 million toys a year and obtaining revenues well in excess of $100 million.

Fisher-Price products were produced in two facilities near Buffalo, New York. The company had operated a plant in Orangeville, Ontario, Canada until 1968 when labor problems forced it to close. Canadian sales accounted for about 10 percent of the company's total sales.

Fifty percent of the company's shipments were made during the three months of September, October, and November. Although the company operated at full production capacity from July through December, this seasonal peak in shipments made it necessary to build up large inventories during the summer months. The expenses connected with financing this inventory, as well as moving it into and out of temporary warehousing, had in the past made management wary of increasing production schedules early in the year.

The company had firm plans to increase its factory and warehouse facilities to handle $50 million of annual sales. Fisher-Price officials foresaw the need for new plant facilities somewhere in the Midwest if the company continued to grow.

Apart from expansion of production facilities, the company was in the process of developing more toys for very young children and for children from 5 to 7 years of age. Several of these toys were slated for the 1969 line. The company was also contemplating the acquisition of another toy company, particularly one with strong summer sales which would offset the current heavy fall sales peak.

MARKET POSITION

Fisher-Price competed primarily in the markets for preschool and educational toys. In the market for toys for children from one to three years old, Fisher-Price executives believed that the company faced no major competitors. Smaller companies made one or two items for this market segment but, according to company officials, did not pose a substantial competitive threat.

According to management, the company's major direct competition came from manufacturers which made toys for children under one year of age and more than three years of age. Among manufacturers of toys for children less than a year old, executives believed Child of Interest to be the major competitor. These executives thought that Fisher-Price sales of products appropriate for children of this age were less than sales of Child of Interest.

In the age grouping of three to six years, Playskool held the dominant market position and was Fisher-Price's closest major competitor. Playskool was acquired in 1968 by Milton Bradley, a major factor in the market for toys for older children. Following the merger, Milton Bradley instituted major changes in the marketing policies of Playskool. A new Detail Sales Force was established to serve retailers which carried both Milton Bradley and Playskool products. This sales force consisted of nine men who worked primarily in large metropolitan areas. These men wrote routine reorders and conducted normal servicing operations, including checking inventory and straightening displays. Apart from changes in Playskool's sales and service force, Milton Bradley was believed to be developing for Playskool a more agressive promotion strategy, which would include some national television advertising. Playskool had done no national TV advertising prior to the merger.

DISTRIBUTION

Fisher-Price sold its products directly to large retail accounts and to jobbers which, in turn, sold Fisher-Price toys to retailers which did not buy directly from the company. Fisher-Price historically had a policy of selling direct to retailers wherever possible. Its salesmen occasionally found themselves competing with the jobber salesman for sales of Fisher-Price products. Sales to retail accounts were made at 40 and 10 percent off the full retail price. (Fisher-Price did not publish a list of suggested retail prices; however, within the toy industry full retail price was generally considered to be twice the price at which manufacturers sold their products to jobbers.) Although there was some price cutting at the retail level, retailers maintained a margin of 30 to 40 percent on most Fisher-Price toys. Company executives believed that retail price cutting on Fisher-Price products was increasing.

The company sold its products to jobbers at 50 percent off the full retail price. Jobbers typically earned margins of 15 to 18 percent, and on some items up to 25 percent, on sales of Fisher-Price toys to retailers.

As was common in the toy industry, Fisher-Price summarized its sales by type of institution. The following table lists for 1967 the percentage of total company sales and number of shipping addresses (points to which Fisher-Price products were shipped) for each of several types of distributors. The number of shipping addresses listed provides only an estimate of the number of stores through which Fisher-Price products were actually sold. Some retailers took

Table 1   Number of Shipping Addresses, Percentage of Company Sales and Sales per Shipping Address, by Type of Distributor (1967 Figures)

Type of distributor	Number of shipping addresses	Percentage of Fisher-Price sales	Sales per shipping address
Jobbers (Wholesalers)	244	29.0	$ 43,875
Retailers			
Discount Chains & Stores	2,065	25.4	3,321
Variety & Drug Chains	1,323	15.9	3,245
Department & Specialty Stores	3,247	11.5	923
Department Store Chains	2,664	6.7	679
Mail Order Houses	7	5.8	223,714
Miscellaneous (Including Export and Government Sales)	159	5.7	9,625
	9,709	100.0	

delivery at a central warehouse (which constituted a shipping address) and re-shipped merchandise to individual stores. Other retailers had merchandise shipped directly to the stores. In this latter case, each store constituted a single shipping address.

By 1969, the percentage of sales accounted for by each type of distributor had changed somewhat. Sales to jobbers had increased to 32.4 percent; sales to discount chains, to 27.4 percent; and sales to mail-order houses, to 6.7 percent. Sales to department store chains had remained about 6 2/3 percent. Sales to variety and drug chains decreased to 11.9 percent; sales to department and specialty stores, to 10.6 percent; and miscellaneous sales had decreased to 4.4 percent.

Company officials noted that these retail institutions were continually changing in ways which made customary classification of institutions imprecise. Many "discounters" had begun to trade up to the point where they were competing directly with department stores, which met the discounters' prices and adopted the self-service operation characteristic of discount and some chain stores. Some department stores had, in addition, attempted to trade up by adding specialty items not directly competitive with merchandise carried by discount stores. Officials also observed that Woolworth, Kresge and other variety chains had opened large discount stores which competed directly with other discounters.

Apart from these continuing changes, management believed that retailers which carried Fisher-Price toys could be classified into two groups on the basis of their sales and service requirements. Executives stated that the first group, which included mail-order houses, almost all the drug and variety chains, about one-third of the department store chains and a small but increasing percentage of the discount chains, required intensive selling effort only once a year. These retailers required no in-store service, and in fact prohibited manufacturers from sending salesmen into their stores. These retailers did, however, insist on prompt and complete shipment of their orders.

Executives stated that early in each year head buyers for these accounts would meet with the headquarters staff of each of several manufacturers to choose particular items from each manufacturer's line. Orders placed ordinarily called for billing and shipment at specified intervals during the remainder of the year. The large seasonal peak in sales made it impossible for manufacturers to fill orders or reorders out of current production during the peak season. Mail-order houses would list the chosen items in their catalogs, and order stock for their centralized shipping operations. Chain stores would place orders for delivery direct to the stores or to a central warehouse which served the stores. Fisher-Price officials stated that chain stores would typically print the selected items on a list from which individual store managers could place orders. Some chains ordered warehouse stock on which individual stores could draw, while other chains forwarded orders from individual stores to the factory for direct shipment to the individual store.

Management estimated that approximately 25 percent of the company's retailers could currently be classified into this first group. Some executives expected this percentage to decline to 15 percent within the next few years, and to stabilize at that level.

Sales and service requirements of retailers in the second group varied considerably. Included in this group were national or regional chains in which many of the buying and operating decisions were made at the store level, as well as some toy departments and smaller toy shops. About half of the retailers in this second group made their major purchase commitments in late winter for all the stores they operated. These commitments specified billing and shipment dates for particular items throughout the year. Buyers for independent stores and central buyers for chains would reorder fast-selling items on a routine basis but could occasionally be persuaded during the year to buy items not included in their initial purchase orders. These retailers welcomed manufacturers' salesmen in their stores for purposes of maintaining displays and making sure adequate stocks were available at the store level. In some instances manufacturers' salesmen had almost complete discretion in making up orders to fill in the stock of a particular store. These orders might be forwarded to the retailer's warehouse or to the manufacturer for direct shipment depending upon the procedures followed by the particular retailer.

The remaining retailers in the second group placed orders throughout the year, rather than simply drawing against a major purchase commitment. These retailers considered manufacturers' salesmen with whom they had established effective working relationships as reliable sources of information on the toy market and on the likely success of particular items. Among these retailers, those which operated more than one store were likely to allow individual stores considerable freedom in deciding what toys to stock from a particular manufacturer, and even to permit some freedom in choice of manufacturer. Salesmen had to work with buyers and store managers in these stores as well as in the independent stores to make up orders and reorders. As a basis for this activity, salesmen took periodic store (and sometimes warehouse) inventories and frequently suggested the addition of new items or larger quantities on the order. In addition, salesmen kept displays and stocks of their products neat, and, when permission could be obtained from the buyer and store manager, set up any displays provided by the manufacturer for in-store use.

Company executives estimated that the percentage of retailers in group two as a whole would gradually increase from 75 percent to 85 percent of all retailers which handled Fisher-Price toys. Within this group, executives thought that central buying and major annual purchase commitments would become much more common within the next five to ten years.

Many retailers in both groups relied to some extent on jobbers to fill in stocks during the Christmas season. Company executives believed that a significant share of Fisher-Price's toys during the Christmas season in these outlets came through jobbers. Apart from Christmas sales, some large retailers and many small retailers were using the major jobbers to service their toy departments throughout the year.

SALES FORCE

The Fisher-Price sales force sold directly to jobbers and retailers which handled the company's products. In 1968, the sales force included ten full-time salesmen and three assistant sales managers. These assistant sales managers devoted part of their time to sales activities and part to supervising salesmen. Together with the sales manager and other senior headquarters personnel, these assistant sales managers handled much of the negotiation involved in obtaining purchase commitments from major customers. Salesmen occasionally participated in or held major responsibility for such negotiations.

Each of the ten salesmen was responsible for a particular territory in which he solicited new customers and worked with existing accounts to arrange special promotions, to develop reorders, and to stock and straighten displays. Each salesman made about 1200 calls per year, some 10 percent of which were made on prospective customers. Fisher-Price salesmen made more calls than the typical toy industry salesman, who might make 600 to 800 calls per year if his work involved primarily service, and 1000 to 1200 calls per year if his work was primarily selling.

Salaries of Fisher-Price salesmen, all of whom were college graduates, ranged from $10,000 to $15,000 per year, plus participation in a company-wide profit-sharing plan. Expenses averaged $5,600 per salesman.

ADVERTISING AND SALES PROMOTION

Fisher-Price customarily relied primarily upon point-of-purchase displays and consumer magazine advertising to promote its products. Since 1966 the company has offered its major customers a formalized display service and reorder advice called Programmed Merchandising For Profit (PM/FP). Working with an assortment of items which the customer had decided to stock and measurements or models of the customer's store fixtures, company marketing personnel developed for each customer merchandise displays that would appeal to the consumer, contain adequate stocks of faster moving items, and minimize item-by-item restocking efforts on the part of store personnel. Along with display suggestions, Fisher-Price proposed that inventory of the stock be taken periodically, and that reorders be made by the store personnel using a manual system for the early part of the year and blanket Christmas season orders determined in October on the basis of earlier sales. By 1969, over 20,000 photos and display diagrams were sent out yearly to customers whose purchases of toys from Fisher-Price totalled to about $16 million.

In 1968, the company spent $438,000[1] to advertise its product in such consumer magazines as *Parents, Woman's Day,* and *Good Housekeeping.* Expenditures on consumer magazine advertising did not exceed $200,000 per year until 1966, when $480,000 was budgeted. The company supplemented its maga-

---

[1] A full-page ad in a major magazine, such as *Good Housekeeping*, cost $27,700 in 1968.

zine advertising with advertisements in newspapers, primarily Sunday supplements, but expenditures in this medium were typically less than expenditures for magazine space. The company did not offer cooperative advertising allowances to retailers.

Prior to 1969 Fisher-Price had not used television advertising, despite the fact that other major toy companies together spent several million dollars each year on television advertising. Management stated that the company had not used television advertising because of the belief that toys advertised on television were frequently used as traffic builders by low-margin retailers. To remain competitive, other retailers were sometimes forced to sell heavily advertised toys at only a few cents above their cost. Management believed that retailers which carried Fisher-Price toys would be reluctant to "push" or display the company's products if those products produced little or no profit for the retailer.

Early in 1969, however, Fisher-Price budgeted $240,000 for television advertising[2] of its products in late 1969. The decision to use television was based to a great extent on results of a test conducted in 1968. In that test, $45,000 was spent on television advertising in a large midwestern city during the months of November and December, 1968. Sales in this test city increased more than 32 percent compared to the same period in the previous year. Sales in a comparable city which received no television advertising of Fisher-Price toys, increased only 13 percent in the same period. Company officials believed that response in the test city would have been greater, had not many retailers run out of stock on the advertised items.

ALTERNATIVES

The first of the three alternatives which Mr. Fisher and Mr. Coords were considering called for the company to increase its present sales force from 10 to 13 men. Proponents of this plan argued that the surest way for the company to increase sales was to expand a sales force which had contributed substantially to the consistent and high rate of growth which the company had enjoyed. Officials who favored this plan pointed out that the addition of three salesmen would enable each salesman to spend more time with each of his accounts.

The second alternative under consideration involved hiring 20 merchandising assistants who would free the salesmen from some of their routine duties.

---

[2] In 1969, typical cost figures for television were as follows:

	Sponsorship of one-hour program	Sponsorship of 15-minute program	60-second spot	30-second spot
Metropolitan area over 1 million	$6,000	$2,400	$2,200	$1,700
Metropolitan area of 300,000	$1,200	$ 500	$ 450	$ 400

These merchandising assistants would check inventories, make up reorders, set up and maintain displays and handle routine dealer servicing and complaints. Merchandising assistants would not necessarily hold college degrees. Executives estimated that competent personnel could be recruited at salaries of $7,500 to $10,000 per year, plus use of a company car and expenses.

The time made available to salesmen through the employment of merchandising assistants would be spent in supervising the assistants' activities and in increased canvassing for new business. Executives who favored this plan argued that the merchandising assistants would more than pay for themselves through more effective servicing of existing accounts and through sales generated from new accounts.

A third proposal would permit each salesman to hire part-time service women as demand warranted. Each salesman would be allowed to spend $10,-000 on part-time service women and allocate them at his discretion. During 1966 two of the salesmen hired part-time help during the fall peak demand season to take inventories and make out reorders. In each case the cost for the year was about $1,200 to $1,400 to cover 25 to 30 stores. In one case, the salesman estimated that the extra servicing was responsible for about half of a $20,-000 to $25,000 sales increase in the stores.

Apart from their discussion of the company's sales and service organization, Fisher-Price executives were considering increased use of national television advertising. One executive proposed that if the $240,000 expended in 1969 proved to be worthwhile, the company increase television expenditures up to several times that amount. Any increase would be financed partly by an increase in the total consumer advertising budget and partly by reduction in expenditures in consumer print media.

Not all executives agreed, however, that promotional expenditures should be increased. As one senior executive put it, "Our products remain the best single promotional device we could have. We enjoy a fine reputation in the trade and among consumers. That reputation has been built on high-quality products which enable a child to learn while he plays. The company's sales have continued to increase despite our competitors' lavish promotional spending. They don't have the product we do, so they have to advertise heavily. We have the kind of product which speaks for itself and doesn't need intensive advertising support."

NOTE ON THE TOY INDUSTRY

This note contains four sections. The first section describes briefly the market for toys. The second section contains an overview of the toy manufacturing industry. The third section of this note discusses toy distribution, and the final section describes typical marketing programs employed in the toy industry.

This note was prepared by Associate Professor Richard N. Cardozo and James E. Haefner, Teaching Associate.

1 The Toy Market

Although precise figures were not available, industry sources estimated that toy sales at the retail level in the United States were between two and three billion dollars in 1968.

A study prepared by the A. J. Wood Research Corporation on behalf of the Toy Manufacturers of America divided total consumption as follows:

	Approximate percent of dollar sales at retail
Riding toys (including bicycles)	22
Dolls, doll clothing and accessories	13
Non-riding transportation	12
Sporting goods	12
Games, puzzles, magic sets	6
Educational and scientific	5
Musical	5
Toy guns	5
Handicraft and models	4
Novelty toys	3
Activity toys	3
Stuffed	2
Child-sized furniture	2
Preschool	2
All others	4
	100

In recent years, approximately one-sixth of the items purchased have accounted for almost two-thirds of the total dollars spent on toys. Table 2, based on data compiled by the A. J. Wood Research Corporation, shows percentage unit and dollar sales of toys by retail price class.

Almost all of the toys consumed in the United States were purchased for children under 12 years of age. Furthermore, almost all toy purchases were made by adults for children. Table 3, based on the A. J. Wood study, lists the percentages of unit purchases made by each of several classes of buyers.

Table 2 Toy Sales by Retail Price Class

	Percent of unit sales	Percent of dollar sales
$15.00 and over	4	33
$10.00–$15.00	3	13
$ 5.00–$ 9.99	10	20
$ 3.00–$ 4.99	14	16
$ 2.00–$ 2.99	12	8
$ 1.00–$ 1.99	20	6
$ .50–$ .99	16	3
$ Under $.50	18	1
Don't remember	3	—
Total	100	100

Table 3   Percent of Unit Sales of Toys, by Purchaser

Parents	73
Grandparents	11
Uncle/aunt	5
Brother/sister	2
Friends	4
Other (including purchases made by child himself)	6

2 Toy Manufacturing

Of the $1.732 billion (manufacturers' prices) of toys consumed in the United States in 1968, domestic manufacturers supplied $1.576 billion, or 91 percent. The remaining nine percent came from imported toys.

Although toy imports accounted for only nine percent of domestic consumption in 1968, their share of the market has increased dramatically during the past 10 years. In 1958, imports amounted to $29 million, or 3.7 percent of total domestic consumption while in 1968, $156 million dollars of finished toys were imported into the United States (see Table 4). During the first seven months of 1968, imports increased 35 percent over the same period in 1967. This rate of increase was substantially higher than in previous periods. Industry sources attributed this increase to the "Kennedy Round" tariff reduction, which became effective at the beginning of 1968. Because additional tariff reductions are scheduled for 1969 and 1970, industry sources expect this uptrend in imports to continue. In recent years, more than 70 percent of all finished toys imported have come from the Far East.

The toy industry is comprised of a few large firms and several hundred small manufacturers. In 1967, some 1,200 firms manufactured toys in the United States. The four largest manufacturers together accounted for 15 percent of sales by domestic manufacturers. The eight largest together accounted for 25

Table 4   Total United States Domestic Production, Exports and Imports of Toys, Selected Years, 1958–1968, Manufacturers' Prices (In Millions of Dollars)

		1958	1962	1964	1966	1968
1	Total Domestic Production	776	1,064	1,180	1,403	1,599
2	Exports	19	18	23	33	23
3	Domestic Production for Domestic Consumption (1 − 2)	757	1,046	1,157	1,370	1,576
4	Imports[1]	29	59	78	97	156
5	Total Domestic Consumption (3 + 4)	786	1,105	1,235	1,467	1,732

[1] These figures do not include toy parts, such as music units, wind-up motors, electric motors, hand-painted components, etc., which are imported in substantial quantities.
Source: U.S. Department of Commerce, Business and Defense Services Administration.

percent of sales, and the largest 20 firms together accounted for 58 percent of sales.[1] The remaining firms generally produced and sold only a few individual specialty items.

In recent years the number of firms producing toys had declined somewhat, due largely to mergers which have occurred within the toy industry. One particularly large merger involved the acquisition of Playskool by Milton Bradley, both large companies which made toys for different age groups. Smaller manufacturers frequently sought as merger partners companies with opposite seasonal peak sales, such as summer peak outdoor equipment, and Christmas peak electric trains. Such mergers were intended to reduce the cash needs of the companies as well as to save money on sales costs. Toy industry sources indicated that the effectiveness of such mergers was limited, however, because the industry as a whole faced peak shipment and service demand in the late fall.

Apart from the intra-industry merger trend, firms having no previous connection with toys have shown great interest in acquiring toy makers. CBS has acquired Creative Playthings, a preschool and kindergarten toy and equipment manufacturer and wholesaler. General Mills acquired Rainbow Crafts, a manufacturer of preschool toys; Parker Brothers, Inc., a manufacturer of games; and Kenner, a manufacturer of toys for children 6–12.

As a result partly of merger and partly of internal growth, 127 manufacturers which hold membership in the Toy Manufacturers Association of America have reported annual growth rates which average 8 percent in each of the last several years. Pre-tax earnings of a selected sample of the publicly-held TMA-member firms ranged from 5.8 percent to 11.5 percent of sales in 1967. After-tax return on equity for these same firms ranged from 6.1 percent to 16 percent in 1967.

The toy industry was highly seasonal in nature. At the retail level 53 percent of all dollar sales and 45 percent of unit sales of toys were made in November and December. As a consequence, more than 50 percent of all toy shipments from manufacturers were made during September, October and November.

Orders placed with toy manufacturers peaked somewhat earlier, in July and August. In addition, at the spring trade shows, manufacturers received major purchase commitments from wholesalers, from almost all large department stores and from chains of all types. These purchase commitments, which the buyer might revise to a limited extent, covered up to 95 percent of a buyer's anticipated purchases from domestic manufacturers for the coming 12 months. More than two-thirds of these commitments were ordinarily backed up with firm purchase orders. (These same wholesalers and large retailers purchased almost all of their European imports at late winter trade shows in Europe.)

Because of the intensity and short duration of the peak retail selling season, manufacturers could not produce enough merchandise during the peak

---

[1] Bureau of the Census, Subcommittee on Antitrust and Monopoly, *Concentration Ratios in Manufacturing Industry 1963* (Washington, D. C., 1967), p. 547.

season to meet demand. Manufacturers therefore operated at a high percentage of capacity during the spring and summer months to build inventories. The large inventories thus accumulated had to be stored. In addition, manufacturers had to obtain substantial amounts of working capital to finance inventory production and storage. The annual cycle of sales, shipments, and production for a typical large product appears in Exhibit 1.

3 Toy Distribution

Toys were sold through approximately 10,000 retail stores. Mail-order houses, department, discount, and variety stores handled the largest volume of sales. Distributions of sales and total stores, by type of retail outlet, appear in Table 5. Because several stores may buy through a central buying office (e.g., chain organizations), the number of stores, or selling points, is greater than the number of buying points.

Toy retailing had become more concentrated in recent years, and industry sources expected this concentration of more sales through few outlets to continue. For example, figures in the Census of Business (1958, 1963) indicated that the number of hobby, toy and game shops had declined five percent between 1958 and 1963. During that same period, however, total sales of these shops increased by more than one-third. According to a study by the Stanford Research Institute, chain stores, particularly discount and variety chains, were likely to continue to be major vendors of toys.

Recently, two major discount chains opened stores which will sell only toys. Both managements believed that their chains could do a specialized year-round business in toys because (1) year-round promotion by toy manufacturers and retailers could create a year-round demand; (2) the youth population (ten

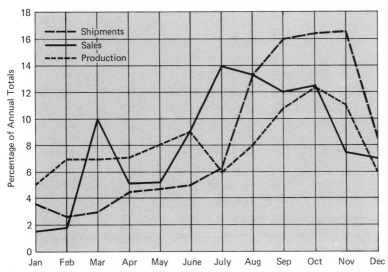

Exhibit 1 Note on the toy industry. Percentage of annual totals by month, of sales, production, and shipments, for typical large producer.

Table 5 Percentage Distributions of Sales and Stores

Type of retail outlet	Percent of dollar sales	Percent of total stores
Department	18	13
Discount	17	18
Chain discount	11	9
Catalog	9	5
Variety	9	21
Auto supply	7	3
Toy	7	8
Hardware	4	2
Drug	3	5
Hobby	2	2
Supermarket	2	4
Sporting goods	2	1
All others	9	9
Total	100	100

and under) was growing, with a 27 percent gain projected for the next decade; and (3) American affluence was increasing: personal disposable income increased 72 percent between 1960 and 1968.[2] Industry sources believed that each of these chains might operate more than 100 stores and gross more than $400 million a year by 1975.

Retailers differ in their buying behavior and their requirements for various types of service. All retail outlets, however, were very concerned with prompt delivery of initial orders and reorders, and with quick replacement of defective products.

The large discount, mail order, and department-store operations which had developed an effective computerized inventory system generally needed no help in inventory checking and reordering. Salesmen were definitely needed to set up and maintain point-of-purchase displays and replace floor samples. An executive of a large, innovative retailer stated; "If we could nail down the floor samples and displays, we would have no need for the salesmen. Unfortunately, no program in any computer system I know of will provide this essential service."

In those retail operations which lacked automated merchandise control systems and in the smaller toy shops, more frequent calls by the individual salesmen were needed. Salesmen helped to make out reorders, provided information to help buyers place initial orders, set up displays and maintain samples. and take occasional inventories. One industry executive believed that simple, yet accurate information and control systems would provide a basis for control and reorders. These systems were rapidly being adopted by even relatively small retailers.

Almost all retailers made some purchases from wholesalers during the

[2] "Toys Should Be Fun," *Forbes,* Vol. 103, No. 6 (March 15, 1969).

peak Christmas selling season. In addition, many retailers preferred to make some or all of their total annual toy purchases from wholesalers, rather than from manufacturers. Major chain store organizations typically purchased a small proportion of their total requirements from wholesalers than did other retailers. One retail executive indicated that he preferred to purchase from wholesalers on a regular basis because:

1   in many instances reorders were filled more quickly,
2   wholesalers would guarantee the sale (any items which were not sold could be returned to the wholesaler for full credit),
3   defective products were replaced promptly,
4   the wholesaler extended long-term credit, and
5   the percentage of mark-up lost by working through a wholesaler was more than offset by decreased inventory costs and improved service.

Some 1,700 toy wholesalers serviced retailers. Of this number, approximately 1,000 were merchant wholesalers.[3] The remainder were commission agents[4] or captive supply organizations of large retailers. Between 1963 and 1967 total sales of the merchant wholesalers of toys increased from $577 million to $755 million, although they numbered about 1,000 throughout the five-year period. This increase in sales was accompanied by an increase in the number of large merchant wholesalers and a decline in the number of smaller merchant wholesalers. The number of merchant wholesalers with sales over $1 million increased by 17 percent from 1963 to 1967, while the number of establishments with sales below $500 thousand declined by more than 13 percent during that period. Despite this increasing concentration of toy wholesaling, industry observers believed that, as of 1970, few if any wholesalers dominated any particular trading area.

Until the mid-1960s, toy wholesalers earned margins of 25 percent on their sales to retailers. By 1970, however, typical wholesaler margins were between 15 and 18 percent, and margins on some high-volume items—which were usually heavily discounted at the retail level—were as low as 10 to 12 percent. Industry sources attributed this decline in wholesalers' margins to pressures for lower prices from retailers, who were themselves facing increasingly intense price competition.

Major manufacturers of toys might ship their products directly to retailers and sell through wholesalers. The smaller manufacturers sold their products through manufacturers' representatives to wholesalers or retailers. Several of these small manufacturers operated leased departments in discount stores, and some are captive supply organizations for large discount chains.

[3] Merchant wholesalers were establishments engaged in buying, taking title to, and physically handling and storing merchandise.

[4] Commission agents typically receive merchandise from their principals, provide storage, find buyers, make deliveries, extend credit, and make collections while never taking title to the goods. In payment for their services, commission agents received an amount equal to five to six percent of the sales they consummated.

4   Marketing Programs in the Toy Industry

There are at least four distinct types of marketing programs currently employed within the toy industry. Each program was associated with a particular type of product: (1) prestige products, (2) staple non-discount toys, (3) semi-discount products, and (4) extreme discount toys.

Prestige items, most of which were European imports, usually permitted the retailer to earn a margin of 40 to 60 percent. These items were sold directly by the manufacturer (or importer) to full-markup retailers, typically prestige department stores. Manufacturers did little or no advertising. Retailers sometimes provided elaborate point-of-purchase displays for these products.

Staple non-discount toys included such basic items as clay sets, doctor kits, and building blocks. Many "educational" toys fell into this category. Retailers earned 30 to 40 percent on these items. Domestic toys might either be sold direct by the manufacturer, or through a wholesaler (jobber) to full-line toy departments and toy stores. Some advertising was done, but its theme generally stressed quality and was directed toward adults. The media typically employed were women's magazines. Point-of-purchase displays were usually simple, but informative.

Semi-discount items called "demand items" (pre-sold merchandise) by the trade, included push and pull toys, riding toys, and games. On these toys, retailers typically obtained a margin of 20 to 30 percent. Semi-discount items were sold directly by the manufacturer or through a wholesaler to all full-line toy departments. Some national advertising was done, but it was essentially "awareness" promotion to keep the name of the product and firm before the consumer. Point-of-purchase displays were simple.

Extreme discount toys included items which were new in a particular season, but whose popularity was short-lived, as well as a few perennial favorites. Many toys imported from the Far East fall into this category. Imported items were sold primarily through wholesalers (jobbers), to discount/department and toy stores, some full-line toy departments, and various non-toy outlets. Extreme discount toys made in the United States were sold to these same types of outlets either directly or through wholesalers. Retailers ordinarily obtained margins of approximately 10 percent on extreme discount items.

With few exceptions, retailers did not promote extreme discount toys aggressively. A retailer might promote a particular toy at a low margin to build store traffic or to reduce excessive inventory.

Many manufacturers of extreme discount toys do, however, engage in extensive promotion. Several of these manufacturers provided retailers with displays, and advertised heavily on television. For example, in 1968, Mattel spent $12.2 million on national television advertising and less than $850,000 in magazine advertising. Mattel sales in that year were $211 million. Milton Bradley, whose sales in 1968 were $69 million, spent $2.1 million on television advertising and less than $100,000 in magazines during that year. As was common in the promotion of extreme discount toys, both companies directed their television advertising primarily toward children.

Any product in the above-mentioned groups (prestige, domestic, semi-discount, and extreme discount) would not necessarily remain in these categories over time. Often a toy sold as a staple item would become a semi-discount or extreme discount item when some retailers in a trading area began to use it as a "loss leader."

For each of the four types of products described above, manufacturers might offer retailers quantity discounts, prepayment of shipping charges, promotional allowances and deferred payment terms. Quantity discounts varied greatly among manufacturers. For one supplier, the first level of discount might begin at $15,000 worth of purchases, while for another it might begin at $300,-000 worth of purchases. Although most large manufacturers required retailers to pay freight charges from the factory to retailer, many smaller toymakers offered some form of freight allowance.

Some manufacturers offered cooperative advertising allowances to retailers, but such allowances were not an established industry practice. Several retail sources indicated, however, that if given the option between the advertising allowance or more margin on the product, they would prefer the latter.

The payment terms offered by most manufacturers depended upon whether the firm was a wholesaler or retailer. Merchandise ordered in quantity for shipment prior to June 1 is payable by October 10 by wholesalers and December 10 by retail accounts. In the case of wholesalers, merchandise shipped after September 24 was payable on a 2/10 EOM basis. Merchandise shipped after December 15 was payable April 10. A few manufacturers had quarterly dating so that all payments were made to them April 10, July 10, October 10 and January 10. The terms which manufacturers offered were frequently negotiable and varied considerably with the relative strength of the seller and buyer.

Chapter 9

Channel Management:
Intermediaries

Even though manufacturers maintain a high stake in the methods by which their output is distributed and presented to final consumers, channel control does not always lie with the producer of the goods. Indeed, control often centers on one of the intermediary positions within the channel. As mentioned earlier, many authors have debated the normative question of which channel institution should be the channel leader. We, on the other hand, focus our attention in this chapter on specific sources and means by which channel intermediaries exert leadership influence on other channel members. The chapter concludes with a discussion of franchising as an alternative channel structure.

CHANNEL MANAGEMENT BY RETAILERS

Many retailers often are able to influence marketing policies and practices of their suppliers. Any time a retailer is able to obtain a price concession, advertising support, or faster delivery from a manufacturer, influence has been exerted over that manufacturer's policies. Previous chapters have discussed power, leadership, and negotiation strategies. In this section attention is focused on retailers' power and their strategies for developing leadership roles in marketing channels.

Sources of Retailer Power

Retailers have many sources of power to draw upon in attempting to develop a leadership role. Some of these sources are structural in nature. For example, market proximity and local monopolies arise strictly as a function of the unique characteristics and functional performance of retail organizations. Other retailer power sources derive from strategic decisions made by the management of retail firms. Development of a customer franchise, use of private label merchandise, horizontal cooperation, and conglomeration are just a few examples of such decisions. These sources of power are discussed in depth in the following parts.

Market Proximity Because retail firms are closest to the final consumer, they have a unique opportunity to gather market information. Consumers often voice their complaints, preferences, desires, and needs to the firms which supply them directly, the retailers. Thus, retailers can act as gatekeepers of market information and can use their proximity to the market as one means of exerting influence over manufacturer and wholesaler decisions. Market proximity can be particularly significant in situations when the retailer is large and has an organized information-gathering network, whereas the suppliers are relatively small and lack ability to gather information through formal research methods. However, even small retailers possess some degree of control due to their closeness to final customers.

Local Monopoly Traditionally, retailing has been considered a highly fragmented and widely dispersed activity. Analysts point to the number of retail institutions in a given industry and assume that the economic conditions of perfect competition—many buyers—have been satisfied. Since there are 68,000 drugstores and 226,000 apparel stores it would appear to ensure that no one buyer can influence the activities of the suppliers, few in comparison to retailers, in those industries. However, lack of concentration in retailing on the national level may be offset by the concentration which exists in any good local *retail* market area.[1]

Within any retail market area, a manufacturer's alternatives are limited. The amount of shelf or display space available in the local market for any specific product is restricted. Since manufacturers often feel that they have excess production capacity, they desire to capture some of that space to display their product line and utilize the excess capacity. However, the retailer can devote the space to any one of a number of different brands or product lines. If a supplier fails to sell to a retailer, those unrealized sales represent revenue lost forever. The retailers, however, can purchase and place other goods in the available space with little relative loss. This concept has been

---

[1] Michael E. Porter, "Consumer Behavior, Retailer Power, and Market Performance in Consumer Goods Industries," *The Review of Economics and Statistics* (November 1974), p. 420.

called the *principle of relative loss* by one writer and derives from the retailer's local monopoly over scarce shelf space.[2]

Monopoly power for retailers can be observed easily in such retail giants as Sears, Penney's, K-Mart, or Kroger's. However, even small retailers, particularly those in isolated rural areas, may exert considerable channel control over suppliers desiring access to those ultimate consumers.[3]

Customer Franchise Related to local monopoly is the concept of retail customer franchise. The ability of a retail firm to develop a strong and/or large customer following can make that firm a critical channel link to a supplier. In effect, the process of developing such loyalty serves to enhance that retailer's monopoly position. The means by which such a franchise is developed, however, is not explained as easily. The strength of a firm's customer franchise depends upon consumer perceptions of the adequacy of that firm's retailing mix. This combination of assortments, locations, hours, prices, facilities, promotions, and services interacts to form a store image in consumers' minds. When the image is extremely favorable with a large number of consumers, a customer franchise is developed.

Again, the existence of a strong customer franchise is more evident with large institutions since those firms have favorable images with many consumers in many locations. However, small stores may also develop a strong loyalty among consumers and make themselves indispensable to suppliers of certain items. Shopping center developers often find that local retail stores have such a strong following within a trade area that those stores are able to negotiate very favorable lease terms. However, not all stores can occupy a prestige or bellwether position; only a few small retailers can claim this source of power.[4]

Private Labels Increasing use of private brands by retailers also increases their power relative to suppliers. Many stores which have developed a strong customer franchise and are trusted by their consumers have included private label merchandise within their product assortments. For example, most grocery chains have devoted a significant amount of effort toward developing store brands of most products. Sears Craftsman tools and Kenmore appliances are two other examples of well-known private label products. This strategy restricts even further the amount of display space available to suppliers of national brand merchandise. Competition among those suppliers to gain the remaining space gives the retailer a considerable amount of control over those manufacturers. To the extent that a manufacturer has developed strong customer

[2] The preceding discussion is based on Roger A. Dickenson, *Retail Management: A Channels Approach* (Belmont, Cal.: Wadsworth Publishing Company, Inc., 1974), p. 37.

[3] Stanley C. Hollander, "Channel Management by Small Retailers," in Robert L. King (ed.), *Marketing and the New Science of Planning* (Chicago: American Marketing Association, 1968), p. 132.

[4] Ibid.

franchises through advertising and promotion, a particular retailer's control over that manufacturer's brand may be reduced or negated.[5] Virtually every grocery store in the United States carries Heinz and Hunt's ketchups because of strong customer loyalty to those brands. Few retailers would be willing to risk loss of customer patronage by failing to carry such widely demanded products.

Horizontal Cooperation Regardless of the above sources of power, small retailers will have little ability to influence and shape the channels in which they operate. The remaining source of power for those firms lies in some form of horizontal cooperation. The cooperation may range from land-buying pools to jointly financed operations such as the familiar cooperative chains discussed in a later section of this chapter.[6] Obviously, a major objective of those activities is to offset the market power of large manufacturers. Such efforts also give small retailers increased ability to compete with large retailers and obtain economies of scale in purchasing, promotion, and other operational aspects. Thus, when suppliers are faced with large retail organizations on the one hand and cooperating smaller firms on the other, their potential dominance is threatened further.[7]

Conglomeration Among large retail organizations the effect of conglomeration has been to reduce dependence upon any one supplier or group of suppliers. Conglomeration—expansion into many different types of retail business —spreads risk for the retailer and opens many new alternatives. Many examples of conglomeration exist. J. C. Penney moved from limited-line soft goods into full-line stores and auto service centers.[8] The May Company, an ownership group for department stores, has moved into the catalog showroom business. On a more limited scale the efforts of many retail firms to expand product lines through scrambled merchandising can be considered conglomeration.

Forms of Retail Channel Management

To a greater or lesser extent all retail firms have access to the sources of power described above. Although almost all interactions between retailers and suppliers involve some attempt to gain concessions by using power, retailers may not always be consciously seeking full channel control.[9] A primary difference among retailers lies in the extent to which any particular firm is able to mobilize

[5] Porter, op. cit., p. 423.

[6] For a more complete discussion of developments in retailers' horizontal cooperation, see C. Merle Crawford, "Needed: A New Look at Retailers' Horizontal Cooperation," *Journal of Retailing* (Summer 1970), pp. 66–71.

[7] Ibid.

[8] Walter Gross, "Retailing in the Seventies: A Projection of Current Trends," *Baylor Business Studies* (February–April, 1969), pp. 19–31.

[9] Roger Dickenson, "Channel Management by Large Retailers," in Robert L. King (ed.), *Marketing and the New Science of Planning* (Chicago: American Marketing Association, 1968), p. 128.

its power and emerge as the channel leader or captain. Two specific forms of organization—chain stores and cooperative groups—have developed and lend themselves to more complete channel control by retail organizations.

Chain Stores The corporate chain, a relatively recent phenomenon in retailing, can now be found in virtually all merchandise lines.[10] As the corporate chains have amassed economic resources, several alternatives have emerged which give the chains even greater ability to exercise leadership and control over the channel.

The first alternative is continued horizontal expansion. With the dollars earned from present operations, new outlets can be opened in new market areas. This alternative has a major impact on suppliers. The chain becomes even more important to those firms needing access to the chain's markets. Supplier dependence is therefore increased. In addition, the increased command of ultimate consumer proximity and loyalty which comes about with the opening of new outlets heightens supplier dependence. Thus, horizontal expansion by a chain increases the power of the retailer and aids that firm in developing its leadership role. Ultimately the chain may become so powerful that it can dictate product designs and innovations to manufacturing firms. Some grocery chains have their own test kitchens which constantly look for new formulations and products to satisfy consumers. Once these products are developed, the chain seeks a manufacturer to act as a source of supply for the item. Other examples can be found in many industries ranging from apparel to furniture where leading retail chains employ their own staff designers and have products manufactured to specification.

The second alternative for the chain store is vertical integration. There is probably no such thing in the United States as a "large retailer" since most of these firms are actually huge, vertically integrated institutions.[11] The most logical first step into vertical integration by retailers is the development and absorption of wholesaler channel functions. Thus, the retailer chain establishes its own warehouses or distribution centers and deals directly with manufacturers. Many examples also exist of retail absorption of manufacturing firms which previously acted as suppliers. Sears' purchase of an interest in Whirlpool, which manufactures the Kenmore line of appliances, and Kroger's purchase of several food processing plants are two of the more outstanding examples.

Cooperative Groups Retailer-sponsored cooperative groups represent another form of organization which may be adopted, especially by small retailers, to increase power and develop channel leadership. In such groups independent retailers organize their own wholesale facility and often use common store de-

[10] J. Barry Mason and Morris L. Mayer, *Modern Retailing: Theory and Practice* (Dallas: Business Publications, Inc., 1978), p. 49.

[11] Robert W. Little, "The Marketing Channel: Who Should Lead This Extra-Corporate Organization?" *Journal of Marketing* (January 1970), p. 34.

signs, share promotional materials, exchange market information, and cooperate in other endeavors.[12] The avowed objective of such groups is to increase the market power and bargaining ability of retailers relative to manufacturers. Thus, the economies which would normally accrue only to chain stores are available also to independents. Examples of retailer-sponsored cooperatives include Associated Grocers in the supermarket industry and Rexall in the drug industry. Once such groups are formed, they have many of the same advantages and abilities as the chain stores in dealing with suppliers.

Retailer Channel Management—Conclusion

Recent developments in the apparel industry demonstrate how retail control can result in functional spinoff to retail organizations. Many retail clothing stores are beginning to buy much closer to their actual selling season and are requiring that manufacturers schedule deliveries to meet store needs. These requirements have forced suppliers to produce in advance of actual orders and to carry larger inventories. The net result is that apparel manufacturers are being forced to assume more risk.

There are many reasons for these changes. First, chain and department stores have increased their share of the business and thus wield greater power in dealing with suppliers. Second, many consumers tend to treat clothes shopping as a leisure activity and visit the same stores repeatedly, expecting to see new merchandise each time. Finally, retailers have become more conscious of the high expenses involved in holding inventories and are determined to reduce such costs. As a result, retailers are demanding faster and more frequent delivery, markdown participation, and buy-back of unsold merchandise. Some suppliers, unable to absorb the risks and higher costs, have been forced out of business. Others have attempted to seek smaller stores as customers or to strengthen their own brand identification. Nevertheless, a significant change in channel control has occurred in the apparel industry in recent years.[13]

The apparel industry provides one example of shifting channel leadership. However, similar developments have occurred in many other industries and can be expected to continue in the future.

CHANNEL MANAGEMENT BY WHOLESALERS

Although wholesaling is one of the oldest forms of economic activity and represents a major segment of the United States economy, the potential for wholesalers to exert control over channels of distribution is limited. This section investigates sources of wholesaler power and organizational methods by which some wholesale institutions have attempted to gain channel control.

---

[12] Mason and Mayer, op. cit., p. 421.
[13] Developed from Deborah Sue Young, "Apparel Makers Face Consolidation as Stores Stiffen Delivery Terms," *Wall Street Journal* (February 6, 1978), p. 1.

Sources of Wholesaler Power

Many of the wholesalers' power sources are similar to those of retailers. Wholesalers enjoy better market proximity relative to manufacturers because of their knowledge of and daily contact with retail outlets in their market area. Some manufacturers wishing access to local retailers have little choice but to contact wholesalers in those local markets. The number of wholesalers doing business in any one line of goods in a market area is extremely limited. This lack of alternatives for manufacturers can increase a wholesaler's power.

As the United States economy has developed over the past century, however, gradual emergence of large-scale retailers and of manufacturers able to perform wholesaling functions has eroded wholesaler power positions. As a result many wholesalers have had to reassess their positions in the channel, change or modify services offered to manufacturers and retailers, and reexamine their product lines.[14] In making these changes, there are four basic reasons why wholesalers may be able to maintain their market positions and perhaps obtain a higher degree of control relative to other channel members:[15]

1   Wholesalers have continuity in and intimacy with the market.
2   Wholesalers have an acute understanding of the costs of holding and handling inventory.
3   Wholesalers can concentrate managerial talent on localized marketing strategies without the distractions of manufacturing problems.
4   Wholesalers have the advantage of local entrepreneurship.

Essentially, then, wholesalers have utilized their specialized knowledge and abilities to strengthen their positions in channels. The specific means by which this specialization has been implemented vary. Some wholesalers, particularly in electronics and plumbing, have instituted automatic reordering systems for retailers.[16] For the retailer this approach frees time normally devoted to the inventory function and reduces total inventory levels. For the wholesaler, the sales staff is able to devote more time to sales programs which benefit both parties. This approach increases retailer dependence upon the wholesaler.

Adoption of distributor brands is another means through which wholesalers have been able to increase retailer dependence. Private distributor brands have been most successful in industries where primary demand is well-established and the products are in common use and frequently purchased.[17] Food and hardware products usually meet these criteria. In these cases wholesalers can successfully rely upon the price appeal of distributors' brands since product differentiation is minimal.

[14] Edwin H. Lewis, "Channel Management by Wholesalers," in Robert L. King (ed.), *Marketing and the New Science of Planning* (Chicago: American Marketing Association, 1968), p. 138.
[15] Richard S. Lopata, "Faster Pace in Wholesaling," *Harvard Business Review* (July–August 1969), p. 132. Copyright © 1969 by the President and Fellows of Harvard College; all rights reserved.
[16] Ibid., p. 138.
[17] Lewis, op. cit., p. 140.

Forms of Wholesaler Channel Management

The above-mentioned sources of power for wholesalers have been used primarily to increase dependence of other channel members upon the wholesale institution. In addition, two organizational trends have emerged which tend to place channel control in the hands of wholesalers. These trends parallel those observed in the retailing industry: integration and voluntary cooperative groups.

Integration Wholesalers have achieved both horizontal and vertical integration, which gives them channel control. Many examples of both forms of integration can be offered:[18]

> **1** Allied Farm Equipment Company is a Chicago-based distributor of farm equipment which now manufactures over 200 items for its international network of distributors.
> **2** Midas International is a distributor of automotive products which today manufactures items for sale through its network of retail shops.
> **3** Distronics Corporation is a joint venture of plumbing and heating wholesalers which provides on-line computer services to its members to aid in their daily operations.

These examples indicate the extent to which wholesalers have integrated to achieve some form of channel control. These trends will likely continue as wholesalers seek new methods of maintaining a viable position within distribution channels.

Voluntary Groups One of the primary forms of organization for wholesaler channel control is the voluntary chain. While such an organization is similar in substance to retailer-sponsored cooperatives, it is a newer development which was spurred by the growth of corporate chains. To establish a voluntary chain the wholesaler solicits independent retail firms to concentrate their merchandising activities through one outlet. Affiliated retailers receive many benefits including group identity, large-scale buying, private labels, centralized promotion, and various management aids. Although control in these organizations rests with the sponsoring wholesale firm, the retail firms are also strengthened and can maintain a more competitive posture.[19]

Many successful voluntary chains exist. In the grocery industry Independent Grocers Association (IGA) has more affiliated retail outlets than does the A&P corporate chain. Western Auto is a well-known hardware voluntary group. In the variety field Ben Franklin Stores is a well-known name.[20]

Voluntary chains have not been universally accepted, however. Voluntary groups have been generally unsuccessful in industries where consumer demand

[18] Lopata, op. cit., p. 136.
[19] Lewis, op. cit., p. 139.
[20] Ibid.

and buying habits have led to intertype competition, large-scale retailing, or selective distribution policies by manufacturers. Because of these reasons voluntary chains have not emerged in the drug, tobacco, and appliance fields.

Wholesaler Channel Management—Conclusion

Despite the trends discussed above, the wholesaler is rarely able to exert channel control. Rather, economic pressures have led wholesalers to seek methods by which they can maintain their position in distribution channels rather than assume leadership. Wholesalers tend to be strong in areas where producers and retailers are large in number, small in size, geographically scattered, and lack resources for major marketing efforts. Unfortunately for wholesalers these market conditions are rarely found in the United States economy today.[21]

THIRD-PARTY CHANNEL MANAGEMENT

In Chapters 3 and 4 the concepts of specialization and dependence as behavioral states which give rise to power were developed in detail. Thus far, however, we have not examined those institutions whose extreme functional specialization places them in a position which many people fail to consider a part of distribution channels. Nevertheless, the existence of these institutions facilitates channel operations and allows the primary channel institutions—manufacturers, wholesalers, and retailers—to achieve their respective goals. The power of these facilitating institutions derives partially from the extreme nature of their functional specialization and partially from the fact that their stake in total channel performance is lower than that of other channel members. In this section the potential for power and leadership among physical distribution specialists, financial institutions, and other facilitating agencies is examined.

Physical Distribution Specialists

Since a distribution channel often uses many physical distribution specialists, their potential for leadership cannot be underestimated. Rather, specialists may be able to capitalize on their unique channel positions and participate actively in coordination and organization of efforts.[22] Many such specialists exist but public warehouses and common carriers appear to be prime candidates as centers of channel control.

Public Warehouses Public warehouses have traditionally performed the storage function for primary channel members on a for-hire basis. In recent years, however, progressive public warehouses have begun to design systems which are made available to logistics managers of manufacturing firms for little

---

[21] Ibid.

[22] James H. Underwood and Adel I. El-Ansary, "Physical Distribution: Marketing Channel Myopia," *Proceedings of the Sixth Annual Transportation and Logistics Educators Conference,* (Columbus, Ohio: The Ohio State University, 1976), p. 79.

investment. These systems include order processing, delivery, inventory, and billing services.[23] These progressive public warehouses are becoming known as distribution centers.[24] As these institutions become marketing oriented, they become more familiar with the needs of their customers and other distribution channel members. Dependence upon the distribution center services is thus increased and the distribution center becomes increasingly powerful. This role has been summarized as follows.[25]

> The greater power of the distribution center primarily emanates from increased expert, informational, and reward power. Coercive, legal legitimate, traditional legitimate, and referent power are not likely to be important bases of power. The customer oriented approach is simply not consistent with emphasis on *coercive* tactics—the distribution center manager's role is that of cooperation and concern with the problems of his clients and not with forcibly manipulating his behavior. The contractual arrangements are also likely not to differ between the traditional public warehouse and the distribution center, and consequently *legal legitimate* power is likely not to differ: i.e., the differences between the two are conceptual while the formal arrangements are the same. At least in the short run, *traditional legitimate* power is not likely to favor the distribution center in that the role expectations will take a while to become institutionalized. Finally, *referent* power is also not going to differ between the traditional warehouseman and the distribution center manager. Behavioral comparisons will still be made with regard to the user's value system.
>
> The key sources of the new power position will emanate from the expertise and informational savvy of the distribution center manager, and eventually from the increased rewards that he can provide. Because he is consumer oriented rather than transaction oriented, he will become actively involved in a wider range of problem areas and examine them in greater depth than the traditional warehouseman. With his experience across a variety of customers, he is likely to develop *expertise* in areas that the user cannot economically obtain himself. At a minimum, he will have extensive knowledge of the *information* that is readily available, and in his activist role, point out contingencies which will assist his customers.

If the distribution center develops its power bases as suggested, the potential for channel control by this institution will increase.

Common Carriers[26]   The functional specialization and concomitant potential for control when practiced in a market-oriented manner is just as evident with common carriers as with public warehouses. Carriers can increase their channel power by making their contributions to total channel performance

[23] See Donald J. Bowersox, *Logistical Management* (New York: The Macmillan Company, 1974), p. 235.
[24] James A. Constantin, et al., "The Distribution Center: A Potential Focus of Power," *Proceedings of the Sixth Annual Transportation and Logistics Educators Conference*, (Columbus, Ohio: The Ohio State University, 1976), p. 38.
[25] Constantin, et al., op. cit., p. 43.
[26] This section is based on Frederick J. Beier, "The Role of the Common Carrier in the Channel of Distribution," *Transportation Journal* (Winter 1969), pp. 12–21.

unique. Two bases of power for common carriers have been identified. The first concerns the use of rewards by carriers in granting rate reduction (a severely restricted practice) and in developing lower cost shipping alternatives by improving performance. For example, carriers may undertake special efforts to reduce damaged merchandise and thus achieve lower total costs for shippers who comply with their control efforts.

The second base of power for carriers rests with their information expertise and control. Carriers can act as advisors to shippers for decisions ranging from routing to plant location. Carriers may also act as clearinghouses for transportation information and as uncertainty absorbers for shippers. Expert power may also be exerted by carriers through their ability to acquire intimate knowledge of the operations of two distinct levels of primary channel participants. For example, the materials handling requirements of both manufacturers and retailers can be readily observed by carriers who deal with both institutions. Recommendations can be developed by carriers which would reduce total handling costs for the channel system. The primary limitation on use of expert power by carriers is the commitment necessary from other channel members to specific carrier organizations so that carriers can see the potential gain in developing and sharing information.

Financial Institutions

As the W. T. Grant situation discussed in Chapter 1 illustrated, financial institutions can substantially affect operations and strategies of primary channel members. In the Grant situation the decision to refuse credit was the final blow to management and led ultimately to Grant's bankruptcy since other creditors were no longer willing to provide financing to the firm.

While such extreme instances of financial institution channel power are rare, there is little doubt that specialization of these firms in the critical marketing functions of financing and risk taking encourages strong channel positions. Field warehouses often finance inventories of wholesale firms. In return, however, field warehouses have the right to approve or disapprove the sale of the financed merchandise, any new purchases, and shipment of merchandise. The field warehouse's control is so complete that physical barriers and safeguards are required on the wholesaler's premises to secure the financed inventory. These actions effectively limit the activities of not only manufacturers and retailers, but also the wholesaler who uses the services of such an agency.

The power of financial institutions can also be observed in shopping center developments. Shopping center developers may be forced to follow the dictates of lending companies because those institutions, in order to grant mortgages, usually require that the developer obtain many tenants with high credit ratings. Financing of major shopping centers is predicated primarily upon the type and value of the leases the developer obtains. The developer is thus forced to seek out major retailing enterprises and offer them advantageous arrangements at the expense of independent merchants.

In this instance financial institutions achieve power because of their available funds. Only a limited number of these institutions are capable of multimillion dollar loans, and the developer must seek one out to finance construction of a shopping center.

Other Facilitating Agencies

Other facilitating agencies exist which have a unique potential for exerting influence or control over marketing channel activities. Resident buying offices are becoming increasingly important in many lines of retail trade.[27] These firms offer retailers specialized market knowledge and instant expertise in major merchandise markets. They also assume a clearinghouse and gatekeeper information function for retailers who choose to utilize their services. Retailers are able to learn quickly about successful styles, trends, and techniques through information provided by a resident buying office. Manufacturers, in turn, can gain contact to many potential retail customers if good will can be cultivated with a resident buyer. Manufacturers also respond very quickly to demands by a resident buyer because of the buyer's contact with many retailers. For example, a retailer in need of a rush shipment may be more likely to receive expedited treatment if the request is placed through the resident buying office rather than directly.

Other facilitators such as advertising agencies and marketing research firms maintain some ability to exert influence over distribution channels. On one hand, this ability arises because of the low stake maintained by such agencies in the operations of any one channel. However, when the functions these institutions perform are relatively unimportant to the total channel or, as is often the case, a number of alternative institutions exist whose services might be utilized within the channel, the power of facilitating firms is greatly diminished.

FRANCHISING

Although franchising is not necessarily a form of intermediary channel management, the leadership potential of all types of channel institutions must be understood before the nature of franchise relationships can be fully appreciated. Therefore, we have delayed a discussion of franchising to this point. Essentially, franchising is a form in which one party is granted the right or privilege to do business and, in return for some payment, is assisted in organizing, training, merchandising, and management. In this section we discuss briefly the history of franchising, types of franchises, advantages and disadvantages of franchise relationships, and some of the problems encountered in the management of franchise systems.

Development of Franchising

Although the past 20 years have seen a tremendous boom in franchising as a form of business, it is by no means a modern phenomenon. Its roots can be

---

[27] Mason and Mayer, op. cit., p. 422.

traced back to kings and chiefs of state who granted land rights to individuals for trade and commercial development. The development of North America was spurred on by just such a franchise, the Hudson's Bay Company. One of the first firms to utilize modern franchising was the Singer Sewing Machine Company, which is still in business today. Established after the Civil War, Singer granted a number of retail outlets the right to distribute its product.

The beginning of this century saw a sudden burst in franchise activity. Both General Motors Corporation and Ford Motor Company chose franchising as the most viable means for distribution of products. With the explosion of the automobile industry, oil companies faced a similar predicament: how to achieve mass distribution rapidly without the capital to open a number of outlets. Those companies also chose the franchise form of business. During those same years Coca-Cola and Pepsi-Cola both began to develop a group of franchise bottlers to mix and distribute their products.

In the 1920s and 1930s the first restaurant franchises were initiated by Howard Johnson's and A & W Root Beer. Franchising also spread into such diverse fields as drugs, mattresses, and variety stores. A slowdown occurred during World War II, but postwar franchising activity boomed again when pent-up demand combined with a proliferation of manufacturers desiring mass distribution. Since 1950 franchising has spread to the motel industry, entertainment and recreation (Kampgrounds of America and Putt-Putt Golf), coin-operated laundries, and other industries.

Types of Franchises

The purpose of the preceding historical discussion has been to develop an understanding of the many different types of franchise organizations which exist. In fact, impetus for development of a franchise system can come from all types of channel members. In various industries manufacturers, wholesalers, and retailers have each taken the lead in using franchising as a means of doing business.

In general, however, franchises can be placed into two basic categories. The first category is the product or service distributorship: The franchisee is licensed to sell products or services actually performed or produced by the franchisor.[28] Several subtypes of distributorships exist. In the *manufacturer-retailer* system, such as in the automobile and petroleum industries, retail outlets are granted the right to distribute the manufacturers' output. *Manufacturer-wholesaler* systems are typified by the arrangements in the soft drink industry. *Wholesaler-retailer* systems are exemplified by IGA and Western Auto Stores.

The second basic category of franchise relationships consists of various forms of trademark licensing systems where all franchises operate under the franchisor's trade name and are identified as a group. Here again a number of subcategories exist. In *trademark franchisor-manufacturer* systems such as Fruit of the Loom, the trademark holder allows others to produce the product

---

[28] Donald N. Thompson, *Franchise Operations and Anti-Trust* (Lexington, Mass.: Heath-Lexington Books, 1971).

as long as strict quality specifications are met. *Trademark franchisor-whole-saler or retailer* systems are found in most service industries. Examples include Holiday Inn, H&R Block, and Hertz. Essentially, retail outlets are granted the right to use the trademark holder's name as long as standard operating policies specified by the holder are followed.

Advantages and Disadvantages of Franchising

Franchising offers a number of advantages to both franchisors and franchisees. Advantages for the franchisor are several. The arrangement allows for rapid entry into new markets since little capital investment is required. At the same time less risk is incurred and the franchisor can withdraw from unsuccessful markets with a minimum of personal loss. Of course, doing so will cause the franchisees to lose their investment and the franchisor's reputation may be damaged. For this reason, McDonald's has a policy of ensuring that no franchisee will lose the money invested in the business. Another advantage for the franchisor is that the daily management problems of operating a retail unit are avoided. Franchisees who have a personal investment in the business are inclined to work harder to ensure that the firm is successful. This would not necessarily be the case if the retail units were company-owned and managed by hired employees.

There are some disadvantages for the franchisor. In successful franchise firms profits accruing through outright ownership would be much larger than those obtained through the franchise relationship. In many instances franchisors have attempted to repurchase the franchise after a few years of operation. Also, the franchisor is limited by law in the exercise of control and thus has limited flexibility since the franchisee is considered an independent business person who has a contractual agreement with the franchisor. It is also often difficult to remove undesirable franchisees.[29]

Franchising offers several advantages to franchisees which may not be available in any other form of business. Franchisees usually receive the benefit of marketing and management aids which have been tried and tested by others. At McDonald's Hamburger University and Burger King's Whopper College, franchisees study all phases of restaurant operations including cooking, personnel management, inventory control, and accounting procedures. In addition, the franchisees are visited monthly and return to their "universities" for brush-up courses on a continuing basis. Franchisees also receive benefits of location research and a recognized trade name.

Of course, the franchisee disadvantages are many. Although it may be easy to get into business, it may be difficult to get out. Since a franchise is usually designed as a continuing relationship, a franchisee may be unable to terminate an undesirable agreement without sacrificing the initial investment. The franchise relationship also implies that franchisees will relinquish some of their independence and agree to operate within certain boundaries established

[29] Mason and Mayer, op. cit., p. 213.

by the franchisor. In addition, while franchisees may benefit from a recognized trade name, the reverse can also hold true. If other franchisees deteriorate in quality or if the franchisor encounters difficulties, the franchisee may suffer from the association. Finally, it is possible that a franchisee can develop over-dependence on the franchisor and abandon the initiative and business judgment so necessary for success.

Problems in Franchise Systems

Franchising can exist only when two parties form a continuing relationship. A franchise contract is developed which establishes the legal rights and responsi-bilities of both franchisor and franchisee. These agreements usually include clauses which define the relationship, methods of payment, location of outlets, and other details. One basic area of concern for the franchisor is the choice of a method of payment. Among the alternatives are an initial franchise fee, royal-ties (such as a percentage of sales), lease or rental of building or equipment, sale of goods or services, and such methods as profit sharing and/or interest.

The agreement also includes regulatory clauses outlining controls which can be exercised by the franchisor and performance requirements for the fran-chisee. In addition, procedures and requirements for termination by either party are detailed.

As the preceding discussion suggests, franchise relationships are prone to manifest some extreme forms of interorganizational behavior. Power, conflict, and cooperation are all readily observed within franchise systems.

Of course, legitimate power in franchising is obvious. The contract speci-fies controls which may be employed by the franchisor to protect the trade name, ensure proper quality and market representation, and help new fran-chisees. Franchisors also have other power sources at their disposal which are often used to increase franchisee motivation. Among these is the use of re-wards such as contests, awards, and prizes for compliance with franchisor re-quests. Coercive power also exists: the threat to invoke the termination clause of the contract.

To counteract franchisor power, the franchisees' power comes from their local market representation and the right to terminate. In some industries fran-chisees have formed trade organizations to counteract franchisor strength. The National Automobile Dealers Association is one example. This organization has amassed such strength that it effectively lobbied in Congress for passage of several laws to enhance automobile dealers' legitimate power. For example, the Monroney Fair-Play Bill of 1956 makes it unfair for manufacturers to force dealers to accept unwanted cars.

As might be expected, the existence of strong power bases of both parties makes conflict a common phenomenon in franchising. Many sources of conflict arise from the basic nature of the franchise agreement. Quite often interests of franchisor and franchisees are in strong conflict. As the relationship between the two parties flourishes, franchisees gain considerable resources and begin to feel that the franchisor does not deserve as much of the profit as the initial agreement calls for. Franchisees may tend to forget the value of the training and aid which were received when the relationship was initiated. Similarly, franchisors may become more active in parent-owned facilities and forget that independent franchisees have a major stake in the success of the relationship.

From time to time some issues have resulted in overt conflict between franchise participants which led to litigation. The more common issues include (1) the right of the franchisee to deal in products of other firms, (2) the franchisee's right to purchase equipment or supplies from sources other than those specified by the franchisor, (3) territorial restrictions, (4) determination of re-sale prices, and (5) termination.

Franchisees also have often complained that communications with franchisors are poor, that franchisor performance in such functions as advertising and promotion is poor, and that profit limitations restrict franchise success unreasonably. Of course, franchise relationships are subject to the same legal restraints discussed in Chapter 5 for other channel relationships. Since a legal contract exists between the parties, however, franchise channel conflicts are usually resolved through litigation.

Although franchising has had a stormy legal history, cooperation is apparent in most highly successful franchise systems. It appears that most overt dysfunctional conflict arises in those franchise systems which show poor profitability. Once both parties realize that franchising is a symbiotic relationship and work together to minimize conflict, profitability is enhanced. However, it is often difficult to determine if these systems exhibit higher profitability because conflict is minimized, or if conflict is minimized because profits are high.

SUMMARY

In this chapter we have been concerned with channel management and leadership by firms other than manufacturers. Retailers have many power sources to draw upon in order to assert a leadership role. Retailer proximity to markets and monopoly of local trading areas increase supplier dependence. Retailers may also attempt to gain control over suppliers by developing a strong customer franchise through effective management of the retail mix. Private label merchandise, horizontal cooperation, and conglomeration are other sources of power for retail firms. Chain stores, particularly vertically integrated chains, and cooperative groups represent two methods by which retailers have asserted their domination over distribution channels.

Wholesaler power sources and methods of domination closely parallel those of retail firms. Market proximity and distributor brands give some degree of control to wholesale firms. In addition, modification of service offerings may enhance wholesaler specialization and develop more channel dependence. Some wholesalers have gained channel dominance through forward and backward vertical integration and by forming voluntary cooperative groups.

A number of facilitating agencies exist to aid in performance of channel activities. Because of the extreme form of functional specialization offered by some of these third parties, an opportunity exists for them to assume leadership of the entire channel. Logistics specialists such as public warehouses and common carriers have unique abilities to influence other channel members. Financial institutions are able to direct certain policies of firms which utilize their services. Other facilitators such as resident buying offices, advertising agencies, and marketing research firms may be able to influence primary channel members but complete control is rare.

Franchising is a channel system in which one party is granted rights to a certain product or service and given assistance in this business in return for payment of some kind. Although hardly a new form of business, franchising has experienced dramatic growth in recent years. Franchises take many forms, ranging from manufacturer-initiated efforts to gain retail outlets to a service firm's efforts to broaden its market penetration. Franchising arrangements involve give and take by both parties since advantages and disadvantages exist for both. Since franchisors and franchisees have many power sources, conflict often arises in franchising relationships. Nevertheless, most successful franchise systems exhibit a high degree of cooperative effort between franchise participants.

QUESTIONS

1 How can the sources of retailer power discussed in this chapter be related to the bases of power discussed in Chapter 4?

2 How can the principle of relative loss be used to explain retailer power over other channel institutions?

3 What generalizations concerning the shifting focus of power in distribution channels can be drawn from the example of changes in the apparel industry?

4 Compare sources of wholesaler power with those of retailers.

5 What forces have led to the relative general decline of wholesaler power in this century? What countervailing forces exist which have allowed some aggressive wholesalers to maintain and enhance their positions in distribution channels?

6 What are the advantages and disadvantages of franchising for the franchisor? The franchisee?

7 Why do you suppose that franchising as a form of business experienced such rapid growth following World War II?

8 Comparing power sources of public warehouses, common carriers, and financial institutions, what generalizations can you develop concerning third-party channel management?

9 What are the alternative means by which retail chains can attempt to exert leadership over channel activities?

10 In the 1940s ARVIN was a small but well-known producer of home appliances. By the late 1950s, however, the company was out of business. Recently, a group of independent retailers has purchased the rights to use the ARVIN name and has considered licensing several small manufacturers to produce a new line of appliances under the ARVIN name. These retailers are primarily discount appliance stores which have gained popularity in many markets. How does this situation fit into the framework of channel management by retailers discussed in this chapter? If you were an appliance retailer, would you consider joining this effort? Why or why not?

CASE 9-1: Rundel's Department Store

On February 2, 1978, Gordon Franklin, men's slacks buyer for Rundel's Department Store, was reflecting on his previous day's meeting with Sue Anderson. As field representative for Davis Manufacturing Company, Ms. Anderson had been trying for some time to increase Davis' volume with Rundel's. In the meeting Franklin had agreed to take on Davis as a major supplier if Davis would agree to several major points in a vendor program Franklin had prepared. Franklin felt confident that Ms. Anderson would meet with Davis executives who would ultimately agree to the program.

COMPANY BACKGROUND

Rundel's Department Store is located in a medium-sized midwestern town with a population of 385,000. With sales in excess of $78 million from its downtown and four suburban branch stores, Rundel's is the dominant retail institution in the market (see Table 1 for Rundel's financial data). There is only one other department store in the market, Youngston's. Since Youngston's is a privately owned company, exact sales data are not known. It is generally assumed, however, that the company's revenue is about half that of Rundel's. The two firms are located about one block apart in the downtown area. Youngston's also has outlets in the same four suburban shopping centers as Rundel's. Youngston's branch outlets, however, average 86,000 square feet, whereas Rundel's branches average 121,000 square feet.

Rundel's is a division of Urban Stores, Incorporated, a major department store ownership group. With sixteen operating divisions in addition to Rundel's, Urban has outlets in most of the major market areas in the United States. In fact, 62 percent of the population of the United States lives within 10 miles of an outlet owned by one of the Urban divisions. Although each division is

Table 1
Rundel's Department Stores
Condensed Income Statements

	1977	1976	1975
Net sales (including leased departments)	$78,200,000	$68,100,000	$58,100,000
Cost of sales (including occupancy and buying costs)	58,100,000	50,100,000	42,600,000
Selling, publicity, delivery and administrative expense	13,200,000	11,500,000	9,900,000
Provision for bad debts	250,000	220,000	200,000
Interest	320,000	290,000	270,000
Income before taxes	$ 6,330,000	$ 5,990,000	$ 5,130,000
Income taxes	3,130,000	3,900,000	2,510,000
Net income	$ 3,200,000	$ 3,100,000	$ 2,620,000

operated autonomously due to variations in local market conditions, there is a tendency for buyers of similar merchandise to correspond regularly. Although Rundel's is one of the smaller stores in the ownership group, buyers in other divisions tend to look to Rundel's for information concerning new products. In fact, because of its relatively small size, Rundel's management is encouraged by Urban to be a leader in trying new concepts. Urban feels that trends can be identified more quickly in this situation and, in the event of a mistake, losses can be minimized.

Men's Slacks Department

As buyer for men's slacks, Gordon Franklin has responsibility for a department which currently contributes about 2.8 percent of all sales to Rundel's. The department has experienced impressive growth in the 3 years that Franklin has been buyer. In 1975 sales for the department were only $755,000, which represented 1.3 percent of total store sales. Much of the growth has occurred because of the addition of new products to the department and the tremendous expansion in the demand for men's clothes.

Franklin had added two major product lines to the department since he became buyer. First, he decided that men's jeans should be represented in his department and in 3 years this line became a major contributor to the department sales. Franklin used three resources for men's jeans: Levi, Farah, and a lower-priced supplier of unbranded jeans. The jeans sold in his department are specifically designed for the over-30 male who, in Franklin's terms, "has lost that youthful trimness but still wants to wear comfortable pants." Thus, these men's jeans are made with a fuller waist and seat, unlike boys' or young men's jeans. They are, however, available with contemporary styling such as patchwork, trim, or suede inserts.

Franklin's second product addition was the new line of coordinated outfits designed by his two principal resources, Levi and Farah. With this addition Franklin expanded the scope of his department beyond men's slacks. Coordinated outfits consist of pants, coats, and vests which can be purchased together as suits or separately for mix-and-match combinations. The development of this line was a recent phenomenon in men's clothing and it met with considerable success. Since a complete coordinated outfit retailed for approximately $100 while the average price for other merchandise was $22, Franklin added this line as soon as it was made available by Levi and Farah. Slacks buyers in twelve other Urban divisions adopted the lines after Franklin reported his early successes.

Franklin's department also carried a full line of regular men's pants. Although suppliers varied from season to season, he typically had slacks from Levi, Farah, Spotwood and at least two other suppliers, including Davis Manufacturing. However, the bulk of his business was done with the first three resources. "Off brands," he commented, "are all right for special sales or the 'Charlie Six-Pack' customer, but most of our business is in regular price, quality merchandise." He explained that "Charlie Six-Pack" was a term used to describe male customers who have the money to buy clothes in quality outlets but lack the clothes consciousness to do so effectively. "You can easily recognize Charlie since he likes to wear Hawaiian print shirts with plaid slacks," he added.

Franklin feels that his major competition comes from Youngston's and the numerous men's specialty shops in the area. A consultant recently conducted research which revealed that 22 percent of all men's slacks were purchased in department stores (see Table 2). Since his department is much larger that his counterpart's at Youngston's and since no specialty store has more than two outlets in the area, he is quite satisfied that his is the primary men's slacks outlet in the area.

DAVIS MANUFACTURING COMPANY

Davis Manufacturing Company is a large manufacturer of a broad line of men's clothing. The firm has a nationally known brand name and ranks among the top five manufacturers of men's apparel. Recent years, however, had not been as successful. See Table 3 for financial data concerning Davis Manufacturing Company. Gordon Franklin explained Davis' problems:

> Rundel's carries Davis products. Three or four years ago we deemphasized them, though, because they simply failed to keep pace with trends in the industry. Whereas our market became much more fashion conscious, demanding new colors and styles, Davis continued to make your basic pants for good ol' Charlie Six-Pack. Their line was fine for discount stores which wanted a well-known name, but most major department stores, including all of Urban stores, deemphasized them. We just didn't want to deal too heavily in that kind of merchandise.

Table 4 presents Davis' performance data in Rundel's Department Store.

Although Franklin's perceptions generally reflected those of other department store buyers, Sue Anderson asserted that Davis was now making a concerted effort to recapture its quality image and regain a considerable share of department store distribution. New designers had been hired and an entire new designer line of slacks, jeans, and coordinates developed. Davis executives and representatives were very excited about the prospects for this line. She said

Table 2 Consultant's Report Concerning Men's Purchasing Patterns in Rundel's Market Area

Store type	Market shares (percent)	
	Men's slacks	Men's jeans
Department	22	15
Specialty	43	40
Discount	22	30
Chain	13	15
	100	100

Table 3
Davis Manufacturing Company
Consolidated Income Statements

	1977	1976	1975
Net sales	$91,000,000	$96,000,000	$112,000,000
Cost of sales	73,100,000	75,200,000	84,400,000
Selling and administrative	19,300,000	20,200,000	21,100,000
Interest	1,500,000	1,200,000	800,000
Income before taxes	$ (3,200,000)	$ (600,000)	$ 5,700,000
Income taxes	cr 1,600,000	cr 300,000	2,800,000
Net income (Loss)	$ (1,600,000)	$ (300,000)	$ 2,900,000

that Davis had made a commitment to men's fashion apparel and, given anticipated growth of the market, was determined to establish itself as a major factor
in the market. Since Davis wanted to regain department store distribution, Anderson had targeted Rundel's as a key account.

THE VENDOR PROGRAM

Sue Anderson and Davis Manufacturing Company executives did not hide their
desire to become a major resource for Rundel's. Franklin was somewhat reluctant to develop a third major resource in addition to Levi and Farah, but decided that if Davis would agree to several points, it would be worth his while to
do so. Thus, he outlined the following program to Anderson:
  Business needs of Rundel's from Davis:

  1 Davis agrees to maintain continuity of supply of regular stock by being
able to fill orders on a 2-week basis.
  2 Ability to maintain markup of 48 percent on basic stock.
  3 Guaranteed turnover rate of 3.5 in 1978, 4.0 thereafter.
  4 Markdown rates on regular in-line merchandise not to exceed 10 percent including vendor participation during sale events.

Table 4
Davis Manufacturing Company
Performance in Rundel's Department Store

	1977	1976	1975	1974
Retail volume (in thousands)	34.0	37.9	72.0	94.1
Cost (in thousands)	21.3	23.6	42.9	56.0
Markup (percent)	37.3	37.7	40.4	40.5
Markdowns (in thousands)	13.0	15.2	14.1	1.5
Turnover	2.9	2.8	3.2	3.1
Cooperative advertising (in thousands)	.6	1.2	2.6	3.4
Source rank (in sales volume)	sixth	fifth	fourth	second

5 Davis cooperative advertising to include 60 percent of all newspaper linage costs, plus full cost of color, to a maximum of 10 percent of Rundel's purchases from Davis.

Rundel's support for Davis:

1 Departmental feature and display of regular running key items.
2 Commitment to develop Davis as a major department vendor including directions toward new product areas to expand commodity base.

Retail Volume Goals

	Spring	Fall	Total
1978	12.0	62.0	74.0
1979	75.0	85.0	160.0
1980	95.0	105.0	200.0
1981	115.0	120.0	235.0

Anderson was very excited about the proposed program. She knew that some of Franklin's requests asked for more than was offered by either Levi or Farah. For example, no other firm could guarantee fill-in or small orders on a 2-week basis. To do so would almost certainly require that either United Parcel Service or air freight be used for these orders. The guaranteed markup on the basic stock was also something that other manufacturers didn't offer. The requested markdown participation on sales events and cooperative advertising levels were somewhat higher than normal for the trade. On the other hand, she felt that such concessions should be granted by Davis if the firm ever hoped to reestablish its position in major department stores. "Perhaps later," she thought, "we can bring our vendor support more in line with the industry. Until then, however, we should offer more than our competitors so we can regain strong distribution."

CASE 9-1: QUESTIONS

1 If you were Sue Anderson or a Davis Manufacturing Company executive, would you agree to the conditions as set forth by Franklin? Why or why not?
2 What basis does Rundel's Department Store have to assume leadership of its channels?
3 If you answered yes to 1 above, would your answer be the same if Rundel's were an independent firm?

CASE 9-2: South Bottling Company

On a warm afternoon in 1978, Sam Stebbins, president of South Bottling Company, was reviewing the consequences of two major strategic decisions he had made in the past 5 years. As he prepared for the annual meeting with the other 739 Coca-Cola franchisees, he was sure he would be questioned closely about the results of his actions regarding addition of the Dr Pepper product line and adoption of an 8-ounce can for Coke. He knew that other Coke bottlers would be very interested in the profit impact of these two actions as well as any problems which might have occurred in the franchise arrangement.

INDUSTRY BACKGROUND

The channel system in the soft drink industry is called a producer-oriented wholesale system. Soft drink producers sell their syrup to franchise bottlers who operate independently of the parent firm. The group producer, such as Coca-Cola, attempts to minimize risks by shifting functions in the channel to its franchise bottlers. The bottlers provide facilities for actual bottling, relieving the producer from considerable investment in production facilities. In addition, the bottler provides local warehousing and delivery to retail outlets. Thus, the bottler actually provides production, storage, warehousing, and delivery facilities within the channel. Bottlers also handle accounting functions and provide a considerable amount of market information concerning tastes and preferences to their present syrup manufacturers. Thus, the major advantages of this distribution system to the producer are reduced investment in fixed facilities, lower inventory requirements, and economies which result from shipping pure syrup rather than the bottled beverage. The bottlers, who serve as warehousers and "manufacturers" of the final product, ship locally and have a lower total inventory expense than would be the case if syrup producers performed the final distribution function.

The bottler in the soft drink industry typically is viewed as the lifeblood of the parent company. The functions performed by this channel member are directly related to the success or failure of the syrup producers. In return, the producer supplies syrup (typically developed from a well-protected recipe) and extensive promotional assistance. The assistance includes expenditures for national advertising, cooperative ad allowances granted to bottlers and retailers, and free sampling.

GROWTH OF DR PEPPER

For the years 1965 to 1975 Dr Pepper was the star of the soft drink industry.[1] The company's cherry-flavored beverage expanded in distribution from the small towns of the South and Midwest into major markets of the United States. In 1974 Dr Pepper completed its national distribution, primarily at the expense of Coca-Cola and PepsiCo, which between them controlled 55 percent of the soft drink market. During the past decade, Dr Pepper was able to double its

---

[1] The situation for South Bottling Company is totally fictitious. Similarity between the decisions described in this case and any real situation is purely coincidental.

sales and profits every 4 years until it reached a sales level of $227 million and profits of $20 million in 1977.

Dr Pepper's strategy generally called for signing the largest bottler in each local market. In almost every case this meant gaining distribution from the local Coca-Cola bottler. Since Coke bottlers were generally independent of that firm, Dr Pepper was able to sign approximately 25 percent of Coke's franchisees by 1975. In doing so, Dr Pepper achieved distribution through many of the strongest bottlers in the industry and gained 5 percent of the total market with its single line product mix. This share placed Dr Pepper fifth in the industry behind Royal Crown (6 percent), Seven-Up (7 percent), and the much larger Coca-Cola and PepsiCo firms. The rapid growth rate during the period 1965 to 1975 caused Dr Pepper executives to project that the firm would pass Royal Crown and Seven-Up in a relatively short period of time.

Dr Pepper executives felt that, in order for sales to increase, it was extremely important for consumers to have an opportunity to sample the product. The unique and distinctive taste of the product made the sale of single drinks a very important aspect in building a strong Dr Pepper franchise. (The single-drink market in the soft drink industry consists of vending machines, fountain sales, and spectator events.) Therefore, Dr Pepper executives planned to put more emphasis on sales promotions such as giveaways at sporting events and shopping center openings. It was felt that this move was necessary before the firm could hope to gain more distribution through supermarkets. It was felt also that the firm should not try to compete directly with Coca-Cola and PepsiCo in advertising since total expenditures for those two firms totaled $130 million— more than Dr Pepper's annual sales. Tables 1 and 2 and Figure 1 present financial summaries for Coca-Cola and Dr Pepper.

Table 1
The Coca-Cola Company and Subsidiaries
Financial Highlights
(In Million Except per Share Data)

	Year ended December 31		
	1977	1976*	Percent increase
Net sales	$3,559.9	$3,094.5	15.0
Profit before taxes on income	605.3	545.5	11.0
Net profit	326.2	290.7	12.2
Net profit per share	2.67	2.38	12.2
Dividends per share	1.54	1.325	16.2
Shareholders' equity	1,557.2	1,418.5	9.8
Percent net profit to net sales	9.2%	9.4%	
Percent net profit to shareholders' equity	20.9%	20.5%	

* 1976 amounts have been restated to include operations of The Taylor Wine Company, Inc., on a pooling of interests basis and to reflect a two-for-one stock split effective in May 1977.
Source: 1977 Coca-Cola Company annual report.

Table 2
Dr Pepper Financial Highlights
(Years Ended December 31, 1977 and 1976)

	1977	1976	Percent change
Net sales	$226,750,000	$187,216,000	+21.1
Earnings			
From continuing operations			
before income taxes	38,504,000	33,426,000	+15.2
Provision for income taxes	18,182,000	15,834,000	+14.8
From continuing operations	20,322,000	17,592,000	+15.5
From discontinued operations,			
net of applicable income taxes	—	193,000	−100.0
Net earnings	20,322,000	17,785,000	+14.3
Number of weighted average			
shares outstanding	20,200,000	20,173,000	—

THE 8-OUNCE CAN

The 8-ounce can of Coca-Cola was introduced by a number of independent bottlers.[2] First brought into the market in Los Angeles, it won quick consumer acceptance there and spread to several other major markets, including New York and Miami. Adoption of this can represented the first time since 1915 that independent bottlers took on a package which the parent firm had not recom-

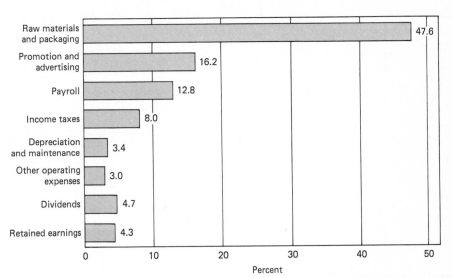

Figure 1 Dr Pepper: distribution of revenue (net revenue of $226,750,000). (*Dr Pepper 1977 Annual Report.*)

[2] Facts for this part of the case were developed from R. S. Smith, "Dr Pepper: Pitted Against the Soft Drink Giants," *Business Week* (October 6, 1975), pp. 70–73.

mended. Since purchase of Coke in 8-ounce cans was more expensive for consumers (2.9¢ per ounce when bought in a six-pack of 8-ounce cans versus 2.3¢ per ounce in a six-pack of 12-ounce cans), marketing executives were puzzled at its rapid acceptance. However, some consumers indicated they eventually threw away some of the contents of the 12-ounce cans because they contained more than would normally be consumed at one time. Thus, the 8-ounce can seemed to fit consumers' needs more closely. Still, Coca-Cola did not give this product its backing either through franchise encouragement or through advertising expenditures.

SOUTH BOTTLING COMPANY

South Bottling Company was located in a major southern metropolitan area with a population of over 700,000.[3] The firm was started as a Coca-Cola bottler by Joshua Stebbins, Sam's father, in 1915. South had enjoyed success commensurate with that of the parent company until Sam took control. Being ambitious, Sam Stebbins added a line of ground coffee to his supermarket distribution network. He also started a packaged sandwich subsidiary which distributed its products through vending machines located in many of the same outlets as his Coke machines.

Stebbins had also added many products intended to make his firm more dominant in the industrial feeding market in his market area. These products included portion-controlled packets of spices and table condiments and a broad base of soft drink products. By 1977 net sales and profits of South Bottling Company, which by this time had become a corporate entity owned by Stebbins and fifteen other relatives (Sam and his immediate family maintained 25 percent ownership), were $27.8 million and $978,000 respectively.

THE CURRENT SITUATION

South Bottling Company became a Dr Pepper bottler in 1973. Stebbins explained that he had added the product because of Dr Pepper's agressiveness in the marketplace and the high level of sales it had achieved. He indicated that Dr Pepper was a very good product and the company did a superb job of promoting it. Since he was not required to take on Coke's competitive product, Mr. Pibb, which had considerably less than 3 percent of the total soft drink market, he felt that it only made sense to add Dr Pepper. He knew that it was extremely unlikely that Coke would sell a Mr. Pibb franchise to Pepsi or Seven-Up bottlers since the regular Coke bottlers would complain bitterly. Thus, by taking on a Dr Pepper franchise, the Coke bottler could virtually monopolize the cherry-flavored market. This was particularly true since Mr. Pibb suffered from low levels of consumer awareness and received little support from Coke.

[3] Facts for this part of the case were developed from "Marketing Observer," *Business Week* (October 3, 1977), p. 64.

South was also one of the first bottlers to begin producing Coke in the 8-ounce can. Stebbins believed that Coke would never give this product a major effort since it had the potential to reduce the total amount of Coke syrup used by local bottlers. On the other hand, he thought bottlers might favor the package since it would reduce their purchases of Coke syrup and increase the per-ounce selling price of their final product. Of course, he realized that this package also increased the number of stock-keeping units required since he felt it would be impossible to eliminate the 12-ounce can entirely. Thus, although there were some drawbacks, Stebbins' experience showed that profits would increase for the bottler by utilizing the 8-ounce can.

Since he was the only bottler in the United States to add Dr Pepper and begin production of 8-ounce cans of Coke, Stebbins was looking forward to the annual bottlers meeting. He knew that he would be the center of attention for other bottlers who were considering the same decisions.

CASE 9-2: QUESTIONS

1 Map the channel network for soft drinks.
2 How does consumer behavior place the bottler in a dominant channel position? What offsetting buyer characteristics tend toward producer dominance?
3 What other sources of buyers does South Bottling Company have over Coca-Cola? What about its position relative to Dr Pepper?
4 What can Coca-Cola do to regain its dominance over a firm such as South Bottling Company?

Chapter 10

Channel Performance
Measurement

One of the most critical aspects of channel management, and yet what seems to be the least managed, is measurement and evaluation of channel performance.[1] The short-run and long-run financial well-being of the channel and its members is based on effective and efficient performance of marketing functions. The management of each institution in the channel must be concerned not only with the performance of its own organization but with the performance of all institutions in the marketing channel. This is necessary because it is the channel system as a whole that competes for customers in the marketplace.

Several explanations are possible for the lack of attention given to channel performance measurement in the literature: the difficulty of measuring channel performance once it has been defined (which in itself may not be easy), the difficulty of quantifying all aspects of channel performance so that an index can be achieved, and lack of published standards for comparison.[2] In this chapter we examine channel performance from both a macro (societal) and a micro (the firm) perspective. Methods for evaluating both overall channel structure

---

[1] Douglas M. Lambert, *The Distribution Channels Decision* (New York: National Association of Accountants; and Hamilton, Ontario: The Society of Management Accountants of Canada, 1978), p. 87.
[2] Ibid., p. 36.

and individual channel members will be presented. Measures of channel efficiency also will be discussed. Channel performance must be measured in order that inadequate achievement by channel members or channel structures can be determined and corrective action taken.

CHANNEL PERFORMANCE MEASUREMENT: A MACRO PERSPECTIVE

The performance of channel structures and channel institutions can be measured on both a macro and a micro level, from the point of view of the total channel system or the individual participants. In this section, channel performance measurement is considered from a macro perspective of the total channel.

Many authors have considered existing methods of measuring the performance of marketing institutions and the relative advantages and disadvantages of each, and some have proposed new methods and research possibilities which promise to rectify shortcomings of established approaches. Established approaches typically measure such factors as size of promotion costs, marketing costs (as related to production costs), marketing productivity, profitability, degree of innovation or progressiveness, amount of choice provided to consumers, degree of consumer satisfaction, characteristics of the products produced, and the efficiency with which marketing functions are performed.[3] It is important that channel participants and channel leaders have the ability to predict changes in channel institutions so that successful responses to those changes can be planned. Given the measurement and interpretation problems associated with many existing approaches, we favor the productivity measurement framework advocated by McCammon and Hammer.[4]

Productivity has been the base for economic and social development in the United States, and continued economic growth depends on improving productivity in the future. Marketing institutions, such as retailing and wholesaling, tend to be labor-intensive. Thus, output per worker-hour is an important measure of productivity. Productivity levels combined with unit labor costs have a direct impact on profitability. In the past labor productivity has risen much less rapidly in wholesaling and retailing than in other sectors of the economy. McCammon and Hammer explain that:[5]

> Lagging wages, in turn, eventually result in the recruitment of marginal personnel which further depresses productivity. The ultimate consequence of this iterative process is a stagnant and depressed industry.

[3] For examples see John R. Grabner and Roger A. Layton "Problems and Challenges in Market Performance Measurement," pp. 163–182; and Robert Buzzell, "Marketing and Economic Performance: Meaning and Measurement," pp. 143–59, both in C. Allvine (ed.), *Public Policy and Marketing Practices* (Chicago: American Marketing Association, 1973); and Stanley C. Hollander, "Measuring the Cost and Value of Marketing," *MSU Business Topics* (Summer 1961), pp. 17–27.

[4] Bert C. McCammon, Jr. and William L. Hammer, "A Frame of Reference for Improving Productivity in Distribution," *Atlanta Economic Review* (September–October 1974), pp. 9–13.

[5] Ibid., p. 10.

Recent trends suggest that retailers are already confronted by a wage gap problem. . . . If the gap between manufacturing and retailing wages continues to widen, retailers will find it increasingly difficult to attract and retain productive personnel.

Efficient use of capital also influences productivity of channel institutions. The strategic profit model shown in Figure 10-1 illustrates that return on net worth (shareholders' investment plus retained earnings) is a function of three factors which are controllable by management: (1) net profit, (2) asset turnover, and (3) financial leverage.

Net profit as a percent of sales is a measure of how efficiently products are manufactured and sold. However, a major drawback in relying exclusively on profit as a measure of performance is that the investment required to achieve a given sales level is not considered. Since the assets employed by a firm can be controlled by management, efficient utilization of assets should also be measured. This measure is important because capital available for expansion of the economy is not unlimited, and efficient employment of capital is a critical variable for sustaining economic growth. Asset turnover (sales divided by total assets) indicates how efficiently assets are used to generate sales for the firm. Return on assets (net profit margin times asset turnover) relates profitability to the value of assets employed.

The third factor is financial leverage, calculated by dividing total assets by net worth (the investment base provided by shareholders and the retained earnings of the firm). Simply stated, if money can be borrowed at 8 percent pretax and invested in assets that return 25 percent pretax, shareholder earnings per share will be larger if expansion is financed by borrowed funds and cash flow rather than by sale of company stock. The critical measure, return on net worth, is equal to the return on assets multiplied by the financial leverage ratio.

Figure 10-2 contains comparative net profit, asset turnover, financial leverage, and return on net worth figures for wholesaling and retailing institutions for the period 1968 to 1972. Although use of the 1968 to 1972 period may be questioned, the approach used by the authors has merit. McCammon and Hammer made the following observations:[6]

As indicated, retailers and wholesalers achieved inadequate rates of return on net worth between 1968 and 1972. Since both types of organizations are already highly leveraged, improved results are most likely to be achieved by companies that simultaneously increase both their profit margins *and* their rates of asset turnover.

The performance mandate is clear. Retailers and wholesalers must significantly improve their labor and capital productivity ratios in the 1970's. In many cases, labor productivity increases of 6% to 8% a year will be required to offset rising wages and to improve profit margins.

Capital productivity ratios must be increased at a comparable rate, primarily through better management of inventories and through more intensive use of both

---

[6] Ibid., p. 11.

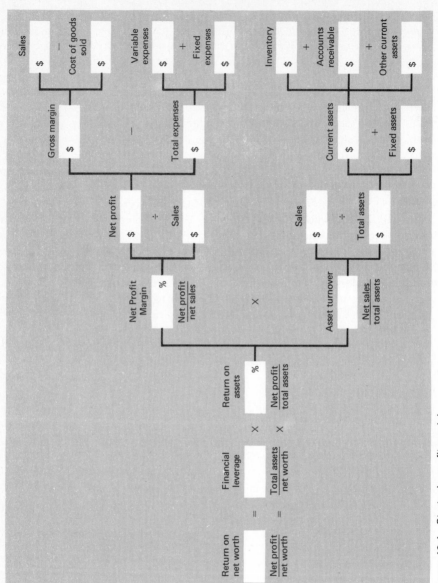

Figure 10-1 Strategic profit model.

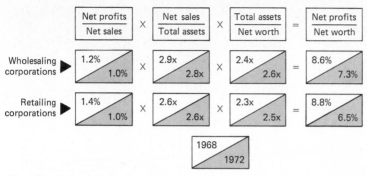

Figure 10-2 Composite strategic profit model for retailing and wholesaling corporations (1968–1972). [*Bert C. McCammon, Jr. and William L. Hammer, "A Frame of Reference for Improving Productivity in Distribution," Atlanta Economic Review (September–October 1974), p. 11.*]

equipment and physical facilities. In short, there must be a concerted attack on the productivity problem in distribution.

In recent years five strategies have been employed by retailers and wholesalers in an attempt to improve productivity and profitability: (1) use of warehouse retailing firms which reduce costs by making use of vertical space, by employing modern materials handling equipment and data processing techniques, and by shifting functions to consumers and suppliers; (2) supermarket retailing for products such as toys, drugs, and home improvement materials; (3) direct marketing using door-to-door sales, television, and/or catalogs; (4) vertical marketing systems; and (5) corporate diversification to improve profitability.[7]

The strategic profit model framework can be used to develop similar data for physical distribution channel members such as public warehouses and carriers. It also can be further developed to measure performance of specific types of retailers and wholesalers. Channel members must conduct this kind of analysis if they are to improve current productivity and anticipate changes in channel institutions and structures. It is interesting to note that during the period when many food wholesalers were disappearing from the food channel, the number of public warehouses providing services to the food industry increased. Anticipation of the shift to direct sales by food manufacturers may have allowed some wholesalers to continue in business by performing the warehousing function.

Evaluation of channel performance from a micro perspective is of critical importance for diagnosing potential short-term and long-term channel problems. Because the data are company-specific, they are of even greater importance to channel management than the broad measure of industry performance discussed above. Performance measurement is necessary to determine if the firm is participating in the most efficient channel systems and to spot ineffi-

[7] Ibid., p. 12.

ciencies on the part of individual channel members. If performance cannot be improved within the existing channel structure or between channel members, channel modification or structural change may be necessary. The remainder of this chapter treats the topic from the micro viewpoint of the individual firm.

CHANNEL PERFORMANCE MEASUREMENT: A MICRO PERSPECTIVE

> The man who reduces the cost of distribution does just as much to increase the standard of living and the well-being of the people as does the inventor of a machine which reduces the cost of production.[8]

Implementation of an efficient and effective channel strategy requires that management measure performance of both structure and members and initiate changes if performance is not satisfactory. In the following pages channel performance will be considered in terms of (1) evaluation of the channel structure used by a firm, and (2) evaluation of individual channel members.

Evaluation of Channel Structure

Bucklin's theory of channel structure (based on the principles of postponement and speculation), the concept of functional spin-off within a channel of distribution, and total cost integration, all of which were discussed earlier in this text, require a substantial amount of cost and revenue data for successful implementation.

Revzan suggests the following steps as components of a necessary beginning analysis on which a series of special studies can be built:[9]

1 The measurement of the size of the potential trading areas. . . .

2 The development of sales potentials for each of these trading areas.

3 The subdivision of (1) and (2) by product lines, if necessary, with accompanying measures of the estimated market penetration ratio of each line.

4 The subdivision of (1) and (2) and (3) by salesmen and salesmen's territories. This involves knowledge, by time-and-duty analyses, of how many customers a given type of salesman can adequately service per working day.

5 The calculation of the cost-of-getting-sales ratios, by product lines, salesmen, territories, etc., in terms of the direct, semidirect, and indirect components based on historical and estimated future bases.

6 The alternative costs, as in (5), for substituting possible channel alternatives.

7 The subdivisions of the cost estimates in (5) and (6) by various size classes of customers.

8 Finally, a comparison of actual sales, cost, and profit results with the bud-

---

[8] Paul D. Converse, *Essentials of Distribution* (New York: Prentice-Hall, Inc., 1936), p. 13.

[9] David A. Revzan, "Evaluation of Channel Effectiveness," *Wholesaling in Market Organizations* (New York: John Wiley & Sons, Inc., 1961), pp. 151–55.

geted potentials, together with a critical explanation of the reasons why the potentials have or have not been realized.

Such a plan can be implemented by using channel profitability analysis and the strategic profit model. In addition, task-oriented measures such as percent of damaged merchandise and size of orders can be applied. These will be discussed later in the chapter.

Channel Profitability Analysis[10]   Channel profitability analysis using contribution analysis offers considerable promise for channel management. Basically, it is a form of segment performance measurement advocated by a number of authors and was introduced in Table 8-2.[11] An example is contained in Table 10-1. By determining the profitability of segments, the manager can spot inade-

Table 10-1   Channel Profitability Analysis—Contribution Approach
($000)

	Total company	Department stores	Discount stores	Drugstores
Net sales	$40,000	$12,000	$10,000	$18,000
Cost of goods sold (Variable manufacturing cost)	20,000	6,000	5,000	9,000
Manufacturing contribution	$20,000	$ 6,000	$ 5,000	$ 9,000
Marketing and physical distribution costs variable (out-of-pocket costs that vary directly with sales to segment)	5,000	1,000	500	3,500
Segment contribution margin	$15,000	$ 5,000	$ 4,500	$ 5,500
Assignable nonvariable costs (costs incurred specifically for segment during the period)	2,000	300	200	1,500
Segment controllable margin	$13,000	$ 4,700	$ 4,300	$ 4,000
Nonassignable costs	5,200			
Fixed-joint costs	3,800			
Total	$ 9,000			
Net profit	$ 4,000			
Segment controllable margin-to-sales ratio	32.5%	39.2%	43.0%	22.2%

Assumptions: (1) Company sells direct to all customers, and (2) all shipments are made from one of the plant locations.

Source: Douglas M. Lambert, *The Distribution Channels Decision* (New York: The National Association for Accountants; and Hamilton, Ontario: The Society of Management Accountants of Canada, 1978), p. 122.

[10] This material is taken from Lambert, op. cit., pp. 121–129.
[11] See W. J. E. Crissy, Paul M. Fischer, and Frank H. Mossman, "Segmental Analysis: Key to Marketing Profitability," *MSU Business Topics* (Spring 1973), pp. 42–49; V. H. Kirpalani and Stanley S. Shapiro, "Financial Dimensions of Marketing Management," *Journal of Marketing* (July 1973), pp. 40–47; Leland L. Beik and Stephen L. Buzby, "Profitability Analysis by Market Segments," *Journal of Marketing* (July 1973), pp. 48–53; Frank H. Mossman, Paul M. Fischer, and W. J. E. Crissy, "New Approaches to Analyzing Marketing Profitability," *Journal of Marketing* (April 1974), pp. 43–48; and Patrick M. Dunne and Harry I. Wolk, "Marketing Cost Analysis: A Modularized Contribution Approach," *Journal of Marketing* (July 1977), pp. 83–94.

quate performance and recommend channel changes that will lead to improved profitability.

Although a full-cost approach has been advocated by some authors,[12] contribution analysis is much better suited to the needs of channel management. When undertaking this type of analysis, it should be recognized that the objective is to enable management to choose a more profitable option if performance standards are not being met. For example, if management decides to eliminate a channel, most allocated fixed costs will not be saved. Even if the decision is to deemphasize a channel, a number of expenses such as nonassignable costs (unable to be traced to a segment), fixed-joint costs (fixed costs shared by more than one segment), and assignable nonvariable costs will remain unchanged. Consequently, a full-cost approach can be misleading.

The approach illustrated in Table 10-1 includes measures of (1) manufacturing contribution margin by channel; (2) the segment contribution by channel, including a charge for inventory and accounts receivable used to support sales of each segment; and (3) segment controllable margin (which includes deductions for nonvariable costs incurred specifically for the segment during the period and which could be eliminated if the segment were discontinued). The segment contribution by channel shows interaction of variable revenues and costs for the segment. Segment controllable margin demonstrates the net advantage of the segment for the operating period. The ratio of segment controllable margin to sales is one method of highlighting an area of weakness. Once this is isolated, further analysis can be undertaken and alternatives can be considered.

As shown in Table 8-2, a charge can be levied for assets employed by each segment. This charge for assets is deducted from the segment controllable margin to produce the net segment margin. This approach, the residual income method, allows the segment controllable margin to be related to the assets employed but avoids some of the problems associated with return on investment measures.[13] It should be emphasized that fixed-joint costs should not be allocated to segments. For example, total order processing costs should not be divided by the number of orders to obtain a per-order cost for assigment to segments because the per-order cost would then include a substantial nonvariable portion.

The segment contribution approach by channel may not provide management with sufficient information. For example, product mix may affect a channel's financial performance. Thus, a channel-product contribution matrix (see Figure 10-3) is recommended so that the individual contributions of products or product groups can be compared across channels. Variations on this type of

[12] See Louis W. Stern and Adel I. El-Ansary, *Marketing Channels* (Englewood Cliffs, N.J.: Prentice-Hall, Inc., 1977), pp. 487–493. Note: Many of the full-cost allocations used by these authors are based on simple averages.
[13] See John Dearden, "The Case Against ROI Control," *Harvard Business Review* (May–June 1969), pp. 124–135.

	Channels Product/ product groups	Department stores	Discount stores	Drug stores	Total
A		2,000	2,000	2,000	6,000
B		1,500	1,150	1,850	4,500
C		1,000	900	1,100	3,000
D		500	450	550	1,500
Total		5,000	4,500	5,500	15,000

Note: Other variations might include a product–territory contribution matrix and/or a customer–channel contribution matrix.

Figure 10-3   Channel-product contribution matrix. [*Douglas M. Lambert, The Distribution Channels Decision (New York: The National Association of Accountants; and Hamilton, Ontario: The Society of Management Accountants of Canada, 1978), p. 125.*]

segmental analysis could include a product-territory contribution matrix or a customer channel contribution matrix.

To demonstrate, refer back to Table 10-1. In this example, sales to drugstores were the largest of the three channels used by the manufacturer, but the segment controllable margin was the lowest. Also, the segment controllable margin-to-sales ratio was almost one-half that of the most profitable segment. Nevertheless, the segment controllable margin at $4 million is still substantial and it is doubtful that elimination of drugstores would be a wise decision. For this reason a product-channel matrix might be generated to study the interaction between channel and product profitability. If this analysis showed, as in Figure 10-3, that product mix was not the source of the problem, then a customer-channel matrix might reveal that small drugstore accounts are the least profitable, medium-sized drug accounts are moderately profitable, and drug chains have a segment controllable margin-to-sales ratio almost as large as that of department stores.

Using this information and distribution cost trade-off analysis (see Figure 7-8), the manager could determine potential channel profitability if small and medium drugstore accounts were served by either drug wholesalers or by strategically located field warehouses. The alternative that would lead to the greatest improvement in corporate profitability would be selected, resulting in the addition of a new channel of distribution. If the drug wholesalers were added as a channel and the company also desired a breakdown of contribution by size of department store, the channel-product contribution matrix shown in Figure 10-2 would be revised to include those changes.

Poor performance by a channel does not necessarily mean the channel should be eliminated. Factors such as the percentage of potential market being reached by the channel, the stage of the product life cycle of the products involved, and the stage in the life cycle of the institutions involved also deserve consideration.[14] In addition, elimination of an unprofitable channel may not be the only viable solution for the firm striving to improve corporate profitability. Changing the logistical system or shifting some of the business to another channel, as in the previous example, may be the most desirable solution. Also, within a channel a customer-product contribution matrix may be used to isolate customers or products as candidates for elimination or revitalization. The strategic profit model introduced earlier also can be used to measure channel structure performance by the individual firm.

The Strategic Profit Model   Another approach to channel performance measurement can be conducted with the strategic profit model. The advantage of this approach is that it explicitly demonstrates the impact of alternative strategies on corporate return on investment (ROI) as well as the contribution of individual channel members to corporate ROI. The strategic profit model can be used with equal effectiveness by both manufacturers and intermediaries. Successful implementation of the concept of functional spin-off within the distribution channel requires that such analysis be performed by all channel members.

The Manufacturer's Perspective[15]   The manufacturer can determine the profit impact of various channel intermediaries by using a framework similar to that shown in Figure 10-4. This particular example concentrates on the profit impact resulting from a manufacturer's decision to use wholesalers/distributors rather than selling direct to retailers. Various factors which influence the manufacturer's return on investment are considered in depth on the right-hand side of the diagram. The model considers corporate return on net worth (ROI) in terms of financial leverage and return on assets. The latter is influenced by the corporate net profit margin and asset turnover.

Net profit is influenced by both sales and expenses. The decision to use a distributor will affect sales in two major ways. Customer service levels are improved as a result of reduced or less erratic lead times which have a favorable impact on sales. However, net sales are reduced somewhat by the volume and/or functional discounts taken by the distributor. The total effect on sales may be positive or negative depending on the business involved and current levels of customer service, as well as the schedule of price breaks on volume purchases. In the majority of companies net sales will probably increase although, in this example, a conservative estimate of no change was made.

The expense categories reduced include (1) lot quantity costs, (2) transportation costs, (3) inventory carrying costs, (4) warehousing costs, (5) bad debt expense, and (6) general and administrative costs. Lot quantity costs are costs

---

[14] For further treatment of contribution by product life cycle and a suggested reporting format, see Sam R. Goodman, "Improved Marketing Analysis of Profitability, Relevant Costs and Life Cycles," *Financial Executive* (June 1967), pp. 28–34.

[15] The following discussion is taken from Douglas M. Lambert and Bernard J. La Londe, "The Economics of Using a Frozen Food Distributor," *Frozen Food Factbook, 1975* (Hershey, Pa.: The National Frozen Food Association, Inc., 1974), pp. 57–63.

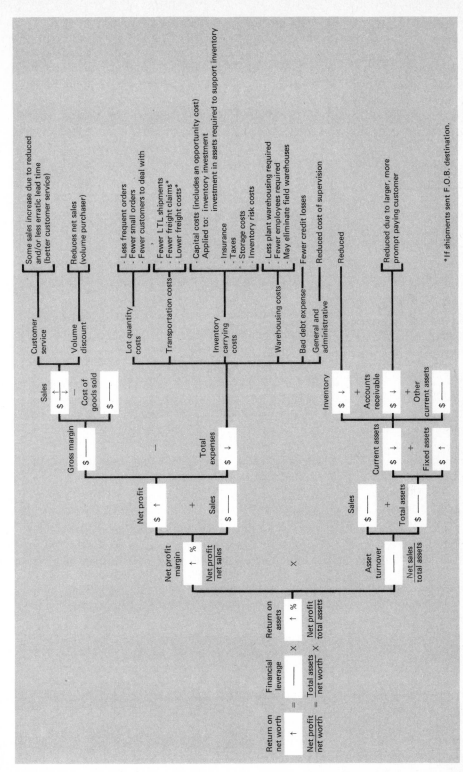

Figure 10-4 Impact of decision to use a distributor on manufacturer ROI. [*Douglas M. Lambert and Bernard J. La Londe, "The Economics of Using a Frozen Food Distributor," Frozen Food Factbook, 1975 (Hershey, Pa.: The National Frozen Food Association, Inc., 1974), p. 62.*]

that are reduced because the manufacturer has fewer customers to deal with, processes fewer small orders, and processes orders less frequently. Savings in transportation costs occur because of a reduction in processing shipping documents for many less than truckload (LTL) shipments. For manufacturers shipping FOB destination, savings are realized from the decrease in freight claims and from lower freight costs since more products are moving by truckload (TL) and carload (CL).

Inventory carrying costs, often ignored when managers plan product distribution, consist of four specific components: capital costs, inventory service costs, storage costs, and inventory risk costs.[16] Warehousing costs refer to fixed costs associated with storage or product throughput costs that can be eliminated by closing field warehouses. In addition, an opportunity cost is attached to capital invested in such facilities, and the cut-off rate applied in the case of the inventory investment should be charged against the book value or, more correctly, the market value of such facilities (if known).

Bad debt expense usually will be reduced because the manufacturer is no longer selling directly to many retailers but to one or more larger distributors who are less likely to default on accounts payable. Any out-of-pocket general and administrative costs that can be reduced or eliminated through reduced supervision and information processing are relevant.

With respect to asset turnover, it is assumed that cash made available by inventory reduction would be invested in fixed assets. These may be revenue-producing or expense-reducing, and the return on the new assets has been included in inventory carrying costs under capital costs (forgone opportunity). This shift from current to fixed assets results in no change in asset turnover or financial leverage.

In this example, corporate ROI is increased by the decision to use a wholesaler-distributor because of the associated improvement in net profit margin. Table 10-2 contains a framework that should be useful to a manufacturer who wants to calculate cost of possession.

The Middleman's Perspective[17]   Although the strategic profit model can be applied by all types of intermediaries, the example in Figure 10-5 is limited to the case of a retailer who wants to determine how use of a wholesaler-distributor will affect ROI.

Three basic differences exist in the case of the retailer versus the manufacturer:

1 Activity within the cost of goods sold account.
2 Treatment of the cost of investment in inventory.
3 The use to which capital generated by the reduction in inventory will be applied.

First, the retailer's lot quantity costs associated with the buying function will be affected. Now they will include the distributor's margin, but cost savings

---

[16] These costs were explained in depth in Chapter 7.
[17] The discussion which follows is taken from Lambert and La Londe, pp. 57–63.

Table 10-2 How to Calculate Your Cost of Possession

Manufacturer

Customer service costs:

   1 Cost of sales lost at retail level due to stockouts resulting
from long and/or erratic lead time $ _____

   2 Return forgone on capital invested in accounts receivable $ _____

   3 Credit losses associated with accounts receivable $ _____

Lot quantity costs:

   4 Cost of dealing with many customers $ _____

   5 Cost of filling small orders $ _____

   6 Cost of filling frequent orders $ _____

Inventory carrying costs:

   7 Return forgone on capital invested in inventory $ _____

   8 Return forgone on capital invested in assets required to
support the inventory $ _____

   9 Insurance paid on inventory $ _____

   10 Taxes paid on inventory $ _____

   11 Storage costs $ _____

   12 Cost of obsolescence $ _____

   13 Cost of damaged product $ _____

   14 Cost of pilferage $ _____

   15 Relocation costs $ _____

Warehousing costs:

   16 Return forgone on capital invested in field warehouses
(if owned) $ _____

   17 Operating expenses associated with such warehouses $ _____

Transportation costs:

   18 Cost of processing shipping documents (for many LTL
shipments) $ _____

   19 Cost of processing freight claims $ _____

   20 Excessive freight costs (associated with LTL shipments) $ _____

General and administrative:

   21 Reduction in management costs associated with holding
and supervising inventory $ _____

Annual cost of possession   Total $ _____

   Less volume discounts to distributor $ _____

Total amount saved by using a distributor $ _____

Source: Douglas M. Lambert and Bernard J. La Londe, ''The Economics of Using a Frozen Food Distributor,''
Frozen Food Factbook, 1975 (Hershey, Pa.: The National Frozen Food Association, Inc., 1974), p. 60.

are possible from larger volume purchases (buying many items from the same distributor), fewer orders, and fewer suppliers with which the company must deal. In any specific situation the cost of goods sold may either increase or decrease but, in many cases, the cost savings associated with use of a distributor will offset the increased purchase price and will result in a no-change position, the assumption made in Figure 10-5.

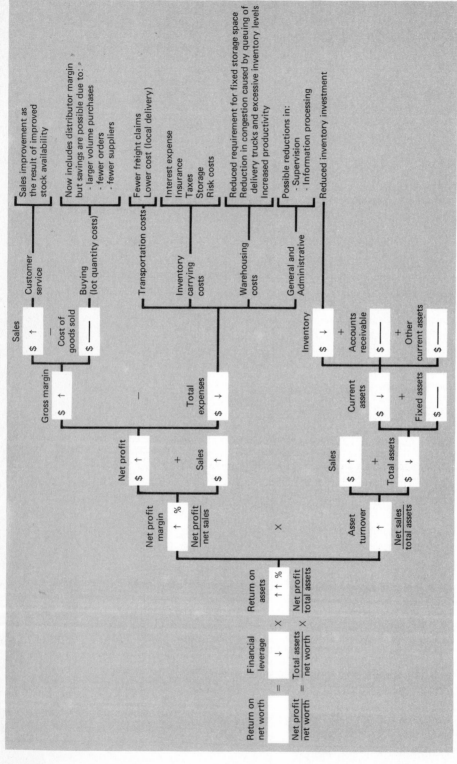

Figure 10-5 Impact of decision to use a distributor on retailer ROI. [*Douglas M. Lambert and Bernard J. La Londe, "The Economics of Using a Frozen Food Distributor," Frozen Food Factbook, 1975 (Hershey, Pa.: The National Frozen Food Association, Inc., 1974), p. 63.*]

Second, many possibilities exist for any firm to find the working capital to finance increased inventories. Working capital can be raised by the issuance of long-term debt, by leaning on one's suppliers and delaying payment on accounts payable, thereby losing any discount terms, or by short-term bank financing. In any case, there is an out-of-pocket cost attached and in this example it is assumed that bank financing has been used. By eliminating excess inventory some or all this financing and the associated interest expense can be avoided. Therefore, in the retailer's case inventory carrying costs do not include an opportunity cost of capital but do include an interest expense.

Third, depending on the financing arrangements explored previously, it is possible for the retailer to invest released capital in inventory of other product lines, thereby improving the product assortment and customer service, or perhaps make in-store improvements. If this were the case, the opportunity cost of capital would be included as an inventory carrying cost. However, in Figure 10-5 it was assumed that the retailer had financed the inventory with bank financing and that the retailer would choose to reduce the amount of this debt. Such a decision would reduce total assets and improve asset turnover, which improves return on assets. *But,* the reduction in debt has an offsetting effect on the debt-to-equity ratio and the company's financial leverage. The result is that improvement in ROI is due solely to the increased profitability obtained by using a distributor.

In summary, Figure 10-5 illustrates how corporate ROI can be improved by using a distributor, and every retailer should consider an analysis similar to the framework given in Table 10-3 to determine cost of possession. In these times of rising costs and the ever-increasing squeeze on corporate profits, management must be open to changes that can improve corporate ROI.

Implementation Problems   Successful implementation of channel profitability analysis and the strategic profit model assumes the availability of adequate accounting information. The accounting system must be able to classify costs in such a way that they can be meaningfully attached to segments. Considerable evidence exists to support the conclusion that required cost and revenue data are not currently available to the decision maker. For example, in a study of how channel decisions were made by eighteen manufacturers, it was found that not one firm used contribution analysis when judging channel performance.[18] In fact, when asked the question "Are there data that are not currently available in the firm which would be useful in measuring channel performance?" three executives replied:[19]

> Yes, but I don't know what I would ask for. We are churning out information that isn't useful operationally. Sales by customer, sales by region would be useful. Profit by customer would be good to have. Transportation cost by customer would be

[18] Douglas M. Lambert, "The Distribution Channels Decision: A Problem of Performance Measurement," *Management Accounting* (June 1978), pp. 60–63.
[19] Ibid., p. 62.

Table 10-3   How to Calculate Your Cost of Possession
(On Excess Inventory)

	Retailer
Customer service costs:	
1 Lost sales due to stockouts (it is possible that a stockout in one brand would result in the purchase of another brand at the same store in some cases)	$ _____
Lot quantity costs:	
2 Cost of writing many frequent small orders	$ _____
3 Cost of dealing with many suppliers	$ _____
4 Cost of purchasing in small quantities	$ _____
Inventory carrying costs:	
5 Interest on inventory investment	$ _____
6 Insurance paid on inventory	$ _____
7 Taxes paid on inventory	$ _____
8 Storage costs	$ _____
9 Cost of obsolescence	$ _____
10 Cost of damaged merchandise	$ _____
11 Cost of pilferage	$ _____
12 Cost of markdowns	$ _____
Warehousing costs (stockroom):	
13 Costs associated with reduced productivity caused by congestion (loading dock and stockroom)	$ _____
14 Reduced future requirements for fixed storage space	$ _____
15 Return on capital no longer required for investment in fixed storage space	$ _____
Transportation costs:	
16 Freight costs associated with buying direct versus buying locally from a distributor	$ _____
17 Freight claims related to 16	$ _____
General and administrative:	
18 Excessive management supervision and information processing costs may be eliminated (buyer's time, etc.)	$ _____
Annual cost of possession Total	$ _____
Less margin paid to distributor	$ _____
Total amount saved by using a distributor	$ _____

Source: Douglas M. Lambert and Bernard J. La Londe, "The Economics of Using a Frozen Food Distributor," *Frozen Food Factbook, 1975* (Hershey, Pa.: The National Frozen Food Association, Inc., 1974), p. 61.

interesting. It leaves me cold sometimes to say I wonder if we make money on sales to X location. . . . I don't know.

We recognize the need for more analysis in the logistics area. The existing data base does not allow this type of analysis. Profitability or profit contribution by channel and along other segments would be useful. Also required are performance standards in order to judge channel members. . . . As far as I know the only constraint would be the time involved in developing such reports.

Better knowledge of where our products are at any given moment. This would help us to direct product to dealers who are selling. Costs associated with selling to different sizes of dealers.

Other studies have verified these results. A survey of 125 firms found that not one distribution executive reported having all the cost components required to implement total cost integration successfully.[20] Total transportation costs were reported to be available in 87 percent of the firms, which made them by far the most accessible numbers. However, by channel, product, and customer, costs were reported to be available by 53, 48, and 31 percent of the respondents respectively. In addition, no firm reported the availability of all cost components necessary to calculate inventory carrying costs.

Mossman et al. have recommended use of a modular data base (Figure 10-6) to improve availability of cost and revenue data: "Such a data base may be viewed as a central storage system which contains revenue and cost information in a readily accessible form."[21] The modular data base can be used to generate traditional accounting reports for external reporting as well as cost reports for each function and segment contribution reports. The input data are coded to enable the cost flows shown in Figure 10-6. The actual costs are used for preparing external reports in the traditional manner. Actual costs also are charged to the functional cost centers responsible for their incurrence. As activity occurs in the functional cost centers, the physical units are charged at a standard cost out of the modular data base into the relevant functional cost center. As the product or service moves from the functional cost center to the market segment, this transfer is made at standard variable cost plus any specific

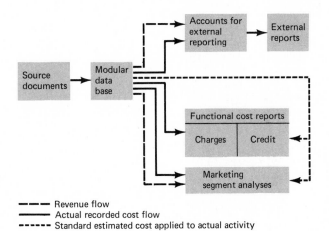

— — — Revenue flow
———— Actual recorded cost flow
- - - - - Standard estimated cost applied to actual activity

Figure 10-6 Marketing cost and revenue flow. [*Frank H. Mossman, Paul M. Fischer, and W. J. E. Crissy, "New Approaches to Analyzing Marketing Profitability," Journal of Marketing, vol. 38 (April 1974), p. 45. Reprinted by permission of the American Marketing Association.*]

[20] Douglas M. Lambert and John T. Mentzer, Jr., "Is Integrated Distribution Management a Reality?" *Journal of Business Logistics* (Fall 1979).
[21] Mossman, Fischer, and Crissy, op. cit., p. 44.

fixed costs. Cost flows to the functional cost centers and market segments occur on a real-time basis.[22]

The modular data base must start with basic documents such as bills of lading or invoices. These documents are coded by function (production, marketing, finance, logistics), territory, product, revenue, or expense, and by further classifications such as selling, advertising, and warehousing. The remainder of the data field can be used for the amount. However, many measurement problems remain unanswered in terms of the ability to trace costs to segments. For example, on a truckload of mixed products to multiple customers in different locations, how should freight costs be attached to customers and to products? The research potential in this area is great.

Other Performance Measures The major shortcoming of channel profitability analysis and the strategic profit model is that current sales are not related to market potential, which was the first step on Revzan's list discussed earlier. Table 10-4 presents a framework that can be used in tandem with these other techniques to measure the extent to which potential markets are being tapped.[23] As the table illustrates, performance indices are constructed by dividing actual sales for each segment (as a percentage of total company sales) by the sales potential for each segment (calculated as a percentage of the total market potential for the firm). This framework can be used to measure relative performance of different channels, products, territories, or sales people.

Other measures of channel effectiveness that could be used as measures of consumer satisfaction are:[24]

1 Lot size: product availability in desired quantities.
2 Delivery time: product availability when needed.
3 Search: product availability in store expected, thus making search time reasonable.
4 Assortment: product availability in model, color, size, and with desired features.
5 Customer service: sales help, delivery, follow-up service, financing, warranty, adjustments for defective products.
6 Strength of brand image.

The next step would be to analyze channel structure to determine if corporate strategy has been implemented successfully. Several criteria may be used to measure the efficiency of the distribution channel structure, including:[25]

[22] The interested reader should refer to Frank H. Mossman, W. J. E. Crissy, and Paul M. Fischer, *Financial Dimensions of Marketing Management* (New York: John Wiley & Sons, Inc., 1978), pp. 37–51.
[23] For additional treatment of this topic, see chapter 7, "Sales Territory Analysis," in Sanford R. Simon, *Managing Marketing Profitability* (American Management Association, Inc., 1969).
[24] Adapted from Adel I. El-Ansary and M. Bixby Cooper, "An Exploratory Framework for Examining Distribution Channel Performance" (unpublished paper, Louisiana State University, 1976), pp. 6–7.
[25] Ibid., pp. 8–9.

Table 10-4 Relating Sales to Market Potential

(1) Channel, product, territory, or sales person	Market potential		Actual sales		Performance indices	
	(2) Dollars	(3) Percent of total	(4) Dollars	(5) Percent of total	(6) Penetration of potential (Column 4 ÷ 2)	(7) Relative to other chan- nels, products, terri- tories, or sales people (Column 5 ÷ 3)
A						
B						
C						
D						
E						

1 Number of channel levels and number of outlets per level.

2 Extent and distribution cost outcome of functional shifting, functional substitution, functional interchange, postponement, and speculation in the channel.

3 Availability of clear channel policies on inventory levels, transportation, warehousing, customer service, pricing and discounts, and promotion.

4 Extent of channel member turnover.

5 Market image of channel members.

6 Financial strength of channel members.

7 Competitive strength of the channel.

During evaluation, attention should be directed toward determination of those marketing functions which can be performed best internally and those which should be performed by external channel members.

Table 10-5 contains a number of "hard" measures of channel performance, and Table 10-6 illustrates qualitative measures managers may use as aids when reevaluating the channel of distribution and specific channel members. Management must set objectives for the channel and measure actual performance against planned performance. Also, trends developed over time could be used to isolate potential problem areas.

Evaluation of Channel Members

Inadequate performance does not necessarily mean that channel structure must be changed. In fact, most changes within a channel of distribution simply require replacing a channel member by another of the same type. Although methods such as the strategic profit model and channel profitability analysis can be used to judge performance of individual channel members for strategic planning purposes, day-to-day operating performance may be monitored successfully by measures that are much less costly to develop and which pinpoint specific problem areas. For example, Table 10-7 contains measures of carrier performance used by seventy-four traffic and distribution executives in three

Table 10-5   Measures of Channel or Channel Member Performance

1   Total distribution cost per unit
2   Transportation cost per unit
3   Warehousing cost per unit
4   Production cost per unit
5   Costs associated with avoiding stockouts
6   Percent of stockout units
7   Percent of obsolete inventories
8   Percent of bad debts
9   Customer service level by product, by market segment
10   Accuracy of sales forecasts
11   Number of errors in order filling
12   Number of new markets entered
13   Percent sales volume in new markets entered
14   Percent of markdown volume
15   Number and percent of discontinued channel intermediaries (distribution turnover)
16   Number and percent of new distributors
17   Percent of damaged merchandise
18   Percent of astray shipments
19   Size of orders
20   Ability to keep up with new technology—data transmission
21   Percent of shipments:
      Less than truckload (LTL) vs. truckload (TL)
      Less than carload (LCL—used with rail shipments)
         vs. carload (CL)
22   Energy costs
23   Number of customer complaints

Source: Adapted from Adel I. El-Ansary, "A Model for Evaluating Channel Performance," unpublished paper, Louisiana State University, 1975, pp. 10–11.

industry groups (canned fruits and vegetables; perfumes, cosmetics, and toilet preparations; and radio and television transmitting, signaling, and detection equipment).[26]

In a recent study of eighteen manufacturers with sales ranging from $9 million to over $1 billion, managers were asked, "What specific data or reports are used to measure and evaluate the performance of channel members?"[27] Sales volume was the most common measure of retailer performance, with gross margin the second most often named measure. Only one company conducted a profitability analysis by customer, and that company used allocations based on volume of sales with percentage allocation rates that were based on total sales. Not one company used segment contribution, which would seem to be the most meaningful measure.

Profitability reports were used for performance appraisal of manufacturer-owned retail outlets and branches where significant investment in assets had been made. One company required monthly profit and loss statements from

[26] James R. Stock, "How Shippers Judge Carriers," *Distribution Worldwide* (August 1976), pp. 32–35.
[27] Lambert, *The Distribution Channels Decision,* pp. 75–88.

Table 10-6   Qualitative Measures of Channel Performance

1	Degree of channel coordination
2	Degree of cooperation
3	Degree of conflict
4	Degree of domain consensus (role prescription and variation)
5	Recognition of superordinate goals
6	Degree of development of channel leadership
7	Degree of functional duplication
8	Degree of commitment to channel
9	Degree of power locus development
10	Degree of flexibility in functional shiftability
11	Availability of information about:

    a Physical inventory
    b Product characteristics
    c Pricing structure
    d Promotional data
        1 Personal selling assistance
        2 Advertising
        3 Point-of-purchase displays
        4 Special promotions
    e Market conditions
    f Services available
    g Organizational changes

12	Assimilation of new technology
13	Innovation in distribution generated within the channel
14	Extent of intrabrand competition
15	Extent of routinization of channel tasks
16	Extent of use of optimal inventory standards
17	Relations with trade associations
18	Relations with consumer groups

Source: Adapted from Adel I. El-Ansary, "A Model for Evaluating Channel performance," unpublished paper, Louisiana State University, 1975, pp. 10–11.

dealers but the most frequently used measures of performance were sales, market potential and/or penetration, and performance to plan.

The company with the most extensive reporting system for dealers used a performance plan that included quarterly marketing reports, the district manager's call report, a report comparing marketing performance to plan, documentation of customer complaints, and a factory order report which contained unit sales by dealer.

At the wholesaler level sales volume, gross margin, and ability to achieve predetermined performance objectives were measures most often used by the manufacturer. Once again, one company used profitability analysis by account, but the method of allocation and the full-cost approach were suspect. For example, the company's total transportation bill was 4 percent of sales and, when transportation cost was assigned to individual accounts, it was done at the rate of 4 percent of sales regardless of the customer's location.

Channel members engaged in physical distribution activities were subjected to a more comprehensive list of performance reports. Almost two-thirds

Table 10-7   Measures of Carrier Performance

Procedures used by firms in evaluating modal performance	MIS*
Review of on-time performance of delivery service	82.1
Review of on-time performance of pickup service	80.8
Analysis of customer complaints	72.9
Review of claims and loss experience (including claims handling)	56.8
Shipment tracing	49.6
Distribution cost studies or audits	41.7

Situations that would cause firms to switch modes or carriers†	MIS
Desire to improve customer service	84.4
Deterioration of service provided by mode	79.8
Desire to reduce overall distribution costs	77.2
Poor pickup and delivery by an existing mode	76.3
Customer complaints	76.1
Desire to reduce transit time	72.2
Changing needs of customers	64.7
Unsatisfactory claims and/or loss experience	63.5
Expansion to new market territories or elimination of old markets	53.5

* MIS = Mean importance score. Respondents were asked to assign importance values from 1 to 100 for each listing on the charts, and the total results were averaged.

† Situations with lower importance scores included solving emergency conditions, existing modes unable to provide additional services, irritation caused by a change in the operational procedures of a mode, development of new product requiring different modes, change in company's geographic distribution plans, and others.

Source: James R. Stock, "How Shippers Judge Carriers," *Distribution Worldwide,* (August 1976), p. 35.

of the firms used damage or claims reports to measure performance of common carriers. Other performance measures included postcard surveys of customers, cost reports, transit time, customer complaints, on-time performance, utilization of leased equipment, data from the freight payment system, and carrier reliability.

With respect to private trucking, performance was most often measured on the basis of cost savings/cost per mile followed by transit time and customer service level.

Performance of public warehousers was judged on the basis of an annual warehouse inspection report, costs, inventory reports, performance reports, customer complaints, and safety and environmental factors. Only three companies indicated that they had no formal measures of public warehouse performance.

Manufacturer-operated distribution centers, including both leased and owned facilities, were evaluated on the basis of performance reports, cost reports by product against budget, total costs, inventory reports, and in-stock availability. One manufacturer said that no formal measures were used.

The manufacturer's sales force was evaluated primarily on the basis of gross sales, with no one reporting a deduction for manageable expenses when measuring performance of the sales force.

The majority of manufacturers had no specific data or reports to measure performance of the total channel. In no case was the contribution to profit measured on a channel basis for comparison between or among channels. These results suggest that performance analysis may be a critical factor to consider in attempts to increase efficiency and productivity in future distribution arrangements.

SUMMARY

A very important area of channel management, and yet one which has been neglected, is channel performance measurement. Channel performance can be viewed from both a macro level using productivity and financial measures, and from a micro level using channel profitability analysis and the strategic profit model which illustrates how various channel alternatives can influence corporate return on investment.

Successful implementation of these financial performance measures depends upon availability of adequate accounting information. The modular data base concept is one method of developing necessary accounting data.

A number of additional performance measures are possible, including relating sales to market potential, measures of channel effectiveness and efficiency, and measures of channel member performance. Empirical research supports the conclusion that significant improvements could be made in channel decision making by developing better accounting systems for reporting performance.

QUESTIONS

1 Why is it that channel systems compete for customers rather than manufacturers competing or retailers competing?
2 What is the major drawback in using profit exclusively as the measure of channel performance?
3 What strategies may be employed by retailers and wholesalers to improve productivity and profitability?
4 Are macro or micro performance measures of greatest importance in channel management? Explain your answer.
5 Why is the contribution approach better than a full-cost approach for evaluation of channel performance?
6 How can channel profitability analysis aid in management of distribution channels?

7 Explain how the strategic profit model can be used to evaluate alternative channel strategies.
8 What problems may prevent successful implementation of channel profitability analysis?
9 What is a modular data base and how does it work?
10 In addition to profit performance, what other types of measures can provide useful means of evaluating channel performance?

CASE 10-1: AUTO Incorporated

In the fall of 1978 Tim Thompson was reflecting on the circumstances which had led to the formation of his company, Automated Updated Transmittal Operations, Incorporated (AUTO). Organized in 1976, the firm provided data consolidation and information processing services for automobile manufacturers and their dealer networks. Thompson was particularly concerned with recent events which suggested that in order to remain a viable enterprise, AUTO would have to engage in a more detailed process of data analysis and performance measurement for the auto manufacturers. Thompson felt that such activities were beyond his scope of expertise and feared the move from single information transmission to information analysis. His firm, located in a large metropolitan area in a southeastern state, had been very successful in obtaining General Motors Corporation dealers and manufacturing divisions as clients. Thompson hoped he could make the proper decisions regarding requests for more service so that the firm could continue its rapid growth rate.

INDUSTRY BACKGROUND

As the largest automobile manufacturer in the United States, General Motors (GM) is organized on a multiple division basis. Five separate divisions exist for automobile production: Buick, Cadillac, Pontiac, Oldsmobile, and Chevrolet. The General Motors Parts Division carries replacement parts for all production divisions and must deal with all GM franchised dealers. General Motors has traditionally adhered to a decentralized management philosophy, allowing each division to maintain operating autonomy. It is generally believed within the organization that such independence will allow each manufacturing division to develop its own unique niche in the auto market. In implementing this strategy, each division has been responsible for establishing its own procedures and network for communications with its dealers.

The distribution channel for the automobile divisions is relatively simple. Manufacturing or assembly plants ship directly to independent dealers who have secured a franchise to market the line of cars from one or more of the divisions. In addition, the dealers are the final link in the channel of distribution for the parts division. This system forces the dealer to be a part of the network for both manufacturing and parts and to utilize the communications procedures unique to each. The situation is further complicated for those dealers who have a franchise with more than one of the manufacturing divisions, which is especially common in many southern or rural areas. These dealers must conform to several reporting systems and procedures, each of which may be radically different. Although the systems and procedures by which communications occur may differ among manufacturing divisions, Figure 1 illustrates the usual type of information and directional flow existing in the channel.

If the dealer has multiple franchises, an identical network exists for communications with each manufacturing division. However, considerable effort

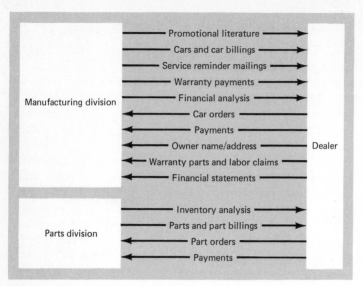

Figure 1   Current information and directional flow.

has been expended over the years to reduce divisional duplication of parts and the resulting communication flows. In a further effort to reduce the complexity of communications, many previous "paper" systems have been replaced with automated computer-oriented devices, such as on-line terminals. However, because GM's channel philosophy relies on a network of *independent* dealers, the corporation has been reluctant to allow each manufacturer to establish direct terminals to each dealer for communication. Conversely, dealers are reluctant to install terminals to support each franchised automobile division plus the parts division due to the differing languages, terminology, and policies required by each.

PRESENT SITUATION

It was with this knowledge of the industry and its communication problems that Tim Thompson had formed AUTO as a data service organization to act as a link between the various manufacturing divisions and their respective dealers. The basic concept of the organization is that it provides terminal communications to dealers and transmits information to the GM divisions. In addition, divisional communications are transmitted to AUTO and passed along to the appropriate dealers. Thompson hoped his firm eventually would take over most communications flows occurring between divisions and dealers. He envisioned that the resulting communications flows would be as illustrated in Figure 2.

Thompson was very pleased with the growth of his company in the 2 years since its formation. He had signed several GM dealers and had obtained cooperation from the manufacturing and parts divisions with his efforts. However, he was concerned that his future growth might be limited because the manufac-

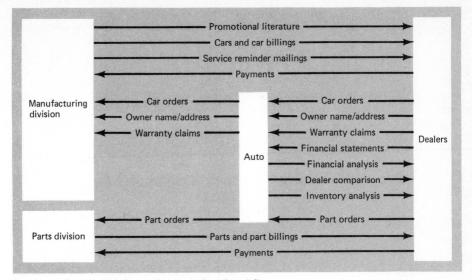

Figure 2 Proposed information and directional flow.

turer desired considerable additional information so that it could maintain its control over dealers as in the past. Thompson explained the problem: "The previous lines of communication were very direct between the dealers and the manufacturer. As a result, the manufacturer had very complete knowledge of dealer operations and performance. GM has been able to analyze sales, inventories, and financial statements for the purpose of ensuring dealer compliance with corporate directives and to compare dealer performance. With data now flowing through service organizations such as AUTO, much of the information needed for performance measurement is lost to the manufacturer. As a result, we are being asked to prepare performance measurements and reports for the manufacturing and parts divisions. Evidently, they desire this information for their own planning purposes as well as for use in obtaining compliance with corporate policies. What we need at AUTO is some direction on how to gather and analyze the proper data, and present these data in a usable form so the manufacturer will continue to support our efforts as an information consolidator."

CASE 10-1: QUESTIONS

1 What kinds of information would be needed by General Motors to analyze dealer performance?

2 How could a firm such as AUTO gather this information? What performance measures would be utilized? What would be the source of the data?

3 How might a firm such as AUTO provide a similar service for dealers to measure performance of various product lines or divisions?

4 What are the implications for channel management raised by the formation of data service organizations in the auto industry?

CASE 10-2: Riverview Distributing Company, Incorporated (B)

In January 1978 David Rose, president and owner of Riverview Distributing Company, began to wonder if sales to certain types of retail outlets were more profitable to his firm than others. As a rack jobber of housewares, batteries, light bulbs, and home entertainment equipment based in Lansing, Michigan, Rose felt opportunities for continued sales growth in his current lines were very limited. He was planning a sales meeting in late January and was not sure which type of account offered the most profit potential for new business development or which of the company's existing accounts deserved the most attention from the sales force.

BACKGROUND

Rose opened Riverview Distributing Company in 1965 when he realized that his earning potential as a ski instructor was low. The first product lines handled by his firm were light bulbs and electrical hardware equipment. His initial success appeared to be due to development of specialized display equipment which presented to customers many different bulbs and hardware items at one time. Previously, most retailers had purchased these products from cash-and-carry wholesalers, but Rose was successful in placing his display units in variety, drug, and grocery stores on a consignment basis. Although Riverview's prices were slightly higher than other wholesalers, the display units and the service provided by his firm were attractive to many retailers. The stores which used Riverview's display units greatly increased their sales in those products.

As the firm continued to grow, several new product lines were added. Because of its success with light bulbs, the firm added a photolamp product line which ultimately led to the inclusion of batteries for the photography market. The tremendous growth of transistorized radios and tape recorders further increased demand for batteries. The firm also expanded into the household products field. Kitchen utensils and supplies provided a steady, but not spectacular, source of income.

During 1973 and 1974 Rose decided his firm could distribute radios and tape recorders since it was currently selling batteries for those products. These two products were successful and other home entertainment equipment was added. By 1977 Riverview's product lines in the home entertainment field included radios, tape recorders, tape players, and stereo components such as speakers, amplifiers, and tuners. The addition of these "brown goods" brought about some changes in the firm's operations. Although each sale had a higher per-unit value than other products, customer financing was required for a longer period of time. Since this merchandise represented the company's fastest growing product line, accounts receivable tripled between 1974 and 1976.

The gross profit margins for products distributed by Rose varied considerably. Although houseware items carried only a 16 percent margin, batteries and related items contributed a much higher margin of about 40 percent. Rose believed that with increases in sales his profit margins would also increase because his firm would qualify for volume discounts from suppliers. An examination of Riverview's income statements in Table 1 shows that gross margins in 1974, 1975, and 1976 were 27 percent, 27 percent, and 19 percent. Table 2 contains balance sheets for the three most recent years.

SALES REPRESENTATIVES AND CUSTOMERS

Riverview operated in three sales territories, each covered by a single sales representative. The three territories were designated North, West, and South,

Table 1
Riverview Distributing Company, Inc.
Statement of Income and Retained Earnings

	For the year ending:		
	1/31/75	1/31/76	1/31/77
Sales	$195,702	$298,683	$385,070
Cost of sales:			
Opening inventory	48,713	76,186	125,600
Purchases	170,500	266,159	352,400
	219,213	342,345	478,000
Closing inventory	76,186	125,600	165,537
	143,027	216,745	312,463
Gross margin	52,675	81,938	72,607
Operating expenses:			
Advertising, travel, and promotion	2,375	4,450	6,158
Truck expenses	4,121	4,587	7,201
Bad and doubtful accounts	249	272	1,892
Bank charges and interest	1,035	1,418	2,406
Depreciation	4,083	4,097	5,510
Insurance	105	770	966
Legal and audit	620	791	2,702
Light, heat, and power	923	1,069	1,254
Municipal taxes	1,300	1,628	2,102
Office supplies	1,221	2,292	4,156
Repairs	551	895	406
Salaries—executive	10,500	10,500	10,500
—other	12,940	22,840	35,496
Telephone	639	672	1,058
	40,662	56,281	81,807
	12,013	25,657	(9,200)
Cash discounts earned	1,098	3,215	3,686
Net income before taxes	13,101	28,872	(5,514)
Income taxes	3,275	7,218	—
Net income	9,826	21,654	(5,514)
Retained earnings, beginning of year	28,850	38,676	60,330
Retained earnings, end of year	$ 38,678	$ 60,330	$ 54,816

Table 2
Riverview Distributing Company, Inc.
Comparative Balance Sheets

	For the year ending:		
	1/31/75	1/31/76	1/31/77
Assets			
Current:			
Cash	$ 300	$ 4,300	$ 200
Accounts receivable, less allowance			
for doubtful accounts	16,876	33,706	58,405
Inventory, valued at the lower			
of cost or market	76,186	125,600	165,537
	93,362	163,606	224,142
Fixed:			
Display racks, building improvements,			
automotive and office equipment, at			
cost less accumulated depreciation	28,506	28,553	34,330
Total assets	$121,868	$192,159	$258,472
Liabilities			
Current:			
Bank loans, secured	$ 5,000	$ 10,000	$ 15,000
Accounts payable and accrued	31,224	70,608	139,052
Income and other taxes payable	1,252	2,607	990
	37,476	83,215	155,042
Long term:			
Loans due to directors	44,716	47,614	47,614
Shareholders' equity:			
Capital stock:			
Authorized—3,600 7% redeemable			
preference shares, par value			
$10 each			
—4,000 common shares			
without par value			
Issued—1,000 common shares	1,000	1,000	1,000
Retained earnings	38,676	60,330	54,816
Total liabilities	$121,868	$192,159	$258,472

with the major cities in each being Lansing, Grand Rapids, and Jackson. Each sales representative had full responsibility for maintaining established accounts and opening new accounts in these territories. The sales representatives carried merchandise in a truck, made sales calls, and replenished stock on the spot. They were also responsible for inventory control in the trucks and for accounts receivable. Sales representatives replenished their inventories from River-

Table 3 Riverview Distributing Company, Inc.: Analysis of Active Accounts by Type and by Route

Type of account	South route	West route	North route (Includes Lansing)	All accounts
Variety stores	62 Accounts	41 Accounts	93 Accounts	195 Accounts
	21 with sales of over $1,000	10 with sales of over $1,000	26 with sales of over $1,000	57 with sales of over $1,000
	1 with sales of less than $100	4 with sales of less than $100	6 with sales of less than $100	11 with sales of less than $100
Grocery stores	18	12	20	50
	6 over $1,000	0	0	6 over $1,000
Drugstores	10	7	8	25
	8 over $1,000	2 over $1,000	1 over $1,000	9 over $1,000
Hardware stores	4	1	13	18
			1 over $1,000	1 over $1,000
Discount stores	1	8	10	19
		5 over $1,000	7 over $1,000	12 over $1,000
Camera shops	9	4	6	19
	7 over $1,000[1]	2 over $1,000	5 over $1,000[2]	14 over $1,000
Department stores	5	5	4	14
		1 over $1,000		
Radio/TV/ appliance	10	14	19	43
	5 over $1,000	3 over $1,000	6 over $1,000	14 over $1,000
Gas stations/ auto supply	9	10	34	53
	2 over $1,000	4 over $1,000	4 over $1,000	10 over $1,000
Miscellaneous	14	16	35	65
	3 over $1,000	5 over $1,000	1 over $1,000	9 over $1,000
	4 less than $100	5 less than $100	8 less than $100	17 less than $100
Total Accounts	142	118	242	502
Sales	$99,058	$107,852	$110,110	$317,220
Sales/account	$699	$914	$455	$632
New accounts (1978)	35	1	72	108
Sales (1978)	$113,825	$148,155	$138,160	$400,140
Sales/account (1978)	$725	$1,245	$440	$656

[1] Includes company's second largest account—$5,575.
[2] Includes company's largest account—$5,653.

view's office-warehouse location in Lansing. They were compensated on a straight commission basis, 7.5 percent of their net collected sales.

Sales representatives were given complete discretion to call on accounts they felt would be potential customers. Informal meetings were held periodically in which Rose discussed the company's plans and encouraged the sales force to discuss problems they had with products and/or customers. Through such meetings and with many sales contests, he emphasized the importance of increased sales volume.

Table 4 Riverview Distributing Company, Inc.: Analysis of Accounts by Type of Account for the Year Ended December 30, 1076

Type of account	All routes		
	Number of accounts	Cumulative sales	Percent of total sales
Variety stores	6	$ 22,040	5.0
	13	39,206	10.0
	24	58,068	15.0
	38	77,416	20.0
	54	96,578	25.0
	77	116,217	30.0
	107	134,870	35.0
	163	154,144	40.0
	195	158,050	41.0
Grocery stores	25	19,379	5.03
	50	22,520	5.8
Drugstores	18	19,465	5.05
	25	20,584	5.34
Hardware stores	18	8,100	2.10
Discount stores	8	20,320	5.27
	19	31,033	8.04
Camera shops	4	18,235	4.90
	19	38,464	9.98
Department stores	14	9,403	2.44
Radio/TV/appliance	8	19,198	4.98
	43	36,560	9.49
Gas stations/auto supply	13	19,798	5.14
	53	32,009	8.31
Miscellaneous	7	18,842	5.01
	65	28,347	7.36

Table 5 Riverview Distributing Company, Inc.: Assorted Data by Product Line

Product	Lead time	Terms	Riverview's margin	Estimated average accounts receivable	Approximate average inventory
Batteries	7–10 days	Net 60 days	25%	$ 4,000	$ 20,000
Electrical hardware	2–4 weeks	Net 30 days	28	500	4,500
Kitchen utensils	5 days	2% 10/net 30	16	500	15,000
Light bulbs	4–10 days	Net 90 days	18	500	9,500
Photo bulbs	4 days	Net 90 days	21	2,500	8,000
Stereo components	Up to 6 months	Net 60 days	22	50,000	124,000
Transistors	Majority 7–10 days	Net 60 days	18	25,000	35,000
Tapes	10 days	Net 30 days	15	18,000	34,000

Table 6 Riverview Distributing Company, Inc.: Sales by Account and Product Category

Type of account		Percentage sales by product categories							
	Batteries	Electrical hardware	Kitchen utensils	Light bulbs	Photo bulbs	Stereo components	Transistors	Tapes	Total, %
Variety stores	20	10	5	5	10	10	20	20	100
Grocery stores	35	5	35	15	10	—	—	—	100
Drugstores	10	5	5	5	5	10	35	25	100
Discount stores	10	—	15	15	30	—	—	30	100
Camera shops	45	—	—	—	55	—	—	—	100
Department stores	10	5	5	10	15	10	15	30	100
Radio/TV/appliance	5	—	—	—	—	35	40	20	100
Gas station/ auto supply	—	—	—	—	—	20	30	50	100
Miscellaneous	5	—	5	5	5	25	30	25	100

An analysis of the company's active customers by type and by route is shown in Table 3. Table 4 shows the sales breakdown by type of account.

COMPANY GROWTH

Rose and his wife initially assumed all management responsibility for the firm. Mrs. Rose handled office duties until the job became so complex that another person was hired to handle all record-keeping. The firm had moved from the basement of the Rose home to an office-warehouse location in Lansing in 1970. As product lines and sales volume grew, Rose hired a warehouse manager who also did some selling in the company's showroom attached to the office.

OBJECTIVES

Rose wanted to increase sales because he wanted the firm to make more money. Until 1965 he had been interested primarily in skiing and enjoying life. But, after Rose married, his father-in-law began to pressure him to build a career. The other members of Mrs. Rose's family had successful professional careers, and Rose was determined to show his father-in-law that he could be just as successful. His objective for Riverview Distributing Company was to achieve a sales volume of $1 million by 1980.

THE CURRENT SITUATION

During 1978 accounts receivable had risen to almost $100,000 and although the year-end inventory count had not yet been made, the book value of inventories was in excess of $250,000. Rose compiled the data in Tables 5 and 6 and felt that he was now ready to begin his analysis.

CASE 10-2: QUESTIONS

1 Which segments of Riverview's business are contributing the most toward corporate profitability?
2 What additional information would be useful for the analysis referred to in question 1?
3 What action should Rose take in order to achieve profitable future growth?

Institutional Change

In Chapter 2 we discussed ideological origins of the distribution system and the emergence of distribution channels, and introduced the concept of channel dynamics. The continuous interaction between function and structure causes channels to be in a constant state of adjustment. The result is that some participants undergo major changes while others are replaced by entirely new channel members.

In this chapter we further examine the dynamic quality of channels to develop an understanding of why channels of distribution never remain static. We then describe some alternative explanations of channel change and propose a change management model.

MARKETING AND THE MANAGEMENT OF CHANGE

To understand why channels of distribution never remain static, it is necessary to explore some additional characteristics of the competitive system. In this section the economics of differentiation and the relationship among innovation, neutralization, and economic growth is developed.

The Economics of Differentiation

In Chapter 2 we discussed the problems of matching heterogeneous supply, produced and distributed by approximately 11.8 million business establishments, with heterogeneous demand, composed of the unique assortments demanded by about 78.4 million centers of demand. In that chapter the solution was primarily logistical, but the need to stimulate exchange through demand-stimulating actions by the 11.8 million suppliers was introduced. These actions must be explored in more detail since they create a competitive system. Suppliers negotiate with sets of buyers, hoping that the buyers will favor their offerings over those of competitive suppliers. If the supplier is successful, supplier and buyer enter into a transaction. Over time buyers must complete a number of transactions and suppliers attempt to establish loyalty among buyers to ensure that the relationship will endure. The suppliers' potential rewards are continuous sales and a predictable share of market.

What do suppliers do to establish buyer loyalty? They seek to differentiate their product in the buyer's mind in such a way that the buyer evaluates the offering of supplier A and interprets it as superior to the offerings of suppliers B, C, and D. The potential for differentiation is limited only by the creativity of the management of the supplying firms. One classification of the ways in which suppliers may differentiate follows:[1]

1 Differentiation in actual product.
2 Psychological differentiation through communication.
3 Differentiation in the purchase environment.
4 Differentiation in physical distribution capability.
5 Differentiation in after-purchase assurances of satisfaction in use.
6 Differentiation in price and terms of sale.

Since suppliers use these means as they negotiate for buyer loyalty, competition is called *competition for differential advantage.* As discussed in Chapter 7, every participant in a channel of distribution engages in some form of differentiating behavior. The manufacturer usually engages in all forms: (1) product differentiation, when it is decided which products will be offered; (2) communication differentiation, with personal selling and advertising which represent the product; (3) purchase environment and physical distribution differentiation, by selecting the channels of distribution in which the product is sold; (4) differentiation through ensuring service, warranties, and guarantees, and in the price and terms of sale at which the product is offered. Likewise, intermediaries, wholesalers, retailers, and facilitators engage in all forms of differentiating behavior as they seek buyer loyalty by performing multiple or specialized functions of marketing. An intermediary in a channel of distribution such as a financial institution or a public warehouse may be very specialized in function, and may represent only a part of all functions performed by the total channel. But

---

[1] Thomas A. Staudt, Donald A. Taylor, and Donald J. Bowersox, *A Managerial Introduction to Marketing,* 3d ed. (Englewood Cliffs, N.J.: Prentice-Hall, Inc., 1976), p. 28.

any single intermediary must view the competitive situation as one composed of many other intermediaries performing similar functions. All participants engage in differentiating behavior and all seek that unique combination of differentiations to capture a satisfactory competitive position.

Innovation, Neutralization, and Economic Growth

The dynamics of competition for differential advantage pay off in economic growth. At any point in time the market shares of each participant are based on past differentiation. Those participants not content with their market shares will enter into a new round of competitive activities to improve their negotiating ability with potential buyers. The new activities may utilize any or all forms of differentiation, but in total they constitute innovation. The differentiations made by the "big three" of the automobile industry may not result in an innovation every year. But the desire to differentiate produced such features as power steering, automatic transmissions, and compact cars. The urge to innovate never stops, not only because participants may not be satisfied with their market share, but also because they never know when a competitor will innovate. The possibility of change forces all participants to continually seek innovation to protect their positions.

Economic growth results from this search for the new and unique. Imagine the competitive situation faced by the transportation carriers in the 1950s as they sought to supply transportation to the automobile industry. At that time the largest share of the market was divided among the railroads. The trucking companies held only a minor share of the market. But an innovation by trucking companies—the development and introduction of the car carrier—coupled with the growth of the highway system, enabled them to capture a dominant share of the automobile hauling business. This innovation *neutralized* the former advantage of the railroads. By the late 1960s the railroads retaliated with the trilevel rail car, which could carry an increased number of units. The result was a significant recapture of market share by the railroads. Two innovations in service capability and two neutralizations occurred. In total, society benefited from the innovations.

Another example is found in the distribution channels for building materials. In the 1950s large timber producers and building material processors and manufacturers utilized a channel of distribution consisting of distributors and retail lumberyards. Varying degrees of vertical integration existed among participants in the channel. Most lumberyards were full-service yards offering mill facilities, delivery, and credit. Two new participants entered the channel simultaneously. First, large discount department stores such as K-Mart and Korvette began to stock selected assortments such as electrical and plumbing supplies, paneling, prefinished wood trim, prefabricated doors and windows, insulation, and tools. Merchandise was attractively displayed and sold with limited service at prices lower than those of lumberyards. This distribution innovation shifted a portion of the traditional lumberyard business to the discount department store. The second new participant to enter was the discount lumberyard, operated as part of a chain by such firms as Wickes Corporation and the 84 Company. These specialists in building materials used a merchandising strategy similar to the discount department stores, but with two exceptions. First, they carried a much larger assortment, especially in milled lumber. Second, they offered expert advice at the point of sale. They also cut heavily into the market shares held by traditional lumberyards. To retaliate, some lumberyards offered two types of service—cash-and-carry and full service—with appropriate pricing for each.

In the lumber case, two innovating participants entered the marketplace and were successful in neutralizing the traditional lumberyards' advantage. The lumberyards retaliated with two types of service. Thus, the availability of building materials, both in number of locations and opportunity of purchase, was increased substantially, and the method of purchase, full service or cash-and-carry, was expanded. Economic growth resulted.

This continual process of innovation, neutralization, and innovation resulting in economic growth led Schumpeter to describe the competitive system as one of "creative destruction."[2] As soon as an innovation is successful, it is destroyed by the next round of retaliatory innovations.

Not all participants understand the system well, and not all are innovators all the time. In fact, innovations that cut into the heart of an industry's market and threaten its existence are usually resisted by all means available, including requests for governmental intervention. All participants, including those in a channel of distribution, are exposed, and channels do change. The process continues and, over time, the neutralization is completed despite resistance. Society benefits from the economic growth of the system. From a managerial perspective every manager is a manager of change, sometimes as initiator, sometimes as responder.

ALTERNATIVE EXPLANATIONS OF CHANNEL CHANGE

In the previous section forces which create the drive for change in the economic system were described. They are too aggregative, however, to give direction to channel managers who wish to anticipate or initiate change. More precise explanations are necessary.

A change in a channel of distribution can occur in two ways. First, existing participants may be forced to change their method of operation so much that their earlier characteristics are barely recognizable. Second, entirely new institutions with different methods of operation may enter the channel, and older participants may recede to a point where they no longer account for a major portion of an industry's output. A number of models of behavior have been developed to aid in understanding these changes. Three of these—the core-fringe, the cycle, and the crisis change model—are the most comprehensive. The following sections describe the models and their limitations.

---

[2] See Joseph Schumpeter, *Capitalism, Socialism, and Democracy,* (New York: Harper & Brothers, 1947), chapter 7.

The Core-Fringe Model

The core-fringe model was developed by Alderson as one of many strategies for survival and growth.[3] The model recognizes that any business institution has a core market for which it has developed expertise, and a fringe market in which it is weak and barely able to compete. Strength in the core market gives the firm time to analyze and develop strategies to either improve its position in the fringe market or to enter new fields through diversification. If the firm's fringe market is ignored, a competitor may recognize the weaknesses and develop a strategy to capitalize on those weaknesses.

The building materials example discussed earlier can be explained by the core-fringe concept. The traditional lumberyard existed at the core, the market comprised of building contractors. Next, a new market comprised of do-it-yourself builders began to develop. This represented a fringe market to the traditional lumberyard, and little adjustment in service was made. The fringe continued to grow, and competitors in the form of discount stores and chain building materials retailers emerged to serve the fringe. In time, the chain building materials retailers began to make inroads into the core market of the lumberyard, the building contractors. The lumberyards then changed their merchandising strategies to cater to both markets. Thus, the institutions involved in the building materials channel changed considerably, with two new entrants and a change in traditional behavior on the part of lumberyards. The stages are diagramed in Figure 11-1. The fringe market in Stage 3, still unknown, will develop in time. Perhaps it will be the large subdivision builder who might bypass all intermediaries in the channel.

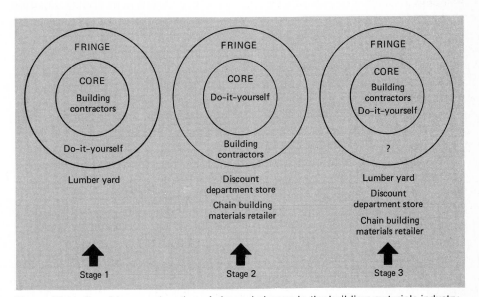

Figure 11-1 Core-fringe explanation of channel change in the building materials industry.

[3] See Wroe Alderson, *Marketing Behavior and Executive Action,* (Homewood, Ill.: Richard D. Irwin, Inc., 1957), p. 56.

A commitment to a core market insulates the firm from attacks by competitors and provides stability for innovative forays into areas with which the firm has had little experience. The lesson to be learned, however, is that commitment to a core market often leaves the firm vulnerable to competitive innovating strategies in the fringe market. In time, an old adage may apply: "The tail wags the dog."

Cycle Models

Cycles have been used to explain the stages a product goes through from introduction to obsolescence. When used to explain channels of distribution, cycle models concentrate on changes which take place in institutions comprising the channel. If it is accepted that institutions do indeed go through a cycle, it is then possible to trace the cycle from historical data, understand the reasons for the changes to date, and anticipate the next change in the cycle.

One of the most popular cycle explanations is the "wheel of retailing" developed by Malcolm P. MacNair to explain changes in retail institutions.[4] Cycle explanations hypothesize that new types of retailers often enter the market as low-status, low-margin, low-price competitors. If the market responds to that marketing mix, the leaders are soon imitated. To compete with each other, the retailers upgrade their establishments and offer additional services, which results in increased capital investment and higher operating costs. Eventually they become high-status, high-margin, and high-price establishments. They are then exposed to new types of competitors who will follow the same cycle.

The cycle is divided into four stages: (1) innovation, (2) accelerated development, (3) maturity, and (4) decline.[5] The *innovation stage* is characterized by rapidly increasing sales, but low profits because of heavy start-up expenditures. In the *accelerated development stage* sales and profits increase rapidly. During the *maturity stage* sales increase but at a slower rate, and profits continue to increase. In the *decline stage* both sales and profits begin to drop. During the accelerated development and maturity stages, retailers are high-status, high-margin, and high-price operators. They are vulnerable to any new institutions entering the innovation stage as low-status, low-margin, low-price competitors.

The evolution of appliance dealers from 1920 to the present depicts the growth and demise of different types of dealers.[6] The stages of development are described in Figure 11-2. During the first stage, from 1920 to 1930, appliance sales began to increase. From 1930 to 1950 sales increased further, but by 1950 the market was glutted with appliances and inefficient dealers and manufac-

---

[4] See Malcolm P. McNair, "Significant Trends and Developments in the Postwar Period," in A. B. Smith (ed.), *Competitive Distribution in a Free High-Level Economy and Its Implications for the University* (Pittsburgh, Pa.: University of Pittsburgh Press, 1958), pp. 17–18.

[5] See William R. Davidson, Albert D. Bates, and Stephen J. Bass, "The Retail Life Cycle," *Harvard Business Review* (November–December 1976), pp. 89–96.

[6] David P. Adams, "A Study of Institutional Change Processes Within the Appliance Industry" (unpublished dissertation, Michigan State University, East Lansing, Michigan, 1977).

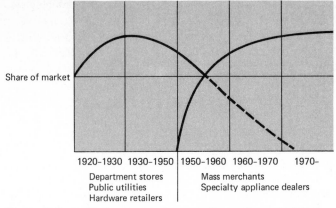

Figure 11-2 Institutional cycle theory in the appliance industry.

turers were forced out of the market. From 1950 to the present has been a period of continued growth, but at a slower rate than before. The original appliance dealers, innovators in retailing, never were low-status, low-margin, low-price operators. Rather, the educational tasks required to introduce a new product line made them full-service establishments from the beginning with high status, high margins, and high prices. After 1950 the share of market shifted to mass merchandisers who entered the innovation stage as low-status, low-margin, low-price operators. Traditional appliance dealers entered into the decline stage.

Other classic examples of this pattern of retail development are the department store replacing the general store, the discount store aggressively competing with the department store in general merchandise lines, and the supermarket replacing the full-service food retailer. If future projections concerning the increase in number of meals eaten outside the home prove accurate the supermarket may be partially replaced by the restaurant.

The Crisis Change Model

This model classifies the phases an organizational system passes through as it confronts a crisis. The phases are described as shock, defensive retreat, acknowledgment, and adaptation and change.[7]

The *shock phase* occurs when an institution recognizes that a threat exists either to its own survival or to achievement of the objectives of the system of which it is a member. Usually this recognition occurs when a new institution enters territory previously considered to be the province of the threatened institution or institutions. Many actions, including noncompetitive moves, are considered as a means of eliminating the intruder. These might include lobbying for political action, agreeing with suppliers to refuse to sell to the intruding

---

[7] See Stephen L. Fink, Joel Beak, and Kenneth Taddeo, "Organizational Crisis and Change," *Journal of Applied Behavioral Science* (January–February 1971), pp. 15–37.

institution, or engaging in cooperative institutional advertising to educate the buying public.

The *defensive retreat phase* occurs when all institutions exposed to the threat begin to cooperate and to seek serious means to reduce the effectiveness of the intruder. In many states retail druggists associations lobbied for political sanctions prohibiting discount stores from selling prescription drugs at reduced prices. Advertisements urging buyers to "support your local businesses" are defensive measures against the chain outsiders that have entered almost every market in the country. During this phase wishful thinking prevails, and often much money and effort is wasted in an attempt to reduce the threat.

The *acknowledgment phase* is characterized by serious self-examination and criticism. If the former phase was an attempt to fit the new situation to an established set of functions, this phase considers adapting functions to the new situation. The threatened institutions examine the problem more closely, and disagreement and confrontation often occur among the members. Some members will be very cautious in making functional adjustments until a leader emerges to show the way. Thus, the threat to grocery wholesalers and independent grocers by chain supermarkets was eventually minimized by formation of wholesaler-sponsored voluntary groups and retailer cooperatives.

The *adaption and change phase* occurs when the threatened institution is able to cope with the situation. This phase usually involves changes in operating procedure and brings with it a new period of growth. Not all institutions reach this phase. Some cling to the traditional way of doing business and disappear eventually. However, those institutions which successfully adapt remain to constitute a threat to the intruder who originally disturbed the status quo. After adaptation, the power position of the originator is no longer as great. For example, the cash-and-carry agricultural chemical retailers posed a threat to the full-service cooperative farm supply houses. The latter passed through all phases until they finally adapted by offering a cash-and-carry service as well.

LIMITATIONS TO EXPLANATIONS

Any one of the models of institutional change could have been used to explain any of the changing channels described above. All three models suffer from the same limitations. All are *ex post,* all are excessively aggregative, and all treat the reasons for change at an immediate level of causation but do not necessarily explain the changes. We will explore these limitations in the following parts.

Ex Post Limitation

In all models interpretation is possible only after the change has taken place. With the benefit of hindsight it is possible to fit the change into any of the constructs, but none of them provides a way to predict or manage changes in channel institutions. With the core-fringe concept, the fact that a competitor is developing a strategy for the fringe market is not known until the competitor actually enters the market. The same holds true for the cycle model: It cannot explain a change until an innovator emerges. Granted, the cycle model provides an awareness that change is rhythmic and, if the reasons for past changes are understood, the next change may be predicted. But there are so many exceptions that attempting to predict changes along a cycle can be very hazardous. Hollander points out a number of nonconforming examples, particularly in underdeveloped countries and in automatic merchandising in the United States. The latter entered the cycle as high-cost, high-margin, high-convenience retailers.[8] Similarly, the first appliance dealers were hardware stores and farm implement dealers who added appliances to their other lines which were merchandised in a full-service, high-margin, high-price manner.

The crisis change model suffers only partially from the *ex post* limitation. It does not specifically describe repetitive actions by the threatened institutions but, based on historical observation, does predict repetitive behavior. Even this statement can be challenged. The transition from home delivery to predominant retailer sale of dairy products was accomplished rather smoothly and often with encouragement from the dairies.

Although the study of past patterns of institutional behavior can provide valuable insights, it must be remembered that "innovation" is synonymous with "new." Repetition is not likely. Each innovation introduces a new pattern of action and usually requires a different response from those threatened.

Aggregation

All explanations are aggregative in the sense that they review past events and lump a number of facts into a single explanation. For example, in the case of the building materials channel, the traditional lumberyards were serving their core markets adequately. The fringe market did not exist until the do-it-yourself market began to grow substantially. A new market was thus created and the discounters and chain lumberyard companies capitalized on it. The traditional lumberyard was not threatened, however, until the innovators began to capture a share of their historical market, the building contractors. These facts are submerged in the aggregation of the usual core-fringe explanation. The cycle explanation is the most aggregative of the models. Hollander points out that statistics on changes in retail margins and expenses, the core of the "wheel" hypothesis, are very scarce. When available, they are usually averages of a line of business which is reported by retailer type in census data. The retailer type category refers to differences in commodity lines carried rather than business practices and price policies.[9]

The crisis change model is only partially aggregative. In any of the phases not all threatened institutions behave in the prescribed way. Some move from awareness of the threat to almost immediate adaptation and change. Rather than participating in the defensive retreat phase, some institutions move imme-

---

[8] See Stanley C. Hollander, "The Wheel of Retailing," *Journal of Marketing* (July 1960), pp. 37–42.

[9] Ibid., p. 144.

diately to acknowledgment, and develop and implement a retaliatory strategy. When mass merchandisers with lower prices threatened traditional department stores, many prestigious department stores collected price information in their markets and advertised that they would not knowingly be undersold. The response was immediate and successful.

Some institutions are resilient; they adapt and change rapidly. Others are resistant. The crisis change model is descriptive of only those institutions that resist change and go through all the phases.

Chain of Causation

Ex post and aggregative limitations result in superficial explanations of the changes observed. The explanations do not extend very far along the chain of causation. They explain change at an immediate level of causation. The tendency of many indirect channels to change to direct channels during the mid-1970s can be placed in the context of the models, but the underlying reasons for the change are not explained. For example, for many products the channel consisted of manufacturer, distributor, dealer, buyer. As inflation eroded gross margins, manufacturers began to exercise stringent inventory control measures to improve their return on investment. This resulted in attempts to spin off inventory responsibility to other channel intermediaries. Faced with the same inflationary pressures the intermediaries refused to accept larger inventories and out-of-stock conditions and lost sales resulted. To remedy the situation, some manufacturers instituted channel separation policies and arranged for their own physical distribution so they could control the flow of inventory and reduce the risk of lost sales. Having absorbed such channel functions, the next logical step was to circumvent distribution and go direct either to the dealer or to the final buyer.

Paradoxically, inflationary pressures have caused some manufacturers selling direct to consider the use of distributors and dealers. This is particularly true among those organizations which require large field sales and service staffs. Selling indirect is an attempt to reduce the excessive financial burden placed on those organizations.

In summary, channel change cannot be adequately explained by existing models of institutional change. McCammon observes that "there is a tendency in marketing to refine analysis beyond the point of maximum usefulness, and this is particularly true when the phenomena under investigation are relatively complex."[10] He goes on to state that "If the market place is viewed as an arena in which firms seek differential advantage and/or react to it, much of what appears to be rather complex behavior can be reduced to fairly simple terms."[11]

---

[10] Bert C. McCammon, Jr., in Stephen A. Geyser (ed.), *Toward Scientific Marketing*, Proceedings of the American Marketing Association (1963), cited in William G. Moller, Jr. and David L. Wilemon, *Marketing Channels: A Systems Viewpoint* (Homewood, Ill.: Richard D. Irwin, Inc., 1971), p. 144.
[11] Moller and Wilemon, ibid., p. 144.

RESISTANCE TO CHANGE

There is considerable resistance to change in channels of distribution and many inefficient institutions in a channel can and do persist for long periods of time. Resistance is not surprising; most innovations create chaos for a period of time. Before the innovation, relationships among the participants are well established, objectives of each are known, and necessary functions are performed. Innovation upsets these relationships and creates uncertainty for the participating institutions. The status quo is the preferred state of affairs for all concerned. The following parts explore specific reasons for resistance.

Some authors suggest that once an institution is successful, complacency sets in and a commitment to a certain business procedure is protected at all costs. Such an institution is often very powerful and is occasionally successful in making incremental adjustments just sufficient to eliminate unwanted intruders. McCammon suggests other reasons for resistance, such as reseller solidarity, entrepreneurial values, organizational rigidity, and the firm's channel position.[12] Each is discussed briefly.

Reseller Solidarity

Resellers, which include wholesalers and retailers in a given line of trade, function as a cohesive group and tend to take group action. If the firms involved have similar problems and expectations, they will cooperate whenever there is any threat to the smooth functioning of the system or to their individual units. This mutual perception of objectives, problems, and expectations results in rather powerful trade associations which reinforce group efforts. There is more of a tendency to take group action under adverse economic conditions rather than during times of prosperity. But a threat from an intruder at any time will be met with group action. To take on the role of innovator in a way that would disturb other participants is contrary to behavioral norms for resellers.

Entrepreneurial Values

Larger resellers are interested in growth and will evaluate any innovation in terms of its growth potential and cost revenue implications. They are thus more inclined to accept change. Smaller resellers, on the other hand, prefer stability. If they are successful in achieving a reasonable scale of operation, they will protect that position. To them, innovation means risk, fear of failure, and possible loss of status in the communities in which they operate. Small resellers are very cautious and, in our economy, cannot be expected to innovate.

Organizational Rigidity

Successful firms have deeply entrenched patterns of behavior supported by substantial sunk costs in systems and procedures developed to perform a

---

[12] Moller and Wilemon, ibid., pp. 137–141.

known set of functions efficiently. They will respond to innovation incrementally over a long period of time in order to recoup their sunk costs, but as a rule they will not take dramatic action unless the innovator begins to penetrate the core market.

The Firm's Channel Position

Every industry has a dominant channel responsible for the bulk of the industry's output. It is comprised of "insiders," those who have made a commitment to the dominant channel and wish to perpetuate it, and "strivers," those outside the dominant channel who strive to become members of that channel. Surrounding the dominant channel are "complementors." They are not part of the dominant channel but they complement the activities of the dominant channel members by serving those markets not served by the dominant channel. There are also "transients," mobile entrepreneurs who switch product lines and who do not wish to become members of the dominant channel. Rarely are these groups the true innovators. The "insiders" are established and resist any innovation which forces a change in relationships. "Strivers" will not upset the status quo for fear of exclusion from the dominant channel. The "complementors" take the leftover markets from dominant channel members and thus want the dominant channel to survive. The "transients" engage in deviant competitive behavior but do not have enough commitment to any product line to innovate. Innovation usually comes from the "outsider" who is sometimes a disgruntled "insider" dissatisfied with the rigidity of the dominant channel. Fervor for the new idea and an uncanny ability to sense economic advantage are characteristics of outside innovators. When they are successful, major institutional realignments must be made.

Since resistance to change in a channel of distribution is strong, innovations are rarely introduced by channel participants. Because of their growth orientation, larger resellers are occasionally innovators, especially if they are leaders of channel systems. Sears, Roebuck has been an innovator in the channel for appliances, and automobile manufacturers have been responsible for innovations in the vertical marketing systems they control. In general, however, innovation will come from those outside the distribution channel.

Although inefficient institutions currently exist in channels, it is not likely that future public policy will permit inefficiencies, even if the economic system can absorb them. From a macroeconomic point of view, inefficient processes anywhere in the system will not be tolerated over the long run.

A CHANGE MANAGEMENT MODEL

Changes in a channel of distribution need not await emergence of an innovator. Any innovation, whether it is a new institution or a new concept that departs from traditional patterns of operation, requires a *change agent* for introduction. Often the change agent is a group other than the original innovator which marks the beginning of a new or reconstituted institution. The major question is: "How can a change in a channel of distribution be managed by the change agent?"

In the following parts we examine the literature of institutionalization, the role of the change agent from the perspective of the kinds of transactions that must be made, and those characteristics of a change agent which facilitate a smooth change.[13]

Institutionalizing Literature

It would be difficult to find the term *institutionalizing process* within social theory literature. But if the introduction of new technologies is to be achieved rapidly and economically, recognition of the process by which it can be most effectively accomplished is essential.[14] Successes and failures can be conveniently attributed to chance, but the probabilities of success can be greatly increased through an understanding of the process by which new ideas are accepted.

Literature related to the institutionalizing process is replete with terms such as "structuralization of organizational behavior," "structuralization of functions," "institutionalization," and "institution building."[15] Although these concepts are explained by their authors, none have clearly defined a process. The difficulty may result from the fact that the theoretical constructions are general but the process is specific. Nevertheless, a historical appreciation of general theoretical constructions is helpful in understanding the institutionalizing process in twentieth-century terms.

Institutional doctrine as it developed following the French Revolution concentrated on the nature of change and the role of organizations or institutions in promoting that change.[16] Recognition of the role of institutions in fashioning social behavior resulted in an emphasis on their organizational nature. Their structures, administrative processes, leadership, and basic functions performed were used to describe the past and predict the future.[17] It cannot be denied that the prevailing institutional structure does influence behavior and its subsequent effect on society. Critics of our capitalistic society attribute its periodic malfunction to the institutional structure of a given industry or industries. To explain an outcome at such an immediate level may be satisfactory for those critics, but it is doubtful that the presence or absence of a given institutional structure can explain change.

---

[13] The characteristics of the change agent and the change management model described were first published in Donald A. Taylor, *Institution Building in Business Administration: The Brazilian Experience,* Michigan State University International Business and Economic Studies, Division of Research, Graduate School of Business Administration, Michigan State University, East Lansing, Michigan, 1968.

[14] Paul Meadows, "Institution Building: A Sociological Perspective," unpublished paper prepared at the request of the Syracuse University Center for Overseas Research for the Inter-University Research Program in Institution Building, 1964.

[15] See J. O. Hertzler, *Society in Action* (New York: The Dryden Press, Inc., 1954).

[16] See Talcott Parsons, *The Social System* (Glencoe: The Free Press, 1951), and Talcott Parsons and N. J. Smetzer, *Economy and Society* (Chicago: The Free Press of Glencoe, Ill., 1956).

[17] "The Guiding Concepts," unpublished paper by the Inter-University Research Program in Institution Building, 1964.

By the middle of the nineteenth century institutional doctrines attempted to describe social phenomena through functional, systems, or organic approaches. That is, a society is viewed as a conglomeration of entities which interact with each other. Over time these entities (institutions) establish relationships with each other which determine the norms and values of that society. These values in turn determine the permissible behavior (function) of the entities (institutions) as they interact with each other. This kind of functionalism is similar to the biological functionalism of the human body. The body consists of a number of related subsystems. The functioning of any single subsystem is dependent upon relationships existing between that subsystem and others. For example, extreme exertion causes the adrenal glands to secrete adrenalin, which in turn causes a change in the functioning of the circulatory system.

The same holistic approach was applied to social behavior. The declining role of agriculture, both economically and politically, is illustrative. Fifty years ago 31 percent of the labor force in the United States was engaged in agriculture and technology was not nearly as advanced as it is today. Under those circumstances the institutional structure of agriculture established firm relationships with the institutional structure of government, the distribution trades, and industry. Those relationships resulted in certain values which were expressed in favorable legislative apportionment in state constitutions, the dominant role of the producers' cooperative in distribution, and a strong bargaining position with the food processing industry. The relationships continue to exist today but the values have changed drastically. These new values have resulted in legislative reapportionment in many states, an almost complete loss of control over the distribution structure, and virtually no bargaining position with agriculture's largest customer, the food processors. The functions of agriculture have changed and the result is a drastically different institutional structure in spite of preventive federal legislation. In 1976 approximately 5 percent of the labor force was engaged in agriculture.

By the beginning of the twentieth century two approaches to the study of social change emerged. On one hand, concern focused on the functional and structural aspects of institutions and, on the other, on the values and norms deriving from relationships existing among institutions. To explain behavior at a given point in time, either concern is satisfactory for most purposes but not for understanding the institutionalizing process. Since we are concerned with managing change, the whole process must be understood and used.

Since World War II there has been a renewed interest in institutional doctrine based on historical development. It is possible to give undue emphasis to functions performed by institutions and structures established for performing those functions, or to emphasize the values and norms resulting from relationships existing among institutions. But both aspects must be utilized in explaining behavior and it must be recognized that both determinant aspects of behavior are not always easily identifiable.

For classification purposes two kinds of institutionalization may occur. First, those changes in values and norms which result in changing functions and structures are not immediately identifiable with any single institution. This kind of institutionalization may be managed and planned but the primary emphasis is communication, or the dissemination of new ideas through a large number of existing agencies. Creation of new agencies to disseminate ideas is of secondary importance. This first kind of institutionalization may be termed *diffused institutionalization*.

Second, some institutionalizations result from the introduction of particular institutions whose sole purpose is to innovate. Changes in values and norms can be easily identified with a particular institution. For example, discount houses have established new relationships with both customers and suppliers. At the time of their introduction the environment was such that manufacturers dominated distribution structures and customers were accustomed to extensive service in the purchase of many commodities. Discount houses established new relationships with suppliers and shattered existing norms, exemplified by the functional and legal breakdown of resale price maintenance. Discount houses gave minimum service in return for a reduction in price.

As an innovator, the new institution recognizes traditional norms and values but it chooses to function in a manner which will change the norms and values of all institutions within its sphere of operation. Its purpose is to create new values calling for a different pattern of behavior by the institutions it seeks to influence. This second kind of institutionalization is termed *institution building*. In many instances change can be managed through the introduction of institutions whose purpose is to promote change.

In summary, the institutionalizing process conforms to certain postulates. First, society consists of an institutional structure in which institutions interact with each other. Second, as a result of relationships between institutions, values and norms emerge which determine the functional behavior and structural composition of the institutions. Third, change can be consciously introduced by creating new institutions for that purpose. Institutionalizing is defined as the planning, structure, and guidance of new or reconstituted organizations which (1) incorporate, foster, and protect normative relationships and action patterns; (2) perform functions and services valued in the environment; and (3) facilitate assimilation of new physical and social technologies.[18]

Research in institutionalizing has not dealt specifically with the economic sector but reference is often made to the economic sector when conceptualizing the approach. The model is broad and equally applicable to economic innovations as well as social innovations.

Role of the Change Agent

A channel of distribution change is an example of institution building: It establishes new norms and values and translates these norms and values into new functions and structures. The institutionalizing process must consider structural and functional aspects of the change agent, that is, the innovating institu-

[18] Ibid., pp. 13–15.

tion and the environment within which it operates. The environment is composed of differing institutions with which the change agent maintains relationships of either a support nature or a service nature. Given the existing pattern of norms, functions, and institutions, the change agent will conflict with existing institutions by espousing a new set of norms and values. Its functions and possibly its structure will be met with hostility within the existing environment. It will function through a series of transactions with the institutions in the environment it seeks to influence. The change agent must identify entities in the environment which it seeks to influence, examine functional transactions it makes with its environment, and evaluate the institutional structure it uses to carry out those transactions.

The following parts examine types of transaction linkages the change agent will make with hostile institutions in the environment and the ideal organizational characteristics for doing so.

Transaction Linkages

Transaction linkages refers to the relationships the change agent must develop with institutions in the environment that are hostile to the change agent's values. Three transaction linkages—enabling, normative, and diffused—are described.[19]

Enabling Linkages   Linkages with organizations which control allocation of resources, both in terms of goods and services and capital needed by the change agent, are essential. Institutions such as suppliers, financial institutions, advertising media, and, more recently, government zoning boards, have the power to prevent the change agent from operating. Unless the relationship of the change agent to enabling institutions is recognized and the functional performance of the change agent is reasonably close to the enabling institutions' values, the chances of success are minimal.

A most familiar example is the discount store. In the beginning of the discount store revolution many suppliers were pressured by nondiscount retailers and refused to sell to discount stores. Many suppliers were willing to forgo substantial sales to discounters until they were convinced of the inevitability of discounting. Similar enabling linkages had to be established with financial institutions to ensure access to capital. Hostility on the part of the enabling institutions had to be overcome by discounters.

Normative Linkages   The ability of a change agent to function may be stifled by institutional norms and values hostile to those of the change agent. Unlike enabling institutions these institutions cannot prevent operations, but they can impair progress. Competitive institutions come to mind, although the change agent does not engage in direct transactions with them. However, open hostility by competitors can be met by the change agent in a manner that does not intensify hostility. Hostile institutions may not be competitors. In the dis-

---

[19] Ibid., pp. 10–12.

count store example, hostility was present among operators of shopping centers and malls. It was almost impossible for early discounters to rent space in shopping centers. Early discount store operations and their followers, the chain mass merchandisers, were freestanding outlets near shopping centers.

Diffused Linkages These linkages refer to public opinion and are relationships with the public as expressed by the news media and other communication channels which crystallize group opinion. If the new institution is to be successful in the long run, its values and norms must find acceptance within the society of which it is a part. It must have sufficient stature and position to encourage society to protect its values and the functions it performs. The change agent must actively seek favorable news coverage, establish cordial relationships with trade associations, and develop active programs with influential groups to secure public acceptance. An institution which failed to concern itself with diffused linkages is the Mappin Department Store in São Paulo, Brazil. In 1957 Mappin opened three general merchandise discount warehouses. Consumers were enthusiastic and welcomed the opportunity to purchase merchandise at one-half the conventional price. However, the news media gave such unfavorable coverage to this revolution in retailing that the outlets were closed in 3 weeks. The media erroneously attacked this form of retailing as uneconomic and potentially destructive to the retailing system. The campaign was so successful that consumers began to question their patronage of such stores. As a result, discounting in general merchandise retailing did not become an accepted practice in São Paulo until 10 years later.

In summary, the change agent must identify those institutions which can prevent or inhibit its progress. Appropriate enabling, normative, and diffused linkages must be made with these institutions.

Characteristics of the Change Agent

A change agent must develop a set of tools for its mission if it is to be successful. These tools have been classified as leadership, doctrine, program, resources, and internal structure. Each is discussed below.

Leadership If the change agent is already a channel leader respected either for innovation or for power held, the task is much easier. But a leadership image can be acquired in other ways. Association of the change agent with the innovative idea by recognized business leaders increases success. Today, informal support of the innovation by recognized government leaders is helpful. Financial backing by prestigious banking institutions also adds an aura of acceptability to the change agent and the idea.

Doctrine There must be a compelling reason why the innovation should replace existing systems and methods of operation. Advantages and benefits of the innovation must be carefully spelled out and reduced to an informative doctrine that supports the innovation. Amway Corporation has developed a very persuasive doctrine in support of in-house buying by appealing to the entrepreneurial spirit of its agents, emphasizing the need to preserve the free enterprise system. Operational changes introduced by the channel leader in a vertical marketing system are usually given catchy phrases such as TDP, "Total Distribution Plan for America," or FITIC, "financial improvement through inventory control." The ideas are then explained in detail to affected participants in order to enlist their support.

Program   While the doctrine elaborates reasons for the innovation, the program spells out how the doctrine will be implemented. Actions must be specified if the innovation is to be introduced in a tangible way. Similar to a marketing plan, the program should detail every part of the innovation with both time and financial budgets. The importance of the program cannot be overstated. Lack of a comprehensive program may have been responsible for failure of the Consumer Products Safety Commission, a new agency in the public sector.

Resources   Until now the change agent has only a set of ideas to promote the innovation. But innovations are costly and require extensive professional management. Are the required financial and human resources available to implement the program? Often, financial resources are available but human resources are lacking. Innovation introduction requires special skills and those involved must understand their responsibilities in implementing the program selected. This is a little different from skills needed to manage an ongoing concern.

Internal Structure   Once human and financial resources are in place, they must be mobilized with procedures and systems which enable them to publicize the doctrine and implement the program. How are the human resources to be organized? Given the mission of the change agent, what is the best organization structure? Standards should also be set to determine progress and to evaluate past actions. The innovator, when it is an existing institution, often reorganizes itself to accomplish introduction of the innovation.

The foregoing characteristics of the change agent represent the ideal. The presence of each characteristic is desirable, but the degree to which they are present will vary among change agents. With these tools linkages can be developed with other institutions in the system to overcome hostility and to facilitate eventual acceptance of the innovation. The change management model is diagramed in Figure 11-3.

SUMMARY

There are a number of forces in the competitive system that explain why channels of distribution are always changing. The economics of differentiation and relationships among innovation, neutralization, and economic growth are integral parts of a system of competition for differential advantage.

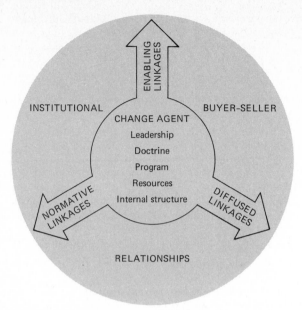

Figure 11-3   A change management model.

A channel change is described as a situation in which existing participants are forced to change their method of operation so much that their earlier characteristics are barely recognizable and/or entirely new institutions enter the channel while older participants recede, ceasing to account for a major portion of an industry's output. Alternative explanations of change are described by three models: the core-fringe, cycle, and crisis change models. Although help ful, these models have limitations. First, they are all *ex post* in their explanation of a change and are of only limited predictive value. Second, they are all aggregative, and a number of explanations for change are submerged in the aggregation. Third, all explain phenomena at an immediate level of causation, rather than examining the roots of the cause. They all suggest that channel change can be explained in fairly simple terms.

Resistance to change by channel institutions may be explained in terms of reseller solidarity, entrepreneurial values, organizational rigidity, and the firm's channel position. In spite of resistance, change occurs at a rapid rate. Innovators are usually either outsiders or large channel leaders in a dominant channel.

Innovators are change agents that can introduce a channel change effectively and smoothly. A change management model may be used to describe orderly change. The change agent, the innovator, reviews all relationships among buyer-seller sets to identify those sets in which either conflict or concurrence will result from innovation. The conflict centers are targets for the change agent. Transaction linkages must be made with these conflict centers by establishing enabling, normative, and diffused relationships. The change agent must also develop certain characteristics to engage effectively in transactions with the environment. These characteristics are leadership, doctrine, program, resources, and internal structure.

QUESTIONS

1 How does innovation and neutralization contribute to economic growth?
2 How does innovation and neutralization relate to changes in channels of distribution? Give examples.
3 What are the similarities and dissimilarities among the core-fringe, cycle, and crisis change models?
4 In the crisis change model does experience indicate that all participants go through all phases? Why or why not?
5 Limitations to available models of channel change are *ex post* limitation, aggregation, and chain of causation. How do these limitations apply to each of the models described in the text?
6 Explain organizational rigidity as a factor in resisting channel change.
7 Give some examples of complementors and transients in a distribution channel of your choice.
8 Can a change in a distribution channel be managed? Explain the underlying institutionalizing process which permits change management.
9 Explain linkages the change agent must make with the environment.
10 What are the characteristics of a successful change agent? Does every company have these characteristics or must they be developed?

CASE 11-1: What is Happening in the Automotive Aftermarket?

The automotive aftermarket in the United States has experienced an unusually rapid growth rate over the past few years. Accompanying this growth has been an inevitable change in the pattern of distribution for automotive parts. In 1968 there were 96.9 million vehicles of all types, including passenger cars, trucks, and buses. By 1976 there were 137.2 million vehicles, and with a manufacturing forecast of 12 million units per year, the total (considering scrappage) is projected to be close to 150 million vehicles by 1980. The prime automotive aftermarket is composed of 3- to 9-year-old vehicles, which represented about 52 percent of the total automotive population in 1965, about 60 percent in 1975, and is projected to reach 70 percent of the vehicle population by 1980.[1]

The rapid increase in 3- to 9-year-old vehicles has been attributed to the following:[2]

1 Increased cost of new vehicles discourages frequent purchase of new cars.
2 A flood of foreign cars whose styling does not change frequently removes new car trading as a status symbol.
3 Increased number of cars per family and financial inability to replace them frequently.
4 Increased number of wearable parts due to new developments—power brakes, steering, and windows; air conditioning; and antipollution devices.
5 Increase in high performance enthusiasts.
6 Increase in number of vehicles in service.

The automotive aftermarket industry has participated in this market growth with an annual volume of $81 billion in 1976 and a projected volume of $125 billion in 1980. As impressive as this sales growth is, the major changes in the industry have taken place in the characteristics of the vehicle owners and channels of distribution which have emerged to serve them.

Until just a few years ago the typical aftermarket consumer was an adult male. In 1976 there were 133.8 million licensed drivers, of which 45 percent were women. The under-25 age group represented 42.3 million license holders in 1976. In 1978, the number of licensed drivers was estimated to be 138 million. These vehicle owners are considerably more knowledgeable about their vehicles. The excessively high cost of auto repair service, lack of confidence in repair services, and the ready availability of parts have been a strong stimulus for the do-it-yourself trend in auto repair. In 1975 it was estimated that 60 percent of car owners worked on their own cars.[3] Figure 1 depicts the most common types of do-it-yourself maintenance.

[1] *Detroit News* (July 25, 1978), p. 1.
[2] Martin E. Goldman, address before the 55th Annual Convention, National Tire Dealers and Retreaders Association.
[3] *Consumers Study*, Autoparts and Accessories Association, 1976.

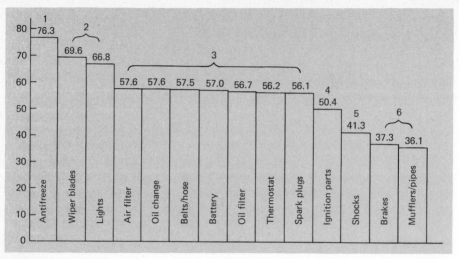

Figure 1 Percentage of do-it-yourself maintenance. (*Unpublished presentation by Charles S. McIntyre, III, president of Monroe Auto Equipment Company, at the 1977 Tri-States Marketing Educators Conference, Eastern Michigan University.*)

The above-mentioned changes have had a dramatic impact on channels of distribution in the industry. As channels developed, they became highly fragmented and specialized, with each institution considering itself a self-contained entity. A recent study revealed twenty-two different channels of distribution, which are graphically displayed in Figure 2. The shaded institutions are primary channels; the others are secondary channels. Many of the institutions did not exist a few years ago. The channels are comprised of a large group of highly specialized wholesale institutions such as jobbers in hard parts, tools, body supplies, fleet products, and high performance parts. Changes at the retail level are equally pronounced, and outlets are no longer limited to service stations, repair shops, and car dealers. Red front stores, chain stores, mass merchandisers, and catalog stores are commonplace today. At the same time there has also been a high degree of integration in some channels. National accounts (direct from manufacturer to retailer) are no longer confined to Sears, Wards, and Penney's, but include such specialty shops as Midas, Tuffy, Aamco, and voluntary chains developed by warehouse distributor programs. Table 1 shows a number of such chains which have organized in the past few years.

About 42 percent of a panel of industry leaders believes that almost half the distributor organizations will be vertically integrated by 1980.[4] Much speculation exists regarding the future of the service station. One school of thought strongly supports a gasoline-and-oil-only operation. Others advocate an increase in sales of tires, batteries, and accessory parts by service stations. Tire companies, on the other hand, are adding batteries, accessories, and services

---

[4] Emil J. Bonkoff, *Summary Report for Panel Members—First Automotive Aftermarket Management "Delphi,"* p. 5.

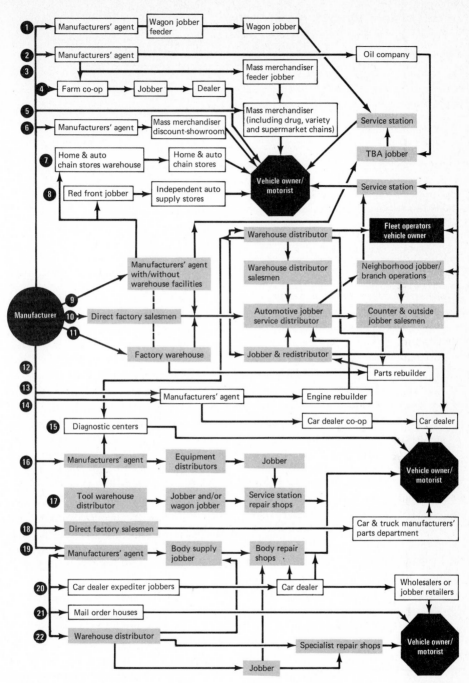

Figure 2 Automotive aftermarket channels of distribution. (*Reprinted by permission of the Furman Advertising Company, Inc., Eastchester, N.Y., Copyright 1972.*)

Table 1 Efforts to Build "Retail Chains"

Name of program and organization	Distribution centers	Jobbers
APA (The Equipment Company)	2	19
APS	32	1,300
APW (Auto Parts Warehouse)	2	40
Autopartner	40	700
Auto Pro (MID-CON)	5	154
Autowize (ITT)	12	500
Bull Parts	13	80
Bumper to Bumper	11	200
The Car Care Man (RAP)	12	200
Carquest	39	1,200
CAPS (Automotive Jobbers WH)	1	40
Goldstar (PDW)	1	100
Greenlight (Mid-America)	10	300
GTC (General Trading Co.)	1	125
IWA (Welco Warehouse)	1	30
Marathon	9	100
Mr. Automotive	3	88
NAPA	64	5,400
Parts Plus	29	850
Pro-Am Partstop (Automotive Dist. Inc.)	3	300
Quick Parts (HLS Dist. Co.)	3	40
RPS	8	118
UCI	8	6
Total	309	11,890

Source: Unpublished presentation by Charles S. McIntyre, III, president of Monroe Auto Equipment Company, at the 1977 Tri-States Marketing Educators Conference, Eastern Michigan University.

to their chain outlets. State automobile dealer associations are entering the parts distribution field by buying parts, warehousing them, and shipping and billing to their members at significantly lower prices than those available from car manufacturers or jobbers. Other groups of new car dealers are entering the warehouse distributor business, buying parts at warehouse distributor prices, and selling to their dealers at jobber prices. One such organization is WISCO in Marshville, Wisconsin. Chrysler Corporation is planning complete distribution of its brand parts throughout the distribution systems. These parts were originally available only through Chrysler dealerships.

All those connected with the automotive aftermarket are attempting to predict future developments in ever-changing channels of distribution. One manufacturer of shock absorbers witnessed an almost complete reversal in the distribution channel over a 7-year period. In 1968 the mass merchant's share of the shock market was 29 percent, while 71 percent went through the warehouse distributor channel. By 1975 mass merchants had 62 percent of the shock market and warehouse distributor jobbers had 38 percent.[5]

[5] Unpublished address by Charles S. McIntyre, III, president, Monroe Auto Equipment Company at the 1977 Tri-States Marketing Educators Conference, Eastern Michigan University.

The mass merchants have experienced very rapid growth in a short period of time. An industry panel estimates that the mass merchant's share of the aftermarket will total 24 percent, or $12.5 billion, by 1980, a 66 percent increase in market share since 1960.[6] In a query of single-outlet parts operators, 80 percent reported that they felt the automotive, discount, tire dealer, and tire company stores were their major competitors.[7] If the competition is felt at the retail level, it is equally felt at the wholesale level, since most mass merchants buy direct from the manufacturer.

Wholesale sales to the retail structure are roughly divided by retailer groups as follows:[8]

Gasoline service stations	32.7%
Tire battery accessory dealers	
Car owners (do-it-yourself)	12.3%
Department stores	
Motor vehicle dealers	16.8%
Farm equipment dealers	2.7%
Heavy-duty establishments (fleets, industrial contractors)	16.3%
General and specialized automotive repair shops	19.2%

The warehouse distributors and jobber operators respond to mass merchant proliferation by claiming that their sales are increasing year after year and that they are not losing business.

CASE 11-1: QUESTIONS

1 Can any of the change models described in Chapter 11 explain the changes observed in the auto parts aftermarket? How?
2 How can managers at any level in the channel of distribution track future institutional changes in this channel?

---

[6] *Home & Auto* (January 1975), p. 28.
[7] *Automotive Chain Store* (October 1976), p. 111.
[8] "The Automotive Aftermarket in the 1970s," *Jobber Topics* (Chicago: The Irving Cloud Publishing Company).

Chapter 12

Future Distribution Arrangements

When he was a General Motors executive, Boss Kettering often criticized his contemporaries for their preoccupation with day-to-day manufacturing and marketing operations at the expense of future planning. Kettering is quoted as having said: "Executives must be concerned with the future because they will spend the rest of their lives there." In this final chapter, we offer our speculations concerning the future of distribution channel arrangements.

To set the stage, the first section of the chapter offers a brief synthesis of the basic ideas around which we have structured this book. Next, we develop a case for increased distribution innovation as a prime source of improved productivity during the decades ahead. The final section of the chapter illustrates four innovative distribution arrangements that may or may not materialize in the future. The important point to remember is that all the "blue sky" arrangements suggested can be developed within the capabilities of today's technology.

CHANNEL MANAGEMENT—A SYNTHESIS

The marketing channel has been described and discussed as an ever-changing system of relationships that exists among institutions involved in buying and selling. Because channels are dynamic it is difficult to crystallize institutional relationships at any point in time into a neat classification. For purposes of differentiation, we identified three basic channel arrangements as being easily observed in contemporary marketing: (1) the vertical marketing system, which may be structured legally on a corporate, contractual, or administered basis; (2) free-flow marketing channels; and (3) single transaction channels. This classification emphasizes the degree of overt expression of mutual dependence between some or all channel members.

Given the above classification structure, six sets of fundamental environmental and behavioral relationships were identified and discussed throughout the background chapters of the text (Chapters 2–5). The six sets of common relationships were (1) legal-social setting, (2) complexity, (3) specialization, (4) routinization, (5) dependence, and (6) disproportionate risk. Our thesis was that the permutation of these six fundamental relationships forms the nucleus around which channels emerge or are strategically planned.

Formulation of a channel strategy by enterprise management represents a significant part of an overall marketing strategy. In the managerial chapters of the text (Chapters 6–11) we introduced and developed four basic considerations in planning channel strategy: (1) enterprise power assessment, (2) separation of transaction and physical distribution performance structure, (3) accurate measurement of channel performance, and (4) the management of change.

In the final analysis the capability to plan the direction and tempo of future channel arrangements rests upon the capability of management to eliminate resistance to change and assume a leadership role. To this end Chapter 11 concluded with a change management model to guide the process of distribution innovation. As a prelude to our speculations regarding tomorrow's distribution arrangements, a brief look at the need for increased distribution innovation in the future is in order.

THE NEED FOR DISTRIBUTION INNOVATION

Although a great deal of change has taken place in the organizational arrangements of marketing channels over the past three decades, a careful look at many basic systems reveals that most significant change has taken place in agreements among participants but not in the basic distribution processes. In other words, a significant degree of functional transfer has occurred among institutions, with the net result that channel participants and their relative roles have changed substantially. However, with few exceptions, the overall process of distribution has remained relatively the same. The retail food industry offers a good example.

The primary method of processed food distribution during the first third of the twentieth century consisted of manufacturers (packers) selling to wholesalers who in turn sold to retailers. In a sense, this is typical of the classic M to W to R channel model that has dominated marketing literature. Over the years, the food distribution system has evolved from a free-flow marketing structure characterized by small retailers to a combination of contractual and administered vertical marketing arrangements dominated by large integrated supermarket organizations. In terms of participant arrangements and functional responsibility, the channel structure has experienced radical changes. At least four stages of evolution or planned change can be identified in retail food distribution:

1 Development of supermarkets to replace small food retailers.
2 Integration of supermarket chains to incorporate the wholesale function leading to development of distribution centers. This stage of development resulted in a significant decline in the number of independent wholesalers.
3 Exercise of pressure by integrated chains on food processors to provide mixed product shipments to retailer distribution centers. This pressure resulted in widespread establishment of mixing distribution centers by processors. Thus, a new activity was introduced into the marketing channel.
4 Continued pressure on the part of integrated chains to push inventory holding responsibility "up the channel" toward processors. This pressure is reflected in such practices as store-sequenced trailer loading which permits the chain to cross-dock products for store delivery without warehousing. Other examples are trailer trip leasing, backhaul allowances, and direct store delivery by processors.

The significant point of this food example is that physical distribution and transaction channel structure has experienced substantial changes, but the process of marketing food for in-home consumption has changed very little.

Invention versus Innovation

At least since World War II a persuasive case can be made that major changes in marketing channels have resulted from a shift in relative power between institutions plus a steady influx of new technology. Returning to the food distribution example, it is clear to industry observers that the relative balance of power has shifted from processors to the retail chain. However, a significant portion of the real change in channel structure can be traced to development of transportation, warehousing, and order processing technology. In a general sense new technology was deployed to perform traditional steps in the distribution process more efficiently. Power was deployed to shift functional responsibility for performance of the function. This deployment of new technology to perform the traditional distribution process more efficiently is in contrast to seeking new and better ways to accomplish necessary marketing functions. Thus, primary emphasis has been placed upon applying technological inventions to the distribution process. Innovation, on the other hand, is directed to seeking totally new ways or processes for accomplishing necessary marketing functions.

The Productivity Gap

The need for innovative distribution arrangements has never been greater. A steady stream of new technology can be expected to emerge during the remainder of the twentieth century. However, the track record of the past two decades suggests that technology alone will not be adequate to achieve the productivity necessary for national and business growth.

Figure 12-1 illustrates the trend in productivity of the United States in comparison to other major industrial nations that function in a free market environment. Productivity is defined as the ratio of real output produced to real resources consumed. The graph clearly shows that the United States is not keeping pace with other industrialized nations. The quarterly figures for the first half of 1978 were even more alarming as the United States experienced no real productivity growth.

Although many different approaches can be utilized to improve productivity, one sure method is to reduce duplication and waste in the distributive process.

INNOVATIVE DISTRIBUTION IDEAS—
FACT OR FICTION?

In this section four basic ideas to innovate traditional distribution practices are highlighted as potential ways to improve productivity. Most of the systems described are or have been studied by existing firms within the specified industry. Rather than including standard cases and discussion questions at the end of this chapter, we offer these four ideas for contemplation. The reader is encouraged to identify the basic changes necessary to make the concept work and to speculate regarding the potential economic validity of the idea. Keep in mind that most innovative system changes have traditionally originated from outside the involved industry and were implemented by people who "didn't know it couldn't be done."[1]

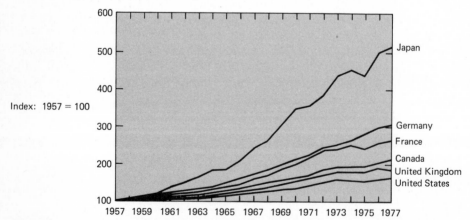

Figure 12-1   Increase in output per labor-hour 1957–1977. (*Bureau of Labor Statistics.*)

[1] Theodore Levitt, "Marketing Myopia," *Harvard Business Review* (July–August 1960), pp. 24–27.

Flying Autos to Market

It has long been a dream of the automobile industry that the day would come when aviation technology would make it economically feasible to fly automobiles from assembly plants to locations close to dealer showrooms. Given today's communication and transportation technology, this form of air-auto distribution may be feasible. The potential benefit to the automobile industry would be the elimination of an average of greater than 20 days of vehicle delivery time from assembly to dealer. Naturally, the cost of air freight will be several times higher than that which is now spent on rail or truck distribution. On the surface it would seem that an air distribution program would be feasible only if the savings from reduced inventories in the distribution channel would be sufficient to offset the increased transportation costs.

However, from an innovative viewpoint the issue must be approached from a much broader perspective. First, what does faster delivery represent to the customer? It would seem that customers would benefit from such rapid delivery only if they were afforded the opportunity to place custom orders. Thus, to make the concept work, it might become necessary to introduce telecommunications so that the customer can in effect build his or her own car using a computer terminal. Such an innovative method of marketing would have far-reaching implications in terms of expertise needed at the dealership level and the dealer's role as a member of the distribution channel.

Second, this concept would have to rely upon greater automation in production. For example, automobiles may have to be preproduced with a primer paint and be limited to a few engine and body styles, with no interiors or accessories attached initially. Upon receipt of a customer order, car assembly could be completed on a customized basis within a relatively short period of time. With this system, an auto ordered on Monday might well run through the customization line on Tuesday, be finished with a paint designed to harden in transit, and be flown to the dealer market late Tuesday or early Wednesday.

Third, for such a concept to work, major changes would have to be made in the relationship between automobile producers and their dealer organizations. Such a program could exist only if given substantial financial support by the manufacturing organization.

Although the above concept is highly speculative in terms of its application in today's economy, its potential rests solidly upon multiple trade-offs between manufacturing, distribution, finance, and coordinated manufacturer-dealer relationships. It is obvious that we cannot afford the transportation cost of flying automobiles unless other system changes are introduced simultaneously to create trade-offs. Is the concept valid? It was sufficiently exciting to stimulate extensive study by General Motors Corporation to evaluate airlift potential and capabilities for automotive transport. Among distribution personnel in the automotive industry, the concept remains a potential but not here-today application. The question is: Will management ever make such a system a reality and, if so, what incentives will be needed to bring about the necessary institutional changes?

Home Delivery of Foods

One of the customer services offered by retail grocery stores before the proliferation of supermarkets was home delivery of groceries. This practice was discontinued by large chains; however, some retailers still keep their foot in the
door by offering specialized delivery routes. One example is the Jewel Companies' home delivery system. All evidence indicates that home delivery has
lost its appeal to both consumers and retailers. Total food delivered to the
home has dropped from 8.6 percent of total sales in 1960 to 1.2 percent in 1977.
Is the concept dead forever or is the timing just not ready for reestablishment
of home delivery?

The potential of telecommunication ordering from the home direct to ware-
house-like supermarkets has been discussed many times in the literature. The
following partial reprint of the introduction to a recent article is typical of how
this subject has been examined.[2]

> The future of retailing, and in particular the prospect of telecommunication systems
> for shopping, has enormous consequences for manufacturers, suppliers, and equip-
> ment manufacturers as well as, of course, retail stores. This article analyzes the vi-
> sions of automation that were described by Edward Bellamy in 1888 and have been
> issuing ever since from various experts. Convinced that likely developments during
> the next few decades are closely connected with past trends, the authors first look
> at the evolution of retail institutions, the shortening of retail life cycles, the influ-
> ence of consumers and their lifestyles on retailing, the rise of specialty stores, and
> other happenings. Next, looking ahead, they see these trends combining and mixing
> with other developments, such as new technologies, to produce a vastly different
> retail scene. While the authors believe that specialty stores will continue to thrive,
> the retailing of routinely ordered staples will be transformed. Telecommunication
> shopping, or "teleshopping," is definitely in prospect for this great area of mark-
> eting.

Naturally, retail store operators are not enthusiastic about teleshopping
systems. However, from a total cost perspective it may be possible to provide
consumers even better services than they now enjoy at a lower total cost if the
whole institution referred to as a supermarket is eliminated from the food distribution channel. Such a radical innovation would require significant institutional
changes and would require a change in consumer shopping habits. Will such a
concept ever become a reality? Some industry experts think so; most do not.

Appliance-Less Dealers

A different form of home delivery offering exciting potential is a system
wherein appliance dealers do not stock inventory for consumer delivery. The
dealers under this distribution arrangement would only stock display models

---

[2] Malcolm P. McNair and Eleanor G. May, "The Next Revolution of the Retailing Wheel,"
Harvard Business Review (September–October 1978), p. 81. Copyright © 1978 by the President
and Fellows of Harvard College; all rights reserved.

for consumer inspection and purchase choice. A consumer order received at a dealer's place of business would be telecommunicated immediately to a distribution center located where it could economically serve many different dealer customers. Upon order receipt, the appropriate appliance would be selected from distribution center inventory and delivered directly to the consumer's home. This direct system of physical distribution would eliminate duplicate handling and transportation at the dealer's place of business. This concept offers potential inventory savings in that retail inventories would be virtually eliminated from the channel. In addition, consolidation of many dealers' inventories in one warehouse would offer better product availability despite lower aggregate channel inventories.

Such systems have been in operation on a test basis for many years. In fact, there are actual cases where an appliance purchased on Monday and delivered on Wednesday from a distant warehouse had not been manufactured at the time of the consumer transaction. The product was obtained directly from the assembly line, loaded on a truck, and transported directly to the consumer's home. When appliance products are warehoused, the trend is toward manufacturing a neutral product without accessories and color attachments. The appliance can be customized by adding a timer or color panel or ice maker after the consumer's order has been received. Thus, one basic stock item can be converted into a variety of products at the warehouse level. As indicated above, the system has been tested, and many people in the industry are convinced it will become the accepted method of marketing and distributing appliances in the near future. This innovation faces some obstacles but it offers the benefit of substantial economies. Will this arrangement become tomorrow's dominant channel for consumer durables?

Purchasing Corporations

Large-scale manufacturing often requires many different production and processing stages in order to produce an end product. In many situations multiple manufacturing and assembly plants are required to produce an end product. An understandable concern in such situations is the maintenance of a continuous supply of materials and labor for conversion into finished products. A persistent problem in such organizations is the maintenance, repair, and operating supply situation (MRO). How can items be purchased in small quantities at an economic price and be available when needed? A new concept is emerging wherein third-party organizations are assuming the role of MRO supply specialists for manufacturing organizations. A master purchase order is negotiated by the manufacturer with vendors. The vendors, in turn, transport products to third-party warehouses when requested. The third party holds items in inventory for support of manufacturing operations. The individual manufacturing plants draw upon the MRO warehouse in much the same way that supermarkets place replenishment orders at their supporting distribution centers. Delivery of critical supplies could be made within an hour. However, the normal order cycle consists of overnight delivery of an assortment truckload of required materials, repair parts, and operating supplies.

The economic advantage of the purchasing corporation is its ability to aggregate large volume purchases geographically close to the point of use coupled with the capability to redistribute exact quantities of MRO items needed to the manufacturing plant rapidly. From the manufacturing plant's viewpoint, many small shipments are consolidated into a single supply order. In addition, it is necessary to manage only the inbound movement and the paperwork involved with a single receipt rather than a wide variety of products flowing in from different locations. Finally, standardization and low-bid purchasing offer additional economies.

The concept of centralized purchasing corporations offers many interesting possibilities. If one firm can enjoy economies of scale with this type of centralized operation, would it be feasible for one supply corporation to purchase for multiple manufacturing destinations? The essential difference between the purchasing corporation and the traditional industrial supplier is an extended commitment and dependence between user organizations and the purchasing and distribution corporation. In certain circumstances the purchasing corporations could expand activities to include joint use of specialized equipment and light manufacturing or fabrication to accompany distribution operations. Such corporations do exist today. Those with the highest visibility now serve Gulf Oil and Dow Chemical. To what extent is this innovative concept practical and will it become a way of doing business in the decades ahead?

CONCLUDING STATEMENT

Throughout this book we have attempted to explain and illustrate the reality of management in marketing channels. In this final chapter, description has given way to speculation. The plea has been for a critical examination of traditional practices in pursuit of increased productivity. The goal is change—but not change purely for the sake of change. Rather, it appears that the challenge of profitable growth for institutions and their respective channels rests upon the ability of management to apply available technology innovatively. The challenge for the future is to negotiate greater productivity through cooperative behavior in contrast to pure functional transfer between firms. It remains to be seen if management can achieve such coordinated behavior in a profit-oriented free market system.

BIBLIOGRAPHY

Books

Alderson, Wroe: "Factors Governing the Development of Marketing Channels," in R. M. Clewett, ed., *Marketing Channels for Manufactured Products* (Homewood, Ill.: Richard D. Irwin, Inc., 1954), pp. 5–34.

——: *Marketing Behavior and Executive Action* (Homewood, Ill.: Richard D. Irwin, Inc., 1957).

——: *Dynamic Marketing Behavior* (Homewood, Ill.: Richard D. Irwin, Inc., 1965).

——: "Cooperation and Conflict in Marketing Channels," in Louis W. Stern, ed., *Distribution Channels: Behavioral Dimensions* (Boston: Houghton Mifflin Company, 1969).

——, and Paul E. Green: "Bayesian Decision Theory in Channel Selection," in Wroe Alderson and Paul E. Green, *Planning and Problem Solving in Marketing* (Homewood, Ill.: Richard D. Irwin, Inc., 1964), pp. 311–317.

Anthony, Robert N.: *Management Accounting,* 4th ed. (Homewood, Ill.: Richard D. Irwin, Inc., 1970).

Aspinwall, Leo V.: "The Depot Theory of Distribution," *in* William Lazer and Eugene J. Kelley, *Managerial Marketing,* rev. ed. (Homewood, Ill.: Richard D. Irwin, Inc. 1962), pp. 652–659.

Balderston, F. E.: "Design of Marketing Channels," *in* Reavis Cox, Wroe Alderson, and Stanley J. Shapiro, eds., *Theory in Marketing* (Homewood, Ill.: Richard D. Irwin, Inc., 1964), pp. 167–175.

——, and A. C. Hoggatt: *Stimulation of Market Processes,* Berkeley Institute of Business and Economic Research (University of California, 1962), chapters 1 and 2.

Baligh, Hemly H.: "A Theoretical Framework for Channel Choice," in P. D. Bennett, *Economic Growth, Competition and World Markets* (Chicago: American Marketing Association, 1965), pp. 631–654.

——, and Leon E. Richartz: *Vertical Market Structures* (Boston: Allyn and Bacon, Inc., 1967).

Ballou, Ronald H.: *Business Logistics Management* (Englewood Cliffs, N.J.: Prentice-Hall, Inc., 1973).

Barger, Harold: *Distribution's Place in the American Economy* (Princeton University Press, 1955).

Bartels, Robert: *Marketing Theory and Metatheory* (Homewood, Ill.: Richard D. Irwin, Inc., 1970).

Baumol, William L.: *Economic Theory and Operations Analysis,* 2d ed. (Englewood Cliffs, N.J.: Prentice-Hall, Inc., 1965).

Beier, Frederick J., and Louis W. Stern: "Power in the Channel of Distribution," *in* Louis W. Stern, ed., *Distribution Channels: Behavioral Dimensions* (Boston: Houghton Mifflin Company, 1969).

Berg, Thomas L.: "Designing the Distribution System," *in* W. D. Stevens, ed., *The Social Responsibilities of Marketing* (Chicago: American Marketing Association, 1962), pp. 481–490.

Beyer, Ralph F.: *Profitability Accounting for Planning and Control* (New York: The Ronald Press Company, 1962).

Bierman, Harold, Jr., and Seymour Smidt: *The Capital Budgeting Decision* (New York: The Macmillan Company, 1966).

Boot, John C. D.: *Mathematical Reasoning in Economics and Management Science* (Englewood Cliffs, N.J.: Prentice-Hall, Inc., 1967).

Boulding, Kenneth E.: *Conflict and Defense* (New York: Harper & Row, Publishers, Inc., 1963).

———: *Economic Analysis,* 4th ed. (New York: Harper & Row, Publishers, Inc., 1966).

———: "The Economics of Human Conflict," *in* Elton B. McNeil, ed., *The Nature of Human Conflict* (Englewood Cliffs, N.J.: Prentice-Hall Inc., 1965), pp. 174–175.

Boudling, Elise, and Robert K. Kahn, eds.: *Power and Conflict in Organizations* (New York: Basic Books, Inc., Publishers, 1964).

Bowersox, Donald J.: *Logistical Management,* rev. ed. (New York: The Macmillan Company, 1978).

———, and E. Jerome McCarthy: "Strategic Development of Planned Vertical Marketing Systems," *in* Louis P. Bucklin, ed., *Vertical Marketing Systems* (Glenview, Ill.: Scott, Foresman and Company, 1970).

———, Edward W. Smykay, and Bernard J. La Londe: *Physical Distribution Management,* rev. ed. (New York: The Macmillan Company, 1971).

Breyer, Ralph, F.: "Some Observations on Structural Formation and the Growth of Marketing Channels," *in* Reavis Cox, Wroe Alderson, and Stanley J. Shapiro, eds., *Theory in Marketing* (Homewood, Ill.: Richard D. Irwin, Inc., 1964), pp. 163–175.

———: *Quantitative System Analysis and Control: Study No. 1, Channel and Channel Group Costing* (Philadelphia: College Offset Press, 1949).

Brickman, Philip: *Social Conflict* (Boston: D. C. Heath and Company, 1974).

Bucklin, Louis P. "The Economic Structure of Channels of Distribution," *in* Martin L. Bell, ed., *Marketing: A Maturing Discipline* (Chicago: American Marketing Association, 1960), pp. 370–385.

———: "The Classification of Channel Structures," *in* Louis P. Bucklin, ed., *Vertical Marketing Systems* (Glenview, Ill.: Scott, Foresman and Company, 1970), pp. 16–30.

———: *Competition and Evolution in the Distributive Trades* (Englewood Cliffs, N.J.: Prentice-Hall, Inc., 1972).

———: "Marketing Channels and Structures: A Macro View," *in* Boris W. Becker and Helmot Becker, eds., *Combined Proceedings: Marketing Education and the Real World and Dynamic Marketing in a Changing World* (Chicago: American Marketing Association, 1972), pp. 28–40.

———: "The Locus of Channel Control," *in* Robert L. King, ed., *Marketing and the New Science of Planning* (Chicago: American Marketing Association, 1973), pp. 28–40.

————., and Leslie Halpert: "Exploring Channels of Distribution for Cement with the Principle of Postponement–Speculation," *in* Peter D. Bennett, ed., *Marketing and Economic Development* (Chicago, Ill.: American Marketing Association, 1965), pp. 699–710.

————, and Stanley F. Stasch: "Preliminary Considerations," *in* Louis P. Bucklin, ed., *Vertical Marketing Systems* (Glenview, Ill.: Scott, Foresman and Company, 1970).

Carr, Charles R., and Charles W. Howe: *Quantitative Decision Procedures in Management and Economics: Deterministic Theory and Applications* (New York: McGraw-Hill, Inc., 1964).

Castenholz, William B.: *The Control of Distribution Costs and Sales* (New York: Harper & Brothers, 1930).

Chambers, Raymond J.: *Accounting, Evaluation and Economic Behavior* (Englewood Cliffs, N.J.: Prentice-Hall, Inc., 1966).

Churchman, C. West: *Prediction and Optimal Decisions: Philosophical Issues of a Science of Values* (Englewood Cliffs, N.J.: Prentice-Hall, Inc., 1961).

————, Russell L. Ackoff, and E. Leonard Arnoff: *Introduction to Operations Research* (New York: John Wiley & Sons, Inc., 1957).

————, and Philburn Ratoosh: *Measurement Definition and Theories* (New York: John Wiley & Sons, Inc., 1959).

Christopher, Martin: *Total Distribution, A Framework for Analysis Costing and Control* (London: Gower Press, 1971).

Clark, Fred E.: *Principles of Marketing* (New York: The Macmillan Company, 1923).

Clewett, Richard M.: *Marketing Channels for Manufactured Products* (Homewood, Ill.: Richard D. Irwin, Inc., 1954).

Commons, John R.: *Institutional Economics* (New York: The Macmillan Company, 1934).

Corley, Robert M., Robert L. Black, and O. Lee Reed: *The Legal Environment of Business,* 4th ed. (New York: McGraw-Hill Book Company, 1977).

Coser, Lewis A.: *The Functions of Social Conflict* (New York: The Free Press, 1956).

Cox, Reavis, Charles Goodman, and Thomas C. Fichander: *Distribution in a High-Level Economy* (Englewood Cliffs, N.J.: Prentice-Hall, Inc., 1965).

————, and Thomas F. Schutte: "A Look at Channel Management," *in* Phillip McDonalds, ed., *Marketing Involvement in Society and the Economy* (Chicago: American Marketing Association, 1969), pp. 99–105.

Dearden, John: *Cost Accounting and Financial Control Systems* (Reading, Mass.: Addison-Wesley Publishing Company, 1973).

Deutsch, Morton: *The Resolution of Conflict* (New Haven: Yale University Press, 1973).

Dickenson, Roger A.: *Retail Management: A Channels Approach* (Belmont, Ca: Wadsworth Publishing Company, Inc., 1974).

Engle, James F., David T. Kollat, and Roger D. Bockwell: *Consumer Behavior* (New York: Holt, Rinehart and Winston, Inc., 1968).

Frank, Ronald, William Massy, and Yoram Wind: *Market Segmentation* (Englewood Cliffs, N.J.: Prentice-Hall, Inc., 1972).

Gardner, John W.: *Self-Renewal* (New York: Harper & Row Publishers, Inc., 1964).

Gill, Lynn E., and Louis W. Stern: "Roles and Role Theory in Distribution Channel Systems," *in* Louis Stern, ed., *Distribution Channels: Behavioral Dimensions* (Boston: Houghton Mifflin Company, 1969).

Goodman, Sam R.: *Financial Manager's Manual and Guide* (Englewood Cliffs, N.J.: Prentice-Hall, Inc., 1973).

Grabner, John R., and L. H. Rosenberg: "Communication in Distribution Channel Systems," *in* Louis Stern, ed., *Distribution Channels: Behavioral Dimensions* (Boston: Houghton Mifflin Company, 1969).

Grisell, T. O.: *Budgetary Control of Distribution* (New York: Harper & Brothers, 1929).

Hall, Margaret: "Economic Analysis of Retail Trade," *in* William G. Moller, Jr., and David L. Wileman, ed., *Marketing Channels: A Systems Viewpoint* (Homewood, Ill.: Richard D. Irwin, Inc., 1971).

Heckert, J. Brooks: *The Analysis and Control of Distribution Costs for Sales Executives and Accountants* (New York: The Ronald Press Company, 1940).

————, and R. B. Milner: *Distribution Costs* (New York: The Ronald Press Company, 1952).

Hertzler, J. O.: *Society in Action* (New York: The Dryden Press, Inc., 1954).

Heskett, James L., Nicholas A. Glaskowsky, and Robert M. Ivie: *Business Logistics,* 2d ed. (New York: The Ronald Press Company, 1973).

Hoglund, Bengt, and Jorgen Ulrich: "Peach Research and the Concepts of Conflict," *in* Bengt Hoglund and Jorgen Ulrich, eds., *Conflict Control and Conflict Resolution* (Copenhagen: C. Olsen and Company, 1972).

Homans, George C.: *The Human Group* (New York: Harcourt, Brace, & World, Inc., 1950).

Horngren, Charles T.: *Cost Accounting: A Managerial Emphasis,* 3d ed. (Englewood Cliffs, N.J.: Prentice-Hall, Inc., 1972).

Howard, Marshall C.: *Legal Aspects of Marketing* (New York: McGraw-Hill Book Company, 1964).

Karrass, Chester L.: *The Negotiating Game* (New York: The World Publishing Company, 1970).

Katz, Daniel, and Robert L. Kohn: *The Social Psychology of Organizations* (New York: John Wiley & Sons, Inc., 1966).

Kollat, David T., Roger D. Blackwell, and James F. Robeson: *Strategic Marketing* (New York: Holt, Rinehart and Winston, Inc., 1972).

Kotler, Philip: *Marketing Management: Analysis, Planning and Control* (Englewood Cliffs, N.J.: Prentice-Hall, Inc., 1967).

————: *Marketing Decision Making: A Model Building Approach* (New York: Holt, Rinehart and Winston, Inc., 1971).

————: *Marketing for Nonprofit Organizations* (Englewood Cliffs, N.J.: Prentice-Hall, Inc., 1975).

————: *Marketing Management* (Englewood Cliffs, N.J.: Prentice-Hall, Inc., 1976).

Lambert, Douglas M.: *The Distribution Channels Decision* (New York: The National Association of Accountants; and Hamilton, Ontario: The Society of Management Accountants of Canada, 1978).

Langman, D. R., and Michael Schiff: *Practical Distribution Cost Analysis* (Homewood, Ill.: Richard D. Irwin, Inc., 1955).

Lesourne, Jacques: *Economic Analysis and Operations Research* (Englewood Cliffs, N.J.: Prentice-Hall, Inc., 1963).

Levin, Richard I., and C. A. Kirkpatrick: *Quantitative Approaches to Management* (New York: McGraw-Hill, Inc., 1963).

Levy, Sidney J., and Gerald Zaltman: *Marketing, Society and Conflict* (Englewood Cliffs, N.J.: Prentice-Hall, Inc., 1975).

Lewis, Edwin H.: "Channel Management by Wholesalers," *in* Robert L. King, ed.,

Marketing and the New Science of Planning (Chicago: American Marketing Association, 1968).

————: *Marketing Channels: Structure and Strategy* (New York: McGraw Hill, Inc., 1968).

Liebhafsky, H. H.: *The Nature of Price Theory* (Homewood, Ill.: The Dorsey Press, 1963).

Lipson, Harry A., and John R. Darling: *Marketing Fundamentals: Text and Cases* (New York: John Wiley & Sons, Inc., 1974).

Lodge, George Cabot: *The New American Ideology* (New York: Alfred A. Knopf, Inc., 1975).

Longman, Donald L., and Michael Schiff: *Practical Distribution Cost Analysis* (Homewood, Ill.: Richard D. Irwin, Inc., 1967).

Luck, David J., and Arthur A. Prell: *Marketing Strategy* (New York: Appleton-Century-Crofts, 1968).

Magee, John F.: "The Computer and the Physical Distribution Network," *in* Wroe Alderson and Stanley J. Shapiro, eds., *Marketing and the Computer* (Englewood Cliffs, N.J.: Prentice-Hall, Inc., 1963).

————: *Physical Distribution Systems* (New York: McGraw-Hill Book Company, 1967).

————: *Industrial Logistics* (New York: McGraw-Hill, Inc. 1968).

Mallen, Bruce: "Conflict and Cooperation in Marketing Channels," *in* L. George Smith, ed., *Reflections on Progress in Marketing* (Chicago: American Marketing Association, 1964), pp. 65–85.

Mao, James C. T.: *Quantitative Analysis of Financial Decisions* (Toronto, Canada: Collier-Macmillan Canada, Ltd., 1969).

March, James G., and Herbert A. Simon: *Organizations* (New York: John Wiley & Sons, Inc., 1959).

Mason, J. Barry, and Morris L. Mayer: *Modern Retailing: Theory and Practice* (Dallas: Business Publications, Inc., 1978).

McCammon, Bert C.: "Alternative Explanations of Institutional Change," *in* Stephen A. Greyser, ed., *Toward Scientific Marketing* (Chicago: American Marketing Association, 1963), pp. 477–490.

————, and Albert D. Bates: "The Emergence and Growth of Contractually Integrated Channels in the American Economy," *in* P. D. Bennett, ed., *Economic Growth, Competition and World Markets* (Chicago: American Marketing Association, 1965), pp. 496–515.

————, and Robert W. Little: "Marketing Channels: Analytical Systems and Approaches," *in* George Schwartz, ed., *Science in Marketing* (New York: John Wiley & Sons, Inc., 1965), pp. 321–385.

Meier, Robert C., William F. Newell, and Harold L. Pazer: *Simulation in Business and Economics* (Englewood Cliffs, N.J.: Prentice-Hall, Inc., 1969).

Merton, Robert K.: *Social Theory and Social Structure* (Glencoe, Ill.: The Free Press, 1949), pp. 179–195.

Michman, Ronald: *Marketing Channels* (Columbus, Ohio: Grid Publishing, Inc., 1974), p. 6.

Mossman, Frank H., and Newton Morton: *Logistics of Distribution Systems* (Boston: Allyn and Bacon, Inc., 1965).

Palamountain, Joseph Cornwall: *The Politics of Distribution* (Cambridge, Mass.: Harvard University Press, 1955).

Parsons, Talcott: *The Social System* (Glencoe, Ill.: The Free Press, 1951).

————, and Neil H. Smelser: *Economy and Society: A Study in the Integration of Economic and Social Theory* (New York: The Free Press, 1956).

Raven, Bertram, and Arie Kruglanski: "Conflict and Power," *in* Paul Swingle, ed., *The Structure of Conflict* (New York: Academic Press, Inc., 1970).

Revzan, David A.: *Wholesaling in Marketing Organizations* (New York: John Wiley & Sons, Inc., 1961).

Robbins, Lionel C.: *An Essay on the Nature and Significance of Economic Science*, 2d ed. (London: Macmillan & Co., Ltd., 1952).

Schelling, Thomas C.: *The Strategy of Conflict* (Cambridge, Mass.: Harvard University Press, 1960).

Schumpeter, Joseph: *Capitalism, Socialism, and Democracy* (New York: Harper & Brothers, 1947).

Schwartz, George: "Breyer Study: Quantitative Systemic Analysis and Control," *in Development of Marketing Theory* (Cincinnati: Southwestern Publishing Company, 1963), pp. 121–125.

Seidler, Lee J., and Lynn Seidler: *Social Accounting: Theory, Issues, and Cases* (New York: Melville Publishing Division of John Wiley & Sons, Inc., 1975).

Selznick, Philip: *Leadership in Administration* (Evanston, Ill.: Row, Peterson & Company, 1957).

Seven, Charles H.: *Marketing Productivity Analysis* (New York: McGraw-Hill Book Company, 1965).

Shuptrine, Kelly, and Ronald Gorman: "Conflict in Distribution Channels: An Exploration," *in* Louis W. Stern, ed., *Distribution Channels: Behavioral Dimensions* (Boston: Houghton Mifflin Company, 1969).

Simmat, Rudolph: *Scientific Distribution*, 2d ed. (London: Sir Isaac Pitman & Sons, Ltd., 1947).

Simon, Sanford R.: *Managing Marketing Profitability* (Chicago: American Management Association, Inc., 1969).

Sims, J. Taylor, J. Robert Foster, and Arch G. Woodside: *Marketing Channels* (New York: Harper & Row, Publishers, Inc., 1977).

Smelser, Neil J.: *The Sociology of Economic Life* (Englewood Cliffs, N.J.: Prentice-Hall, Inc., 1963).

Starr, Martin K.: *Systems Management of Operations* (Englewood Cliffs, N.J.: Prentice-Hall, Inc., 1971).

Stasch, Stanley F.: "The Stability of Channel Systems: Two Dynamic Models," *in* Raymond M. Haas, ed., *Science, Technology, and Marketing* (Chicago: American Marketing Association, 1966), pp. 436–442.

Staubus, George J: *Activity Costing and Input-Output Accounting* (Homewood, Ill.: Richard D. Irwin, Inc., 1971).

Staudt, Thomas A., Donald A. Taylor, and Donald J. Bowersox: *A Managerial Introduction to Marketing*, 3d ed. (Englewood Cliffs, N.J.: Prentice-Hall, Inc., 1976).

Stern, Louis W.: "Channel Control and Interorganizational Management," *in* Peter D. Bennett, ed., *Marketing and Economic Development* (Chicago: American Marketing Association, 1965), pp. 655–665.

————, and Jay W. Brown: "Distribution Channels: A Social Systems Approach," *in* Louis Stern, ed., *Distribution Channels: Behaviorial Dimensions* (Boston: Houghton Mifflin Company, 1969).

———, and Adel I. El-Ansary: *Marketing Channels* (Englewood Cliffs, N.J.: Prentice-Hall, Inc., 1977).

———, and Ronald H. Gorman: "Conflict in Distribution Channels: An Exploration," *in* Louis Stern, ed., *Distribution Channels: Behavioral Dimensions* (Boston: Houghton Mifflin Company, 1969).

———, and J. L. Heskett: "Conflict Management in Interorganization Relations: A Conceptual Framework," *in* Louis Stern, ed., *Distribution Channels: Behavioral Dimensions* (Boston: Houghton Mifflin Company, 1969).

Sturdivant, Frederick D.: "Determinants of Vertical Integration in Channel Systems," *in* Peter D. Bennett, ed., *Marketing and Economic Development* (Chicago: American Marketing Association, 1965), pp. 462–479.

———, et. al.: *Managerial Analysis in Marketing* (Glenview, Ill.: Scott, Foresman and Company, 1970).

Thompson, Donald N.: *Franchise Operations and Anti-Trust* (Lexington, Mass.: Heath-Lexington Books, 1971).

Thompson, James D.: *Organizations in Action* (New York: McGraw-Hill Inc., 1967).

Tousley, Rayburn D., Eugene Clark, and Fred E. Clark: *Principles of Marketing* (New York: The Macmillan Company, 1962).

von Neumann, J., and O. Morgenstern: *Theory of Games and Economic Behavior* (Princeton: Princeton University Press, 1947).

Wagner, Harvey M: *Principles of Operations Research with Applications of Managerial Decisions* (Englewood Cliffs, N.J.: Prentice-Hall, Inc., 1969).

Walters, Glenn C.: *Marketing Channels* (New York: The Ronald Press Company, 1974), pp. 15–16.

Walton, Richard E., and Robert B. McKersie: *A Behavioral Theory of Labor Negotiations* (New York: McGraw-Hill Book Company, 1965).

White, Percival: *Scientific Marketing Management* (New York: Harper & Brothers, 1927).

Journal Articles

Alderson, Wroe: "Marketing Efficiency and the Principle of Postponement," *Cost and Profit Outlook* (September 1950).

———, and Miles W. Martin: "Toward a Formal Theory of Transactions and Transvections," *Journal of Marketing Research* (May 1965), pp. 117–126.

Artle, Robert, and Sture Berglund: "A Note on Manufacturer's Choice of Distribution Channels," *Management Science* (July 1959), pp. 460–471.

Assael, Harry: "The Political Role of Trade Associations in Distributive Conflict Resolutions," *Journal of Marketing* (April 1968), pp. 21–28.

Balderston, F. E.: "Communication Networks in Intermediate Markets," *Management Science* (January 1958), pp. 154–171.

Baligh, Helmy H., and Leon E. Richartz: "An Analysis of Vertical Market Structures," *Management Science* (July 1964), pp. 667–689.

Bauer, Raymond A., and Dan H. Fenn, Jr.: "What *is* a Corporate Social Audit?" *Harvard Business Review* (January–February 1973).

Beier, Frederick J.: "The Role of the Common Carrier in the Channel of Distribution," *Transportation Journal* (Winter 1969).

Beik, Leland L., and Stephen L. Buzby: "Profitability Analysis by Market Segments," *Journal of Marketing* (July 1973), pp. 48–53.

Boulding, Kenneth E.: "Organization and Conflict," *Journal of Conflict Resolution* (June 1957).

Bowersox, Donald J.: "Physical Distribution Development, Current Status and Potential," *Journal of Marketing* (January 1969), pp. 63–70.

———: "The Need for Innovative Distribution Management," *Distribution Worldwide* (December 1977).

Brendel, Louis H.: "18 Tips for Working With Distributors," *Industrial Marketing* (August 1961), pp. 89–92.

Bucklin, Louis P.: "Retail Strategy and the Classification of Consumer Goods," *Journal of Marketing* (January 1963).

———: "Postponement, Speculation and the Structure of Distribution Channels," *Journal of Marketing Research* (Febryary 1965), pp. 26–31.

———: "A Theory of Channel Control," *Journal of Marketing* (January 1973), pp. 29–37.

Buzzell, Robert D., Bradley T. Gale, and Ralph G. M. Sulton: "Market Share—A Key to Profitability," *Harvard Business Review* (January–February 1975), pp. 97–106.

Cooper, S. Kerry, and Mitchell H. Raiborn: "Accounting for Corporate Social Responsibility," *MSU Business Topics* (Spring 1974), pp. 19–26.

Coser, Lewis A.: "Collective Violence and Civil Conduct," *Journal of Social Issues* (vol. 28, no. 1, 1972).

Cox, Reavis, and Charles S. Goodman: "Marketing of House Building Materials," *Journal of Marketing* (July 1959), pp. 36–61.

Crawford, C. Merle: "Needed: A New Look at Retailers' Horizontal Cooperation," *Journal of Retailing* (Summer 1970).

Crissy, W. J. E., Paul Fischer, and Frank H. Mossman: "Segmental Analysis: Key to Marketing Profitability," *MSU Business Topics* (Spring 1973), pp. 42–49.

———, and Robert M. Kaplan: "Matrix Models for Market Planning," *MSU Business Topics* (Summer 1963).

Dahl, R. A.: "The Concept of Power," *Behavioral Science* (no. 2, 1957), pp. 201–218.

Davidson, Sidney: "The Day of Reckoning—Managerial Analysis and Accounting Theory," *Journal of Accounting Research* (Autumn 1963).

Davidson, William R.: "Changes in Distributive Institutions," *Journal of Marketing* (January 1970), pp. 7–10.

———, Albert D. Bates, and Stephen J. Bass: "The Retail Life Cycle," *Harvard Business Review* (November–December 1976).

Dearden, John: "The Case Against R.O.I. Control,"*Harvard Business Review* (May–June 1969), pp. 124–135.

Dixon, Donald F.: "The Emergence of Marketing Systems," *Economic and Business Bulletin* (June 1965), pp. 1–8.

Doherty, Philip A.: "A Closer Look at Operations Research," *Journal of Marketing* (April 1963).

Dommermuth, William P., and R. Clifton Anderson: "Distributive Systems—Firms, Functions and Efficiencies," *MSU Business Topics* Spring 1969), pp. 51–56.

Douglas, Edna: "Size of Firm and the Structure of Costs in Retailing," *The Journal of Business* (April 1962), pp. 158–189.

Dunn, Patrick M., and Harry I. Wolk: "Marketing Cost Analysis: A Modularized Contribution Approach," *Journal of Marketing* (July 1977), pp. 83–94.

El-Ansary, Adel I., and Robert A. Robicheaux: "A Theory of Channel Control: Revisited," *Journal of Marketing* (January 1974), pp. 2–7.

——, and Louis W. Stern: "Power Measurement in the Distribution Channel," *Journal of Marketing* (February 1972), pp. 47–52.

Emerson, Richard: "Power-Dependence Relations," *American Sociological Review* (February 1962).

Emery, F. E., and E. L. Trist: "The Casual Texture of Organizational Environments," *Human Relations* (February 1965), pp. 21–32.

Evan, William M.: "Toward A Theory of Inter-Organizational Relations," *Management Science* Series B (August 1965), pp. B217–B320.

Ferrara, William L.: "Responsibility Accounting and the Contribution Approach," *NAA Bulletin* (December 1963), pp. 11–19.

Fink, Stephen L., Joel Beak, and Kenneth Taddeo: "Organizational Crisis and Change," *Journal of Applied Behavioral Science* (January–February 1971).

Fischer, Ronald J.: "Third Party Consultation: A Method for the Study and Resolution of Conflict," *Journal of Conflict Resolution* (March 1972).

French, John R. P., Jr.: "A Formal Theory of Social Power," *Psychological Review* (May 1956).

Goodman, Sam R.: "Improved Marketing Analysis of Profitability, Relevant Costs and Life Cycles," *Financial Executive* (June 1967), pp. 28–34.

Hollander, Stanley C.: "The Wheel of Retailing," *Journal of Marketing* (July 1960), pp. 37–42.

——: "Measuring the Cost and Value of Marketing," *MSU Business Topics* (Summer 1961), pp. 17–27.

Holton, Richard H.: "A Simplified Capital Budgeting Approach to Merchandise Management," *California Management Review* (Spring 1961), pp. 82–98.

Horngren, Charles T.: "Choosing Accounting Practices for Reporting to Management," *National Association of Accountants* (September 1962).

Hovde, Howard T., special ed.: "Wholesaling in our American Economy," *Journal of Marketing,* supplementary issue (September 1949).

Hudig, John: "Marketing Costs and Their Control," *The Controller* (July 1963), pp. 16–20.

Hunt, Shelby D., and John R. Nevin: "Tying Agreements in Franchising," *Journal of Marketing* (July 1975).

Kaufman, Felix: "Data Systems that Cross Company Boundaries," *Harvard Business Review* (January–February 1966), pp. 141–155.

Kelly, Edward W.: "Marketing Cost Analysis—The Accountant's Most Neglected Opportunity," *NAA Bulletin* (July 1960), pp. 11–21.

Laczniak, Gene R., Robert F. Lusch, and John G. Udell: "Marketing in 1985: A View from the Ivory Tower," *Journal of Marketing* (October 1977).

La Londe, Bernard J., John R. Grabner, and James F. Robeson: "Integrated Distribution Systems: A Management Perspective," *International Journal of Physical Distribution* (October 1970).

La Londe, Bernard J., and Douglas M. Lambert: "Inventory Carrying Costs: Significance, Components, Means Functions," *International Journal of Physical Distribution* (vol. 6, no. 1, 1975), pp. 51–63.

Lambert, Douglas M.: "The Distribution Channels Decision: A Problem of Performance Measurement," *Management Accounting* (June 1978).

Lambert, Eugene W., Jr.: "Financial Considerations in Choosing a Marketing Channel," *MSU Business Topics* (Winter 1966), pp. 17–26.

Levine, Robert A.: "Anthropology and the Study of Conflict: An Introduction," *Journal of Conflict Resolution* (March 1962).

Lewis, Richard J., and Leo G. Erickson: "Marketing Functions and Systems: A Synthesis," *Journal of Marketing* (July 1969), pp. 10–14.

Lewis, Ronald J.: "Strengthening Control of Physical Distribution Costs," *Management Services* (January–February 1956).

Little, Robert W.: "The Marketing Channel: Who Should Lead This Extra-Corporate Organization," *Journal of Marketing* (January 1970), pp. 31–38.

Lopata, Richard S.: "Faster Pace in Wholesaling," *Harvard Business Review* (July–August 1969).

Lowes, Bryan, and John R. Sparkes: "Fitting Accounting to Social Goals," *Business Horizons* (June 1974), pp. 53–57.

Lusch, Robert F.: "Channel Conflict: Its Impact on Retailer Operating Performance," *Journal of Retailing* (Summer 1976).

Mack, Raymond W., and Richard C. Snyder: "The Analysis of Social Conflict—Toward an Overview and Synthesis," *Journal of Conflict Resolution* (June 1956), pp. 212–248.

Mallen, Bruce: "A Theory of Retailer-Supplier Conflict, Control, and Cooperation," *Journal of Retailing* (Summer 1963).

———: "Introducing the Marketing Channel to Price Theory," *Journal of Marketing* (July 1964), pp. 29–33.

———: "Interaction of Channel Selection Policies in the Marketing Systems," an extension of: Bruce Mallen, "A Conceptual Foundation for a General Theory of Marketing," *The Marketer: Journal of the Marketing Association of Canada* (Spring 1965), pp. 14–16.

———: "Functional Spin-off: A Key to Anticipating Changes in Distribution Structure," *Journal of Marketing* (July 1973), pp. 18–25.

———, and Stephen D. Silver: "Modern Marketing and the Accountant," *Cost and Management* (February 1964), pp. 75–85.

March, James G.: "An Introduction to the Theory and Measurement of Influence," *American Political Science Review* (1955).

McCammon, Bert C., Jr., and William L. Hammer: "A Frame of Reference for Improving Productivity in Distribution," *Atlanta Economic Review* (September–October 1974), pp. 9–13.

McDonald, A. L. Jr.: "Do Your Distribution Channels Need Reshaping?" *Business Horizons* (Summer 1964), pp. 29–38.

McGann, Thomas J.: "Yes! The Controller Belongs on the Marketing Team," *The Controller* (August 1961), pp. 377–382.

McGarry, Edmund: "The Contractual Function in Marketing," *Journal of Business* (April 1951), pp. 108–112.

McVey, Phillip: "Are Channels of Distribution What the Textbooks Say?" *Journal of Marketing* (January 1960), pp. 61–64.

Merton, Robert K.: "The Role-Set: Problems in Sociological Theory," *British Journal of Sociology* (vol. 8, 1957), pp. 110–112.

Michman, Ronald: "Channel Development and Innovation," *Marquette Business Review* (Spring 1971), pp. 45–49.

Moore, Jack: "Protection of Small Firms Has Been Keystone of U. S. Regulatory Efforts," *Supermarket News* (October 24, 1977).

Mossman, Frank H., Paul M. Fischer, and W. J. E. Crissy: "New Approaches to Analyzing Marketing Profitability," *Journal of Marketing* (April 1974), pp. 43–48.

Parker, Donald D.: "Improved Efficiency and Reduced Cost in Marketing," *Journal of Marketing* (April 1962).

Pearson, Michael: "The Conflict-Performance Assumption," *Journal of Purchasing* (February 1973).

Pondy, Louis R.: "Organizational Conflict: Concepts and Models," *Administrative Science Quarterly* (September 1967), pp. 300–306.

Porter, Michael E.: "Consumer Behavior, Retailer Power, and Market Performance in Consumer Goods Industries," *The Review of Economics and Statistics* (November 1974).

Ray, David: "Distribution Costing: The Current State of the Art," *International Journal of Physical Distribution* (vol. 6, no. 2, 1975), pp. 75–106.

Rayburn, L. Gayle: "Setting Standards for Distribution Costs," *Management Services* (March–April 1967), pp. 42–52.

Ridgeway, Valentine F.: "Administration of Manufacturer-Dealer Systems," *Administrative Science Quarterly* (March 1957), pp. 464–483.

Robicheaux, Robert A., and Adel I. El-Ansary: "A General Model for Understanding Channel Member Behavior," *Journal of Retailing* (Winter 1975–76).

Rosenberg, Larry J., and Louis W. Stern: "Toward the Analysis of Conflict in Distribution Channels: A Descriptive Model," *Journal of Marketing* (October 1970), pp. 40–46.

——, and——: "Conflict Measurement in the Distribution Channel," *Journal of Marketing Research* (November 1971), pp. 437–442.

Rosenbloom, Bert: "Conflict and Channel Efficiency: Some Conceptual Models for the Decision Maker," *Journal of Marketing* (July 1973), pp. 26–30.

Ruhuke, H. O.: "Vertical Integration: Trend for the Future," *Advanced Management Journal* (January 1966), pp. 69–73.

Sheth, Jagdish N.: "A Model of Industrial Buyer Behavior," *Journal of Marketing* (October 1963), pp. 50–56.

Smith, Wendell R.: "Product Differentiation and Market Segmentation as Alternative Marketing Strategies," *Journal of Marketing* (July 1956).

Soppington, Lewis B., and C. G. Browne: "The Skills of Creative Leadership," *Journal of Retailing* (Spring 1957).

Stern, Louis W.: "Antitrust Implications of a Sociological Interpretation of Competition, Conflict, and Cooperation in the Marketplace," *The Antitrust Bulletin* (Fall 1971), pp. 509–530.

——, and C. Samuel Craig: "Interorganizational Data Systems: The Computer and Distribution," *Journal of Retailing* (Summer 1971), pp. 73–91.

——, Brian Sternthal, and C. Samuel Craig: "A Parasimulation of Interorganizational Conflict," *International Journal of Group Tensions* (vol. 3, no. 1 and 2, 1973), pp. 68–90.

Stewart, Wendell M.: "Physical Distribution: Key to Improved Volume and Profits," *Journal of Marketing* (January 1965).

Stigler, George: "The Division of Labor is Limited by the Extent of the Market," *Journal of Political Economy* (June 1951), pp. 185–193.

Stock, James R.: "How Shippers Judge Carriers," *Distribution Worldwide* (August 1976).

Terreberry, Shirley: "The Evolution of Organizational Environments," *Administrative Science Quarterly* (March 1968), pp. 509–613.

Weigand, Robert E.: "The Marketing Organization, Channels and Firm Size," *Journal of Business* (April 1963), pp. 228–236.

————: "The Accountant and Marketing Channels," *The Accounting Review* (July 1963), pp. 584–590.

————"Fit Products and Channels to Your Markets," *Harvard Business Review* (January–February 1977), pp. 95–105.

Weiss, Edward B.: "How Much of a Retailer is the Manufacturer?" *Advertising Age* (July 21, 1958).

Willett, Ronald P., and P. Ronald Stephenson: "Determinants of Buyer Response to Physical Distribution Service," *Journal of Marketing Research* (August 1969), pp. 270–283.

Wittreich, Warren J.: "Misunderstanding the Retailer," *Harvard Business Review* (May–June 1962), pp. 147–155.

Wren, Daniel A.: "Interface and Interorganizational Coordination," *Academy of Management Journal* (March 1967).

Zikmunic, William G., and William J. Stanton: "Recycling Solid Wastes: A Channels-of-Distribution Problem," *Journal of Marketing* (July 1971), p. 35.

Special Publications

Adams, David: *A Study of Institutional Change Processes Within the Appliance Industry,* unpublished doctoral dissertation, Department of Marketing and Transportation Administration, Michigan State University, East Lansing, Michigan, 1977.

Allvine, Fred C., and James M. Patterson: *Competition, Ltd.: The Marketing of Gasoline* (Bloomington, Ind.: Indiana University Press, 1972).

Assael, Henry, ed.: *The Politics of Distributive Trade Associations: A Study in Conflict Resolution* (Hempstead, N.Y.: Hofstra University Press, 1967).

Balderston, F. E.: "Theories of Marketing Structure and Channels," *in Proceedings: Conference of Marketing Teachers from Far Western States,* Delbert J. Duncan, ed., (Berkeley, Calif.: University of California, 1958), pp. 139–140.

Bailey, Earl L.: "Manufacturers' Marketing Costs," *Conference Board,* vol. VIII, no. 10 (October 1971).

Bowersox, Donald J., et al.: *Simulated Product Sales Forecasting,* (East Lansing, Mich.: Michigan State University Bureau of Business Research, 1979).

Brion, John M.: *Marketing Through the Wholesaler/Distributor Channel* (Chicago: American Marketing Association, 1965), pp. 53–57.

Bucklin, Louis P.: *A Theory of Distribution Channel Structure,* (Berkeley, Cal.: Institute of Business and Economic Research, University of California, 1966).

Buzzell, Robert D.: *Value Added by Industrial Distributors and Their Productivity,* (Columbus, Ohio: Bureau of Business Research, The Ohio State University, 1959).

————: "Marketing and Economic Performance: Meaning and Measurement," *in* C. Allvine, ed., *Public Policy and Marketing Practices* (Chicago: American Marketing Association, 1973).

Cartwright, Dorwin: "Influence, Leadership, and Control," *in* James G. March, ed., *Handbook of Organization* (Chicago: Rand McNally & Company, 1965).

Cole, Robert: *Vertical Integration in Marketing* (Urbana, Ill.: University of Illinois College of Commerce and Business Administration, Bureau of Business and Economic Research, 1952).

Constantin, James A., et al.: "The Distribution Center: A Potential Focus of Power," *Proceedings of the Sixth Annual Transportation and Logistics Educators Conference* (1976).

Craig, David R., and Werner Gabler: "The Competitive Struggle for Market Control," *in Marketing in the American Economy,* vol. 209, The Annals of the American Academy of Political Science (Philadelphia: American Academy of Political and Social Science, May 1940).

Diamond, William M.: *Distribution Channels for Industrial Goods* (Columbus, Ohio: Bureau of Business Research, The Ohio State University, 1963).

Dickenson, Roger: "Channel Management by Large Retailers," *in* Robert L. King, ed., *Marketing and the New Science of Planning* (Chicago: American Marketing Association, 1968).

Distribution System Costing: Concepts and Procedures, Proceedings of the Fourth Annual James R. Riley Symposium on Business Logistics, John R. Grabner and William S. Sargent, eds., Transportation and Logistics Research Foundation, The Ohio State University (April 9–11, 1972).

Epstein, Marc J., Eric G. Flamholtz, and John L. McDonough: *Corporate Social Performance: The Measurement of Product and Service Contributions* (New York: The National Association of Accountants, 1977).

French, John R. P. Jr., and Bertram Raven: "Bases of Social Power," *in Studies in Social Power,* Dorwin Cartwright, ed. (Ann Arbor: University of Michigan Press, 1959).

Grabner, John R. and Roger A. Layton: "Problems and Challenges in Market Performance Measurement," *in* C. Allvine, ed., *Public Policy and Marketing Practices* (Chicago: American Marketing Association, 1973).

Gross, Walter: "Retailing in the Seventies: A Projection of Current Trends," *Baylor Business Studies* (February–April 1969).

"The Guiding Concepts" unpublished paper by the Inter-University Research Program in Institution Building, Syracuse University Center for Overseas Research, 1964.

Harrison, Mary C., and M. Bixby Cooper: "An Analysis of Retailer Participation in Product Recalls," *Proceedings of the Southern Marketing Association Conference* (Starkville, Miss.: Mississippi State University, 1976).

Hollander, Stanley C.: "Channel Management by Small Retailers," *in* Robert L. King, ed., *Marketing and the New Science of Planning,* (Chicago: American Marketing Association, 1968).

La Londe, Bernard J., and Paul H. Zinszer: *Customer Service: Meaning and Measurement* (Chicago: National Council of Physical Distribution Management, 1976).

Lambert, Douglas M.: *The Development of an Inventory Costing Methodology: A Study of the Costs Associated with Holding Inventory* (Chicago: National Council of Physical Distribution Management, 1976).

———, and Bernard J. La Londe: "The Economics of Using a Frozen Food Distributor," *Frozen Food Factbook, 1975* (Hershey, Pa.: The National Frozen Food Association, Inc., 1974).

———, and John T. Mentzer, Jr.: "The Availability of Distribution Cost Information," unpublished research paper, Michigan State University, 1977.

Lewis, Ronald: *Accounting Consequences of Physical Distribution System Changes,* unpublished doctoral dissertation, Michigan State University, 1965.

Madden, Donald L.: *An Approach to Budgetary Planning in Marketing Channels,* unpublished doctoral dissertation, The University of Texas at Austin, 1967.

Magee, John F.: *Quantitative Analysis of Physical Distribution Systems, The Social Responsibilities of Marketing* (Chicago: American Marketing Association, Winter 1961).

Market Processes in the Recife Area of Northeast Brazil, Marketing in Developing Communities Series, Research Report No. 2, Latin American Studies Center, Michigan State University, East Lansing, Michigan, 1969.

Market Processes in La Paz, Bolivia, Marketing in Developing Communities Series, Research Report No. 3, Latin American Studies Center, Michigan State University, East Lansing, Michigan, 1969.

Market Coordination in the Development of the Cauca Valley Region, Colombia, Marketing in Developing Communities Series, Research Report No. 5, Latin American Studies Center, Michigan State University, East Lansing, Michigan, 1970.

Marketing Definitions: A Glossary of Marketing Terms (Chicago: American Marketing Association, 1960).

Mathews, William E.: "Challenge for Industrial Marketers: Changing Channels of Distribution," working paper published by the Marketing Science Institute, Cambridge, Massachusetts, 1972.

McNair, Malcolm O.: "Significant Trends and Developments in the Postwar Period," *in* A. B. Smith, ed., *Competitive Distribution in a Free High-Level Economy and Its Implications for the University* (Pittsburgh: University of Pittsburgh Press, 1958).

Meadows, Paul: "Institution Building: A Sociological Perspective," unpublished paper prepared at the request of the Syracuse University Center for Overseas Research for the Inter-University Research Program in Institution Building, 1964.

Moore, James R.: "A Comparative Analysis of Decision Criteria Used in Channel Formation by Fifteen Industry Groups," *1974 Combined Proceedings,* Ron C. Curhan, ed. (Chicago: The American Marketing Association, 1974).

Mossman, Frank H.: *Differential Cost and Revenue Analysis, Marketing and Transportation Paper #10,* (East Lansing, Michigan: Bureau of Business Research, Michigan State University, 1962).

Rosenberg, Larry J.: *An Empirical Examination of the Causes, Level, and Consequences of Conflict in a High Stake Distribution Channel,* unpublished doctoral dissertation, Ohio State University, 1969.

Schiff, Michael: *Accounting and Control in Physical Distribution Management* (Chicago: National Council of Physical Distribution Management, 1972).

Selecting and Evaluating Distributors, Studies in Business Policy #116 (New York: National Industrial Conference Board, 1965).

Seven, Charles H.: *How Manufacturers Reduce Their Distribution Costs* (Washington, D.C.: U.S. Department of Commerce Economic Series #72, 1958).

Sherif, Muzafer, et al.: *Intergroup Conflict and Cooperation: The Robbers Cave Experiment* (Norman, Okla.: University of Oklahoma Press, 1961).

Taylor, Donald A.: *Institution Building in Business Administration: The Brazilian Experience,* Michigan State University International Business and Economic Studies, Division of Research, Graduate School of Business Administration, East Lansing, Michigan, 1968.

Underwood, James H., and Adel I. El-Ansary: "Physical Distribution: Marketing Channel Myopia," *Proceedings of the Sixth Annual Transportation and Logistics Educators Conference,* Columbus, Ohio: The Ohio State University, 1976.

U.S. Department of Commerce, Bureau of Foreign and Domestic Commerce, *Distribution Cost Analysis,* 1946.

Wayman, Wilbur S.: "Harnessing the Corporate Accounting System for Physical Distribution Cost Information," from *Proceedings of the Fourth Annual James R. Riley Symposium on Business Logistics,* John R. Grabner and William S. Sargent, eds., Ohio State University, 1972.

Name Index

Adams, David, 51*n.*, 340*n.*
Alderson, Wroe, 7*n.*, 36*n.*, 73*n.*, 75*n.*, 81*n.*,
    113*n.*, 158, 161*n.*, 162*n.*, 170*n.*, 339
Allvine, Fred C., 72*n.*
Assael, Henry, 79

Bartels, Fred E., 201
Bass, Stephen J., 340*n.*
Bates, Albert D., 340*n.*
Beak, Joel, 341*n.*
Beier, Frederick J., 104*n.*, 105*n.*
Beik, Leland L., 305*n.*
Bentham, Jeremy, 30
Black, Robert L., 130*n.*, 136*n.*
Blackwell, Roger D., 5*n.*
Boulding, Kenneth E., 31, 73*n.*, 80, 81*n.*, 82*n.*
Bowersox, Donald J., 2*n.*, 3*n.*, 13*n.*, 31*n.*, 39*n.*,
    165*n.*, 170*n.*, 198*n.*, 199*n.*, 205*n.*, 207*n.*,
    243*n.*, 280*n.*
Bucklin, Louis P., 9*n.*, 41, 106*n.*, 201*n.*, 215,
    304
Buzby, Stephen L., 305*n.*

Buzzell, Howard D., 49, 300*n.*

Cartwright, Dorwin, 101*n.*
Clark, Eugene, 67*n.*
Clark, Fred E., 67*n.*, 201*n.*
Commons, John R., 160
Constantin, James A., 280*n.*
Converse, Paul D., 304*n.*
Cooper, M. Bixby, 144, 316*n.*
Corley, Robert M., 130*n.*, 136*n.*
Coser, Lewis, 80*n.*
Cox, Reavis, 6*n.*, 28*n.*, 236*n.*
Craig, David R., 48, 49*n.*
Crawford, C. Merle, 274*n.*
Crissy, W. J. E., 305*n.*, 315, 316*n.*

Dahl, Robert A., 99*n.*
Darling, John R., 137*n.*
Davidson, William R., 340*n.*
Dearden, John, 306
Dickenson, Roger A., 273*n.*, 274*n.*
Dunne, Patrick M., 305*n.*

Subject Index